Destiny, NY

Volume One:
Who I Used to Be

D0217566

PAT
For Amy, my love.

MANUEL
To Mom and Dad, who made it possible.
To Jennifer, who listened to my complaints.
To Steve, who believed in me.
To Rick, whose stories are the best inspiration.
To all of You, readers! Believe in your Destiny!

BLACK MASK

Written by
Pat SHAND

Illustrated by
Manuel PREITANO

Lettered and Designed by
Jim CAMPBELL

Edited by
Shannon LEE

Created by
SHAND & PRETIANO

Cover by
Elisa ROMBOLI

● ● ●

For this edition

Produced by
Matt PIZZOLO

Production Artist
Phil SMITH

● ● ●

A Space Between Production

Published by Black Mask Entertainment, Inc.

DESTINY, NY volume 1. First Printing. JULY 2021.
DESTINY, NY is © 2021 Pat Shand & Manuel Preitano. All rights reserved.
Produced by Black Mask Entertainment, Inc. Office of publication: 254 N Lake
Ave #853 Pasadena CA 91101. Originally published in single magazine form as
DESTINY, NY no. 1-5. No part of this publication may be reproduced or transmitted,
in any form or by any means (except for short excerpts for journalistic or review
purposes) without the express written permission of Pat Shand, Manuel Preitano
or Black Mask Entertainment, Inc. All names, characters, events, and locales in
this publication are entirely fictional. Any resemblances to actual persons (living or
dead), events, or places, without satiric intent, is coincidental.
Printed in China.

www.blackmaskcontent.com

For licensing information, contact: licensing@blackmaskcontent.com

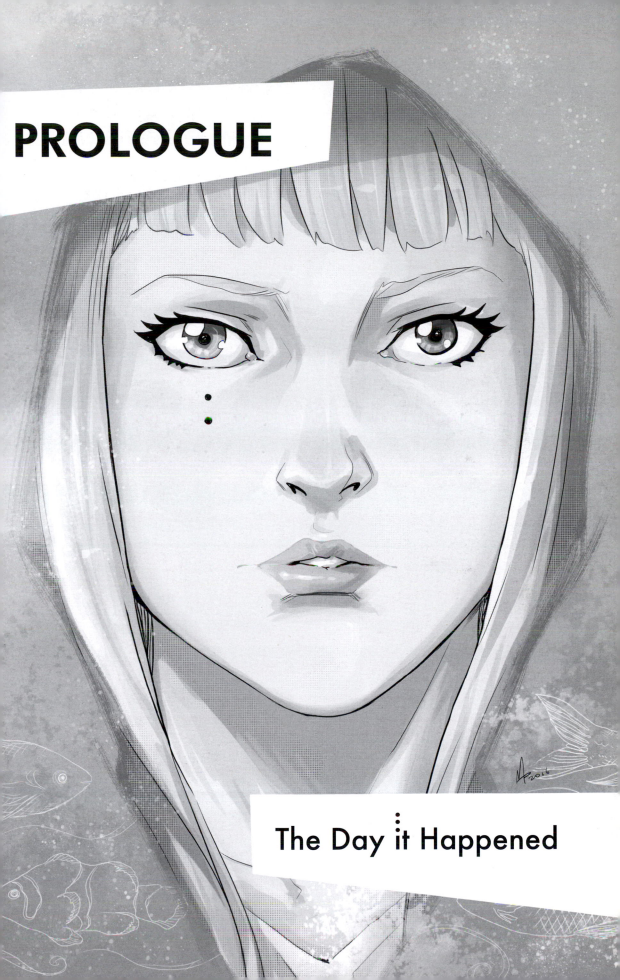

PROLOGUE

The Day it Happened

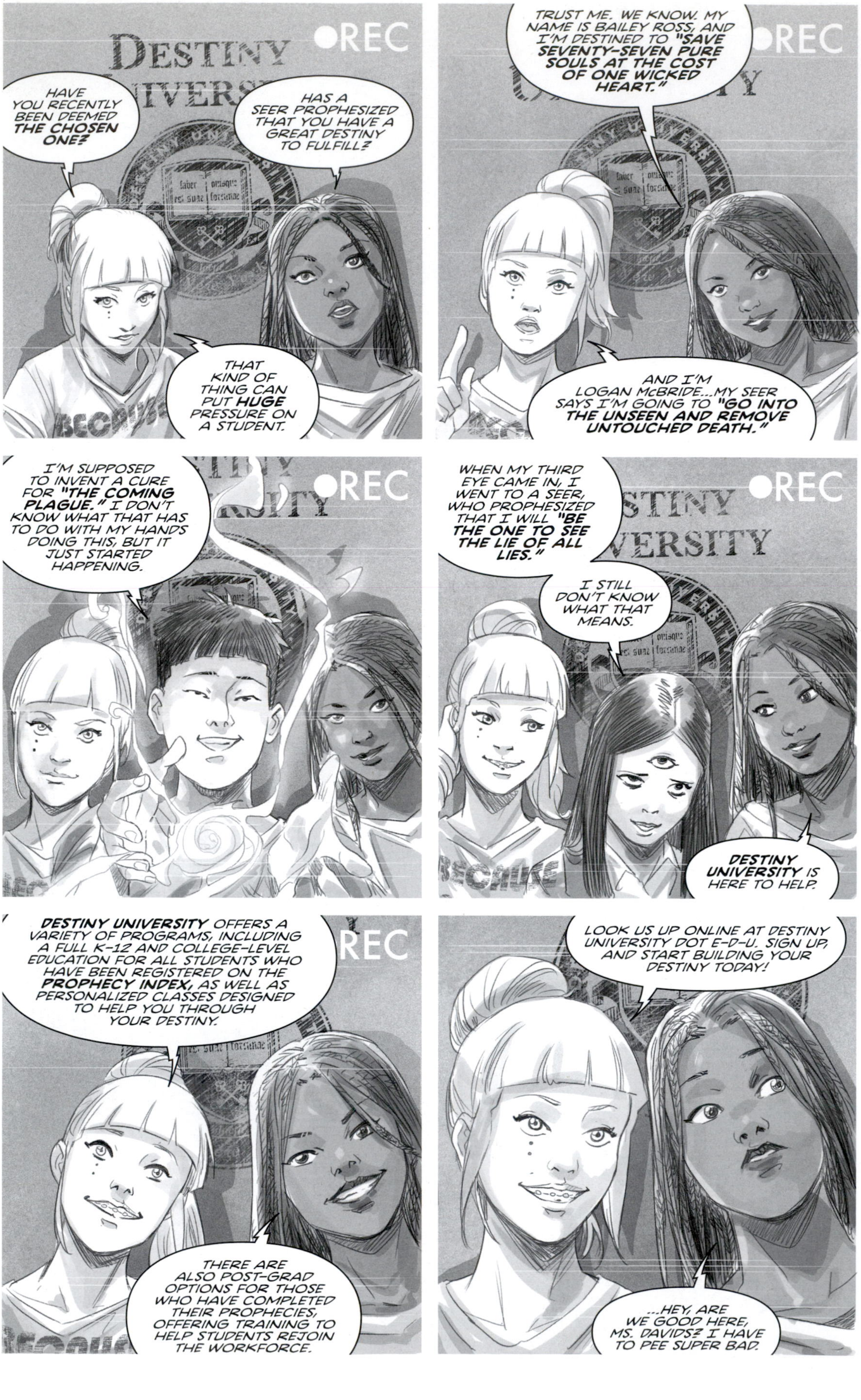

REC
DESTINY UNIVERSITY
HAVE YOU RECENTLY BEEN DEEMED **THE CHOSEN ONE?**
HAS A SEER PROPHESIZED THAT YOU HAVE A GREAT DESTINY TO FULFILL?
THAT KIND OF THING CAN PUT **HUGE** PRESSURE ON A STUDENT.
REC
TRUST ME. WE KNOW. MY NAME IS BAILEY ROSS, AND I'M DESTINED TO **"SAVE SEVENTY-SEVEN PURE SOULS AT THE COST OF ONE WICKED HEART."**
AND I'M LOGAN McBRIDE...MY SEER SAYS I'M GOING TO **"GO INTO THE UNSEEN AND REMOVE UNTOUCHED DEATH."**
REC
I'M SUPPOSED TO INVENT A CURE FOR **"THE COMING PLAGUE."** I DON'T KNOW WHAT THAT HAS TO DO WITH MY HANDS DOING THIS, BUT IT JUST STARTED HAPPENING.
REC
WHEN MY THIRD EYE CAME IN, I WENT TO A SEER, WHO PROPHESIZED THAT I WILL **"BE THE ONE TO SEE THE LIE OF ALL LIES."**
I STILL DON'T KNOW WHAT THAT MEANS.
DESTINY UNIVERSITY IS HERE TO HELP.
REC
DESTINY UNIVERSITY OFFERS A VARIETY OF PROGRAMS, INCLUDING A FULL K-12 AND COLLEGE-LEVEL EDUCATION FOR ALL STUDENTS WHO HAVE BEEN REGISTERED ON THE **PROPHECY INDEX,** AS WELL AS PERSONALIZED CLASSES DESIGNED TO HELP YOU THROUGH YOUR DESTINY.
THERE ARE ALSO POST-GRAD OPTIONS FOR THOSE WHO HAVE COMPLETED THEIR PROPHECIES, OFFERING TRAINING TO HELP STUDENTS REJOIN THE WORKFORCE.
LOOK US UP ONLINE AT DESTINY UNIVERSITY DOT E-D-U. SIGN UP, AND START BUILDING YOUR DESTINY TODAY!
...HEY, ARE WE GOOD HERE, MS. DAVIDS? I HAVE TO PEE SUPER BAD.

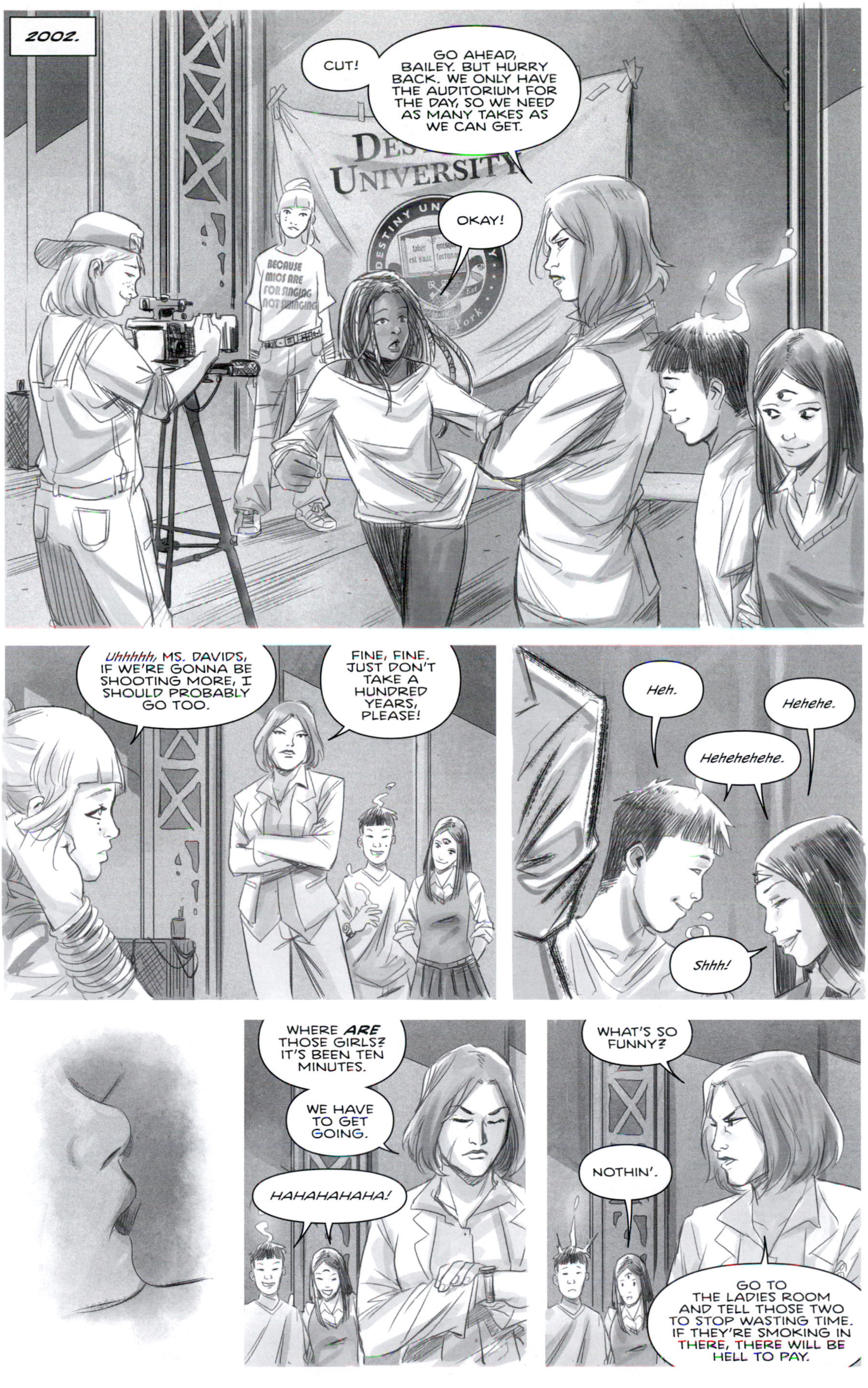
2002.
CUT!
GO AHEAD, BAILEY. BUT HURRY BACK. WE ONLY HAVE THE AUDITORIUM FOR THE DAY, SO WE NEED AS MANY TAKES AS WE CAN GET.
DESTINY UNIVERSITY
OKAY!
BECAUSE MICS ARE FOR SINGING NOT SWINGING
Uhhhhh, MS. DAVIDS, IF WE'RE GONNA BE SHOOTING MORE, I SHOULD PROBABLY GO TOO.
FINE, FINE. JUST DON'T TAKE A HUNDRED YEARS, PLEASE!
Heh.
Hehehe.
Hehehehehe.
Shhh!
WHERE ***ARE*** THOSE GIRLS? IT'S BEEN TEN MINUTES.
WE HAVE TO GET GOING.
HAHAHAHAHA!
WHAT'S SO FUNNY?
NOTHIN'.
GO TO THE LADIES ROOM AND TELL THOSE TWO TO STOP WASTING TIME. IF THEY'RE SMOKING IN THERE, THERE WILL BE HELL TO PAY.

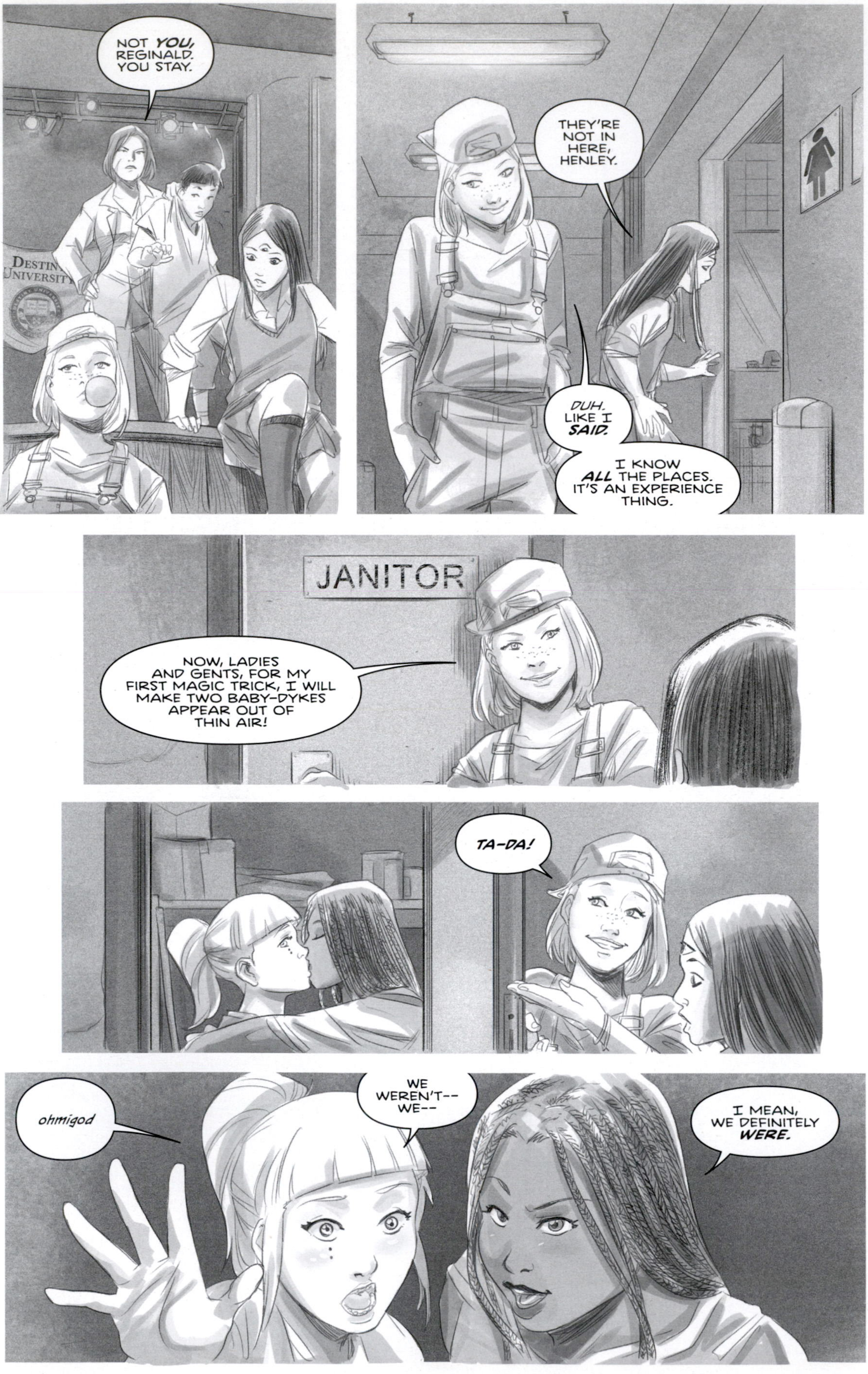
NOT YOU, REGINALD. YOU STAY.
DESTINY UNIVERSITY
THEY'RE NOT IN HERE, HENLEY.
DUH. LIKE I SAID.
I KNOW ALL THE PLACES. IT'S AN EXPERIENCE THING.
JANITOR
NOW, LADIES AND GENTS, FOR MY FIRST MAGIC TRICK, I WILL MAKE TWO BABY-DYKES APPEAR OUT OF THIN AIR!
TA-DA!
ohmigod
WE WEREN'T-- WE--
I MEAN, WE DEFINITELY WERE.

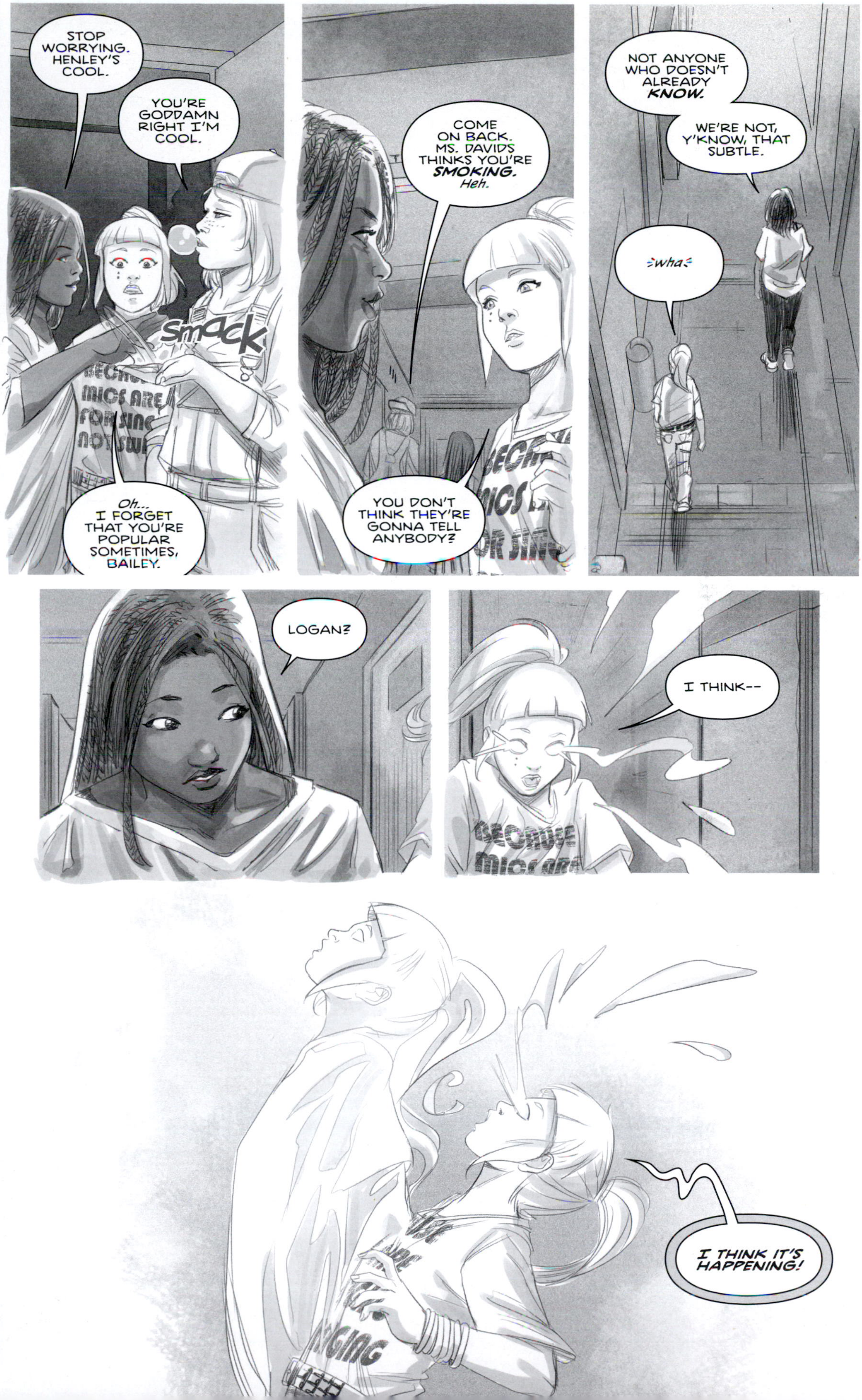
STOP WORRYING. HENLEY'S COOL.
YOU'RE GODDAMN RIGHT I'M COOL.
SMACK
Oh... I FORGET THAT YOU'RE POPULAR SOMETIMES, BAILEY.
COME ON BACK. MS. DAVIDS THINKS YOU'RE SMOKING. Heh.
YOU DON'T THINK THEY'RE GONNA TELL ANYBODY?
NOT ANYONE WHO DOESN'T ALREADY KNOW.
WE'RE NOT, Y'KNOW, THAT SUBTLE.
wha
LOGAN?
I THINK--
I THINK IT'S HAPPENING!

CHAPTER ONE

There Will Be Time

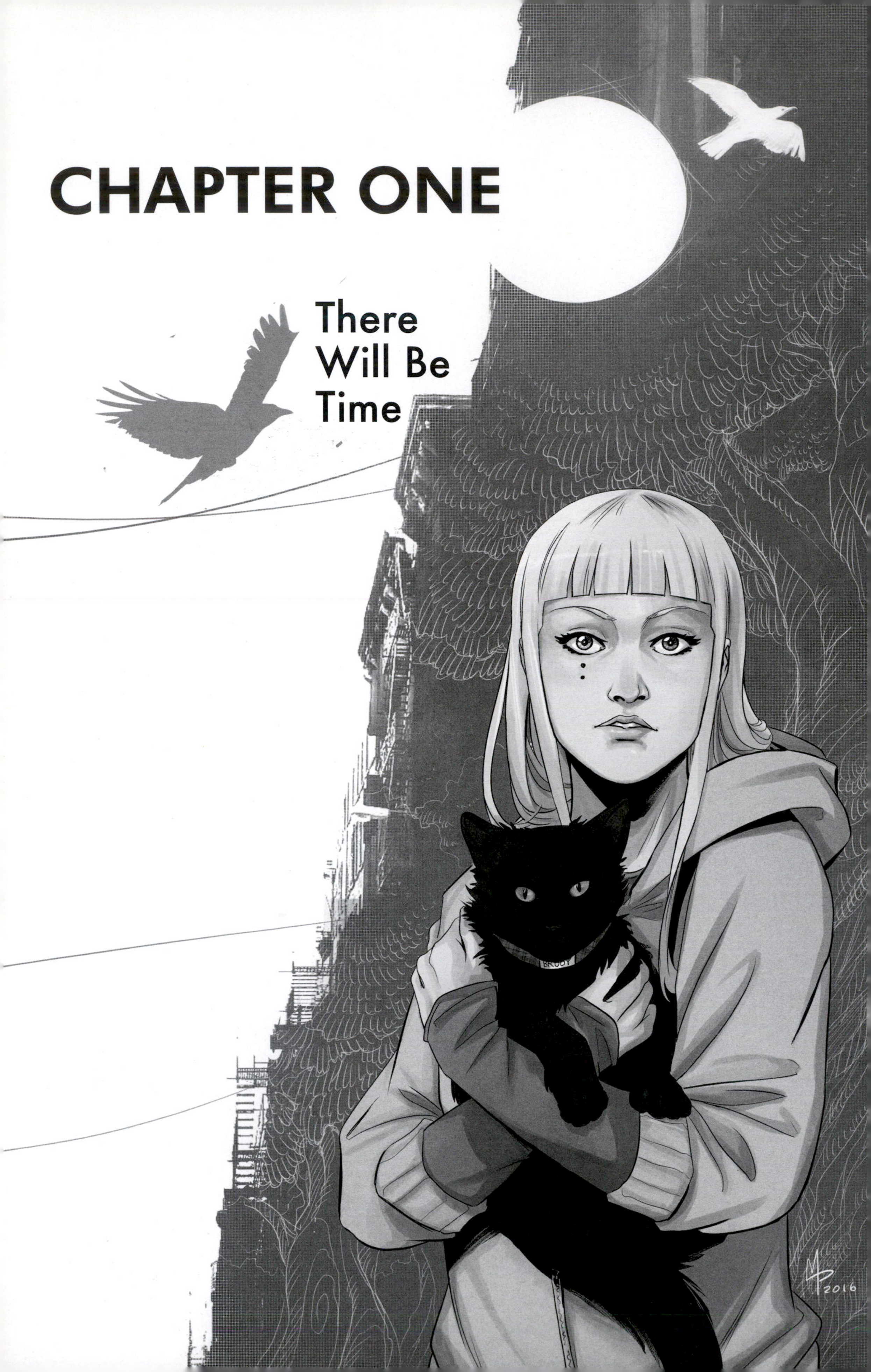

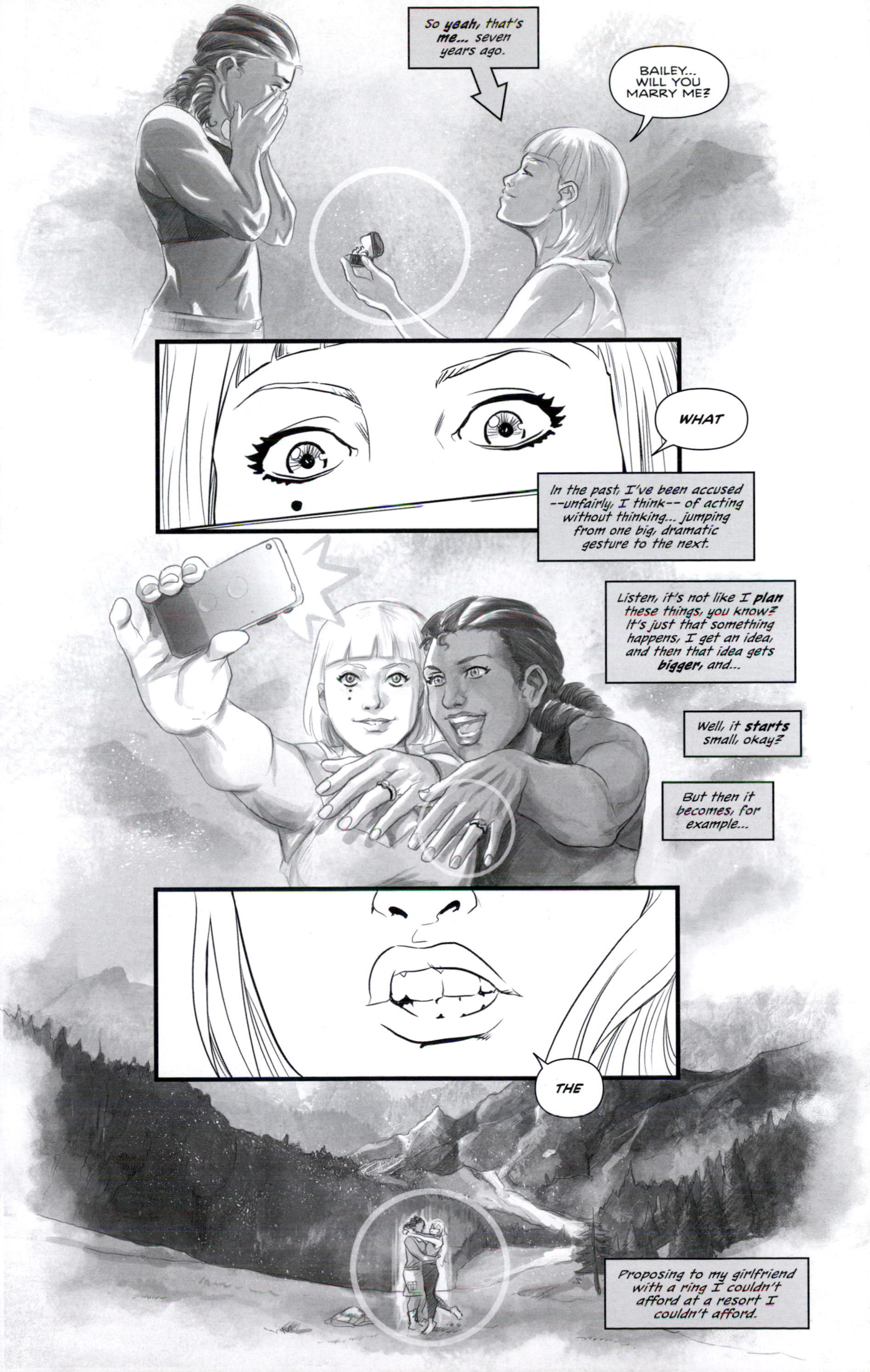
So yeah, that's me... seven years ago.
BAILEY... WILL YOU MARRY ME?
WHAT
In the past, I've been accused --unfairly, I think-- of acting without thinking... jumping from one big, dramatic gesture to the next.
Listen, it's not like I plan these things, you know? It's just that something happens, I get an idea, and then that idea gets bigger, and...
Well, it starts small, okay?
But then it becomes, for example...
THE
Proposing to my girlfriend with a ring I couldn't afford at a resort I couldn't afford.

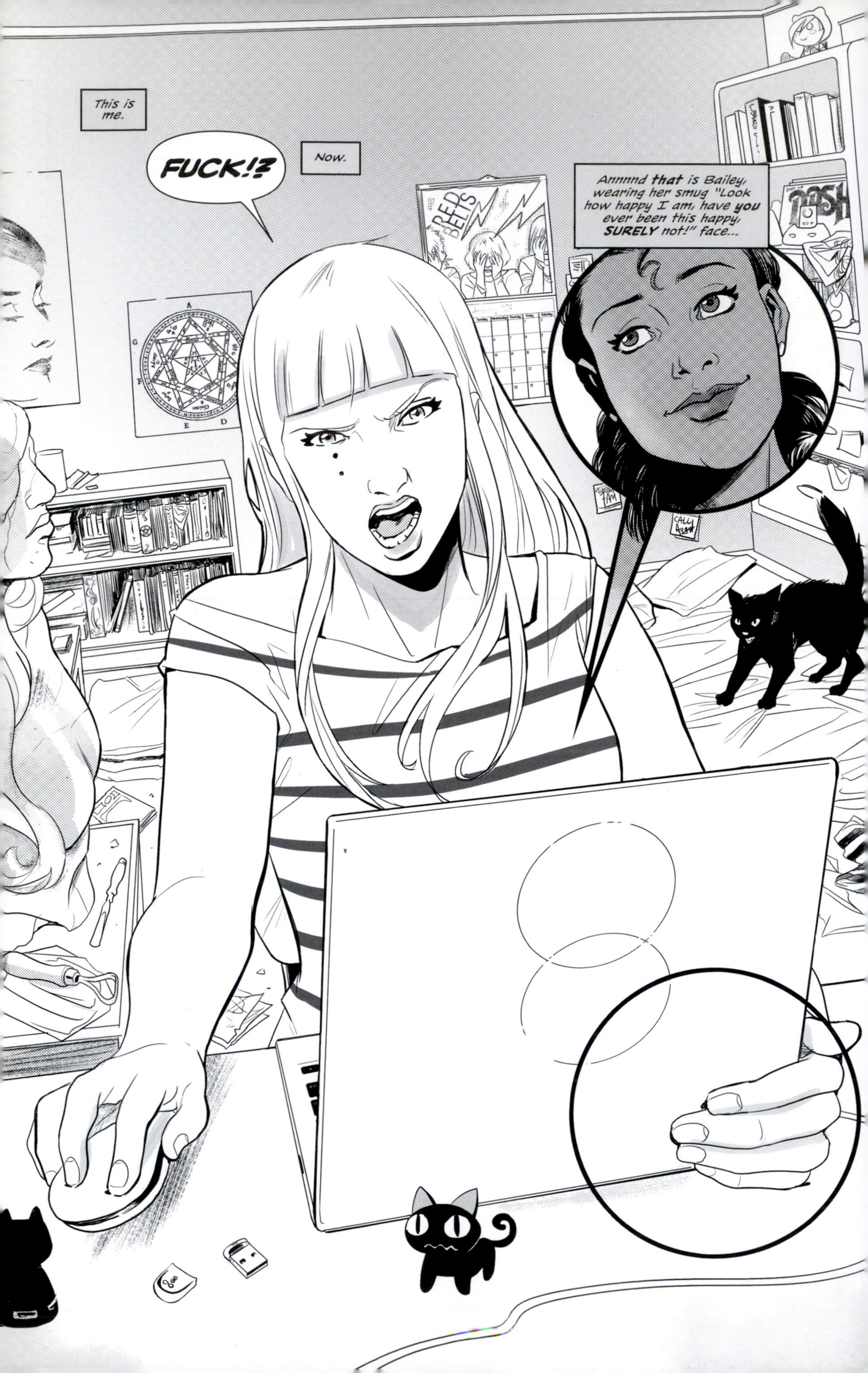
This is me.
FUCK!?
Now.
Annnnd **that** is Bailey, wearing her smug "Look how happy I am, have **you** ever been this happy, **SURELY** not!" face...

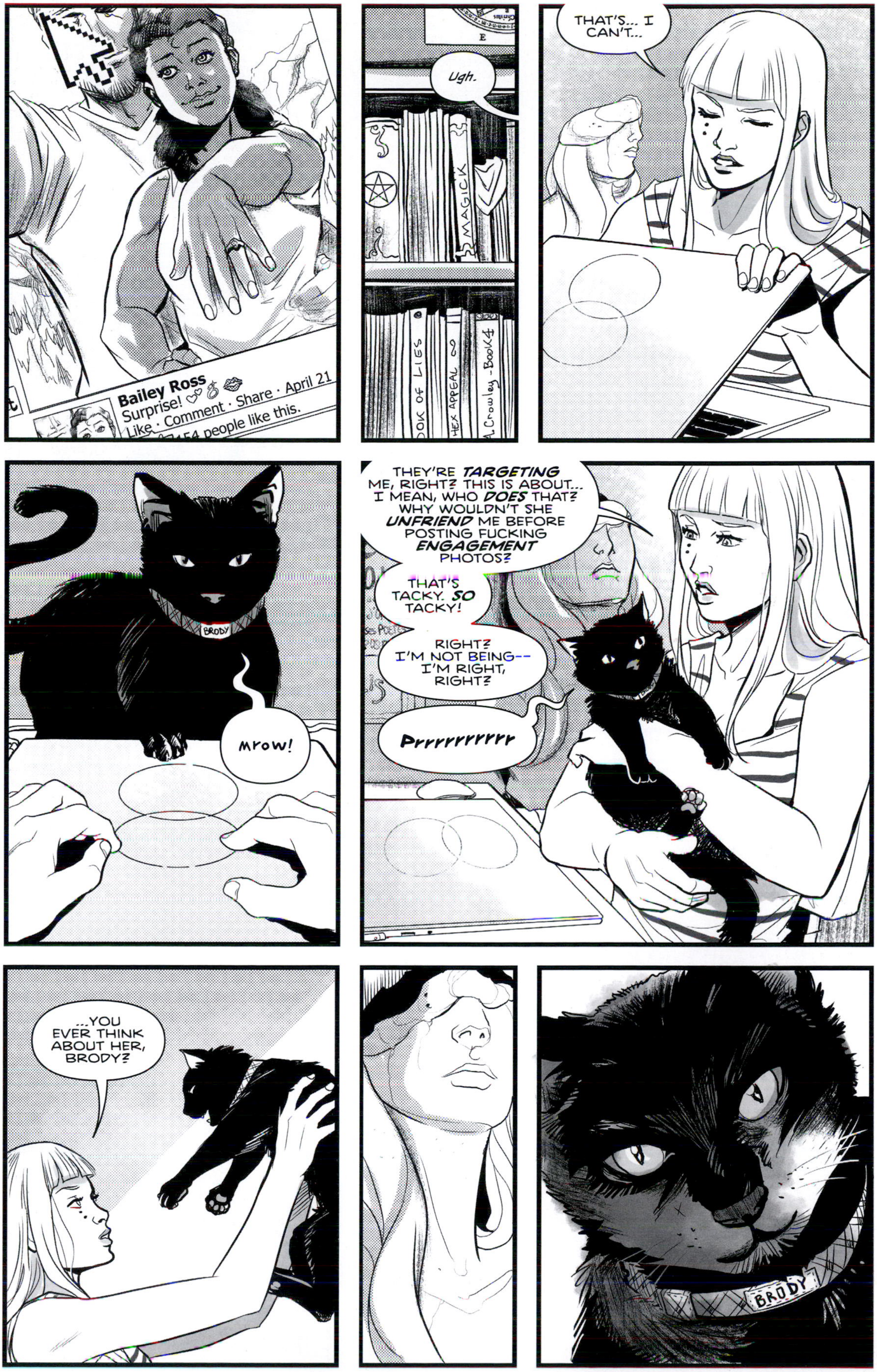
Bailey Ross
Surprise!
Like · Comment · Share · April 21
154 people like this.
Ugh.
MAGICK
BOOK OF LIES
HEX APPEAL
A. Crowley - Book 4
THAT'S... I CAN'T...
BRODY
mrow!
THEY'RE TARGETING ME, RIGHT? THIS IS ABOUT... I MEAN, WHO DOES THAT? WHY WOULDN'T SHE UNFRIEND ME BEFORE POSTING FUCKING ENGAGEMENT PHOTOS?
THAT'S TACKY. SO TACKY!
RIGHT? I'M NOT BEING-- I'M RIGHT, RIGHT?
Prrrrrrrrrr
...YOU EVER THINK ABOUT HER, BRODY?
BRODY

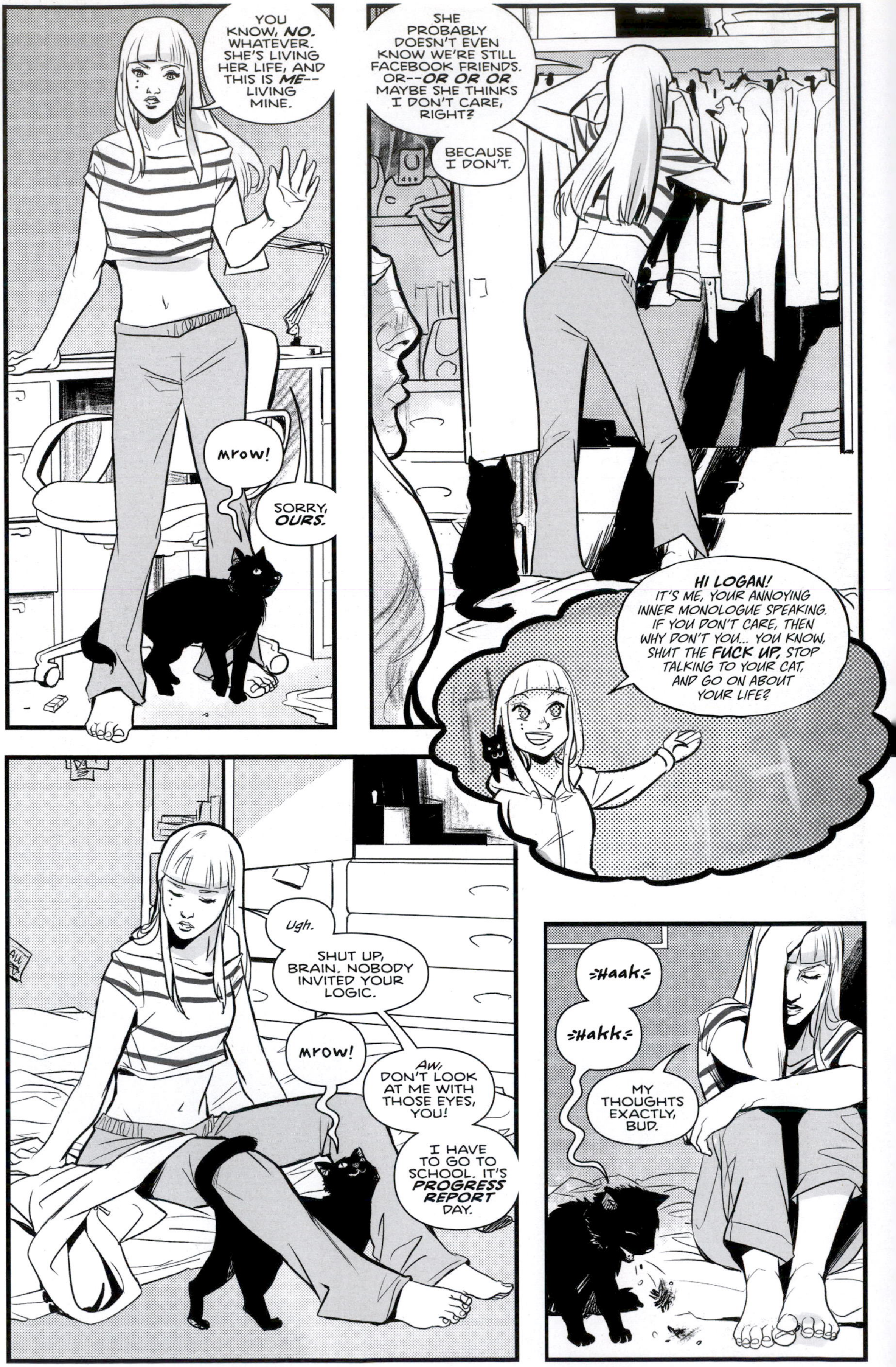
YOU KNOW, NO. WHATEVER. SHE'S LIVING HER LIFE, AND THIS IS ME-- LIVING MINE.
MROW!
SORRY, OURS.
SHE PROBABLY DOESN'T EVEN KNOW WE'RE STILL FACEBOOK FRIENDS. OR--OR OR OR MAYBE SHE THINKS I DON'T CARE, RIGHT?
BECAUSE I DON'T.
HI LOGAN! IT'S ME, YOUR ANNOYING INNER MONOLOGUE SPEAKING. IF YOU DON'T CARE, THEN WHY DON'T YOU... YOU KNOW, SHUT THE FUCK UP, STOP TALKING TO YOUR CAT, AND GO ON ABOUT YOUR LIFE?
Ugh.
SHUT UP, BRAIN. NOBODY INVITED YOUR LOGIC.
MROW!
AW, DON'T LOOK AT ME WITH THOSE EYES, YOU!
I HAVE TO GO TO SCHOOL. IT'S PROGRESS REPORT DAY.
HAAK
HAKK
MY THOUGHTS EXACTLY, BUD.

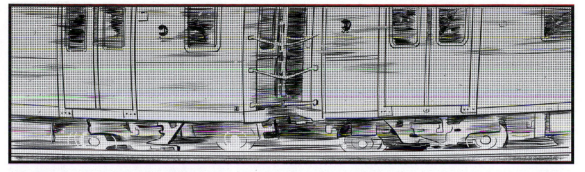

Stop it. You're powerful. You're strong.

You're magic... literally! You can do **anything**. You can do **everything**.

You're **important**.

Stop.

STONE OF HEARTH

Blessed by the goddess **Hearth**, it is supposed to absorb your anxiety, your worries, your sadness...and give it back to you as positive energy.

Still waiting for it to work.

Ms. Davids said all you have to do is rub the smooth surface of the stone and--

HEY, SWEETHEART.

...concentrate.

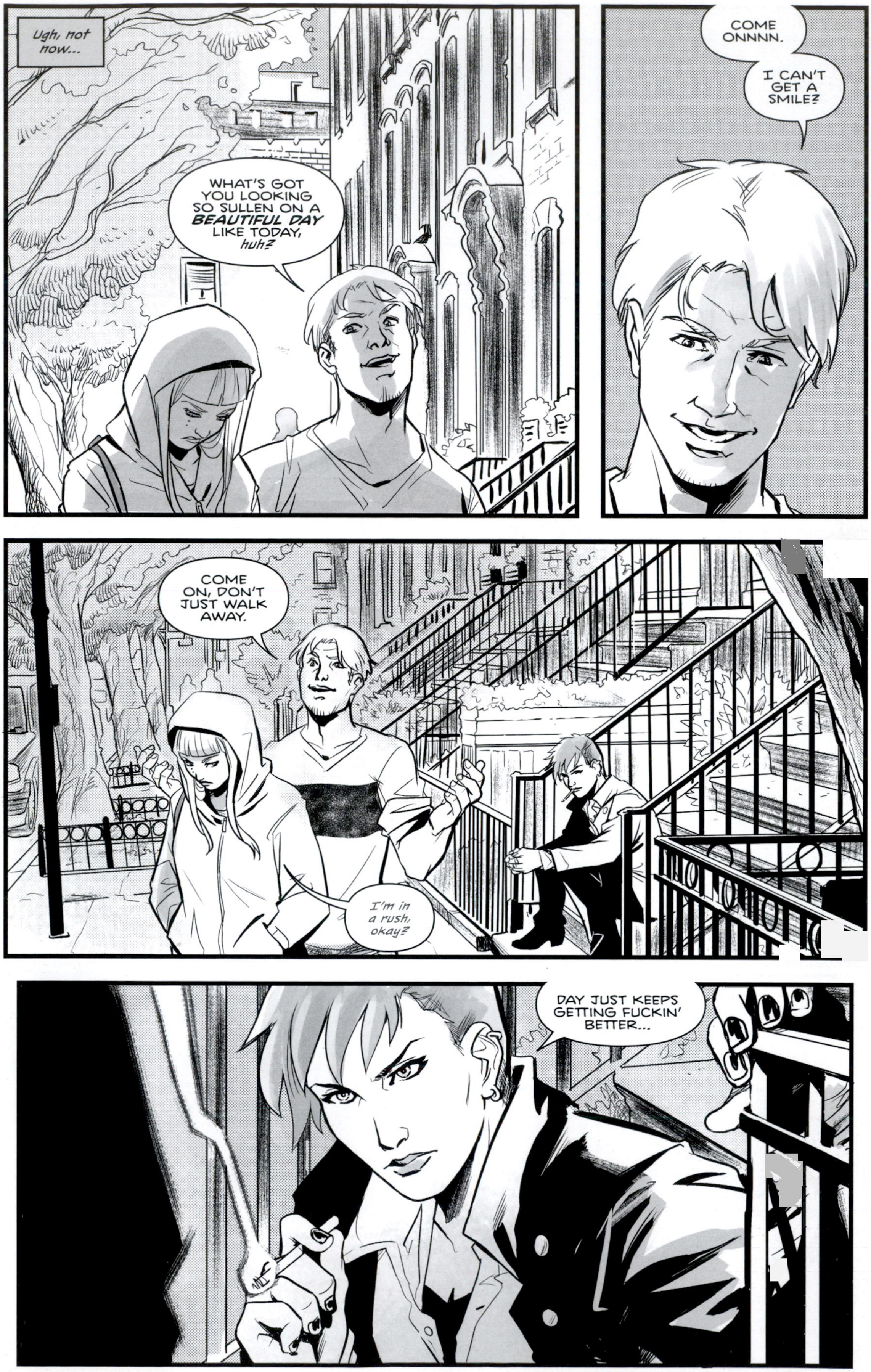
Ugh, not now...
WHAT'S GOT YOU LOOKING SO SULLEN ON A BEAUTIFUL DAY LIKE TODAY, huh?
COME ONNNN.
I CAN'T GET A SMILE?
COME ON, DON'T JUST WALK AWAY.
I'm in a rush, okay?
DAY JUST KEEPS GETTING FUCKIN' BETTER...

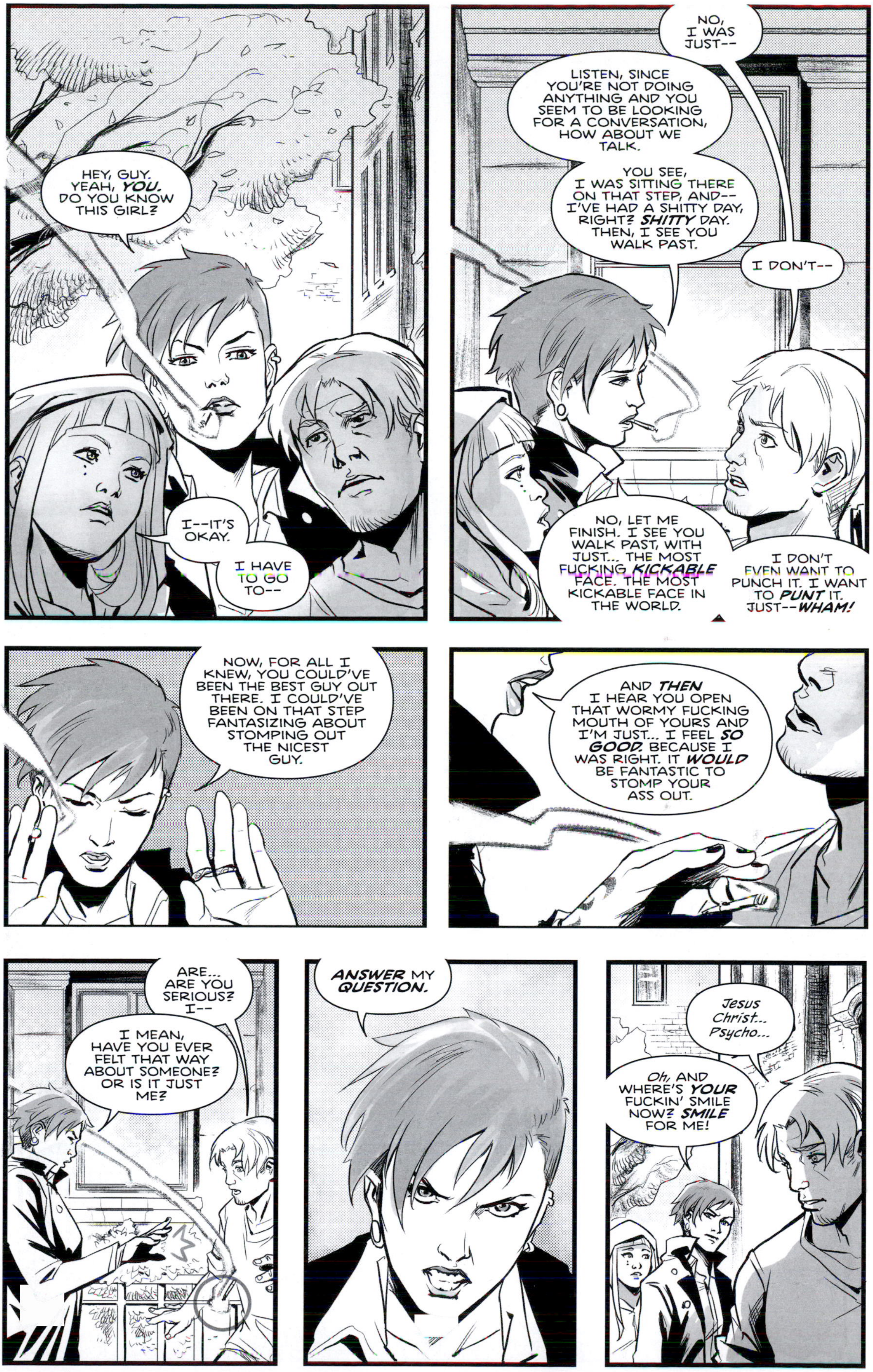
HEY, GUY. YEAH, YOU. DO YOU KNOW THIS GIRL?
I--IT'S OKAY.
I HAVE TO GO TO--
NO, I WAS JUST--
LISTEN, SINCE YOU'RE NOT DOING ANYTHING AND YOU SEEM TO BE LOOKING FOR A CONVERSATION, HOW ABOUT WE TALK.
YOU SEE, I WAS SITTING THERE ON THAT STEP, AND-- I'VE HAD A SHITTY DAY, RIGHT? SHITTY DAY. THEN, I SEE YOU WALK PAST.
I DON'T--
NO, LET ME FINISH. I SEE YOU WALK PAST, WITH JUST... THE MOST FUCKING KICKABLE FACE. THE MOST KICKABLE FACE IN THE WORLD.
I DON'T EVEN WANT TO PUNCH IT. I WANT TO PUNT IT. JUST--WHAM!
NOW, FOR ALL I KNEW, YOU COULD'VE BEEN THE BEST GUY OUT THERE. I COULD'VE BEEN ON THAT STEP FANTASIZING ABOUT STOMPING OUT THE NICEST GUY.
AND THEN I HEAR YOU OPEN THAT WORMY FUCKING MOUTH OF YOURS AND I'M JUST... I FEEL SO GOOD. BECAUSE I WAS RIGHT. IT WOULD BE FANTASTIC TO STOMP YOUR ASS OUT.
ARE... ARE YOU SERIOUS? I--
I MEAN, HAVE YOU EVER FELT THAT WAY ABOUT SOMEONE? OR IS IT JUST ME?
ANSWER MY QUESTION.
Jesus Christ... Psycho...
Oh, AND WHERE'S YOUR FUCKIN' SMILE NOW? SMILE FOR ME!

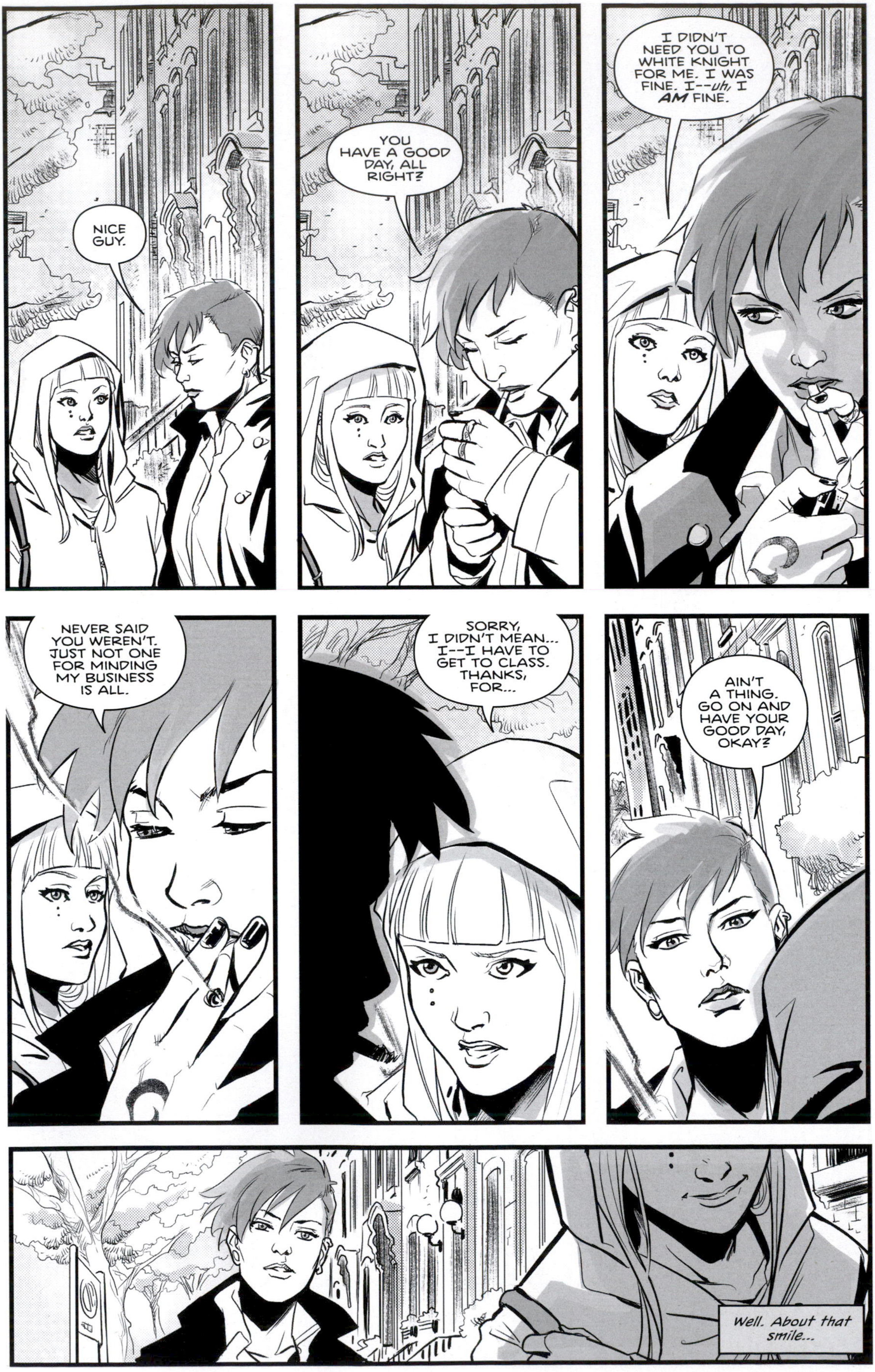

NICE GUY.
YOU HAVE A GOOD DAY, ALL RIGHT?
I DIDN'T NEED YOU TO WHITE KNIGHT FOR ME. I WAS FINE. I--*uh,* I ***AM*** FINE.
NEVER SAID YOU WEREN'T. JUST NOT ONE FOR MINDING MY BUSINESS IS ALL.
SORRY, I DIDN'T MEAN... I--I HAVE TO GET TO CLASS. THANKS, FOR...
AIN'T A THING. GO ON AND HAVE YOUR GOOD DAY, OKAY?
Well. About that smile...

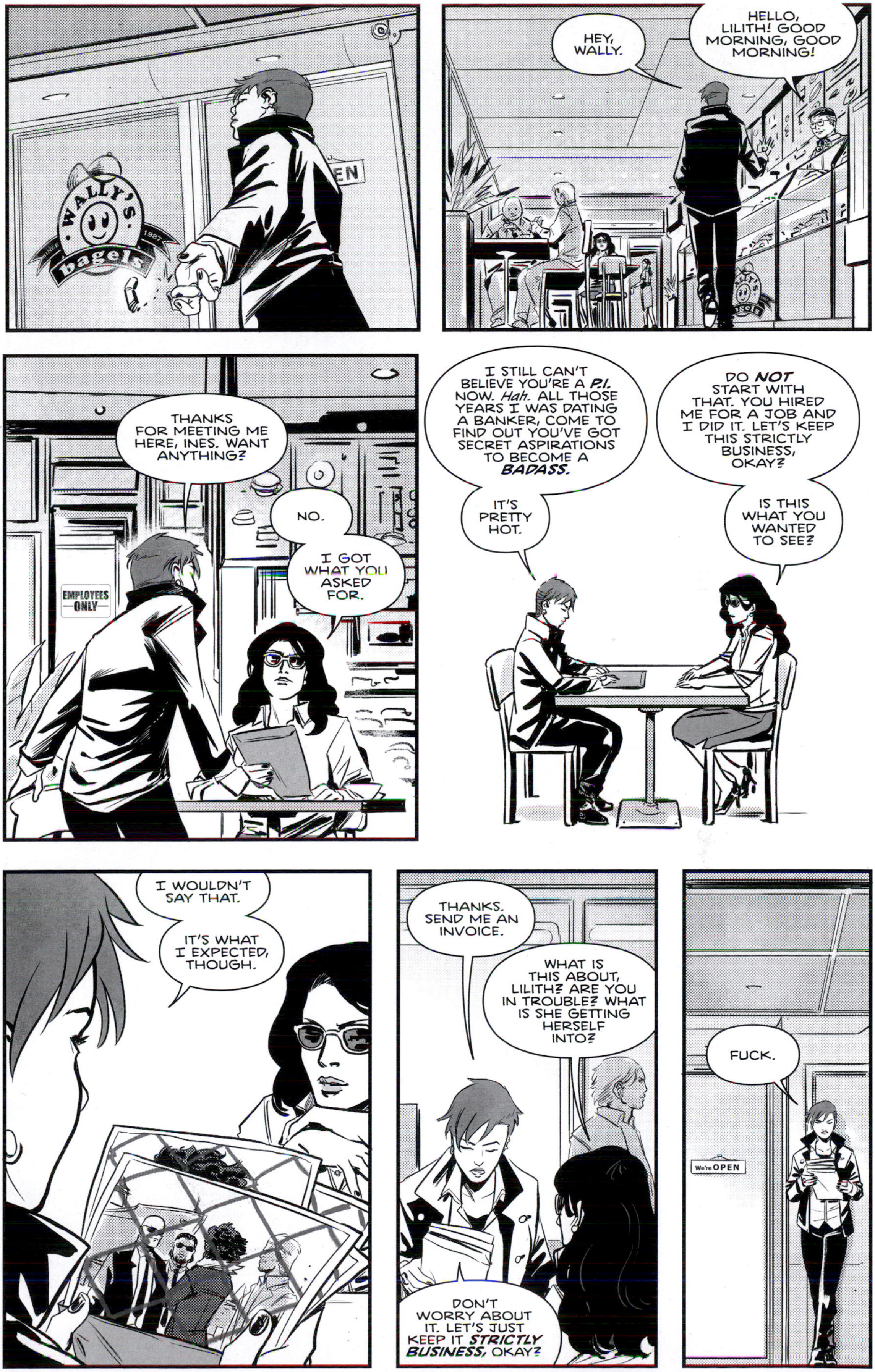

WALLY'S
SINCE 1987
bagels
EN
HEY, WALLY.
HELLO, LILITH! GOOD MORNING, GOOD MORNING!
THANKS FOR MEETING ME HERE, INES. WANT ANYTHING?
NO.
I GOT WHAT YOU ASKED FOR.
EMPLOYEES ONLY
I STILL CAN'T BELIEVE YOU'RE A P.I. NOW. Hah. ALL THOSE YEARS I WAS DATING A BANKER, COME TO FIND OUT YOU'VE GOT SECRET ASPIRATIONS TO BECOME A BADASS.
IT'S PRETTY HOT.
DO NOT START WITH THAT. YOU HIRED ME FOR A JOB AND I DID IT. LET'S KEEP THIS STRICTLY BUSINESS, OKAY?
IS THIS WHAT YOU WANTED TO SEE?
I WOULDN'T SAY THAT.
IT'S WHAT I EXPECTED, THOUGH.
THANKS. SEND ME AN INVOICE.
WHAT IS THIS ABOUT, LILITH? ARE YOU IN TROUBLE? WHAT IS SHE GETTING HERSELF INTO?
DON'T WORRY ABOUT IT. LET'S JUST KEEP IT STRICTLY BUSINESS, OKAY?
We're OPEN
FUCK.

Sometimes, I can't help but think in terms of ***me*** *and* ***them.***

There's ***them...*** *the people on the street who never doubt their ability to get out of bed in the morning. The people who, if they heard my complaints, my problems-- they'd probably just think I need to get over it. And maybe they're right. It's not like I'm homeless, I don't suffer from any disabilities, I'm not* ***poor...*** *well, not* ***very*** *poor. There are good people who have it pretty bad in this city.*

And then there's ***me...*** *Logan McBride, girl wonder, whose brain can overanalyze every aspect of her life at the speed of a flying bullet, who jumps to the worst conclusions in a single bound! The girl who met her destiny less than a week after she got her first kiss.*

There's also the ***other*** *them... the* ***them*** *that live a normal life. Get married (maybe after being proposed to at a fucking resort,* ***twice***--*ugh), have kids, get old, die. The kind of people who get to tell their own story.*

And then there's ***me...*** *the girl who goes to a magical graduate school with all of the other* ***Chosen Ones.***

Yeah, don't get excited. it couldn't be ***less*** *what you think.*

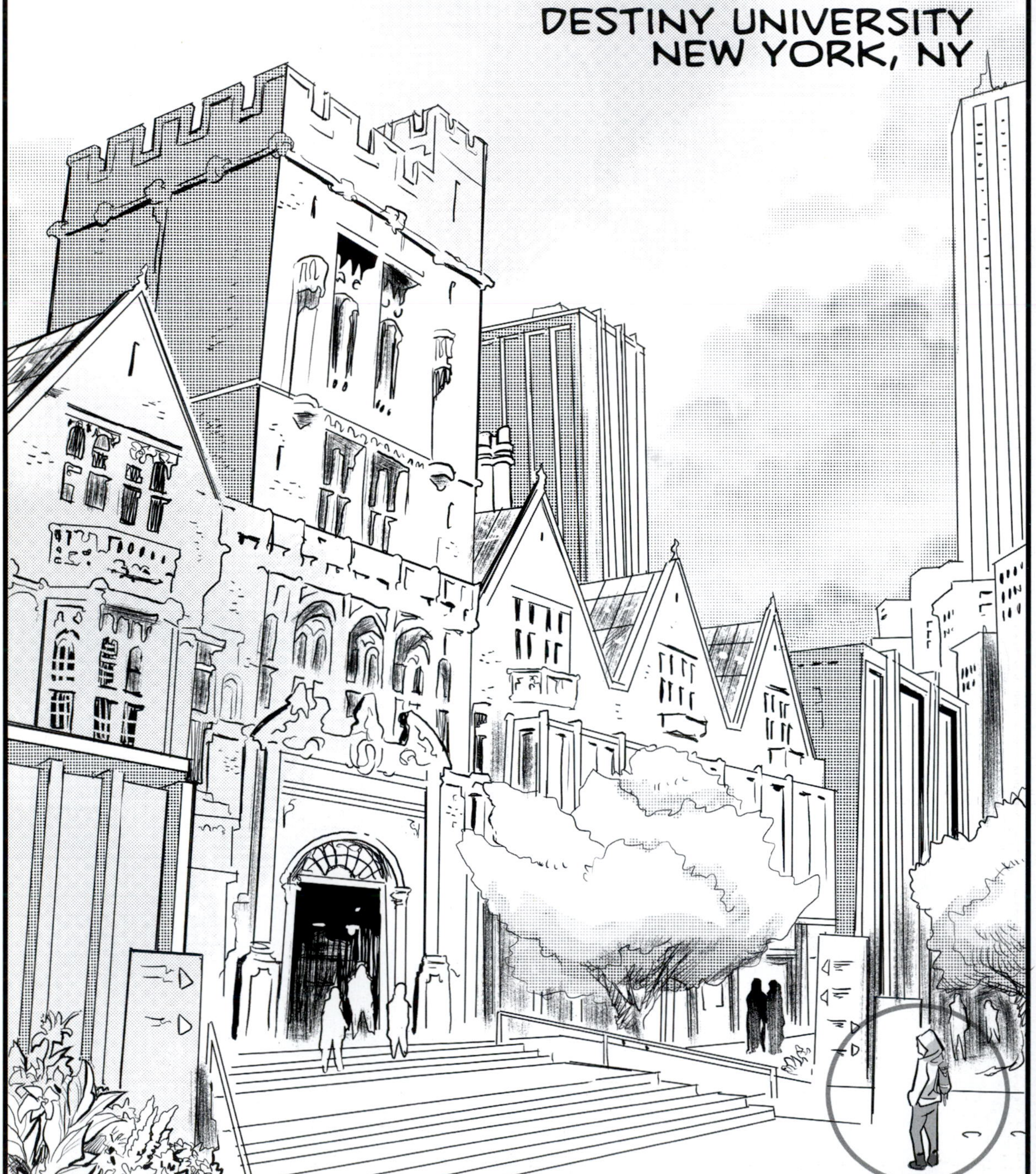
DESTINY UNIVERSITY
NEW YORK, NY

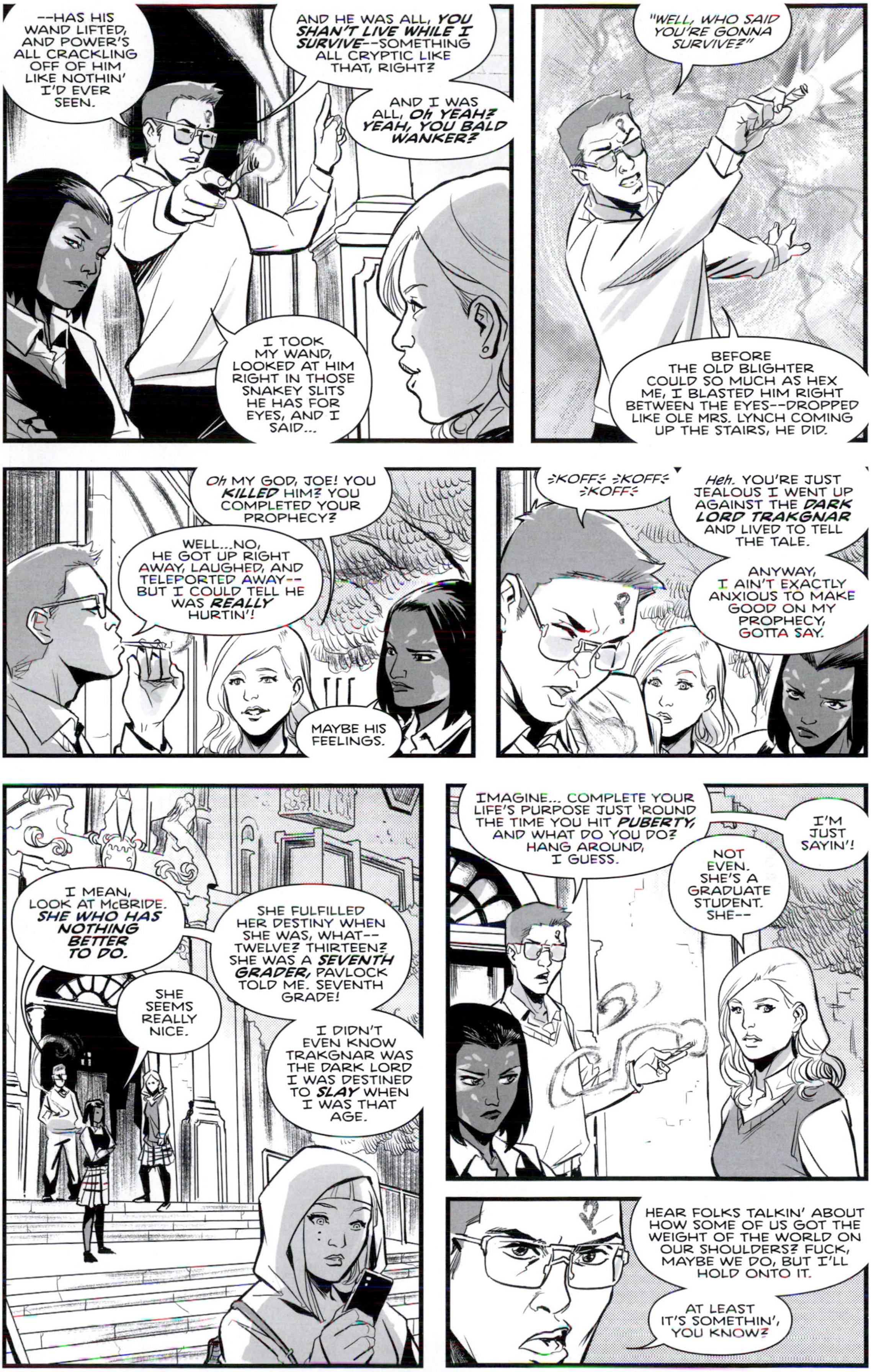
--HAS HIS WAND LIFTED, AND POWER'S ALL CRACKLING OFF OF HIM LIKE NOTHIN' I'D EVER SEEN.
AND HE WAS ALL, ***YOU SHAN'T LIVE WHILE I SURVIVE***--SOMETHING ALL CRYPTIC LIKE THAT, RIGHT?
AND I WAS ALL, ***Oh YEAH? YEAH, YOU BALD WANKER?***
I TOOK MY WAND, LOOKED AT HIM RIGHT IN THOSE SNAKEY SLITS HE HAS FOR EYES, AND I SAID...
"WELL, WHO SAID YOU'RE GONNA SURVIVE?"
BEFORE THE OLD BLIGHTER COULD SO MUCH AS HEX ME, I BLASTED HIM RIGHT BETWEEN THE EYES--DROPPED LIKE OLE MRS. LYNCH COMING UP THE STAIRS, HE DID.
Oh MY GOD, JOE! YOU ***KILLED*** HIM? YOU COMPLETED YOUR PROPHECY?
WELL...NO, HE GOT UP RIGHT AWAY, LAUGHED, AND TELEPORTED AWAY--BUT I COULD TELL HE WAS ***REALLY*** HURTIN'!
MAYBE HIS FEELINGS.
KOFF *KOFF* *KOFF*
Heh. YOU'RE JUST JEALOUS I WENT UP AGAINST THE ***DARK LORD TRAKGNAR*** AND LIVED TO TELL THE TALE.
ANYWAY, I AIN'T EXACTLY ANXIOUS TO MAKE GOOD ON MY PROPHECY, GOTTA SAY.
I MEAN, LOOK AT McBRIDE. ***SHE WHO HAS NOTHING BETTER TO DO.***
SHE FULFILLED HER DESTINY WHEN SHE WAS, WHAT--TWELVE? THIRTEEN? SHE WAS A ***SEVENTH GRADER,*** PAVLOCK TOLD ME. SEVENTH GRADE!
SHE SEEMS REALLY NICE.
I DIDN'T EVEN KNOW TRAKGNAR WAS THE DARK LORD I WAS DESTINED TO ***SLAY*** WHEN I WAS THAT AGE.
IMAGINE... COMPLETE YOUR LIFE'S PURPOSE JUST 'ROUND THE TIME YOU HIT ***PUBERTY,*** AND WHAT DO YOU DO? HANG AROUND, I GUESS.
I'M JUST SAYIN'!
NOT EVEN. SHE'S A GRADUATE STUDENT. SHE--
HEAR FOLKS TALKIN' ABOUT HOW SOME OF US GOT THE WEIGHT OF THE WORLD ON OUR SHOULDERS? FUCK, MAYBE WE DO, BUT I'LL HOLD ONTO IT.
AT LEAST IT'S SOMETHIN', YOU KNOW?

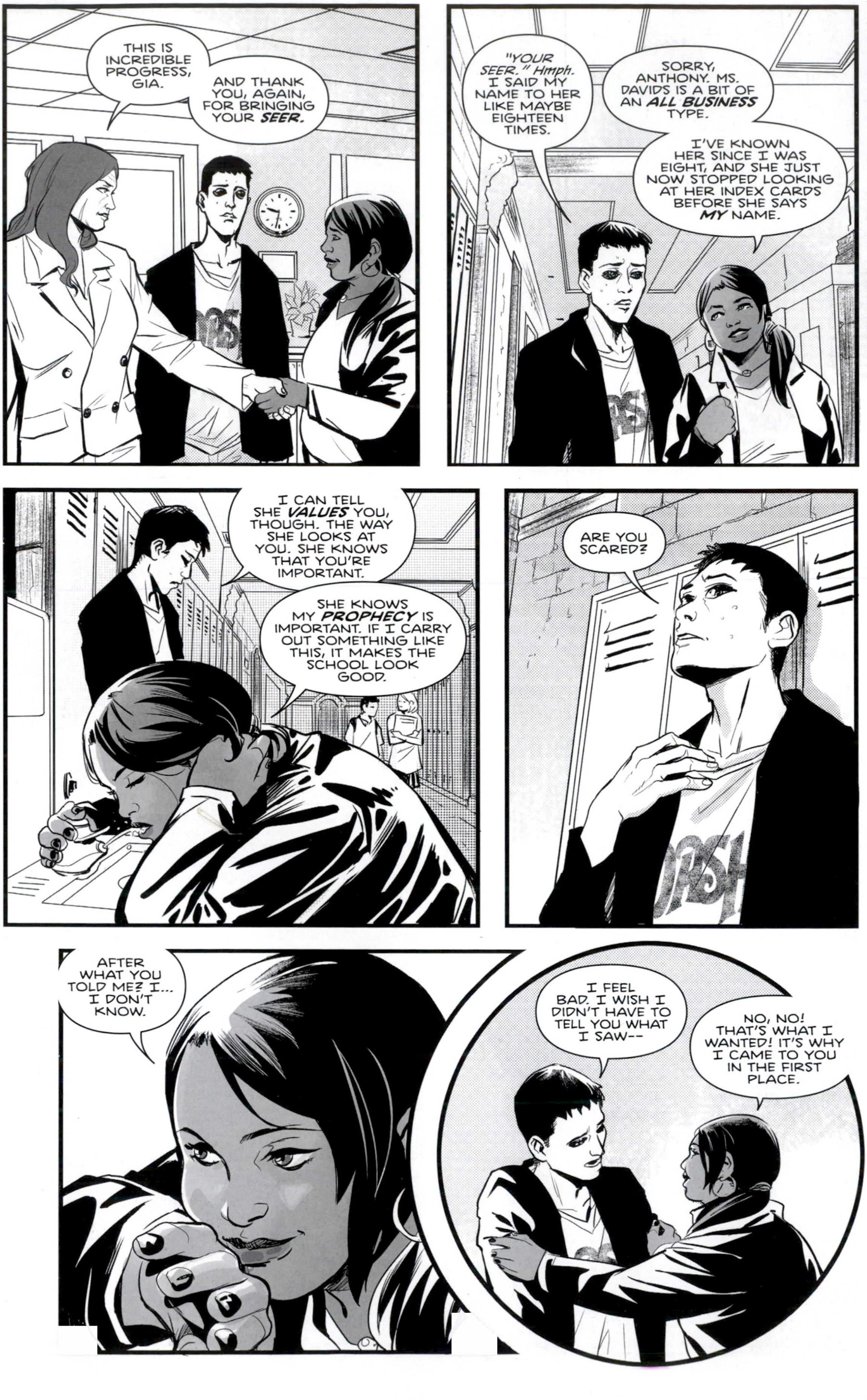
THIS IS INCREDIBLE PROGRESS, GIA.
AND THANK YOU, AGAIN, FOR BRINGING YOUR *SEER.*
"YOUR SEER." Hmph. I SAID MY NAME TO HER LIKE MAYBE EIGHTEEN TIMES.
SORRY, ANTHONY. MS. DAVIDS IS A BIT OF AN *ALL BUSINESS* TYPE.
I'VE KNOWN HER SINCE I WAS EIGHT, AND SHE JUST NOW STOPPED LOOKING AT HER INDEX CARDS BEFORE SHE SAYS *MY* NAME.
I CAN TELL SHE *VALUES* YOU, THOUGH. THE WAY SHE LOOKS AT YOU. SHE KNOWS THAT YOU'RE IMPORTANT.
SHE KNOWS MY *PROPHECY* IS IMPORTANT. IF I CARRY OUT SOMETHING LIKE THIS, IT MAKES THE SCHOOL LOOK GOOD.
ARE YOU SCARED?
AFTER WHAT YOU TOLD ME? I... I DON'T KNOW.
I FEEL BAD. I WISH I DIDN'T HAVE TO TELL YOU WHAT I SAW--
NO, NO! THAT'S WHAT I WANTED! IT'S WHY I CAME TO YOU IN THE FIRST PLACE.

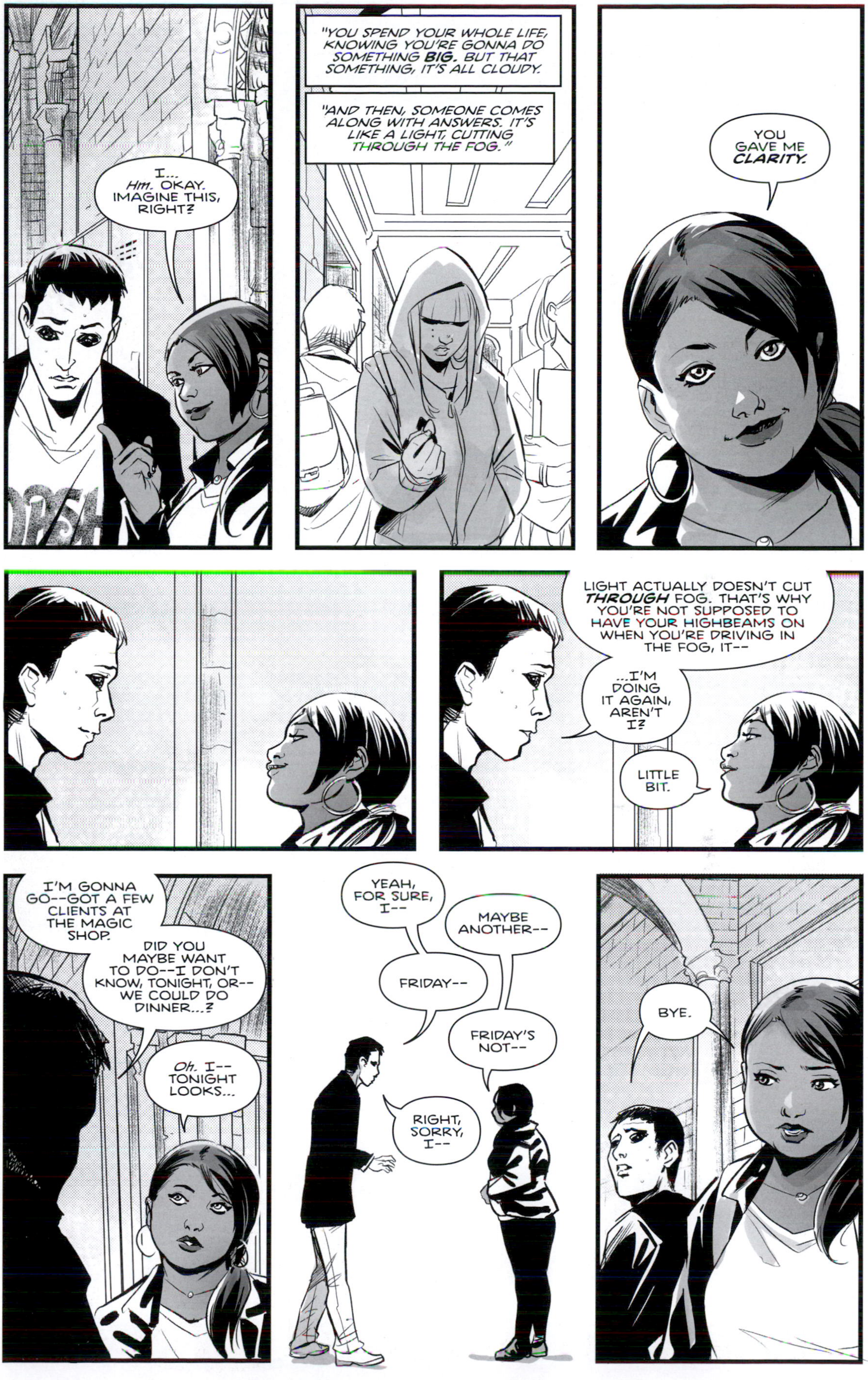
I... Hm. OKAY. IMAGINE THIS, RIGHT?
"YOU SPEND YOUR WHOLE LIFE, KNOWING YOU'RE GONNA DO SOMETHING BIG. BUT THAT SOMETHING, IT'S ALL CLOUDY.
"AND THEN, SOMEONE COMES ALONG WITH ANSWERS. IT'S LIKE A LIGHT, CUTTING THROUGH THE FOG."
YOU GAVE ME CLARITY.
LIGHT ACTUALLY DOESN'T CUT THROUGH FOG. THAT'S WHY YOU'RE NOT SUPPOSED TO HAVE YOUR HIGHBEAMS ON WHEN YOU'RE DRIVING IN THE FOG, IT--
...I'M DOING IT AGAIN, AREN'T I?
LITTLE BIT.
I'M GONNA GO--GOT A FEW CLIENTS AT THE MAGIC SHOP.
DID YOU MAYBE WANT TO DO--I DON'T KNOW, TONIGHT, OR--WE COULD DO DINNER...?
Oh. I--TONIGHT LOOKS...
YEAH, FOR SURE, I--
MAYBE ANOTHER--
FRIDAY--
FRIDAY'S NOT--
RIGHT, SORRY, I--
BYE.

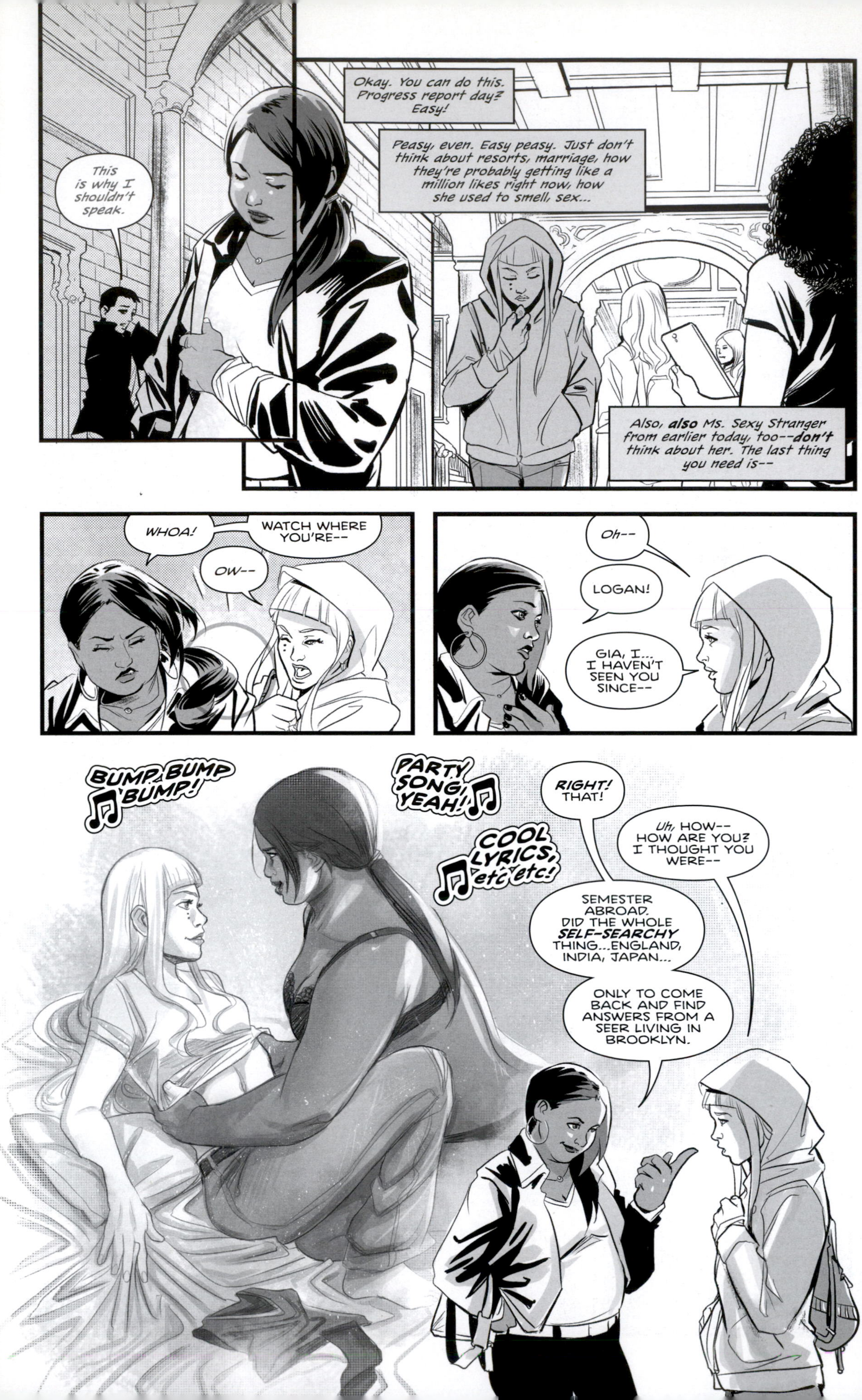
This is why I shouldn't speak.
Okay. You can do this. Progress report day? Easy!
Peasy, even. Easy peasy. Just don't think about resorts, marriage, how they're probably getting like a million likes right now, how she used to smell, sex...
Also, **also** Ms. Sexy Stranger from earlier today, too--**don't** think about her. The last thing you need is--
WHOA!
WATCH WHERE YOU'RE--
OW--
Oh--
LOGAN!
GIA, I... I HAVEN'T SEEN YOU SINCE--
BUMP BUMP BUMP!
PARTY SONG, YEAH!
COOL LYRICS, etc etc!
RIGHT! THAT!
Uh, HOW-- HOW ARE YOU? I THOUGHT YOU WERE--
SEMESTER ABROAD. DID THE WHOLE ***SELF-SEARCHY*** THING...ENGLAND, INDIA, JAPAN...
ONLY TO COME BACK AND FIND ANSWERS FROM A SEER LIVING IN BROOKLYN.

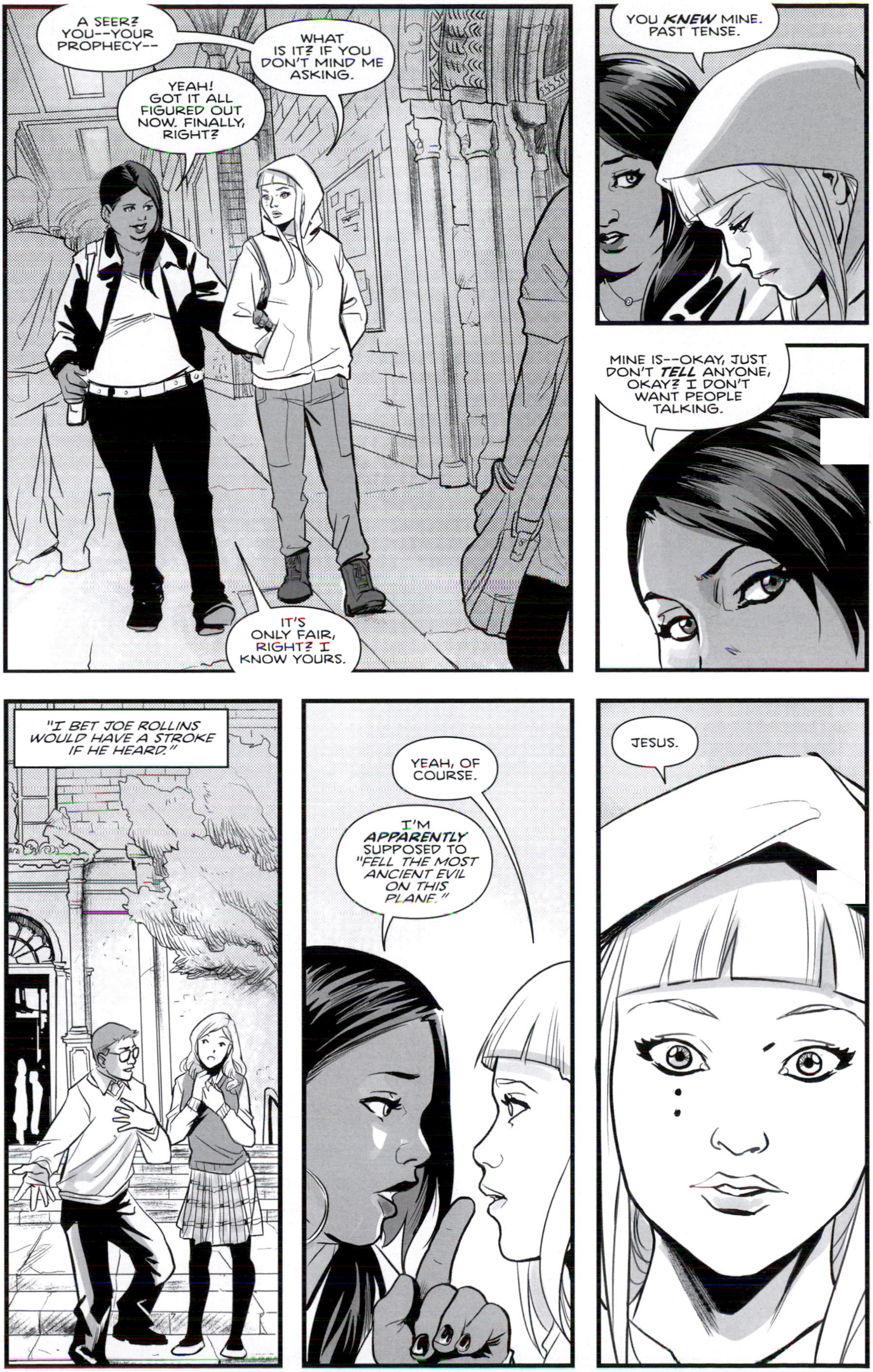
A SEER? YOU--YOUR PROPHECY--
YEAH! GOT IT ALL FIGURED OUT NOW. FINALLY, RIGHT?
WHAT IS IT? IF YOU DON'T MIND ME ASKING.
IT'S ONLY FAIR, RIGHT? I KNOW YOURS.
YOU KNEW MINE. PAST TENSE.
MINE IS--OKAY, JUST DON'T TELL ANYONE, OKAY? I DON'T WANT PEOPLE TALKING.
"I BET JOE ROLLINS WOULD HAVE A STROKE IF HE HEARD."
YEAH, OF COURSE.
I'M APPARENTLY SUPPOSED TO "FELL THE MOST ANCIENT EVIL ON THIS PLANE."
JESUS.

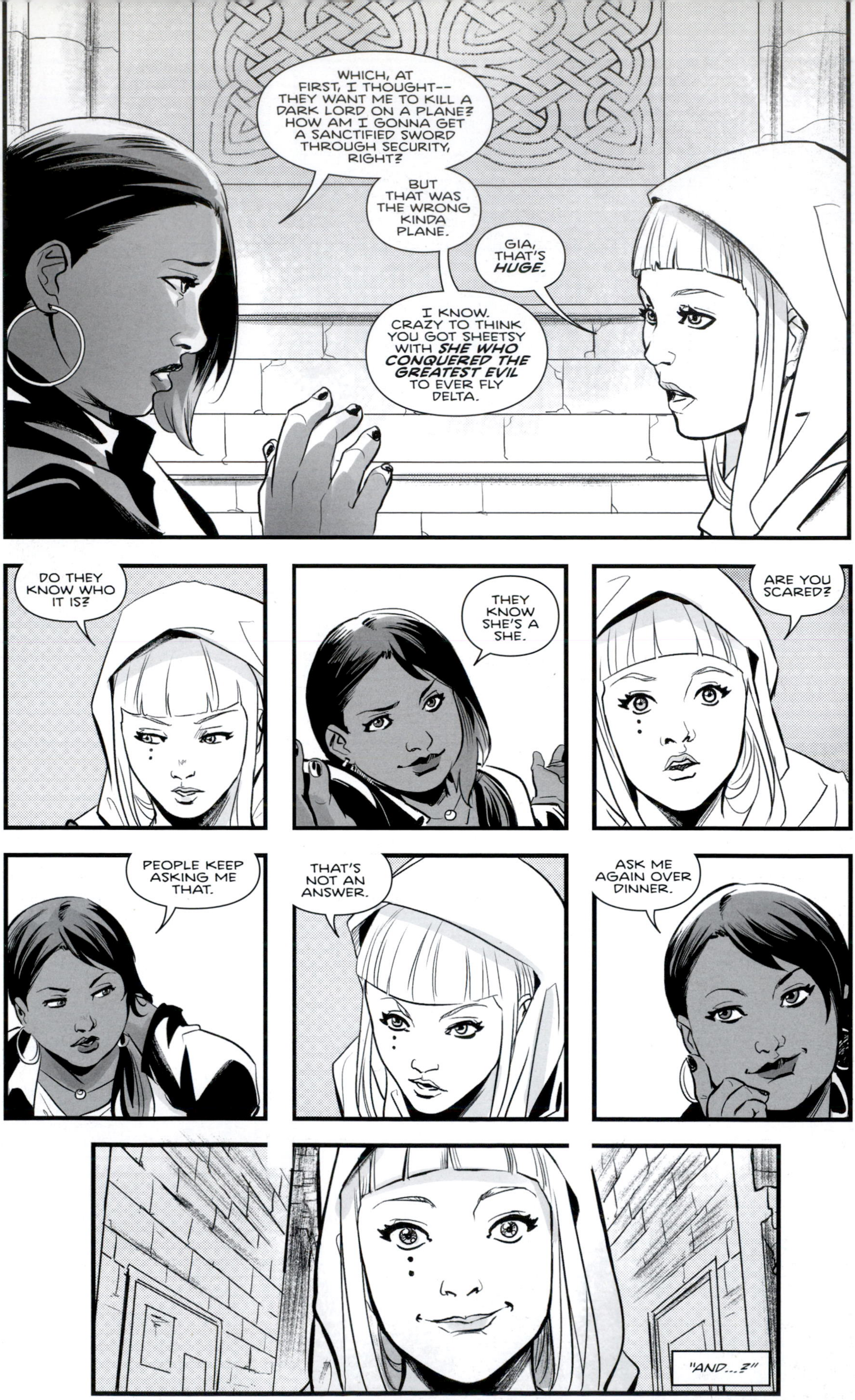
WHICH, AT FIRST, I THOUGHT-- THEY WANT ME TO KILL A DARK LORD ON A PLANE? HOW AM I GONNA GET A SANCTIFIED SWORD THROUGH SECURITY, RIGHT?
BUT THAT WAS THE WRONG KINDA PLANE.
GIA, THAT'S *HUGE.*
I KNOW. CRAZY TO THINK YOU GOT SHEETSY WITH ***SHE WHO CONQUERED THE GREATEST EVIL*** TO EVER FLY DELTA.
DO THEY KNOW WHO IT IS?
THEY KNOW SHE'S A SHE.
ARE YOU SCARED?
PEOPLE KEEP ASKING ME THAT.
THAT'S NOT AN ANSWER.
ASK ME AGAIN OVER DINNER.
"AND...?"

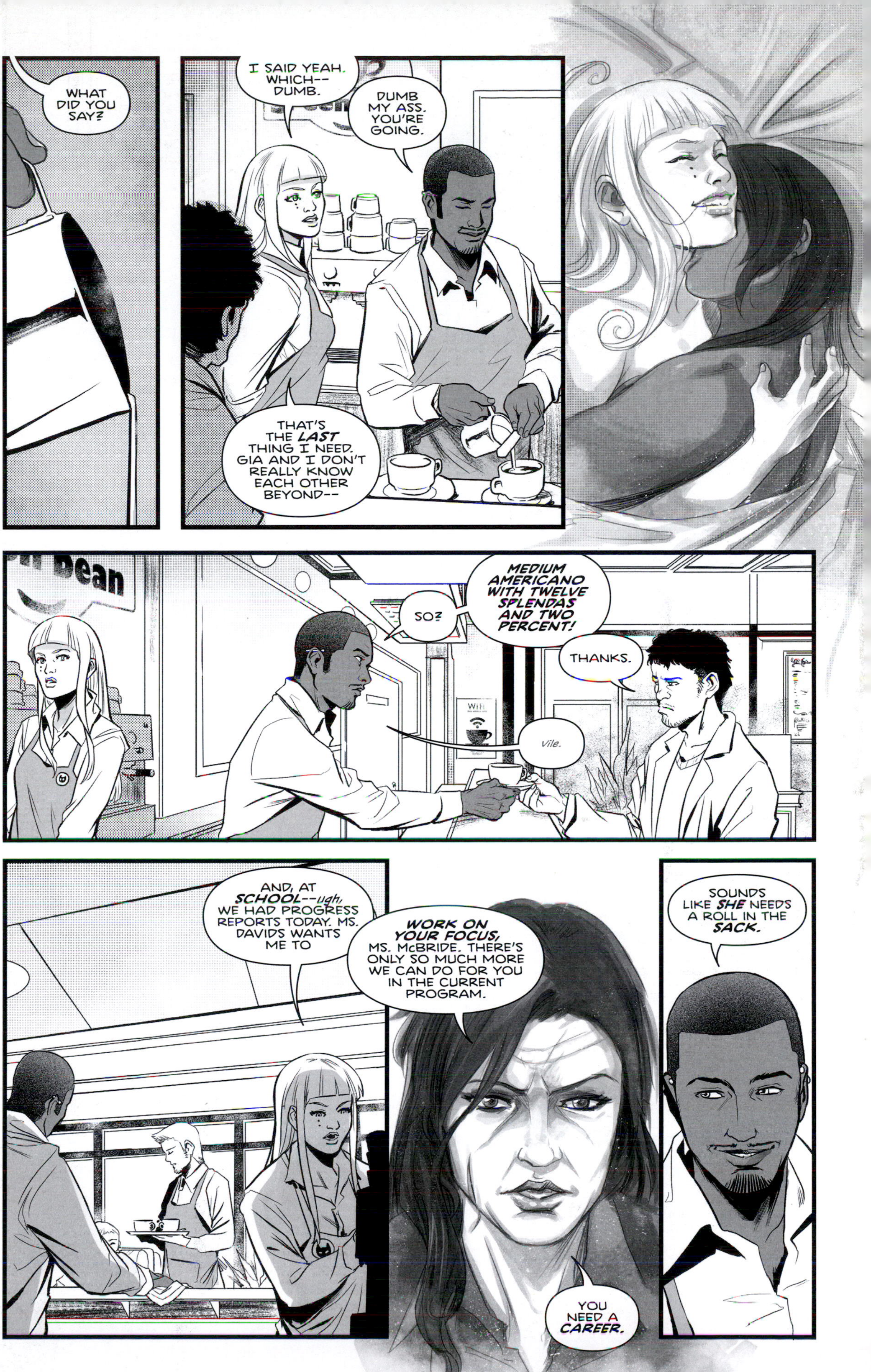
WHAT DID YOU SAY?
I SAID YEAH. WHICH-- DUMB.
DUMB MY ASS. YOU'RE GOING.
THAT'S THE LAST THING I NEED. GIA AND I DON'T REALLY KNOW EACH OTHER BEYOND--
SO?
MEDIUM AMERICANO WITH TWELVE SPLENDAS AND TWO PERCENT!
THANKS.
Vile.
AND, AT SCHOOL--ugh, WE HAD PROGRESS REPORTS TODAY. MS. DAVIDS WANTS ME TO
WORK ON YOUR FOCUS, MS. McBRIDE. THERE'S ONLY SO MUCH MORE WE CAN DO FOR YOU IN THE CURRENT PROGRAM.
YOU NEED A CAREER.
SOUNDS LIKE SHE NEEDS A ROLL IN THE SACK.

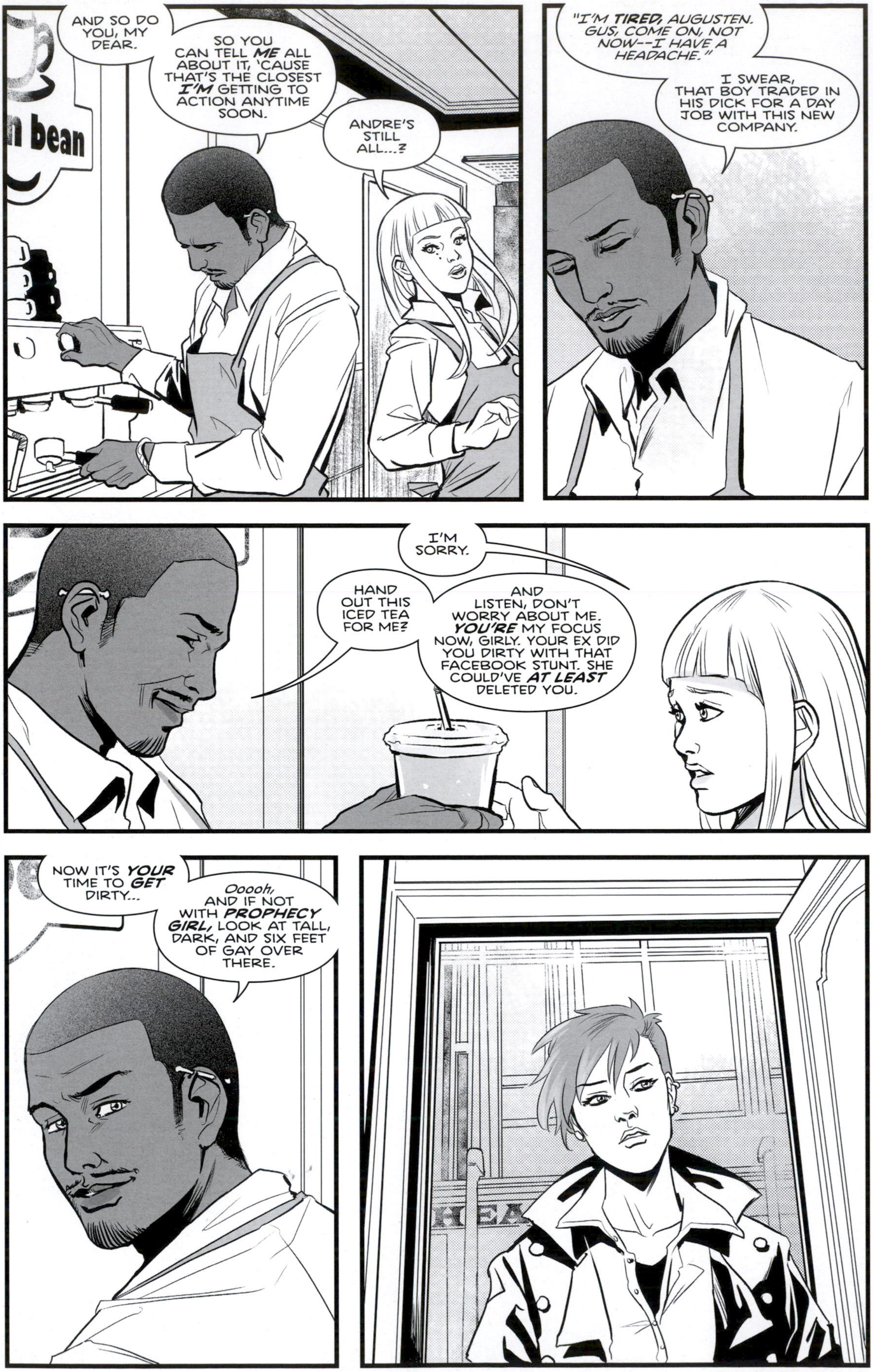

AND SO DO YOU, MY DEAR.
SO YOU CAN TELL ME ALL ABOUT IT, 'CAUSE THAT'S THE CLOSEST I'M GETTING TO ACTION ANYTIME SOON.
ANDRE'S STILL ALL...?
"I'M TIRED, AUGUSTEN. GUS, COME ON, NOT NOW--I HAVE A HEADACHE."
I SWEAR, THAT BOY TRADED IN HIS DICK FOR A DAY JOB WITH THIS NEW COMPANY.
I'M SORRY.
HAND OUT THIS ICED TEA FOR ME?
AND LISTEN, DON'T WORRY ABOUT ME. YOU'RE MY FOCUS NOW, GIRLY. YOUR EX DID YOU DIRTY WITH THAT FACEBOOK STUNT. SHE COULD'VE AT LEAST DELETED YOU.
NOW IT'S YOUR TIME TO GET DIRTY...
Ooooh, AND IF NOT WITH PROPHECY GIRL, LOOK AT TALL, DARK, AND SIX FEET OF GAY OVER THERE.

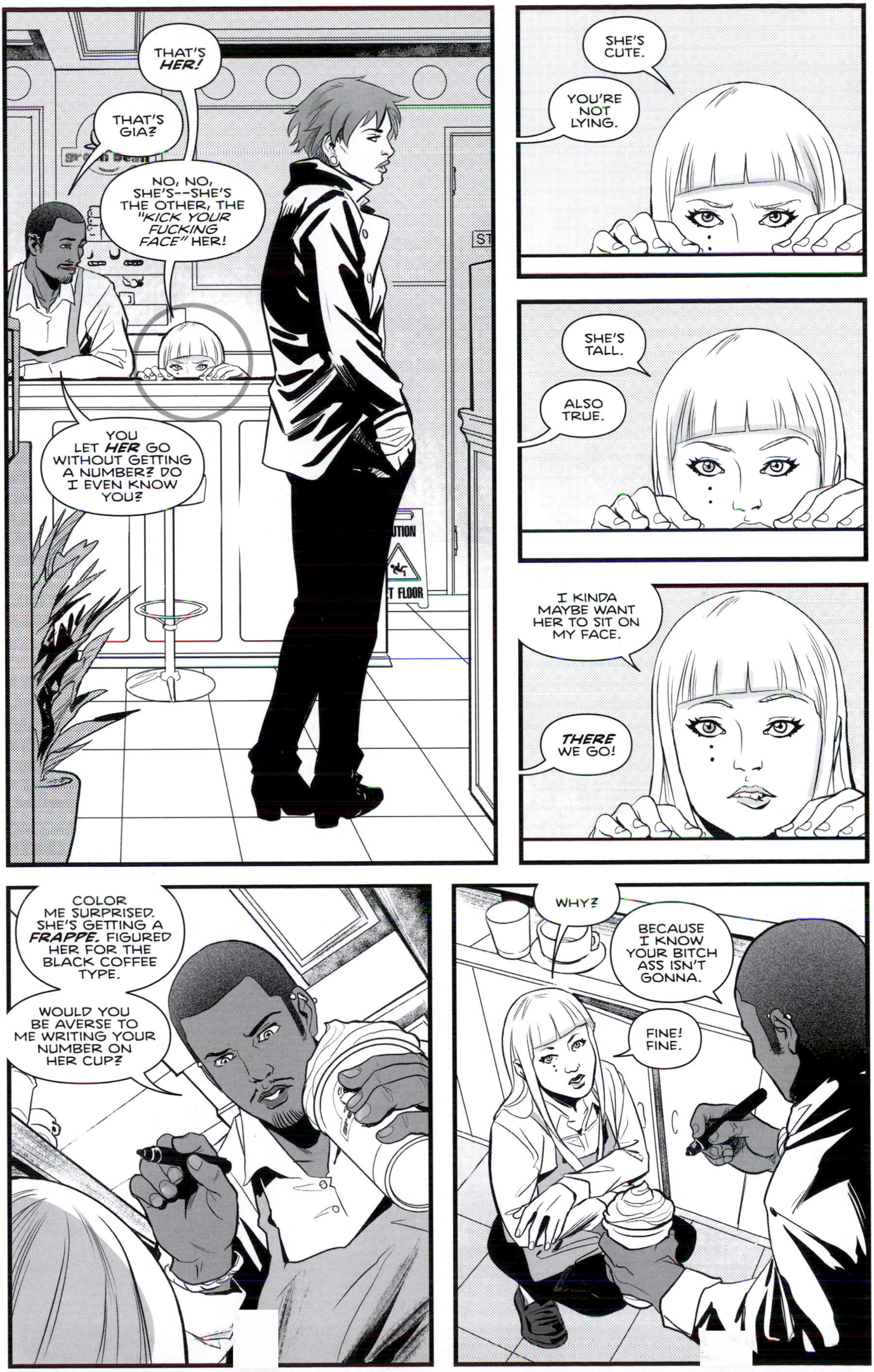
THAT'S GIA?
THAT'S *HER!*
NO, NO, SHE'S--SHE'S THE OTHER, THE *"KICK YOUR FUCKING FACE"* HER!
YOU LET *HER* GO WITHOUT GETTING A NUMBER? DO I EVEN KNOW YOU?
SHE'S CUTE.
YOU'RE NOT LYING.
SHE'S TALL.
ALSO TRUE.
I KINDA MAYBE WANT HER TO SIT ON MY FACE.
THERE WE GO!
COLOR ME SURPRISED. SHE'S GETTING A *FRAPPE.* FIGURED HER FOR THE BLACK COFFEE TYPE.
WOULD YOU BE AVERSE TO ME WRITING YOUR NUMBER ON HER CUP?
WHY?
BECAUSE I KNOW YOUR BITCH ASS ISN'T GONNA.
FINE! FINE.

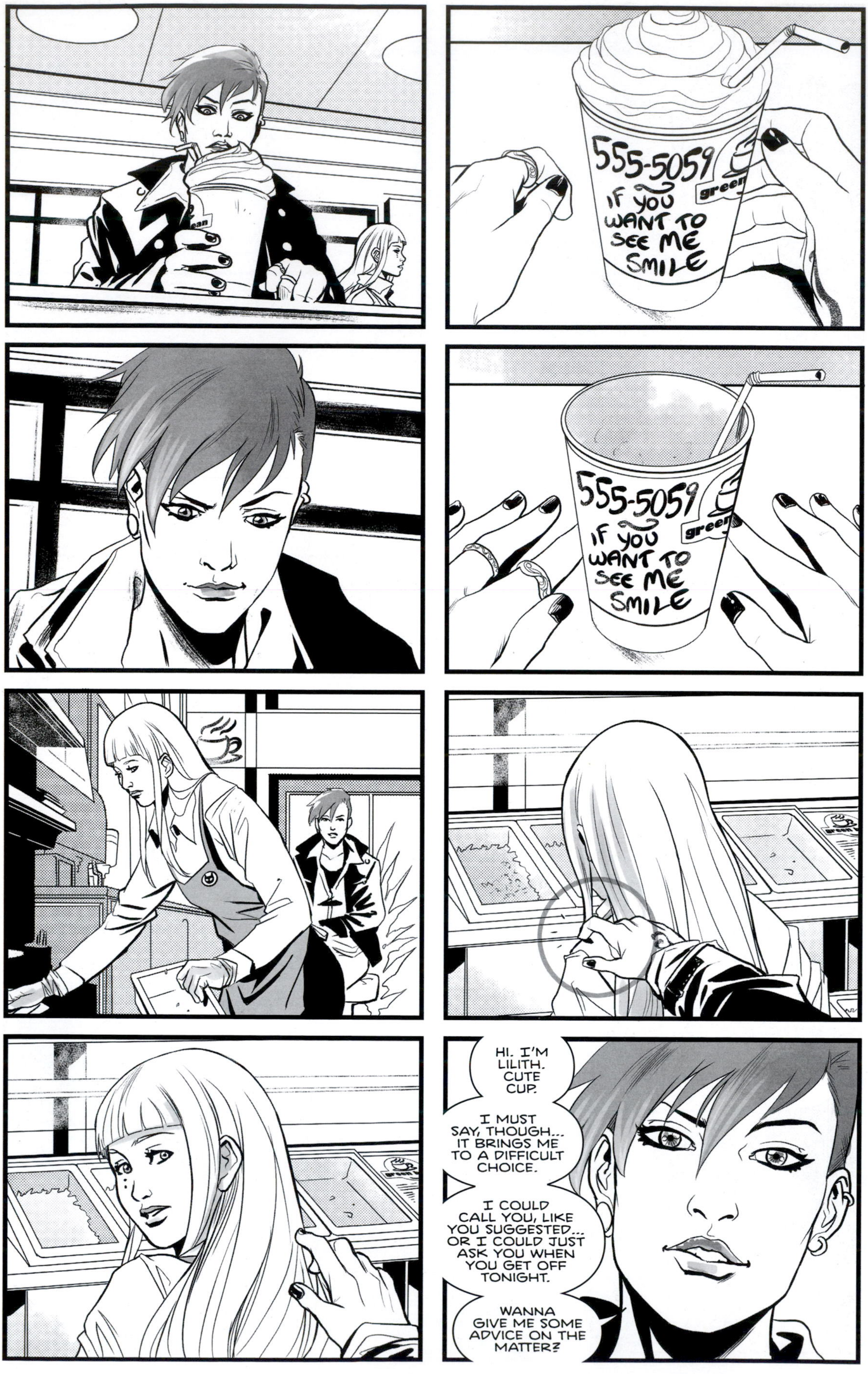
555-5059
IF YOU WANT TO SEE ME SMILE
555-5059
IF YOU WANT TO SEE ME SMILE
HI. I'M LILITH. CUTE CUP.
I MUST SAY, THOUGH... IT BRINGS ME TO A DIFFICULT CHOICE.
I COULD CALL YOU, LIKE YOU SUGGESTED... OR I COULD JUST ASK YOU WHEN YOU GET OFF TONIGHT.
WANNA GIVE ME SOME ADVICE ON THE MATTER?

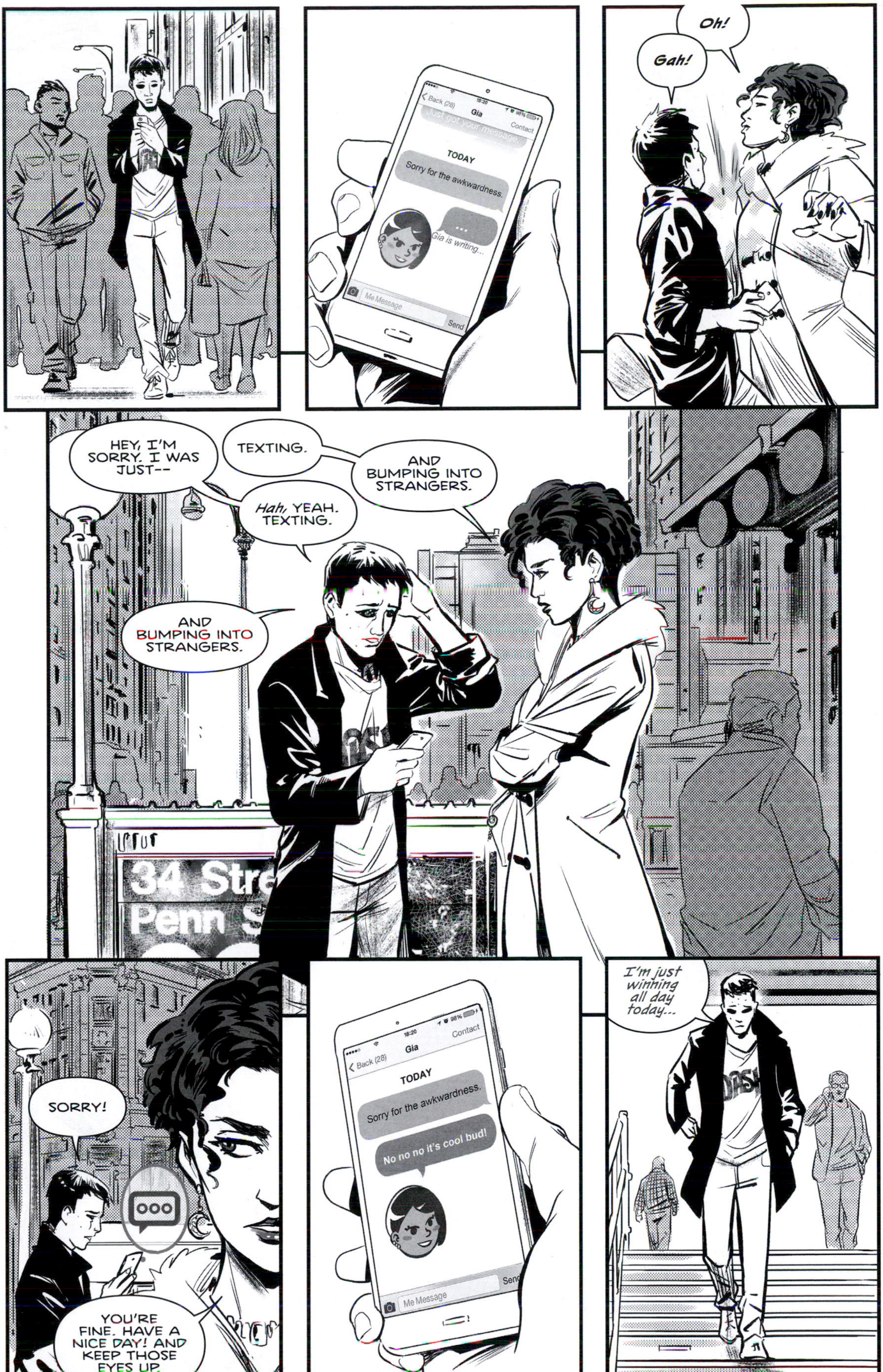

Back (28)
Gia
Contact
Just got your message.
TODAY
Sorry for the awkwardness.
Gia is writing...
Me Message
Send
Gah!
Oh!
HEY, I'M SORRY. I WAS JUST--
TEXTING.
AND BUMPING INTO STRANGERS.
Hah, YEAH. TEXTING.
AND BUMPING INTO STRANGERS.
34 Stre
Penn S
SORRY!
YOU'RE FINE. HAVE A NICE DAY! AND KEEP THOSE EYES UP.
Back (28)
Gia
Contact
TODAY
Sorry for the awkwardness.
No no no it's cool bud!
Me Message
I'm just winning all day today...

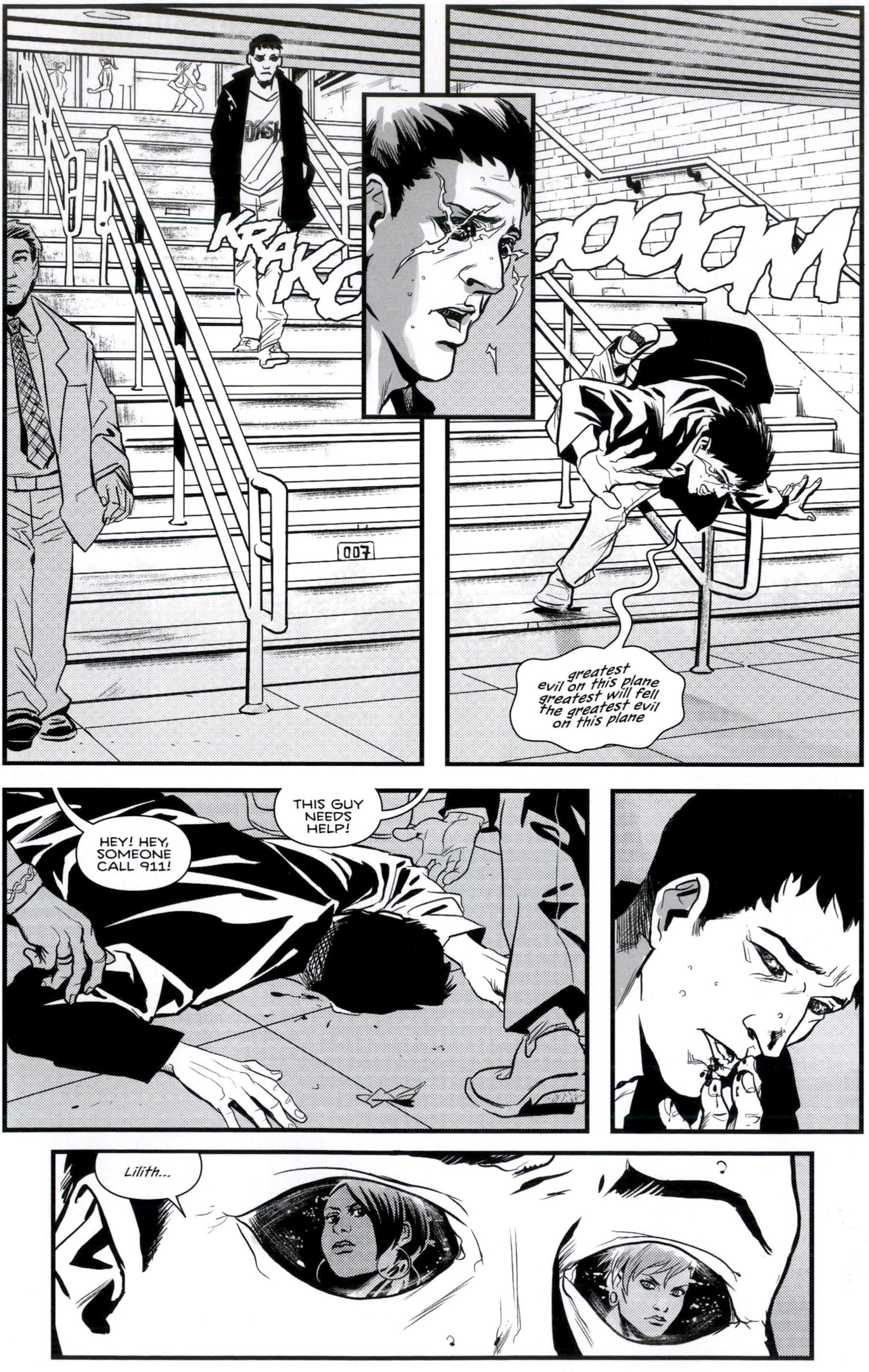
KRAKOOOOOOM
greatest evil on this plane greatest will fell the greatest evil on this plane
HEY! HEY, SOMEONE CALL 911!
THIS GUY NEEDS HELP!
Lilith...

The way today started, I felt like...

Like there was static electricity trapped in my chest, squeezing my heart, my lungs... making it so it hurt to breathe.

But I let that happen.

I opened a door and let the past in.

I do that. Think in terms of the past. Who I used to be, who I **should** be...

But you know... with all that happened...

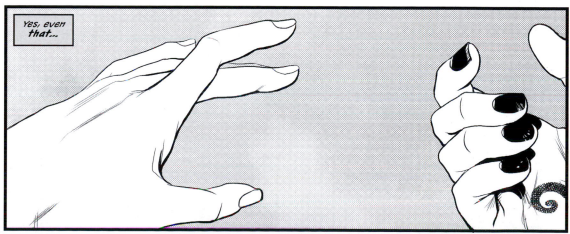

Yes, even **that**...

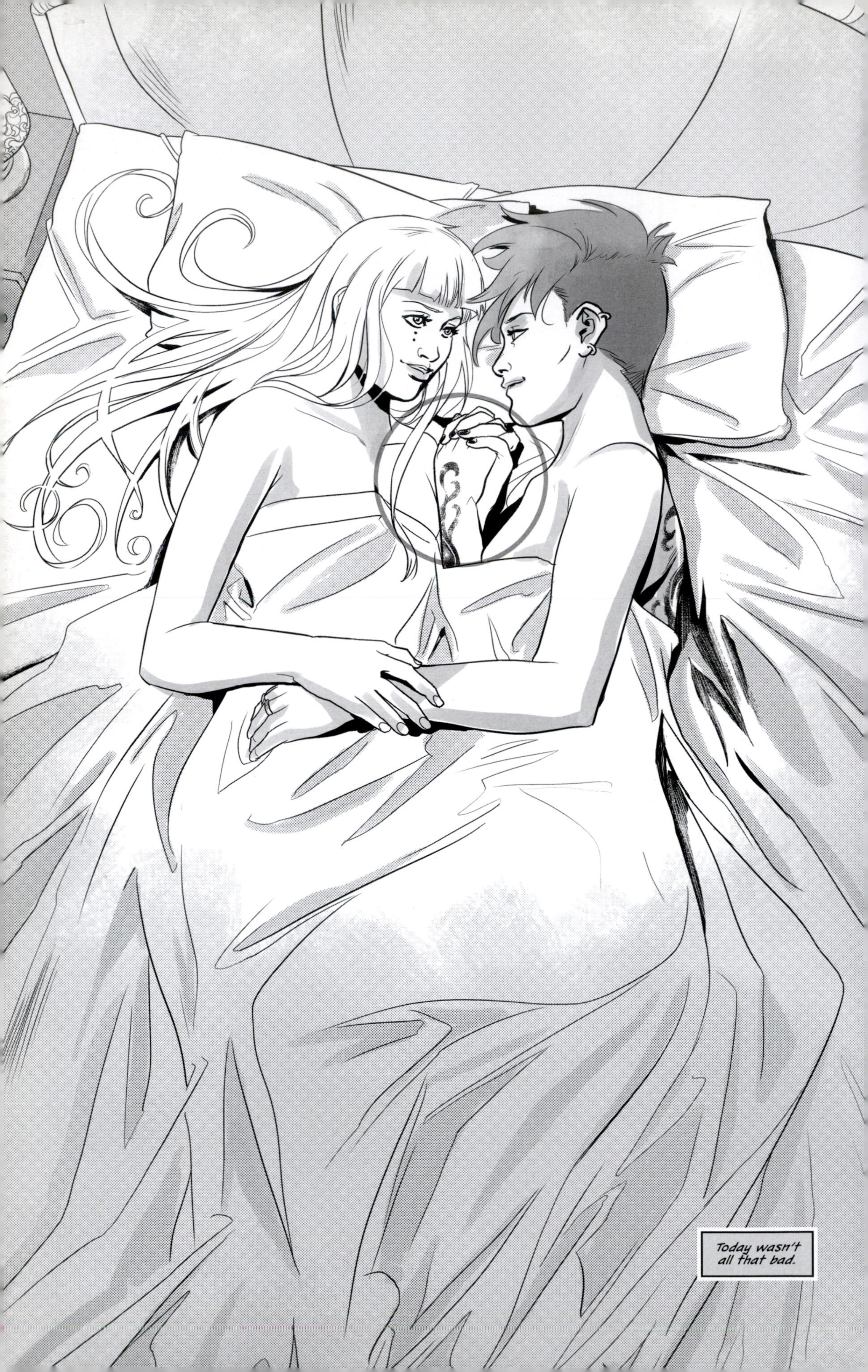
Today wasn't all that bad.

CHAPTER TWO

What Do You Do?

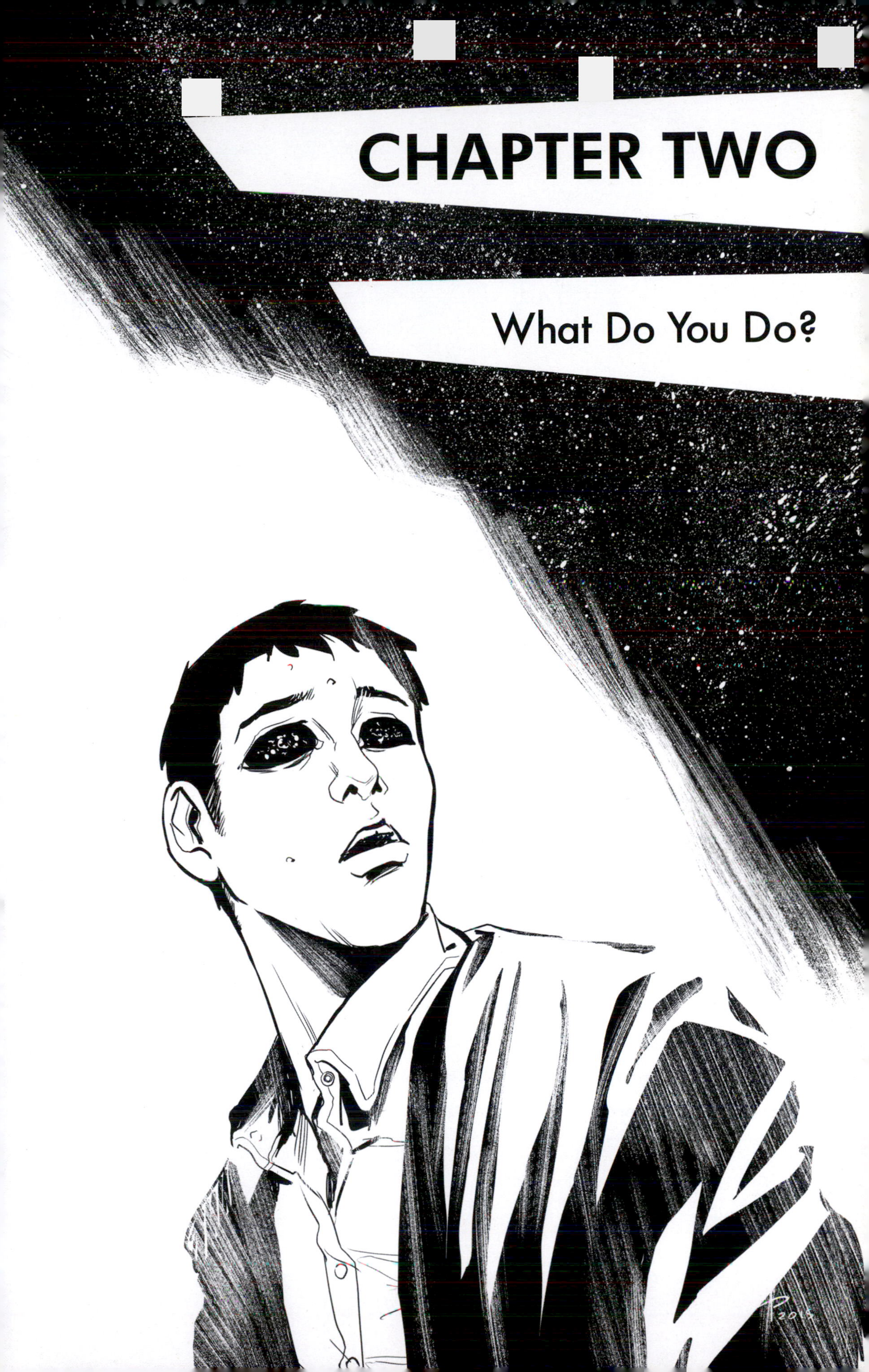

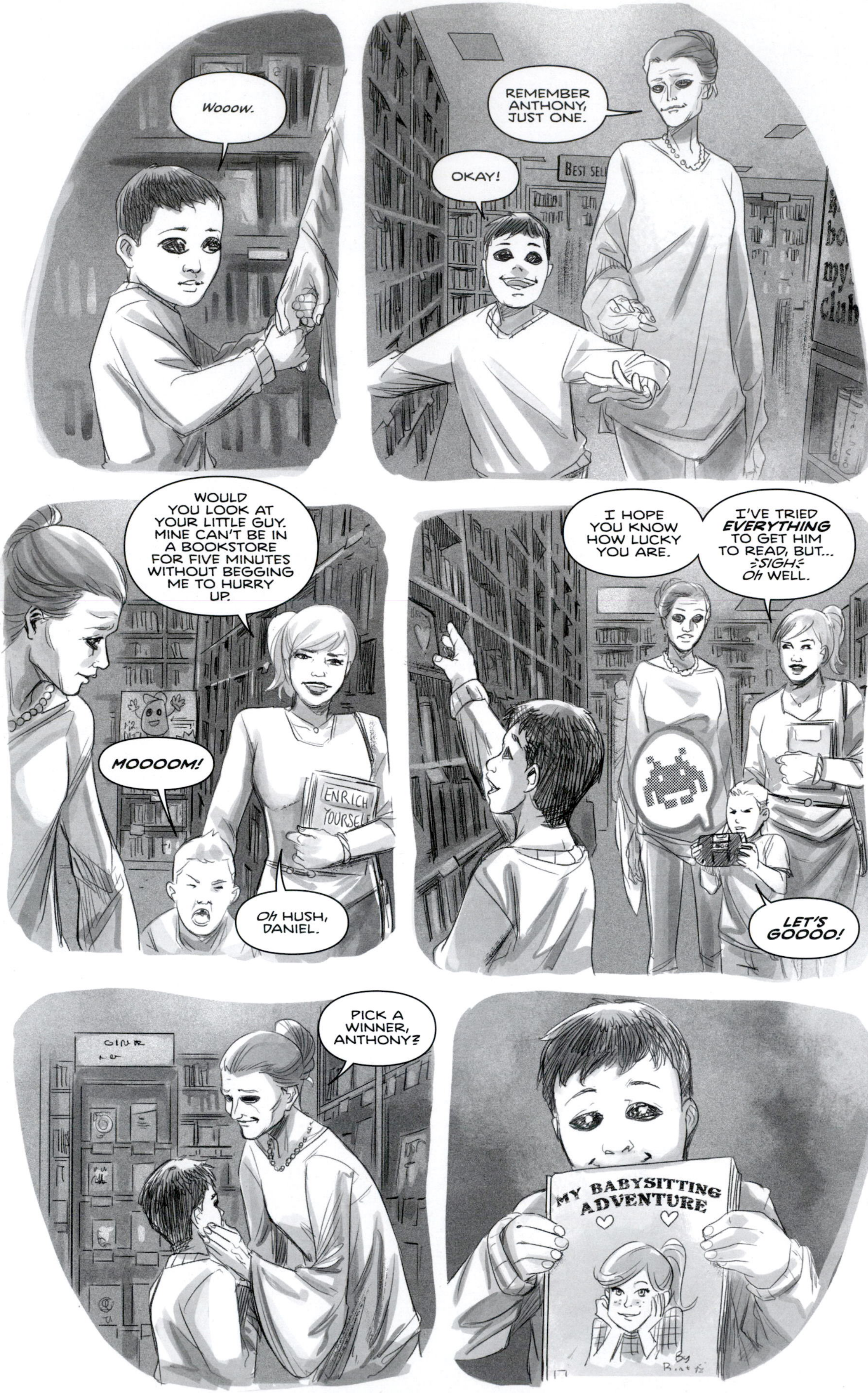

Wooow.
REMEMBER ANTHONY, JUST ONE.
OKAY!
BEST SELL
WOULD YOU LOOK AT YOUR LITTLE GUY. MINE CAN'T BE IN A BOOKSTORE FOR FIVE MINUTES WITHOUT BEGGING ME TO HURRY UP.
MOOOOM!
ENRICH YOURSELF
Oh HUSH, DANIEL.
I HOPE YOU KNOW HOW LUCKY YOU ARE.
I'VE TRIED EVERYTHING TO GET HIM TO READ, BUT... SIGH Oh WELL.
LET'S GOOOO!
PICK A WINNER, ANTHONY?
MY BABYSITTING ADVENTURE

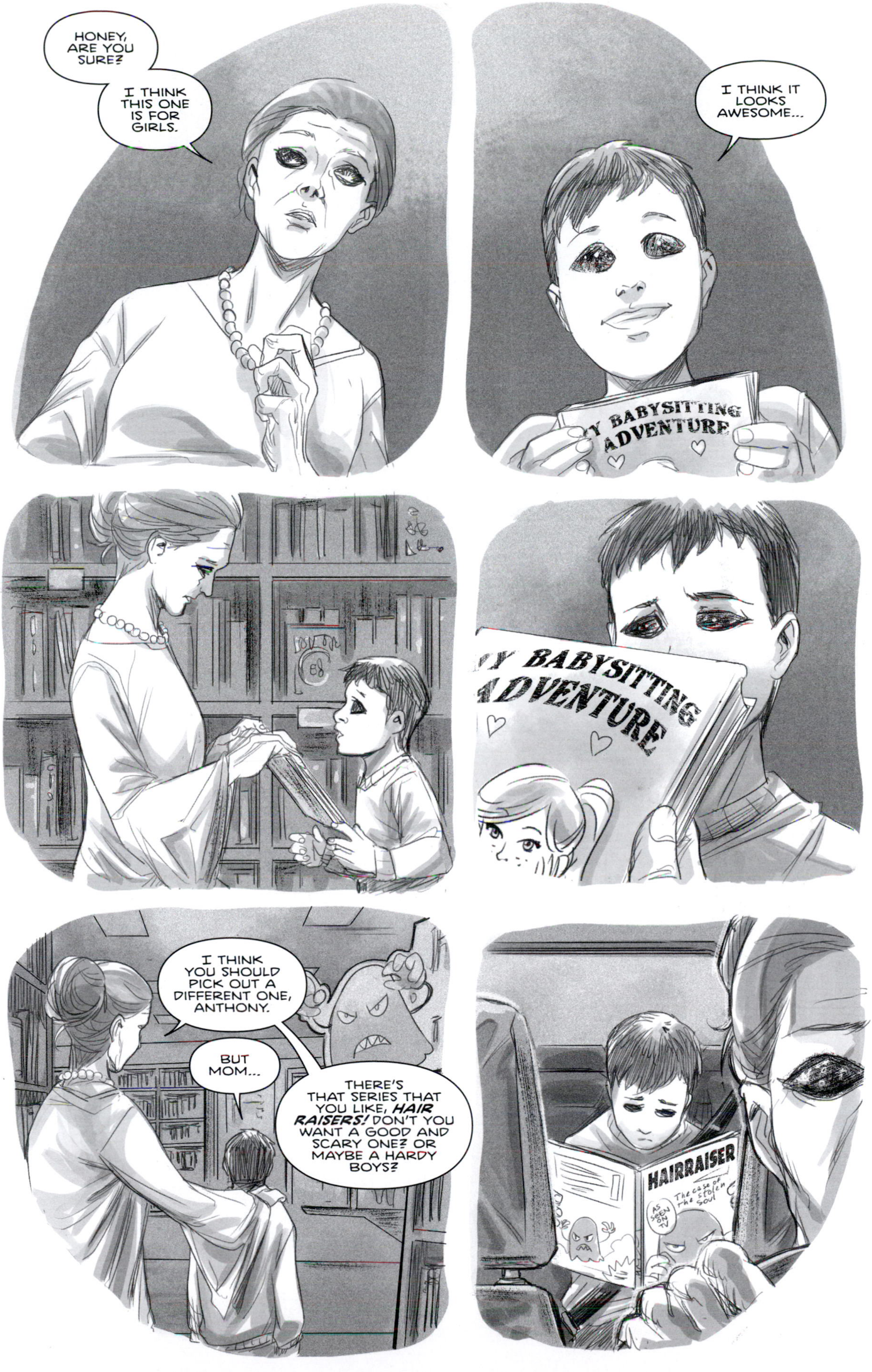
HONEY, ARE YOU SURE?
I THINK THIS ONE IS FOR GIRLS.
I THINK IT LOOKS AWESOME...
Y BABYSITTING ADVENTURE
BABYSITTING ADVENTURE
I THINK YOU SHOULD PICK OUT A DIFFERENT ONE, ANTHONY.
BUT MOM...
THERE'S THAT SERIES THAT YOU LIKE, *HAIR RAISERS!* DON'T YOU WANT A GOOD AND SCARY ONE? OR MAYBE A HARDY BOYS?
HAIRRAISER
The case of the stolen Soul
AS SEEN ON TV

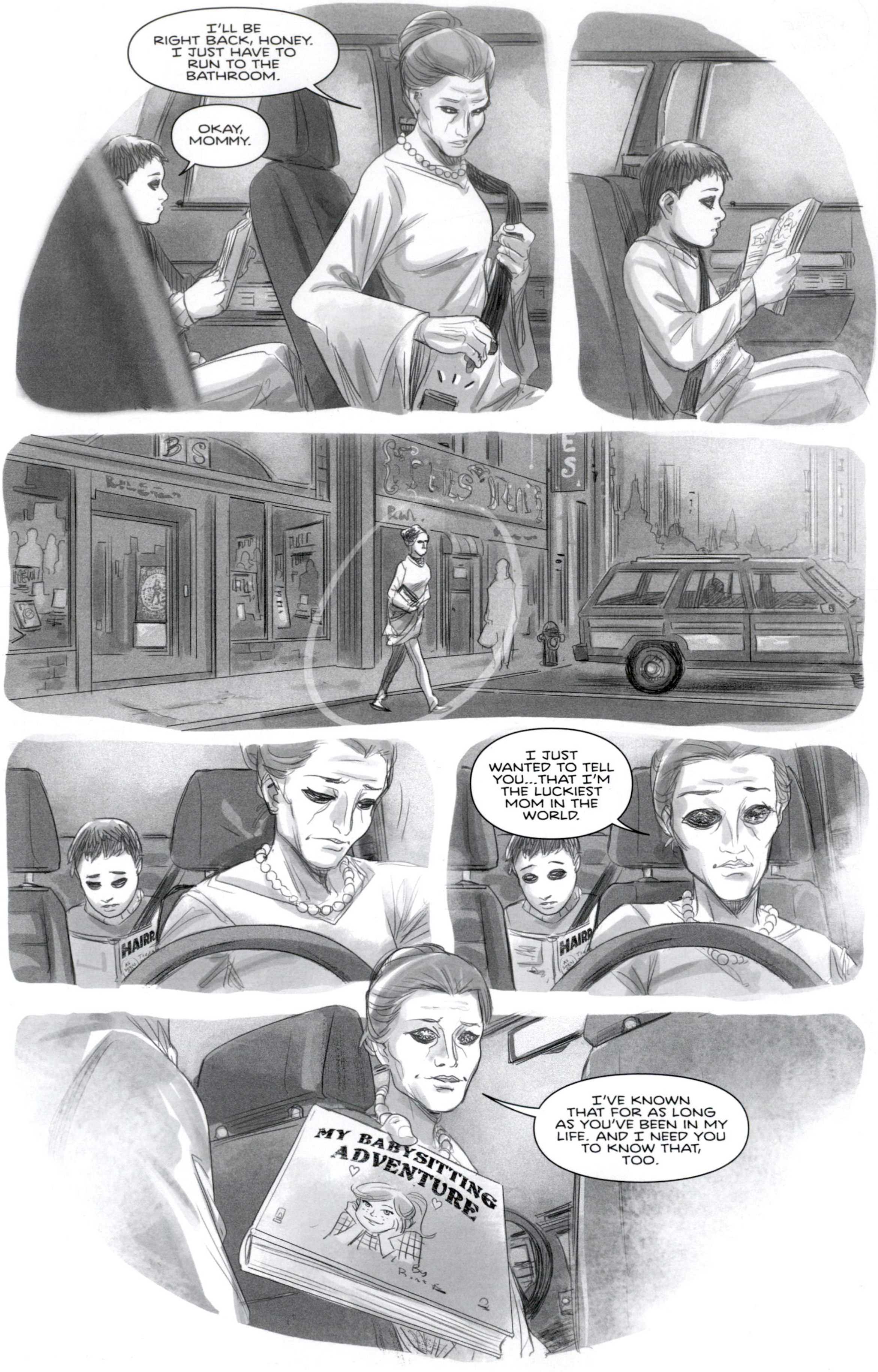
I'LL BE RIGHT BACK, HONEY. I JUST HAVE TO RUN TO THE BATHROOM.
OKAY, MOMMY.
I JUST WANTED TO TELL YOU...THAT I'M THE LUCKIEST MOM IN THE WORLD.
I'VE KNOWN THAT FOR AS LONG AS YOU'VE BEEN IN MY LIFE. AND I NEED YOU TO KNOW THAT, TOO.
MY BABYSITTING ADVENTURE

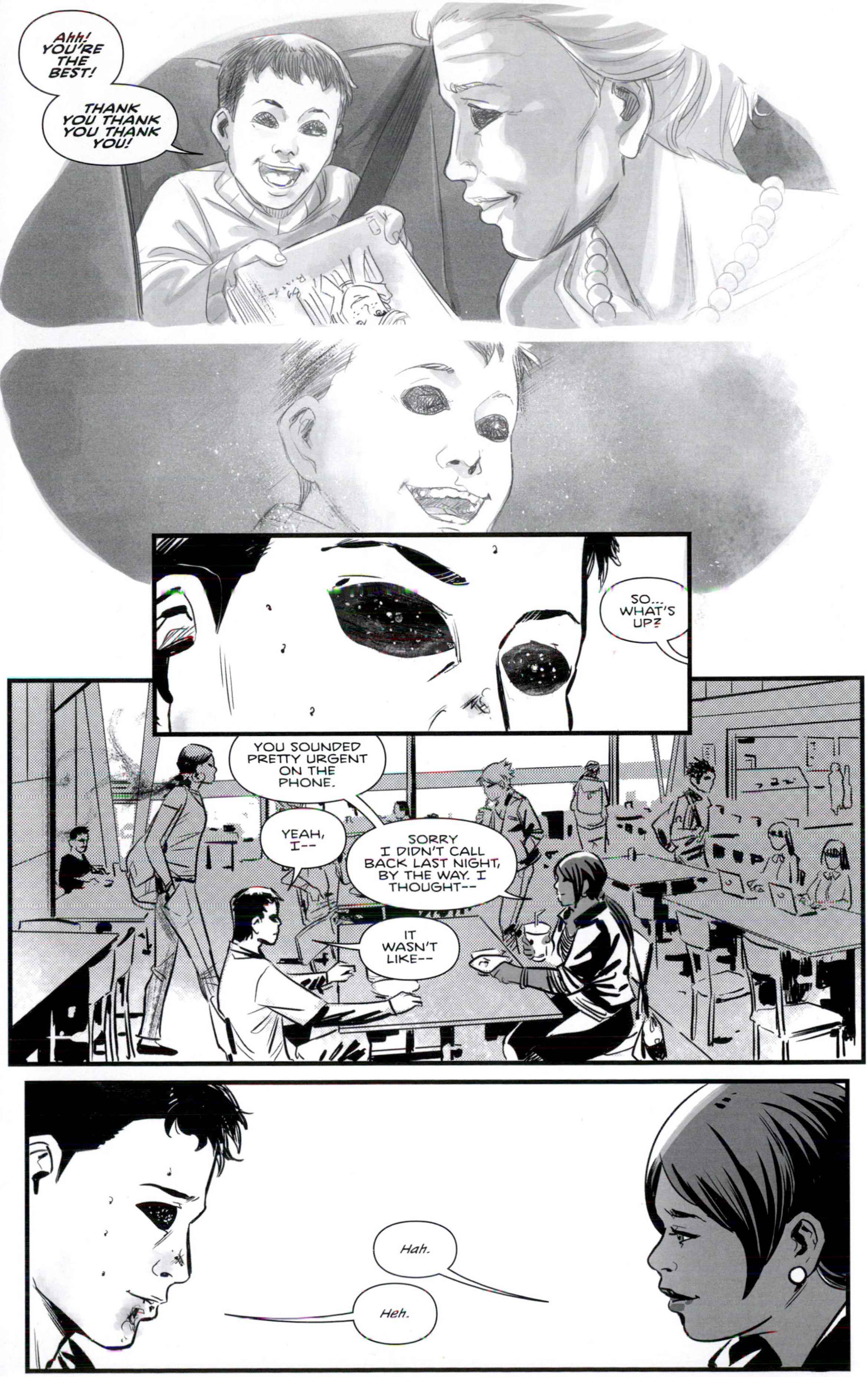
Ahh! YOU'RE THE BEST!
THANK YOU THANK YOU THANK YOU!
SO... WHAT'S UP?
YOU SOUNDED PRETTY URGENT ON THE PHONE.
YEAH, I--
SORRY I DIDN'T CALL BACK LAST NIGHT, BY THE WAY. I THOUGHT--
IT WASN'T LIKE--
Hah.
Heh.

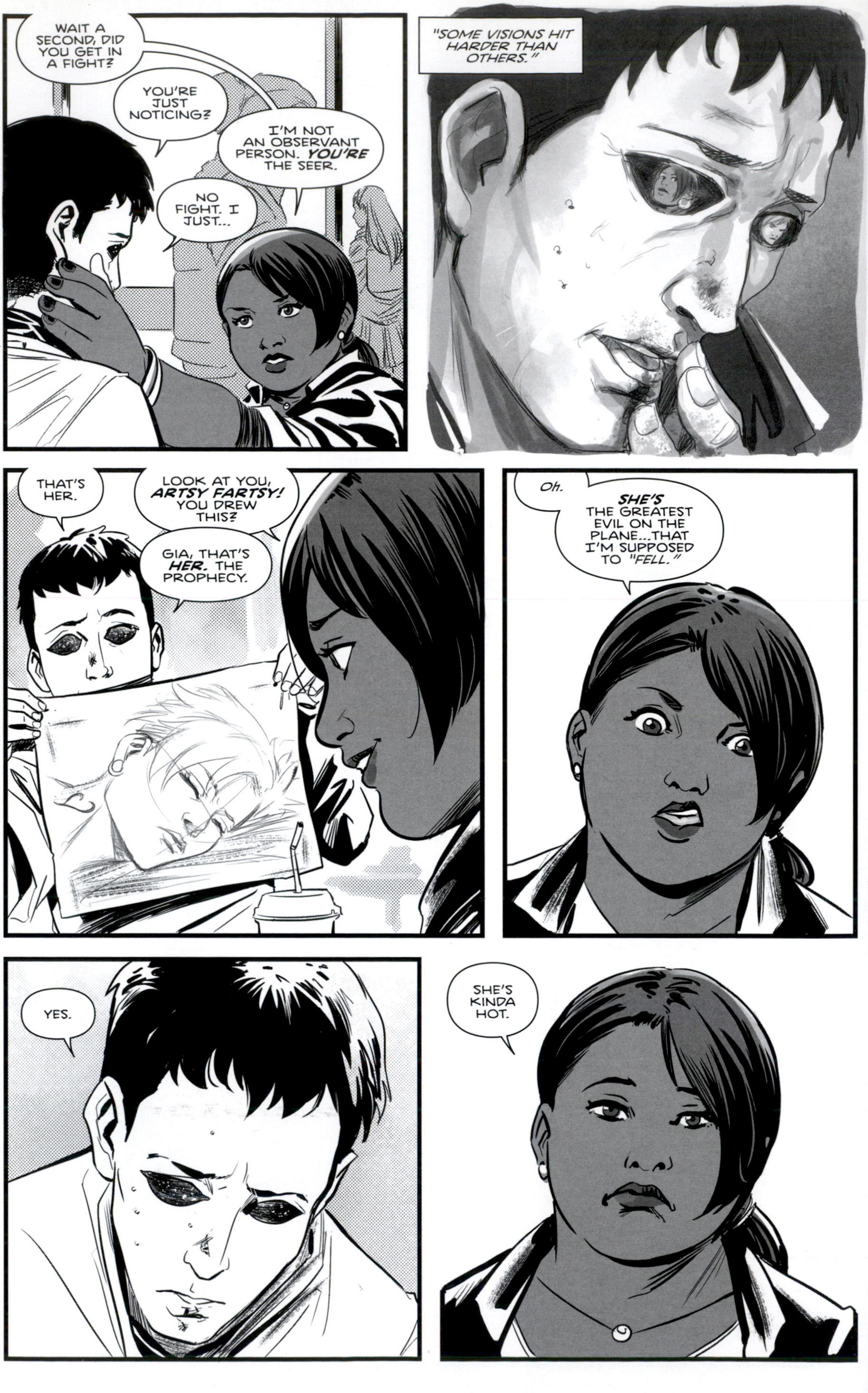
WAIT A SECOND, DID YOU GET IN A FIGHT?
YOU'RE JUST NOTICING?
I'M NOT AN OBSERVANT PERSON. YOU'RE THE SEER.
NO FIGHT. I JUST...
"SOME VISIONS HIT HARDER THAN OTHERS."
THAT'S HER.
LOOK AT YOU, ARTSY FARTSY! YOU DREW THIS?
GIA, THAT'S HER. THE PROPHECY.
Oh.
SHE'S THE GREATEST EVIL ON THE PLANE...THAT I'M SUPPOSED TO "FELL."
YES.
SHE'S KINDA HOT.

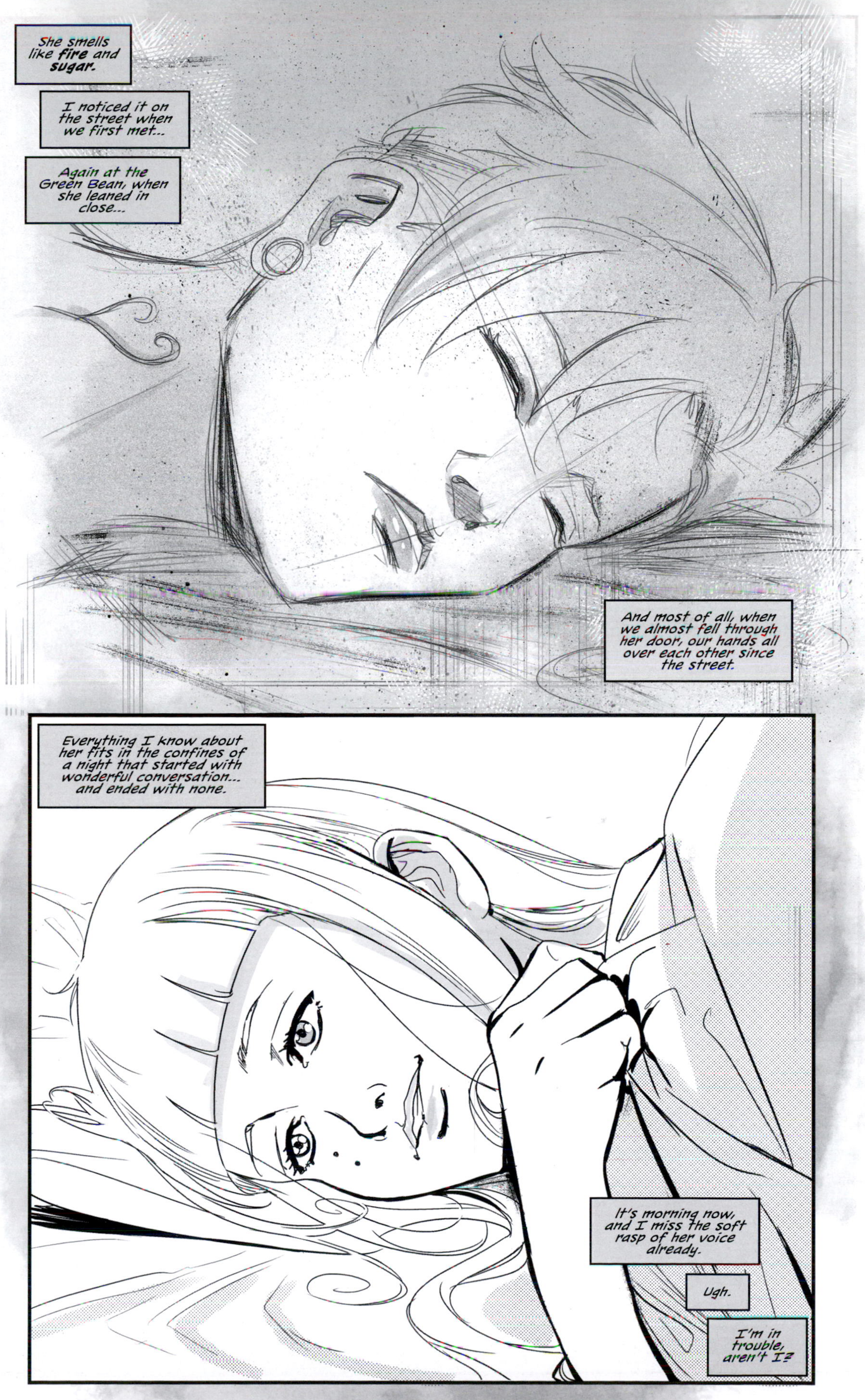
She smells like **fire** and **sugar.**
I noticed it on the street when we first met...
Again at the Green Bean, when she leaned in close...
And most of all, when we almost fell through her door, our hands all over each other since the street.
Everything I know about her fits in the confines of a night that started with wonderful conversation... and ended with none.
It's morning now, and I miss the soft rasp of her voice already.
Ugh.
I'm in trouble, aren't I?

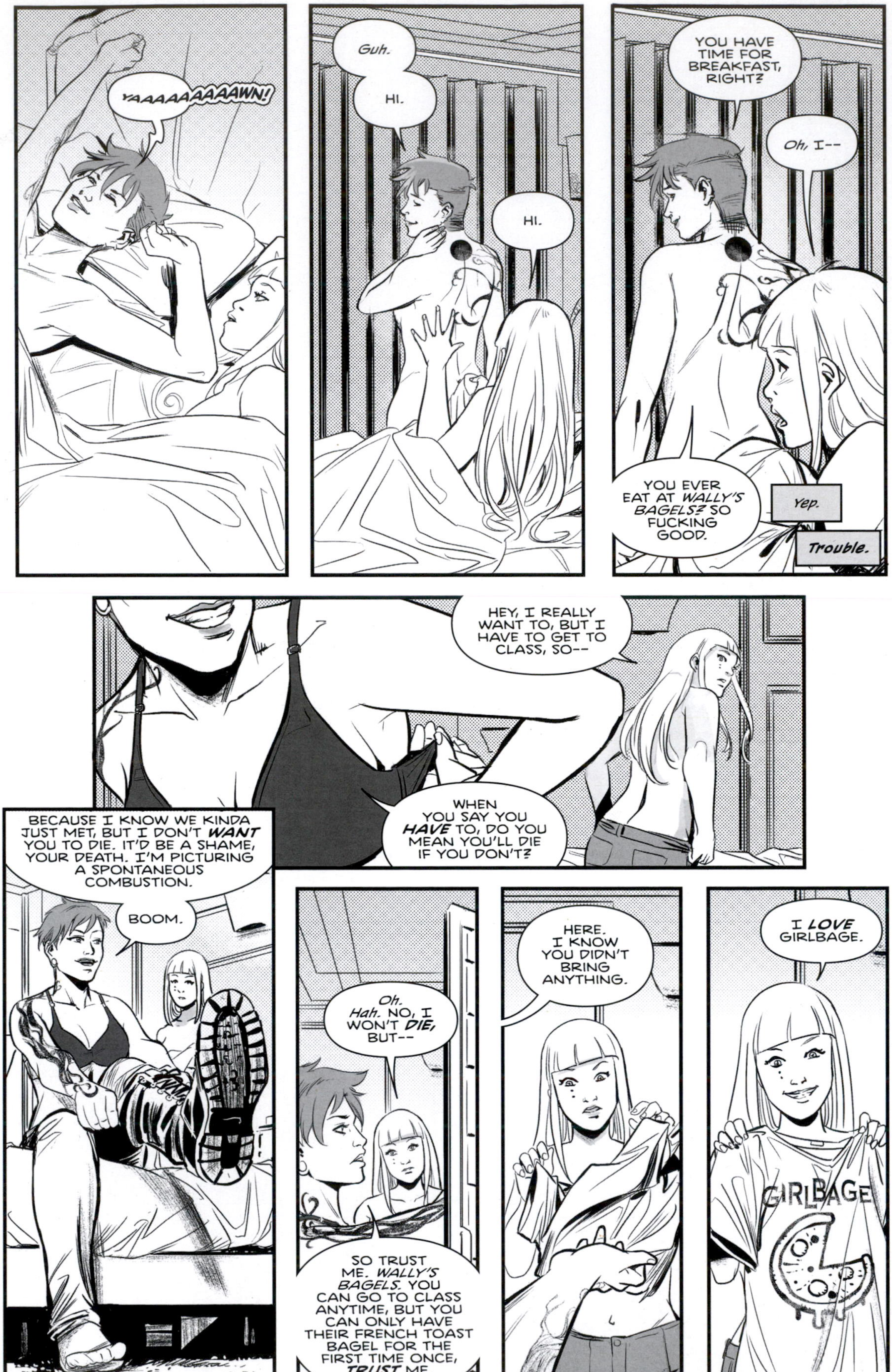
YAAAAAAAAAWN!
Guh.
HI.
HI.
YOU HAVE TIME FOR BREAKFAST, RIGHT?
Oh, I--
YOU EVER EAT AT WALLY'S BAGELS? SO FUCKING GOOD.
Yep.
Trouble.
HEY, I REALLY WANT TO, BUT I HAVE TO GET TO CLASS, SO--
WHEN YOU SAY YOU HAVE TO, DO YOU MEAN YOU'LL DIE IF YOU DON'T?
BECAUSE I KNOW WE KINDA JUST MET, BUT I DON'T WANT YOU TO DIE. IT'D BE A SHAME, YOUR DEATH. I'M PICTURING A SPONTANEOUS COMBUSTION.
BOOM.
Oh. Hah. NO, I WON'T DIE, BUT--
SO TRUST ME. WALLY'S BAGELS. YOU CAN GO TO CLASS ANYTIME, BUT YOU CAN ONLY HAVE THEIR FRENCH TOAST BAGEL FOR THE FIRST TIME ONCE, TRUST ME.
HERE. I KNOW YOU DIDN'T BRING ANYTHING.
I LOVE GIRLBAGE.
GIRLBAGE

HEY, FUCK YOU!

GO DIE, MOTHER-FUCKER!

WALLY'S bagels SINCE 1987

Oh MY GOD, THIS IS HEAVEN.

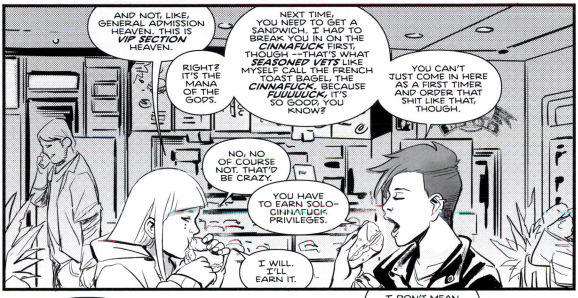

AND NOT, LIKE, GENERAL ADMISSION HEAVEN. THIS IS *VIP SECTION* HEAVEN.

RIGHT? IT'S THE MANA OF THE GODS.

NEXT TIME, YOU NEED TO GET A SANDWICH. I HAD TO BREAK YOU IN ON THE *CINNAFUCK* FIRST, THOUGH --THAT'S WHAT *SEASONED VETS* LIKE MYSELF CALL THE FRENCH TOAST BAGEL, THE *CINNAFUCK.* BECAUSE *FUUUUUCK*, IT'S SO GOOD, YOU KNOW?

YOU CAN'T JUST COME IN HERE AS A FIRST TIMER AND ORDER THAT SHIT LIKE THAT, THOUGH.

NO, NO OF COURSE NOT. THAT'D BE CRAZY.

YOU HAVE TO EARN SOLO-CINNAFUCK PRIVILEGES.

I WILL. I'LL EARN IT.

YOU'RE CUTE, YOU KNOW. I THOUGHT IT ON THE STREET WHEN I SAW YOU THE FIRST TIME, BUT CONSIDERING THE SITUATION, THAT DICKBAG RUNNING HIS MOUTH, IT DIDN'T FEEL APPROPRIATE TO SAY.

BUT YOU'RE REALLY BEAUTIFUL, YOU KNOW THAT?

Er...

I DON'T MEAN TO TO BE NOSY, BUT...YOUR APARTMENT, IT'S *AMAZING.*

IT'S OKAY. SOLID *DEFLECTION* OF THAT COMPLIMENT, BY THE WAY. YOU'RE WELL-PRACTICED.

NO, REALLY, YOUR APARTMENT-- IT'S INSANE. NOT IN A BAD WAY, I MEAN... IT'S *GORGEOUS.*

WHAT DO YOU *DO?*

DON'T YOU REMEMBER I PURPOSELY DODGED THAT QUESTION LAST NIGHT?

I SEAMLESSLY CHANGED THE SUBJECT WITHOUT MISSING A BEAT IN THE CONVERSATION.

Oh. Uh... WHY? ARE YOU A HITMAN OR SOMETHING?

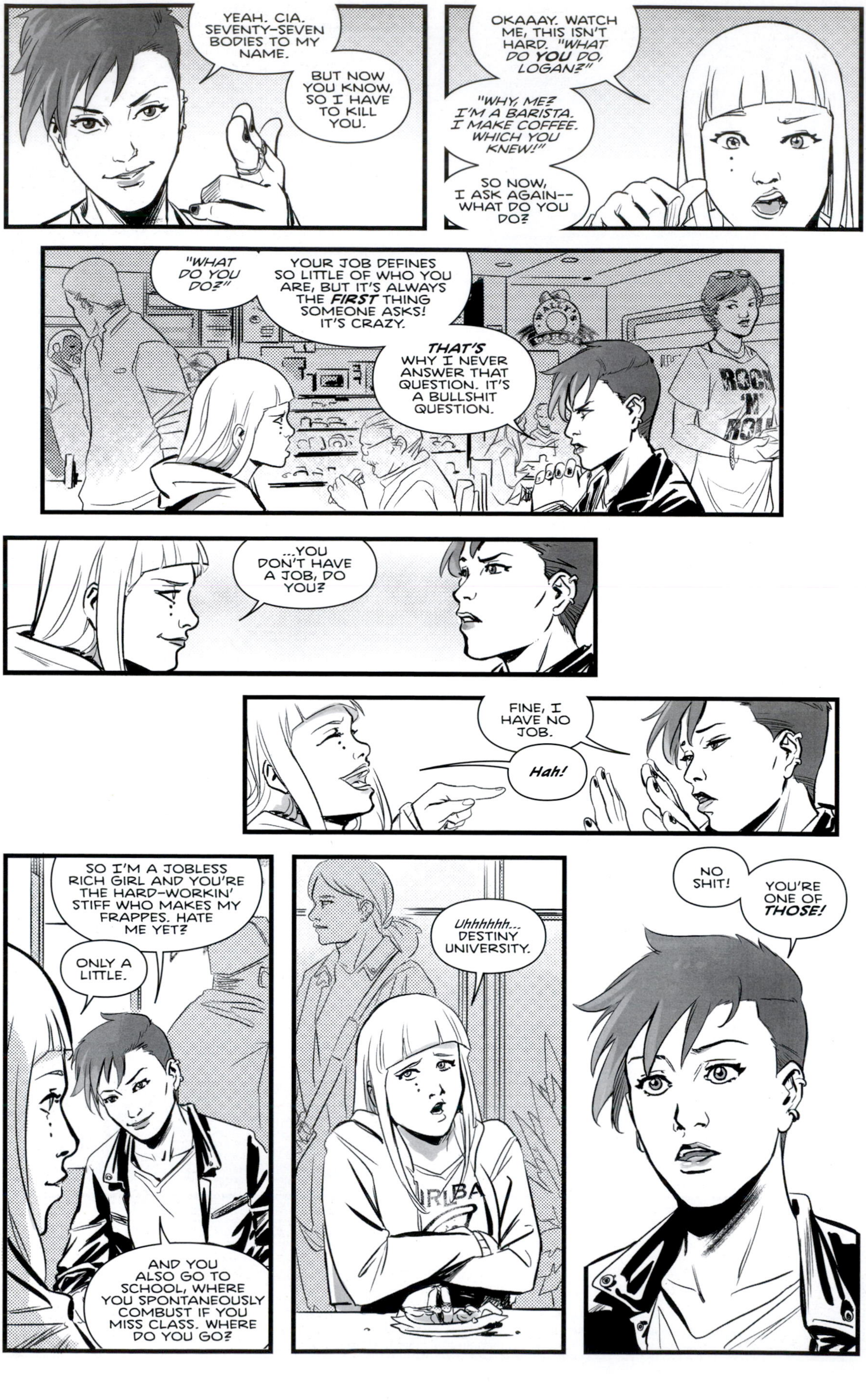
YEAH. CIA. SEVENTY-SEVEN BODIES TO MY NAME.
BUT NOW YOU KNOW, SO I HAVE TO KILL YOU.
OKAAAY. WATCH ME, THIS ISN'T HARD. "WHAT DO YOU DO, LOGAN?"
"WHY, ME? I'M A BARISTA. I MAKE COFFEE. WHICH YOU KNEW!"
SO NOW, I ASK AGAIN-- WHAT DO YOU DO?
"WHAT DO YOU DO?"
YOUR JOB DEFINES SO LITTLE OF WHO YOU ARE, BUT IT'S ALWAYS THE FIRST THING SOMEONE ASKS! IT'S CRAZY.
THAT'S WHY I NEVER ANSWER THAT QUESTION. IT'S A BULLSHIT QUESTION.
...YOU DON'T HAVE A JOB, DO YOU?
FINE, I HAVE NO JOB.
Hah!
SO I'M A JOBLESS RICH GIRL AND YOU'RE THE HARD-WORKIN' STIFF WHO MAKES MY FRAPPES. HATE ME YET?
ONLY A LITTLE.
AND YOU ALSO GO TO SCHOOL, WHERE YOU SPONTANEOUSLY COMBUST IF YOU MISS CLASS. WHERE DO YOU GO?
Uhhhhhh... DESTINY UNIVERSITY.
NO SHIT!
YOU'RE ONE OF THOSE!

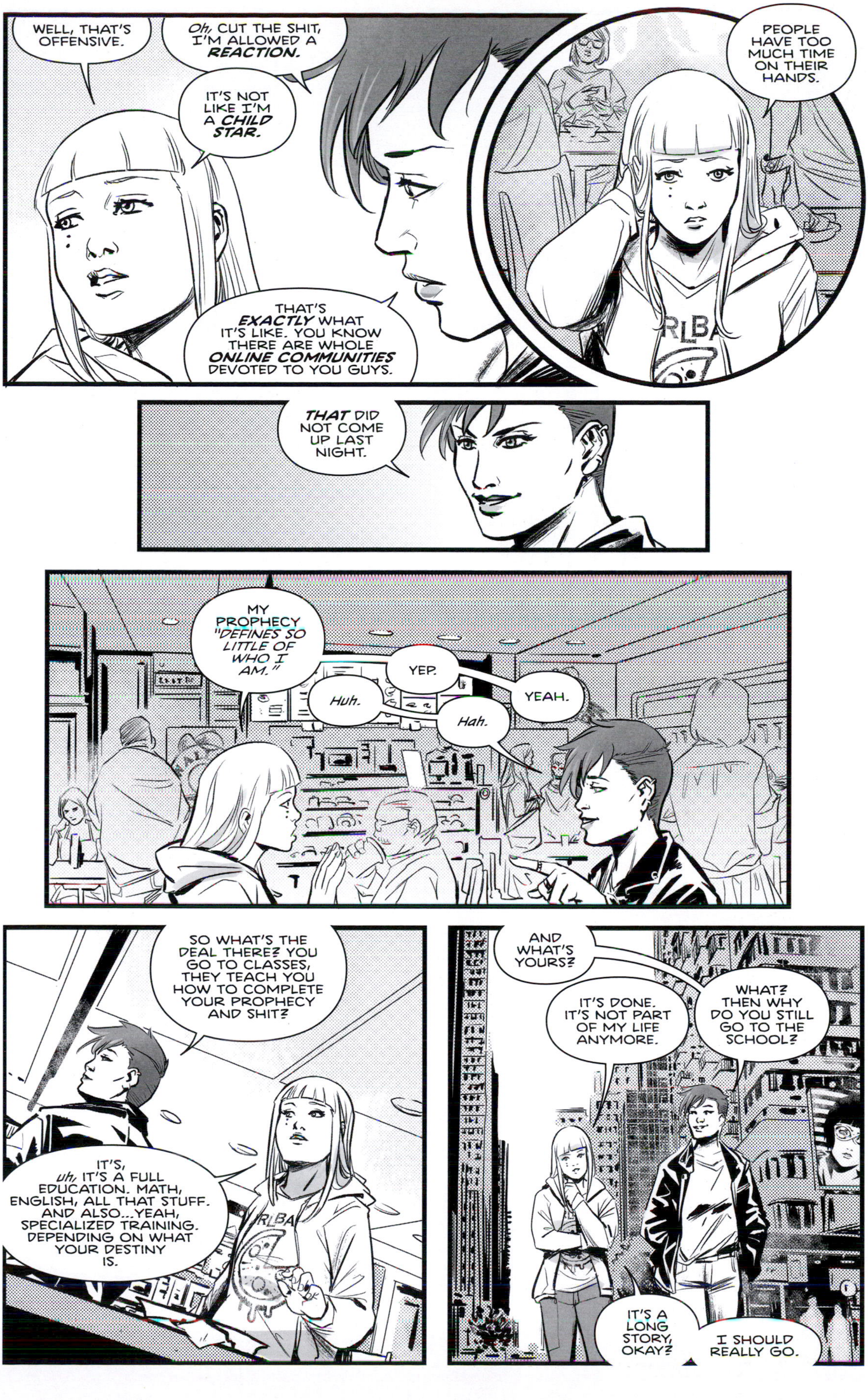
WELL, THAT'S OFFENSIVE.
Oh, CUT THE SHIT, I'M ALLOWED A **REACTION.**
IT'S NOT LIKE I'M A ***CHILD STAR.***
THAT'S ***EXACTLY*** WHAT IT'S LIKE. YOU KNOW THERE ARE WHOLE ***ONLINE COMMUNITIES*** DEVOTED TO YOU GUYS.
PEOPLE HAVE TOO MUCH TIME ON THEIR HANDS.
THAT DID NOT COME UP LAST NIGHT.
MY PROPHECY *"DEFINES SO LITTLE OF WHO I AM."*
Huh.
YEP.
Hah.
YEAH.
SO WHAT'S THE DEAL THERE? YOU GO TO CLASSES, THEY TEACH YOU HOW TO COMPLETE YOUR PROPHECY AND SHIT?
IT'S, *uh,* IT'S A FULL EDUCATION. MATH, ENGLISH, ALL THAT STUFF. AND ALSO...YEAH, SPECIALIZED TRAINING. DEPENDING ON WHAT YOUR DESTINY IS.
AND WHAT'S YOURS?
IT'S DONE. IT'S NOT PART OF MY LIFE ANYMORE.
WHAT? THEN WHY DO YOU STILL GO TO THE SCHOOL?
IT'S A LONG STORY, OKAY?
I SHOULD REALLY GO.

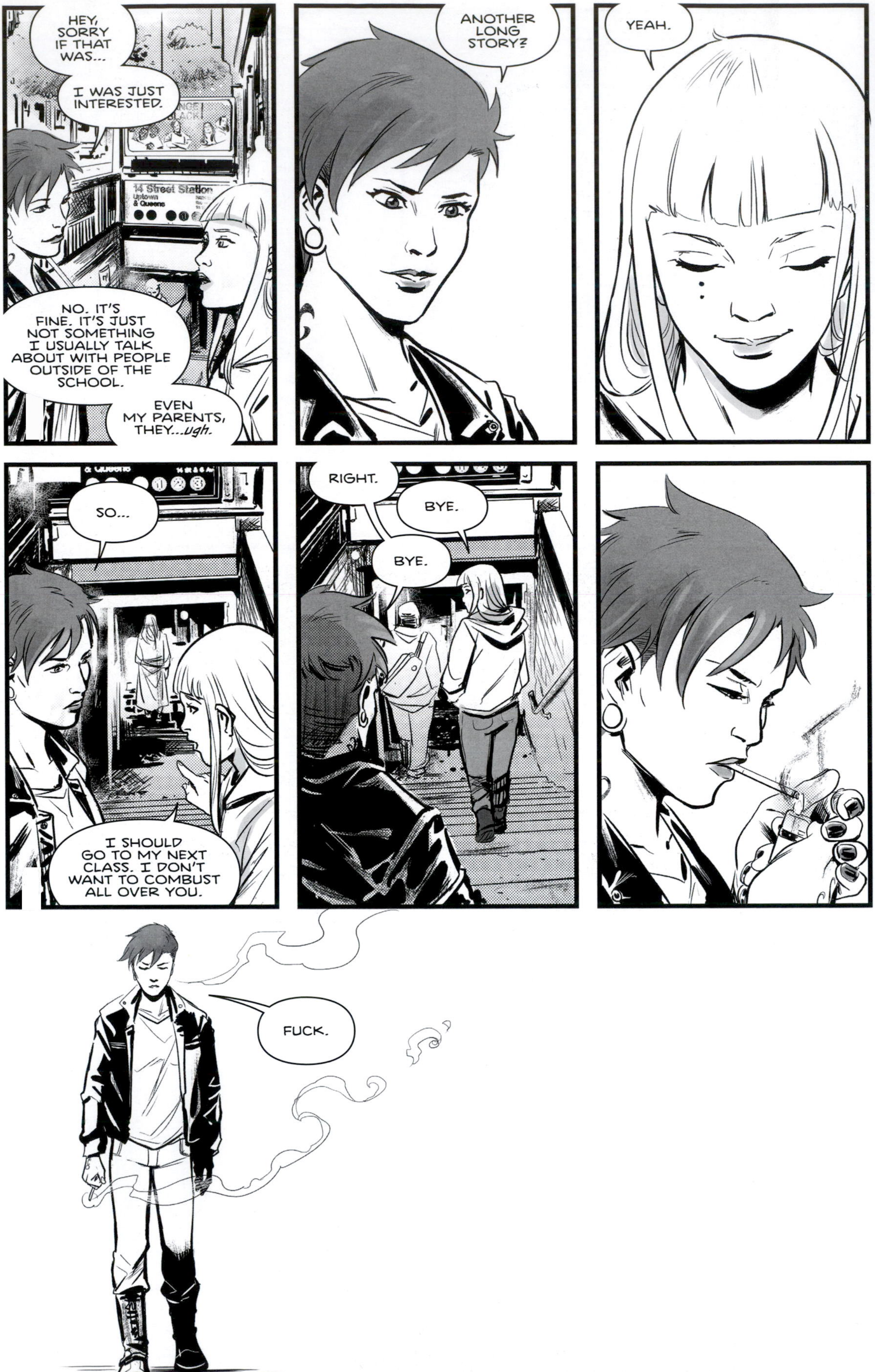
HEY, SORRY IF THAT WAS...
I WAS JUST INTERESTED.
14 Street Station
Uptown & Queens
NO. IT'S FINE. IT'S JUST NOT SOMETHING I USUALLY TALK ABOUT WITH PEOPLE OUTSIDE OF THE SCHOOL.
EVEN MY PARENTS, THEY...*ugh*.
ANOTHER LONG STORY?
YEAH.
SO...
I SHOULD GO TO MY NEXT CLASS. I DON'T WANT TO COMBUST ALL OVER YOU.
RIGHT.
BYE.
BYE.
FUCK.

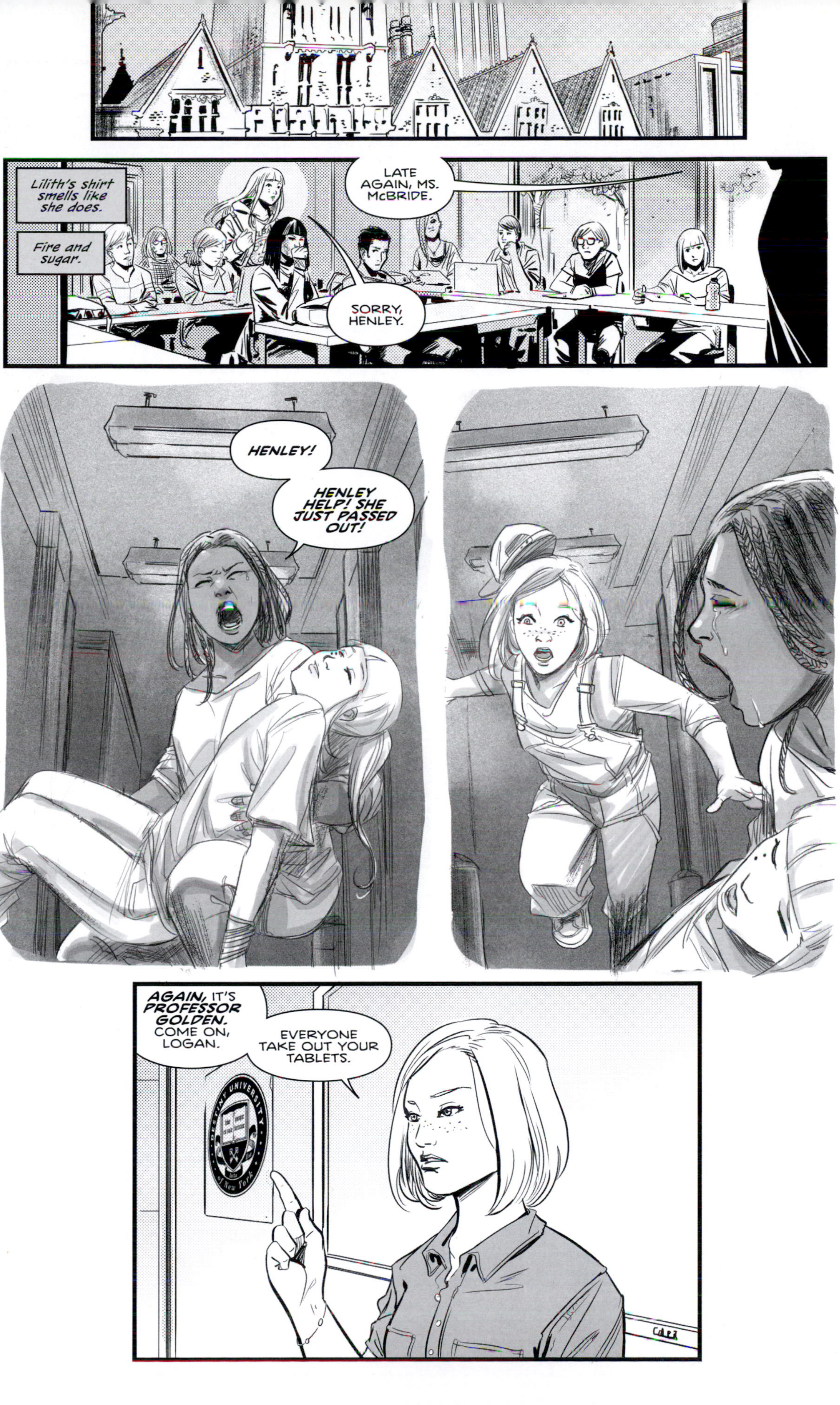

Lilith's shirt smells like she does.
Fire and sugar.
LATE AGAIN, MS. McBRIDE.
SORRY, HENLEY.
HENLEY!
HENLEY HELP! SHE JUST PASSED OUT!
AGAIN, IT'S PROFESSOR GOLDEN. COME ON, LOGAN.
EVERYONE TAKE OUT YOUR TABLETS.

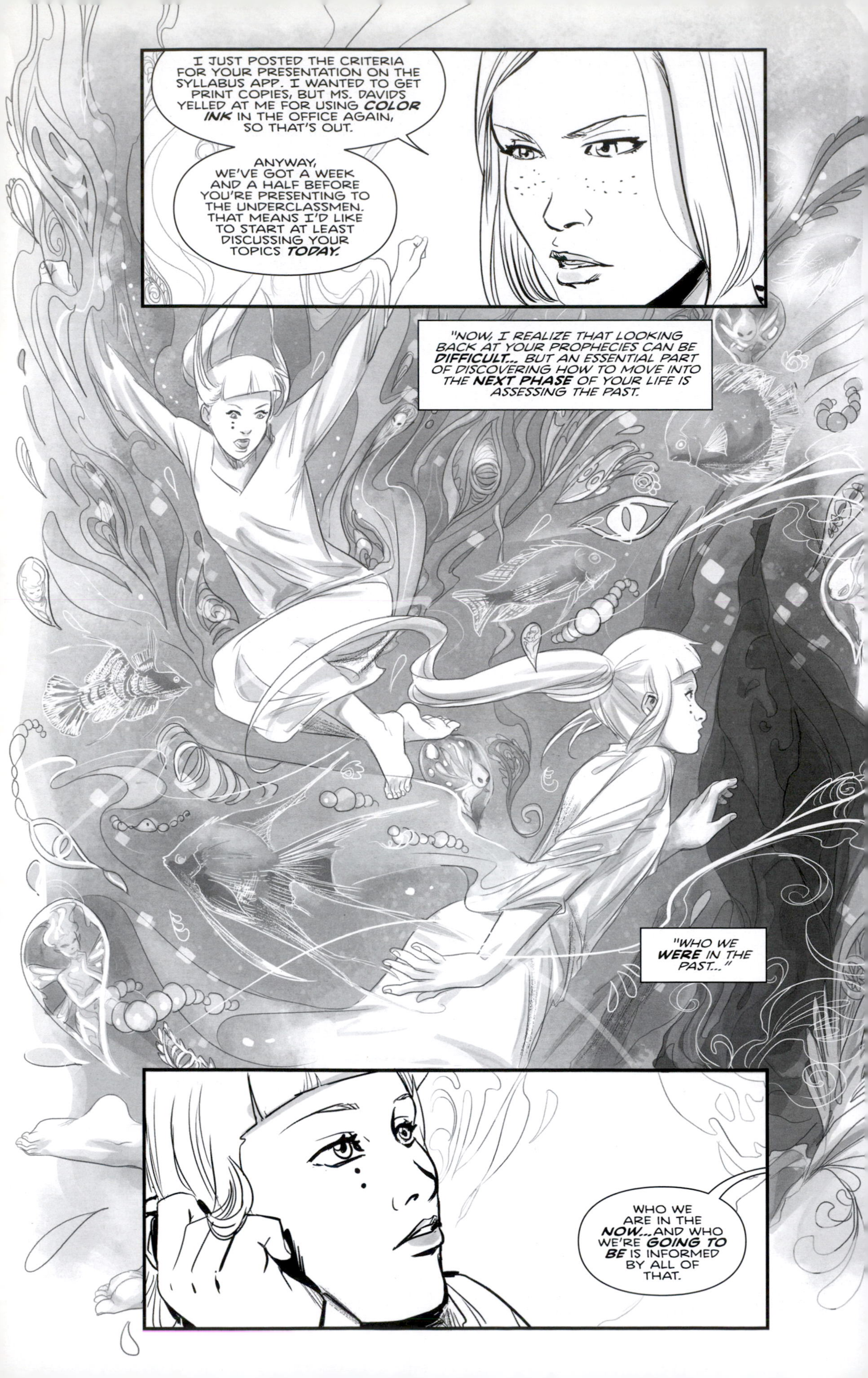
I JUST POSTED THE CRITERIA FOR YOUR PRESENTATION ON THE SYLLABUS APP. I WANTED TO GET PRINT COPIES, BUT MS. DAVIDS YELLED AT ME FOR USING COLOR INK IN THE OFFICE AGAIN, SO THAT'S OUT.
ANYWAY, WE'VE GOT A WEEK AND A HALF BEFORE YOU'RE PRESENTING TO THE UNDERCLASSMEN. THAT MEANS I'D LIKE TO START AT LEAST DISCUSSING YOUR TOPICS TODAY.
"NOW, I REALIZE THAT LOOKING BACK AT YOUR PROPHECIES CAN BE DIFFICULT... BUT AN ESSENTIAL PART OF DISCOVERING HOW TO MOVE INTO THE NEXT PHASE OF YOUR LIFE IS ASSESSING THE PAST.
"WHO WE WERE IN THE PAST..."
WHO WE ARE IN THE NOW... AND WHO WE'RE GOING TO BE IS INFORMED BY ALL OF THAT.

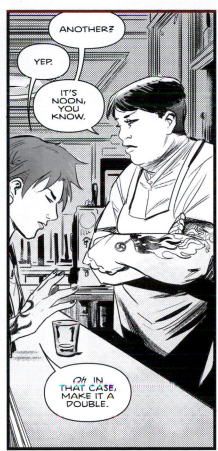

ANOTHER?

YEP.

IT'S NOON, YOU KNOW.

Oh IN THAT CASE, MAKE IT A DOUBLE.

EARLY TO BE DRINKING, NO?

NOT INTERESTED, SO MIND YOUR FUCKING--

business...

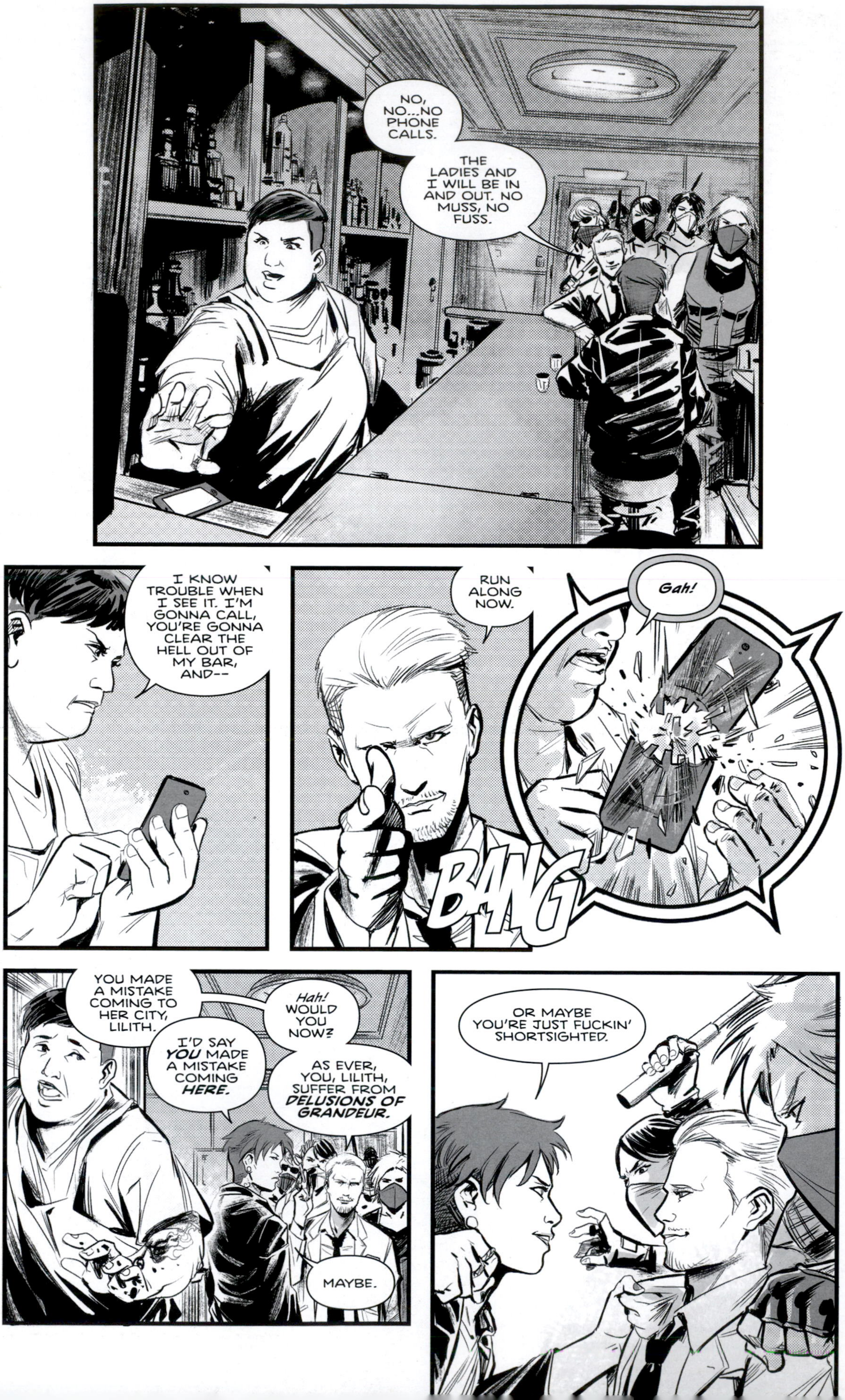

NO, NO...NO PHONE CALLS.
THE LADIES AND I WILL BE IN AND OUT. NO MUSS, NO FUSS.
I KNOW TROUBLE WHEN I SEE IT. I'M GONNA CALL, YOU'RE GONNA CLEAR THE HELL OUT OF MY BAR, AND--
RUN ALONG NOW.
BANG
Gah!
YOU MADE A MISTAKE COMING TO HER CITY, LILITH.
Hah! WOULD YOU NOW?
I'D SAY YOU MADE A MISTAKE COMING HERE.
AS EVER, YOU, LILITH, SUFFER FROM DELUSIONS OF GRANDEUR.
MAYBE.
OR MAYBE YOU'RE JUST FUCKIN' SHORTSIGHTED.

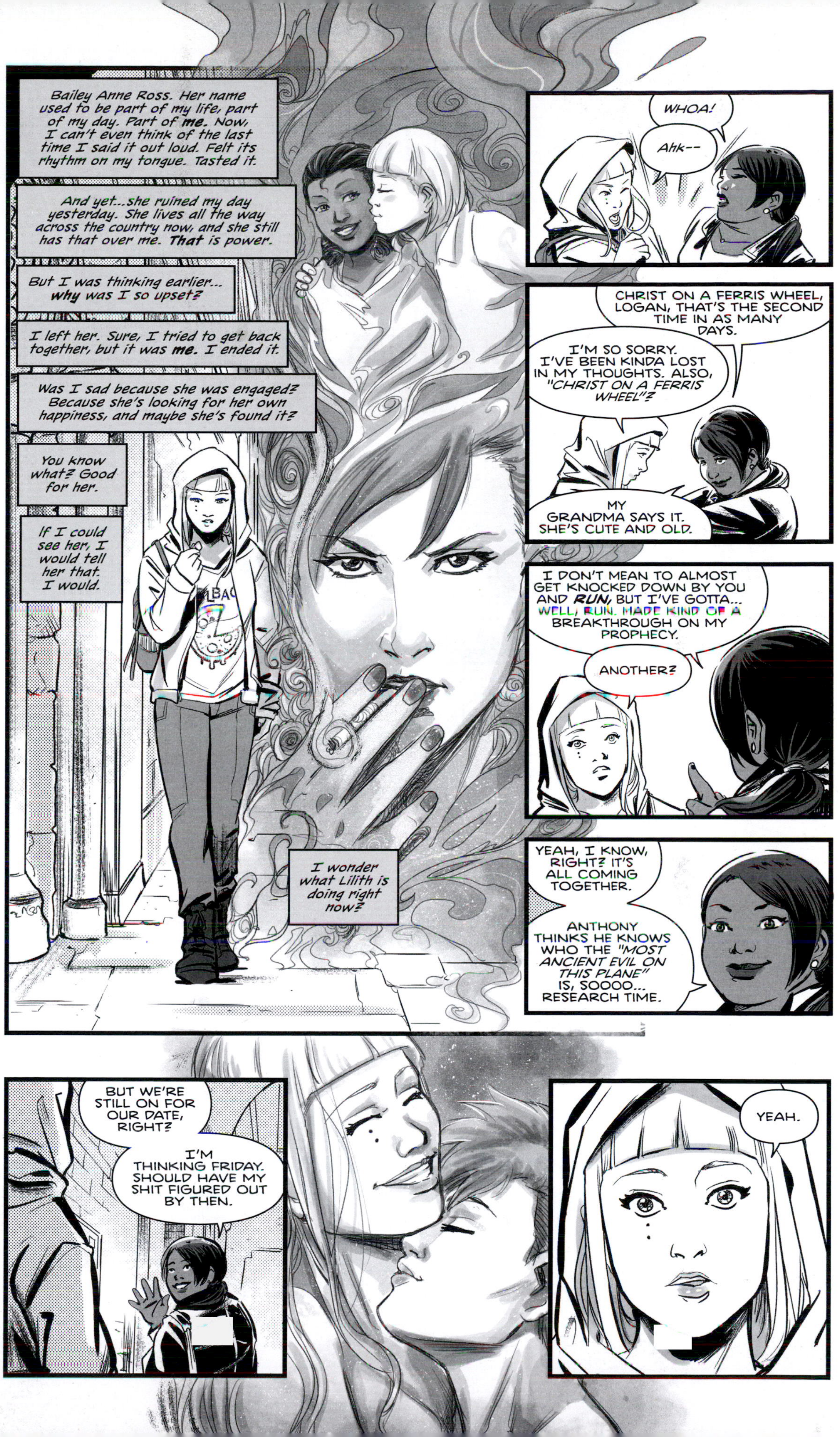

Bailey Anne Ross. Her name used to be part of my life, part of my day. Part of me. Now, I can't even think of the last time I said it out loud. Felt its rhythm on my tongue. Tasted it.
And yet...she ruined my day yesterday. She lives all the way across the country now, and she still has that over me. That is power.
But I was thinking earlier... why was I so upset?
I left her. Sure, I tried to get back together, but it was me. I ended it.
Was I sad because she was engaged? Because she's looking for her own happiness, and maybe she's found it?
You know what? Good for her.
If I could see her, I would tell her that. I would.
I wonder what Lilith is doing right now?
WHOA!
Ahk--
CHRIST ON A FERRIS WHEEL, LOGAN, THAT'S THE SECOND TIME IN AS MANY DAYS.
I'M SO SORRY. I'VE BEEN KINDA LOST IN MY THOUGHTS. ALSO, "CHRIST ON A FERRIS WHEEL"?
MY GRANDMA SAYS IT. SHE'S CUTE AND OLD.
I DON'T MEAN TO ALMOST GET KNOCKED DOWN BY YOU AND RUN, BUT I'VE GOTTA... WELL, RUN. MADE KIND OF A BREAKTHROUGH ON MY PROPHECY.
ANOTHER?
YEAH, I KNOW, RIGHT? IT'S ALL COMING TOGETHER.
ANTHONY THINKS HE KNOWS WHO THE "MOST ANCIENT EVIL ON THIS PLANE" IS, SOOOO... RESEARCH TIME.
BUT WE'RE STILL ON FOR OUR DATE, RIGHT?
I'M THINKING FRIDAY. SHOULD HAVE MY SHIT FIGURED OUT BY THEN.
YEAH.

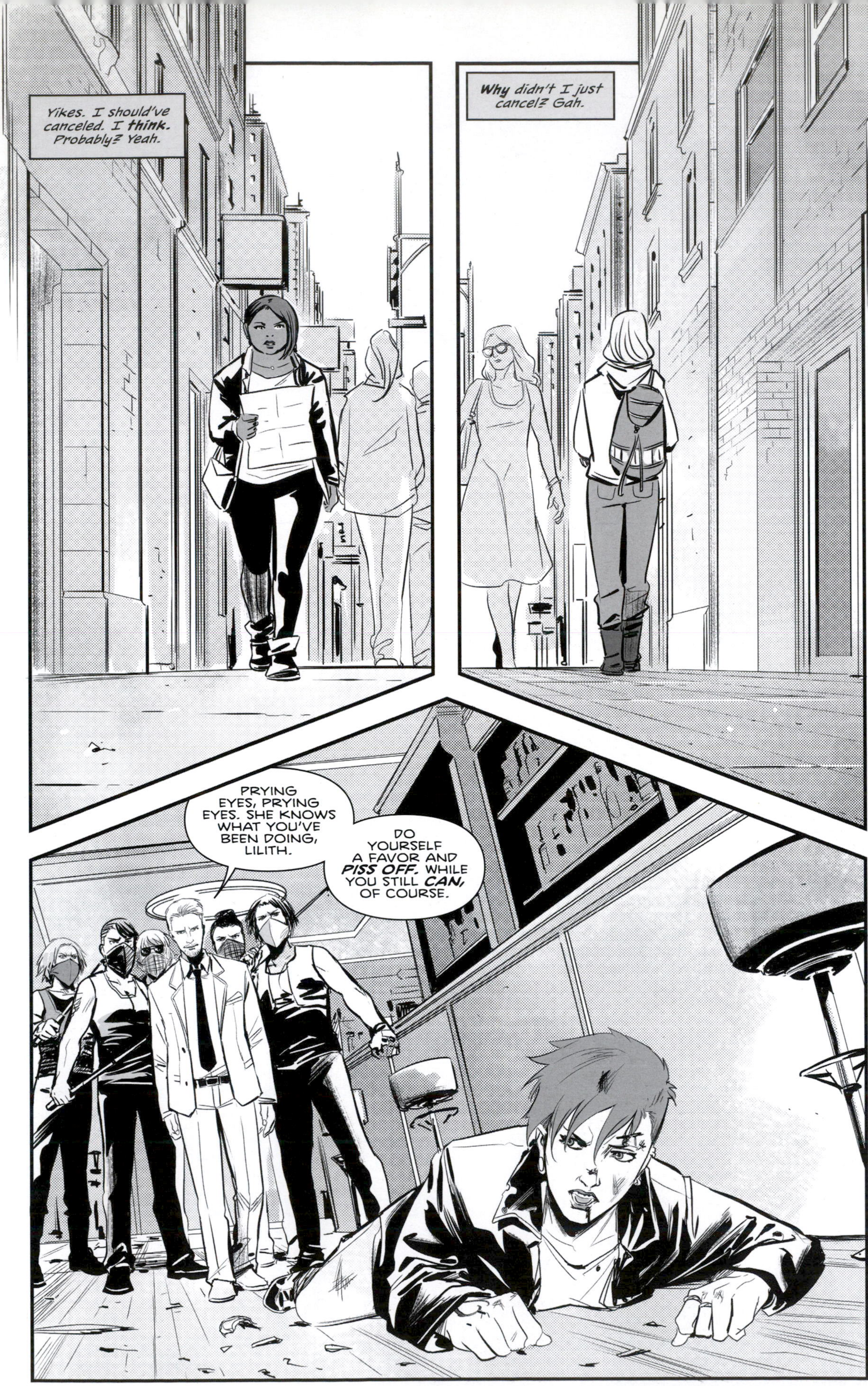
Yikes. I should've canceled. I **think.** Probably? Yeah.
Why didn't I just cancel? Gah.
PRYING EYES, PRYING EYES. SHE KNOWS WHAT YOU'VE BEEN DOING, LILITH.
DO YOURSELF A FAVOR AND ***PISS OFF.*** WHILE YOU STILL ***CAN,*** OF COURSE.

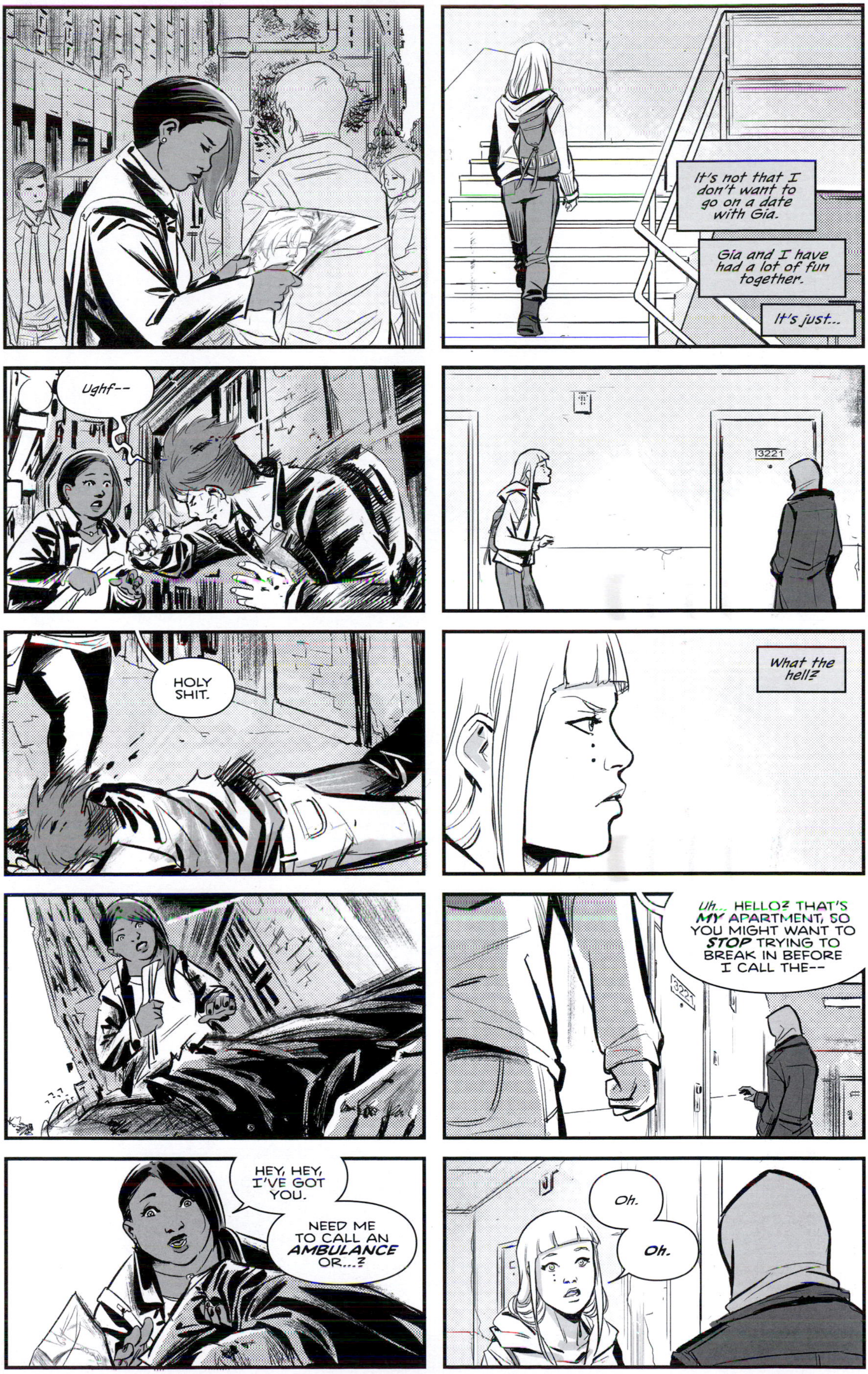
It's not that I don't want to go on a date with Gia.
Gia and I have had a lot of fun together.
It's just...
Ughf--
3221
HOLY SHIT.
What the hell?
Uh... HELLO? THAT'S MY APARTMENT, SO YOU MIGHT WANT TO STOP TRYING TO BREAK IN BEFORE I CALL THE--
3221
HEY, HEY, I'VE GOT YOU.
NEED ME TO CALL AN AMBULANCE OR...?
Oh.
Oh.

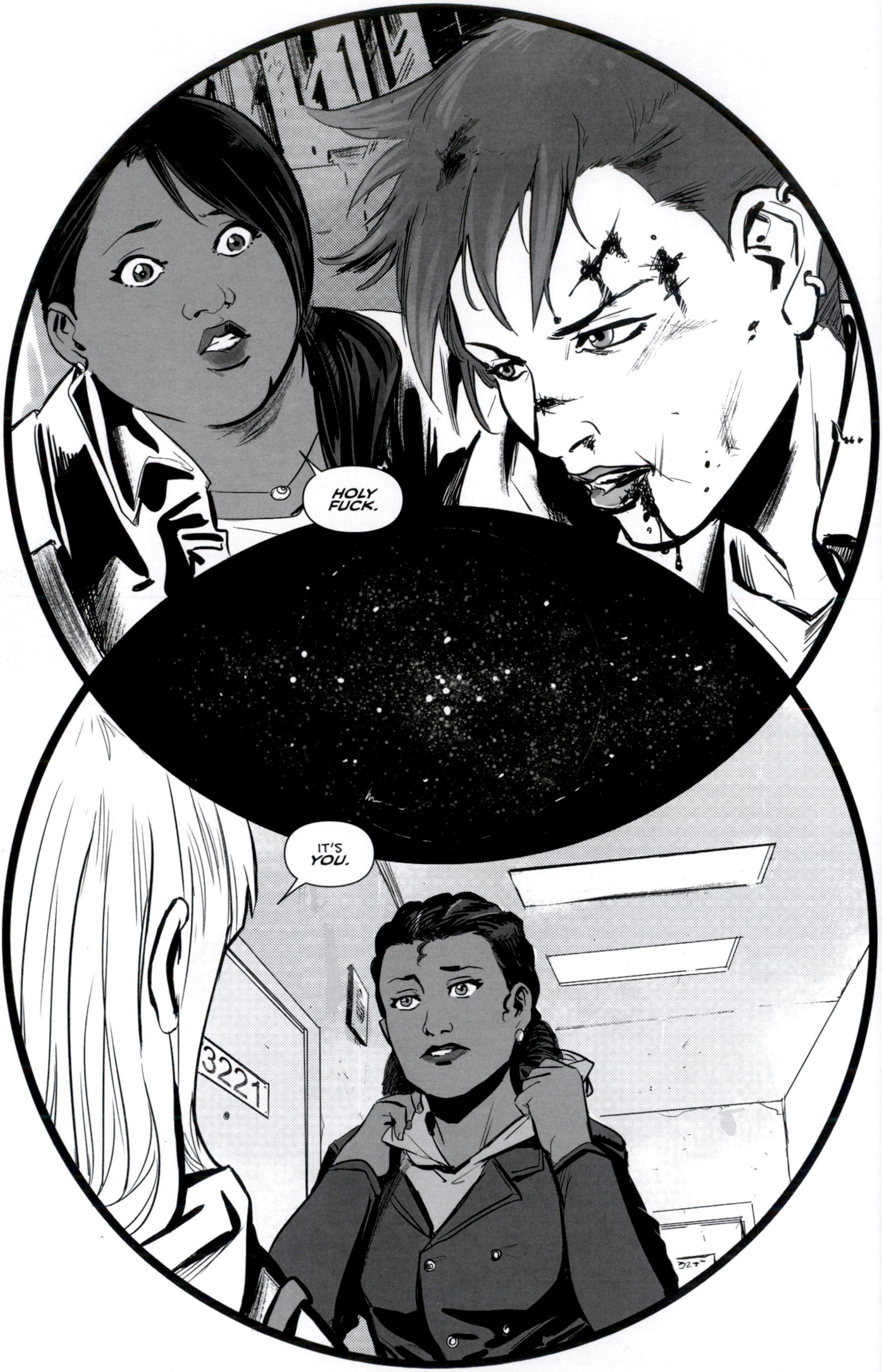
HOLY FUCK.
IT'S YOU.
3221

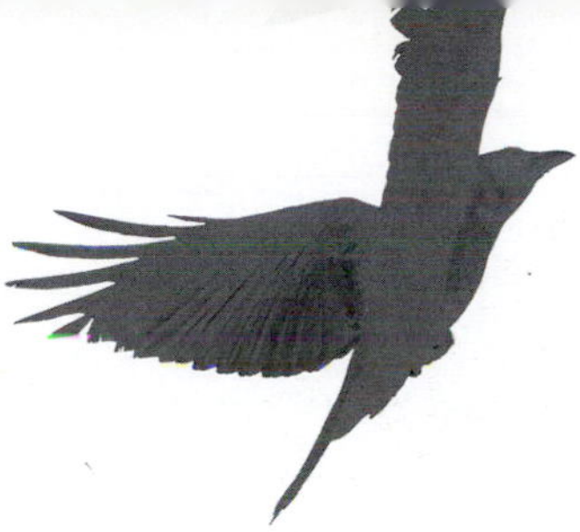

CHAPTER THREE
Circle, Circle

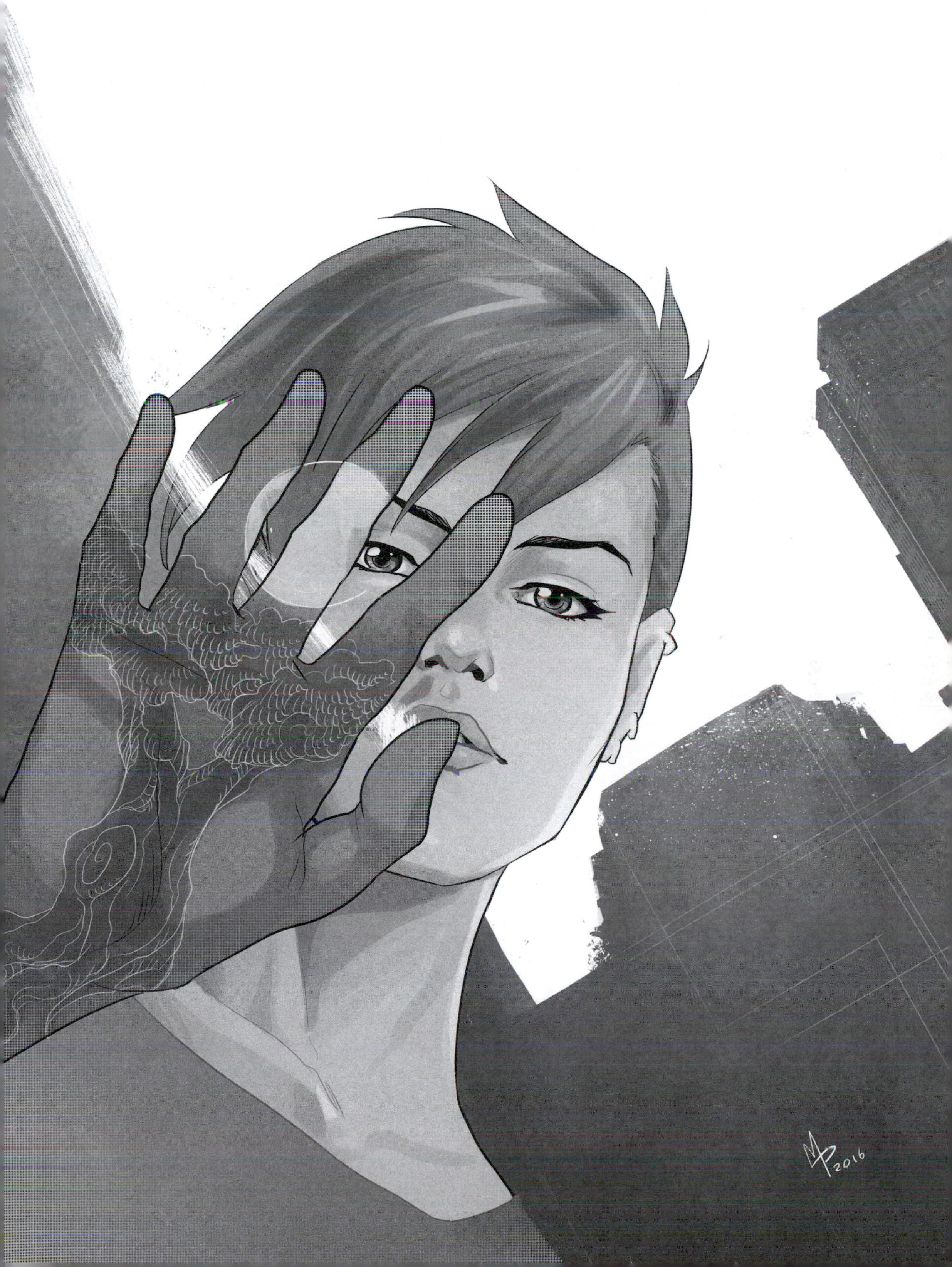

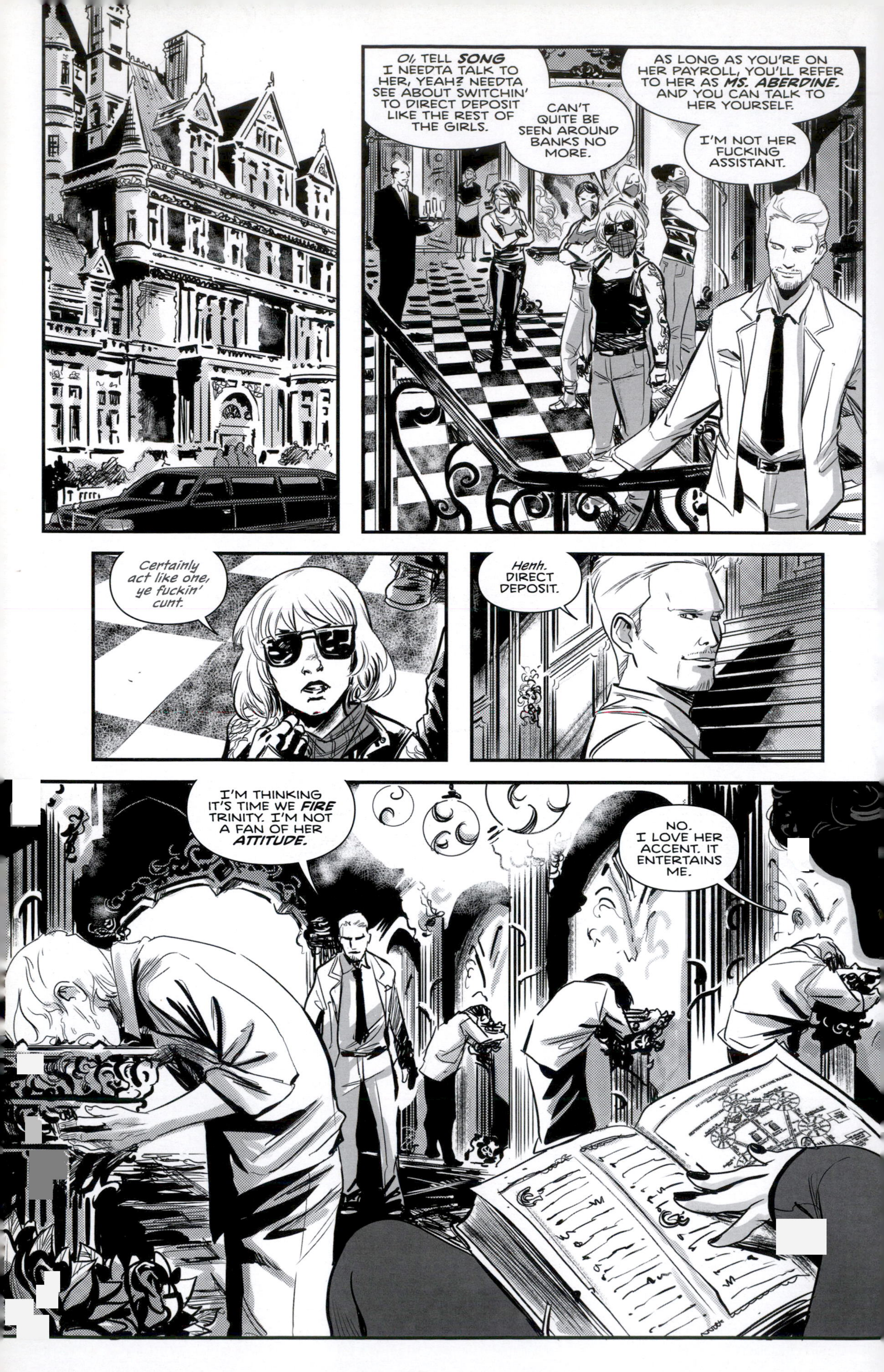
OI, TELL SONG I NEEDTA TALK TO HER, YEAH? NEEDTA SEE ABOUT SWITCHIN' TO DIRECT DEPOSIT LIKE THE REST OF THE GIRLS.
CAN'T QUITE BE SEEN AROUND BANKS NO MORE.
AS LONG AS YOU'RE ON HER PAYROLL, YOU'LL REFER TO HER AS MS. ABERDINE. AND YOU CAN TALK TO HER YOURSELF.
I'M NOT HER FUCKING ASSISTANT.
Certainly act like one, ye fuckin' cunt.
Henh. DIRECT DEPOSIT.
I'M THINKING IT'S TIME WE FIRE TRINITY. I'M NOT A FAN OF HER ATTITUDE.
NO. I LOVE HER ACCENT. IT ENTERTAINS ME.

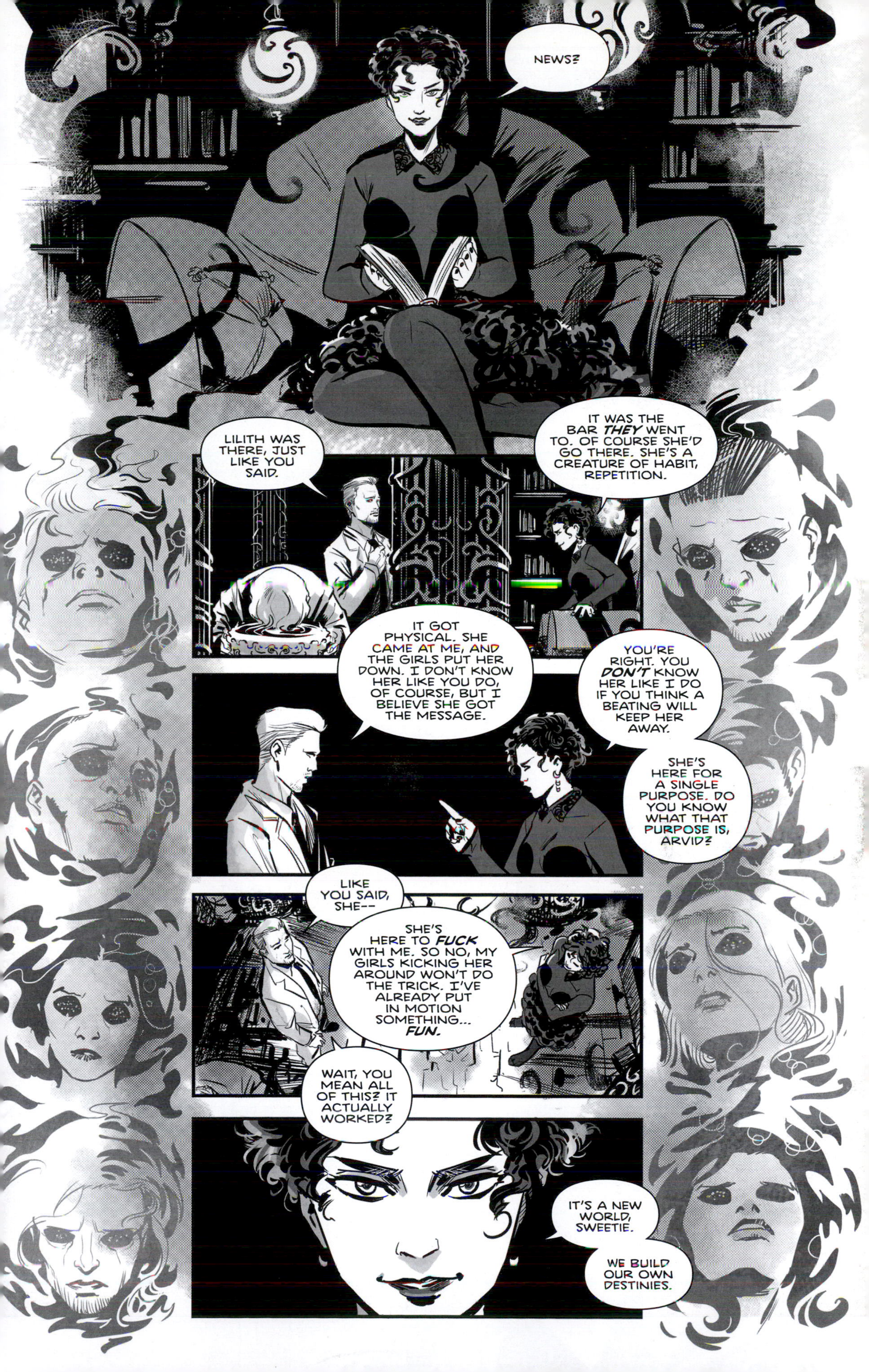
NEWS?
LILITH WAS THERE, JUST LIKE YOU SAID.
IT WAS THE BAR *THEY* WENT TO. OF COURSE SHE'D GO THERE. SHE'S A CREATURE OF HABIT, REPETITION.
IT GOT PHYSICAL. SHE CAME AT ME, AND THE GIRLS PUT HER DOWN. I DON'T KNOW HER LIKE YOU DO, OF COURSE, BUT I BELIEVE SHE GOT THE MESSAGE.
YOU'RE RIGHT. YOU *DON'T* KNOW HER LIKE I DO IF YOU THINK A BEATING WILL KEEP HER AWAY.
SHE'S HERE FOR A SINGLE PURPOSE. DO YOU KNOW WHAT THAT PURPOSE IS, ARVID?
LIKE YOU SAID, SHE--
SHE'S HERE TO *FUCK* WITH ME. SO NO, MY GIRLS KICKING HER AROUND WON'T DO THE TRICK. I'VE ALREADY PUT IN MOTION SOMETHING... *FUN.*
WAIT, YOU MEAN ALL OF THIS? IT ACTUALLY WORKED?
IT'S A NEW WORLD, SWEETIE.
WE BUILD OUR OWN DESTINIES.

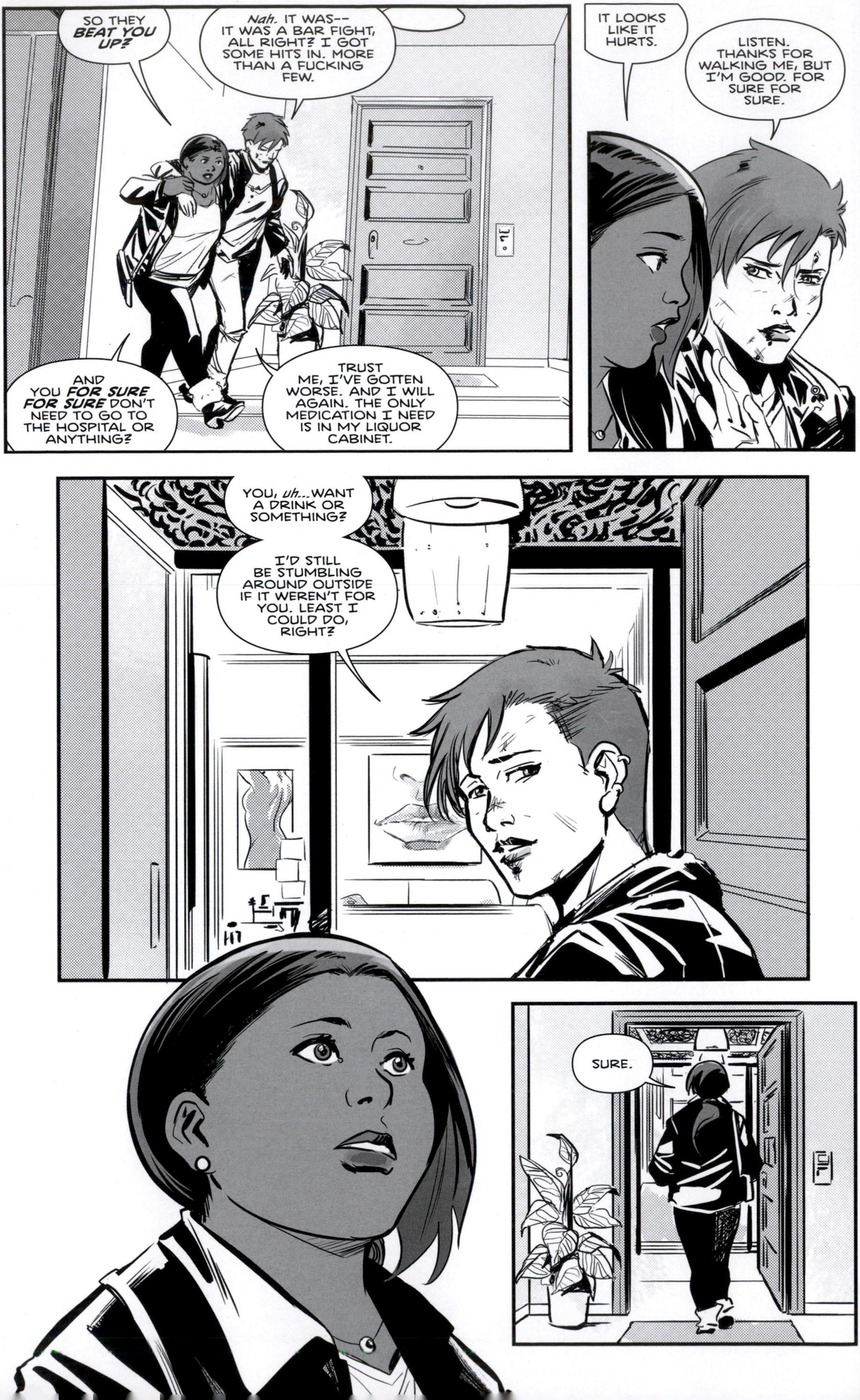
SO THEY *BEAT YOU UP?*
Nah. IT WAS-- IT WAS A BAR FIGHT, ALL RIGHT? I GOT SOME HITS IN. MORE THAN A FUCKING FEW.
AND YOU *FOR SURE FOR SURE* DON'T NEED TO GO TO THE HOSPITAL OR ANYTHING?
TRUST ME, I'VE GOTTEN WORSE. AND I WILL AGAIN. THE ONLY MEDICATION I NEED IS IN MY LIQUOR CABINET.
IT LOOKS LIKE IT HURTS.
LISTEN. THANKS FOR WALKING ME, BUT I'M GOOD. FOR SURE FOR SURE.
YOU, *uh...*WANT A DRINK OR SOMETHING?
I'D STILL BE STUMBLING AROUND OUTSIDE IF IT WEREN'T FOR YOU. LEAST I COULD DO, RIGHT?
SURE.

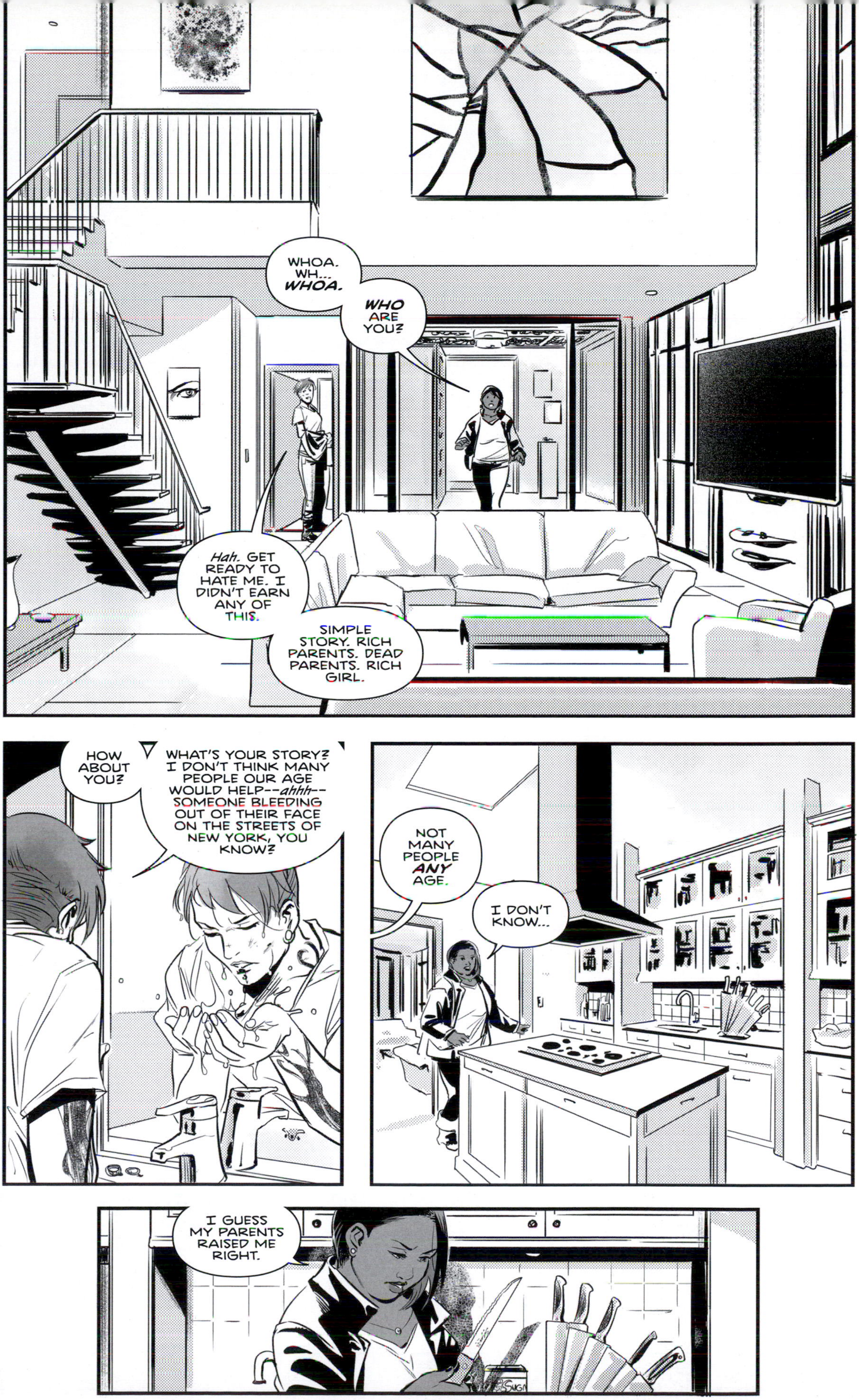
WHOA. WH... WHOA.
WHO ARE YOU?
Hah. GET READY TO HATE ME. I DIDN'T EARN ANY OF THIS.
SIMPLE STORY. RICH PARENTS. DEAD PARENTS. RICH GIRL.
HOW ABOUT YOU?
WHAT'S YOUR STORY? I DON'T THINK MANY PEOPLE OUR AGE WOULD HELP--ahhh--SOMEONE BLEEDING OUT OF THEIR FACE ON THE STREETS OF NEW YORK, YOU KNOW?
NOT MANY PEOPLE ANY AGE.
I DON'T KNOW...
I GUESS MY PARENTS RAISED ME RIGHT.

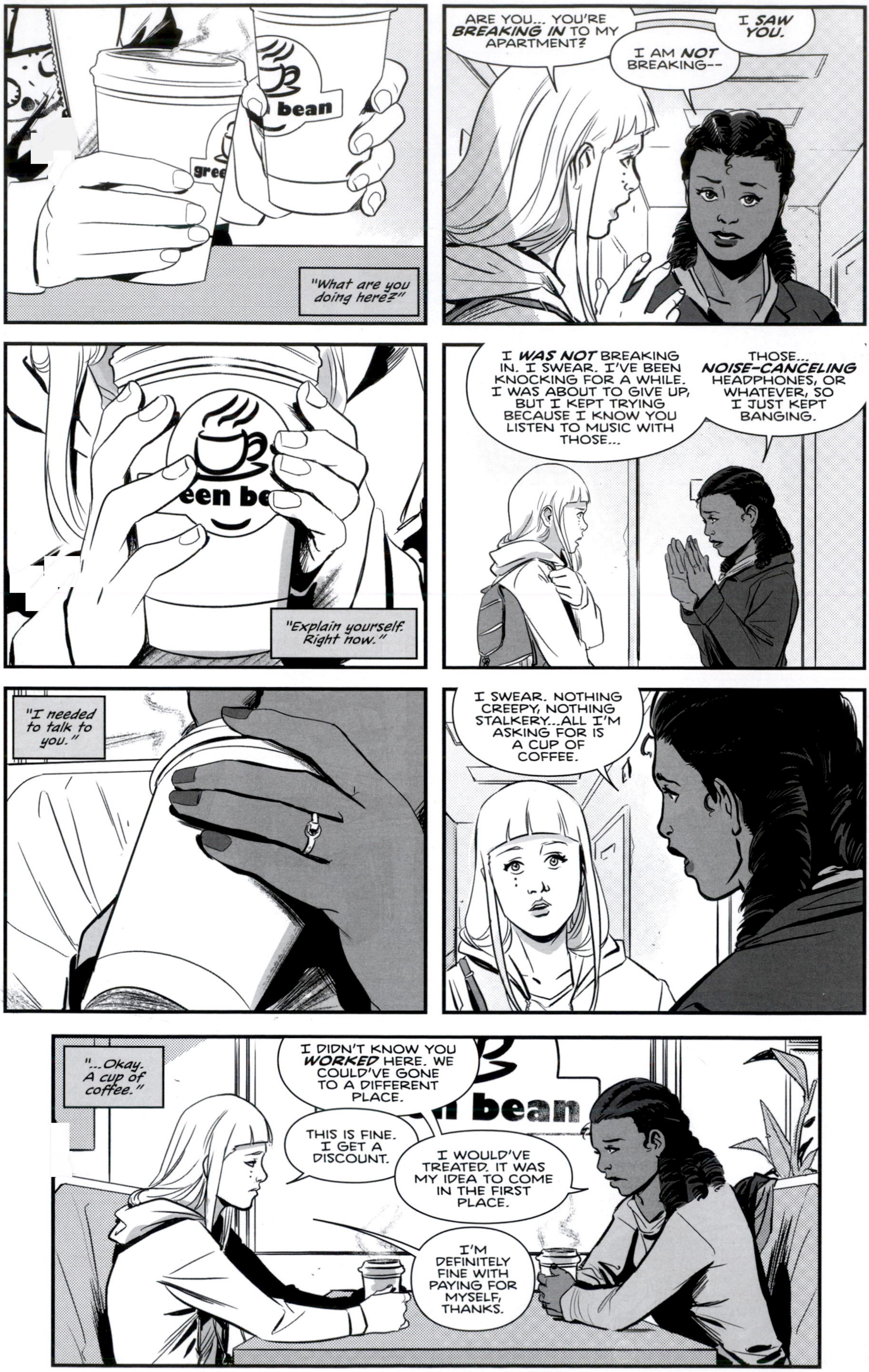
"What are you doing here?"
ARE YOU... YOU'RE BREAKING IN TO MY APARTMENT?
I AM NOT BREAKING--
I SAW YOU.
"Explain yourself. Right now."
I WAS NOT BREAKING IN. I SWEAR. I'VE BEEN KNOCKING FOR A WHILE. I WAS ABOUT TO GIVE UP, BUT I KEPT TRYING BECAUSE I KNOW YOU LISTEN TO MUSIC WITH THOSE...
THOSE... NOISE-CANCELING HEADPHONES, OR WHATEVER, SO I JUST KEPT BANGING.
"I needed to talk to you."
I SWEAR. NOTHING CREEPY, NOTHING STALKERY...ALL I'M ASKING FOR IS A CUP OF COFFEE.
"...Okay. A cup of coffee."
I DIDN'T KNOW YOU WORKED HERE. WE COULD'VE GONE TO A DIFFERENT PLACE.
THIS IS FINE. I GET A DISCOUNT.
I WOULD'VE TREATED. IT WAS MY IDEA TO COME IN THE FIRST PLACE.
I'M DEFINITELY FINE WITH PAYING FOR MYSELF, THANKS.

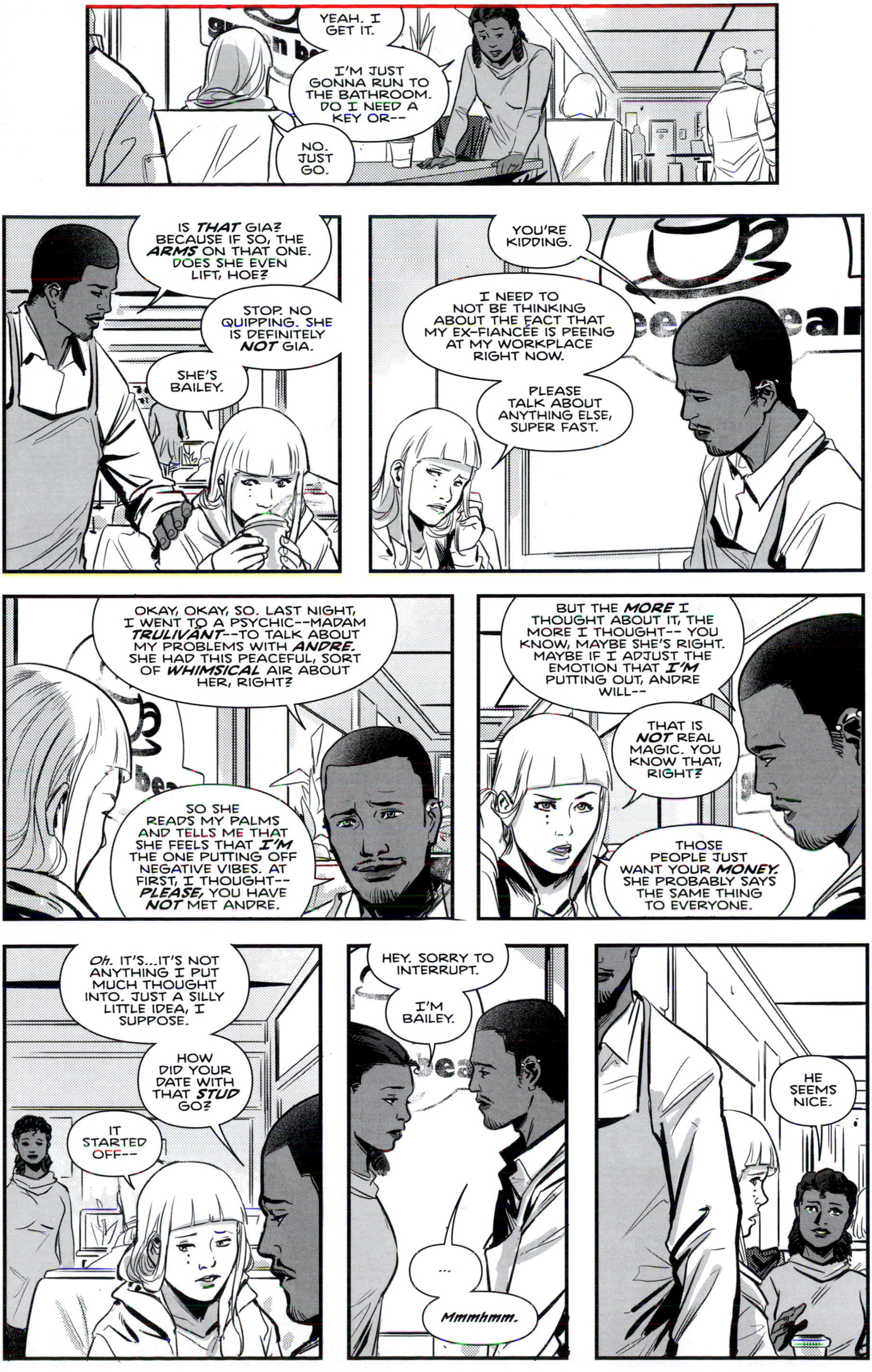
YEAH. I GET IT.
I'M JUST GONNA RUN TO THE BATHROOM. DO I NEED A KEY OR--
NO. JUST GO.
IS THAT GIA? BECAUSE IF SO, THE ARMS ON THAT ONE. DOES SHE EVEN LIFT, HOE?
STOP. NO QUIPPING. SHE IS DEFINITELY NOT GIA.
SHE'S BAILEY.
YOU'RE KIDDING.
I NEED TO NOT BE THINKING ABOUT THE FACT THAT MY EX-FIANCÉE IS PEEING AT MY WORKPLACE RIGHT NOW.
PLEASE TALK ABOUT ANYTHING ELSE, SUPER FAST.
OKAY, OKAY, SO. LAST NIGHT, I WENT TO A PSYCHIC--MADAM TRULIVANT--TO TALK ABOUT MY PROBLEMS WITH ANDRE. SHE HAD THIS PEACEFUL, SORT OF WHIMSICAL AIR ABOUT HER, RIGHT?
SO SHE READS MY PALMS AND TELLS ME THAT SHE FEELS THAT I'M THE ONE PUTTING OFF NEGATIVE VIBES. AT FIRST, I THOUGHT-- PLEASE, YOU HAVE NOT MET ANDRE.
BUT THE MORE I THOUGHT ABOUT IT, THE MORE I THOUGHT-- YOU KNOW, MAYBE SHE'S RIGHT. MAYBE IF I ADJUST THE EMOTION THAT I'M PUTTING OUT, ANDRE WILL--
THAT IS NOT REAL MAGIC. YOU KNOW THAT, RIGHT?
THOSE PEOPLE JUST WANT YOUR MONEY. SHE PROBABLY SAYS THE SAME THING TO EVERYONE.
Oh. IT'S...IT'S NOT ANYTHING I PUT MUCH THOUGHT INTO. JUST A SILLY LITTLE IDEA, I SUPPOSE.
HOW DID YOUR DATE WITH THAT STUD GO?
IT STARTED OFF--
HEY. SORRY TO INTERRUPT.
I'M BAILEY.
...
Mmmhmm.
HE SEEMS NICE.

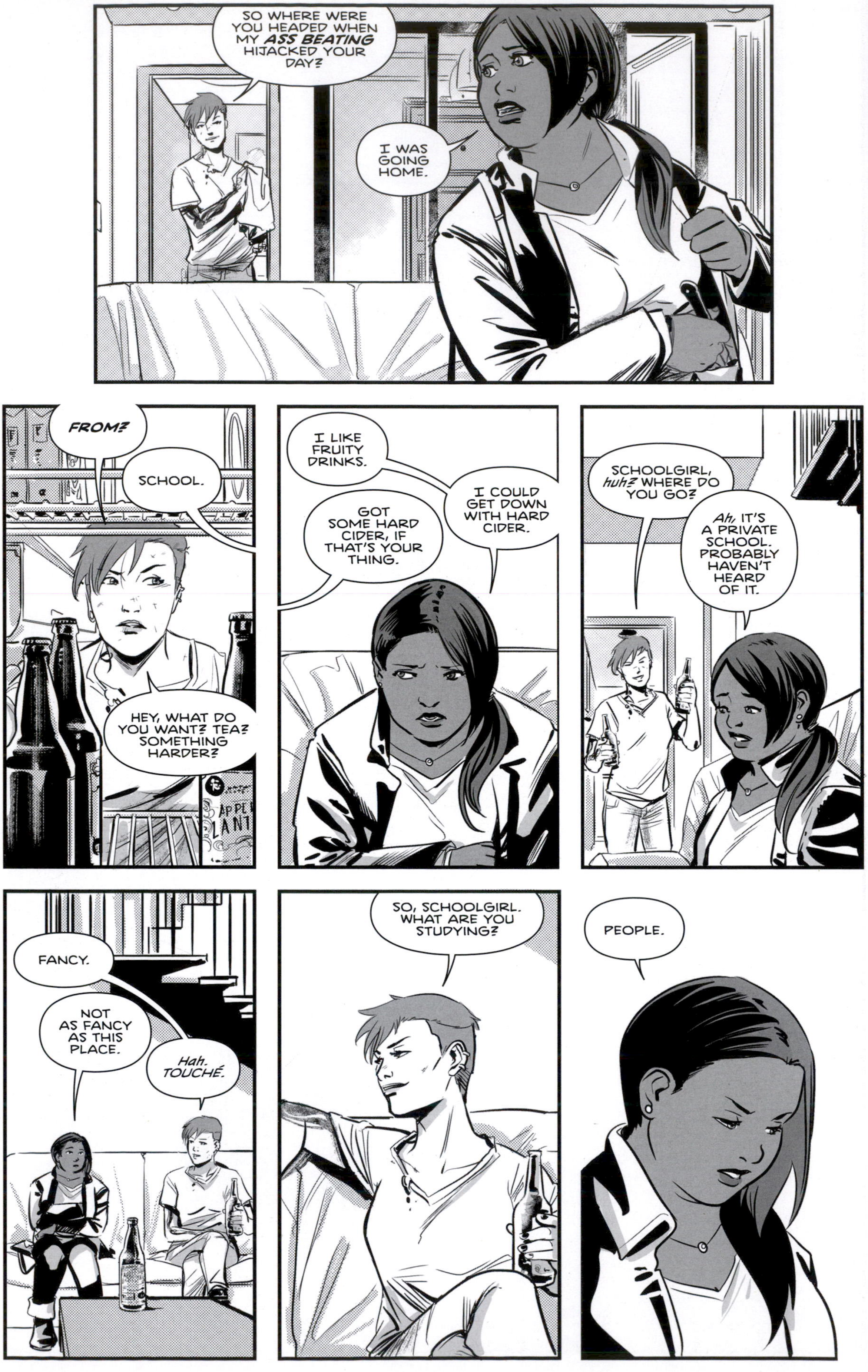
SO WHERE WERE YOU HEADED WHEN MY ASS BEATING HIJACKED YOUR DAY?
I WAS GOING HOME.
FROM?
SCHOOL.
HEY, WHAT DO YOU WANT? TEA? SOMETHING HARDER?
I LIKE FRUITY DRINKS.
GOT SOME HARD CIDER, IF THAT'S YOUR THING.
I COULD GET DOWN WITH HARD CIDER.
SCHOOLGIRL, huh? WHERE DO YOU GO?
Ah, IT'S A PRIVATE SCHOOL. PROBABLY HAVEN'T HEARD OF IT.
FANCY.
NOT AS FANCY AS THIS PLACE.
Hah. TOUCHÉ.
SO, SCHOOLGIRL. WHAT ARE YOU STUDYING?
PEOPLE.

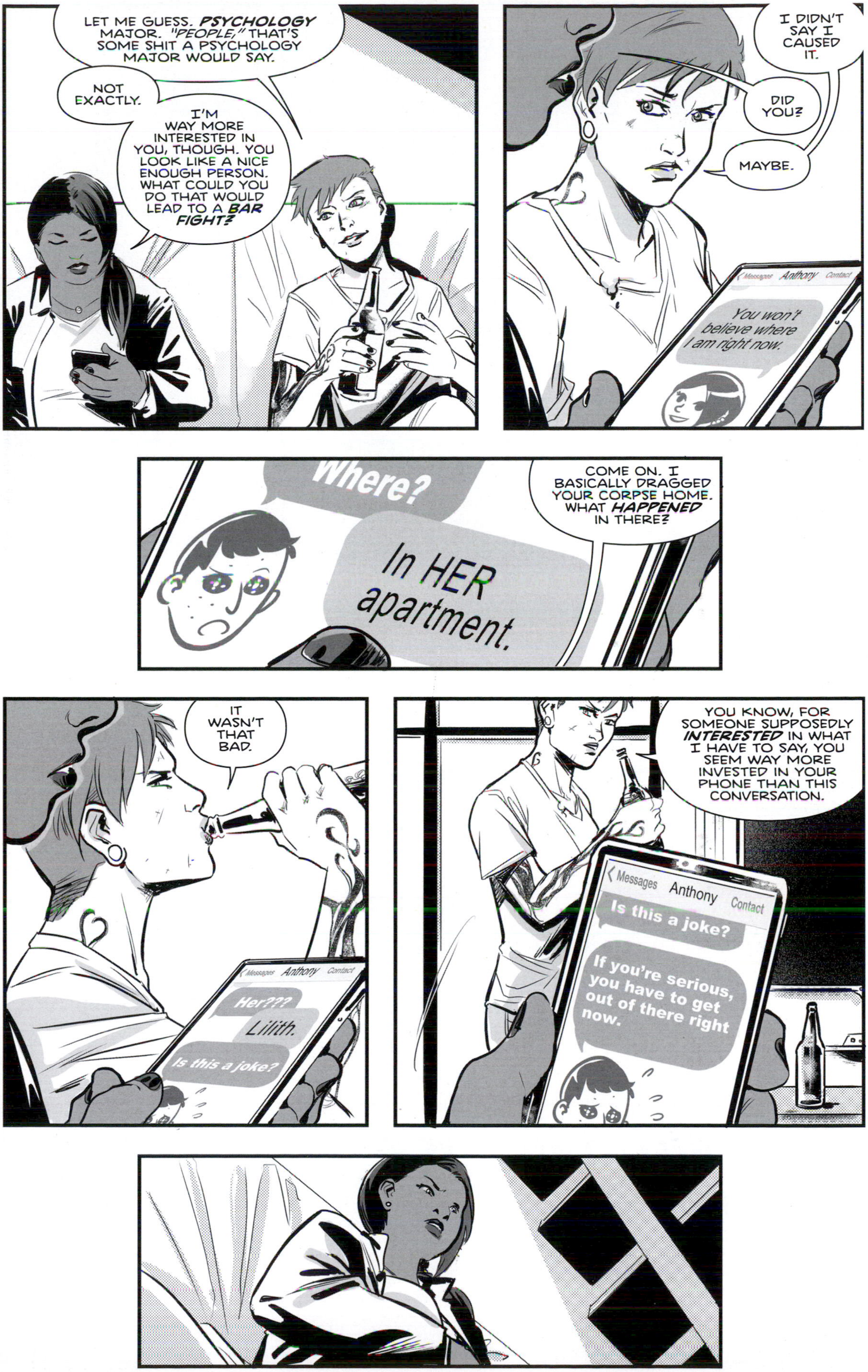
LET ME GUESS. PSYCHOLOGY MAJOR. "PEOPLE," THAT'S SOME SHIT A PSYCHOLOGY MAJOR WOULD SAY.
NOT EXACTLY.
I'M WAY MORE INTERESTED IN YOU, THOUGH. YOU LOOK LIKE A NICE ENOUGH PERSON. WHAT COULD YOU DO THAT WOULD LEAD TO A BAR FIGHT?
I DIDN'T SAY I CAUSED IT.
DID YOU?
MAYBE.
Messages Anthony Contact
You won't believe where I am right now.
Where?
In HER apartment.
COME ON. I BASICALLY DRAGGED YOUR CORPSE HOME. WHAT HAPPENED IN THERE?
IT WASN'T THAT BAD.
Messages Anthony Contact
Her???
Lilith.
Is this a joke?
YOU KNOW, FOR SOMEONE SUPPOSEDLY INTERESTED IN WHAT I HAVE TO SAY, YOU SEEM WAY MORE INVESTED IN YOUR PHONE THAN THIS CONVERSATION.
Messages Anthony Contact
Is this a joke?
If you're serious, you have to get out of there right now.

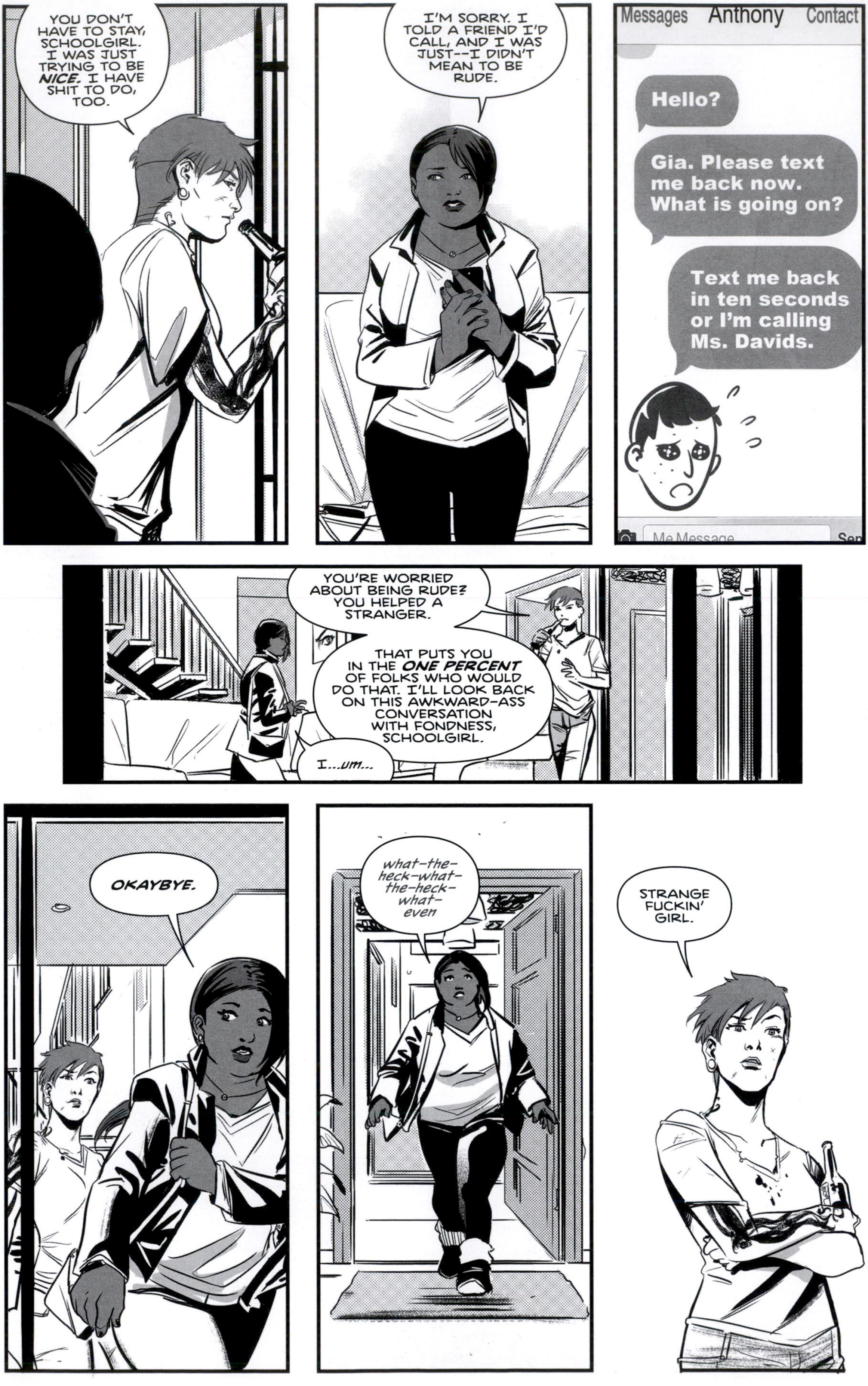
YOU DON'T HAVE TO STAY, SCHOOLGIRL. I WAS JUST TRYING TO BE NICE. I HAVE SHIT TO DO, TOO.
I'M SORRY. I TOLD A FRIEND I'D CALL, AND I WAS JUST--I DIDN'T MEAN TO BE RUDE.
Messages Anthony Contact
Hello?
Gia. Please text me back now. What is going on?
Text me back in ten seconds or I'm calling Ms. Davids.
YOU'RE WORRIED ABOUT BEING RUDE? YOU HELPED A STRANGER.
THAT PUTS YOU IN THE ONE PERCENT OF FOLKS WHO WOULD DO THAT. I'LL LOOK BACK ON THIS AWKWARD-ASS CONVERSATION WITH FONDNESS, SCHOOLGIRL.
I...UM...
OKAYBYE.
what-the-heck-what-the-heck-what-even
STRANGE FUCKIN' GIRL.

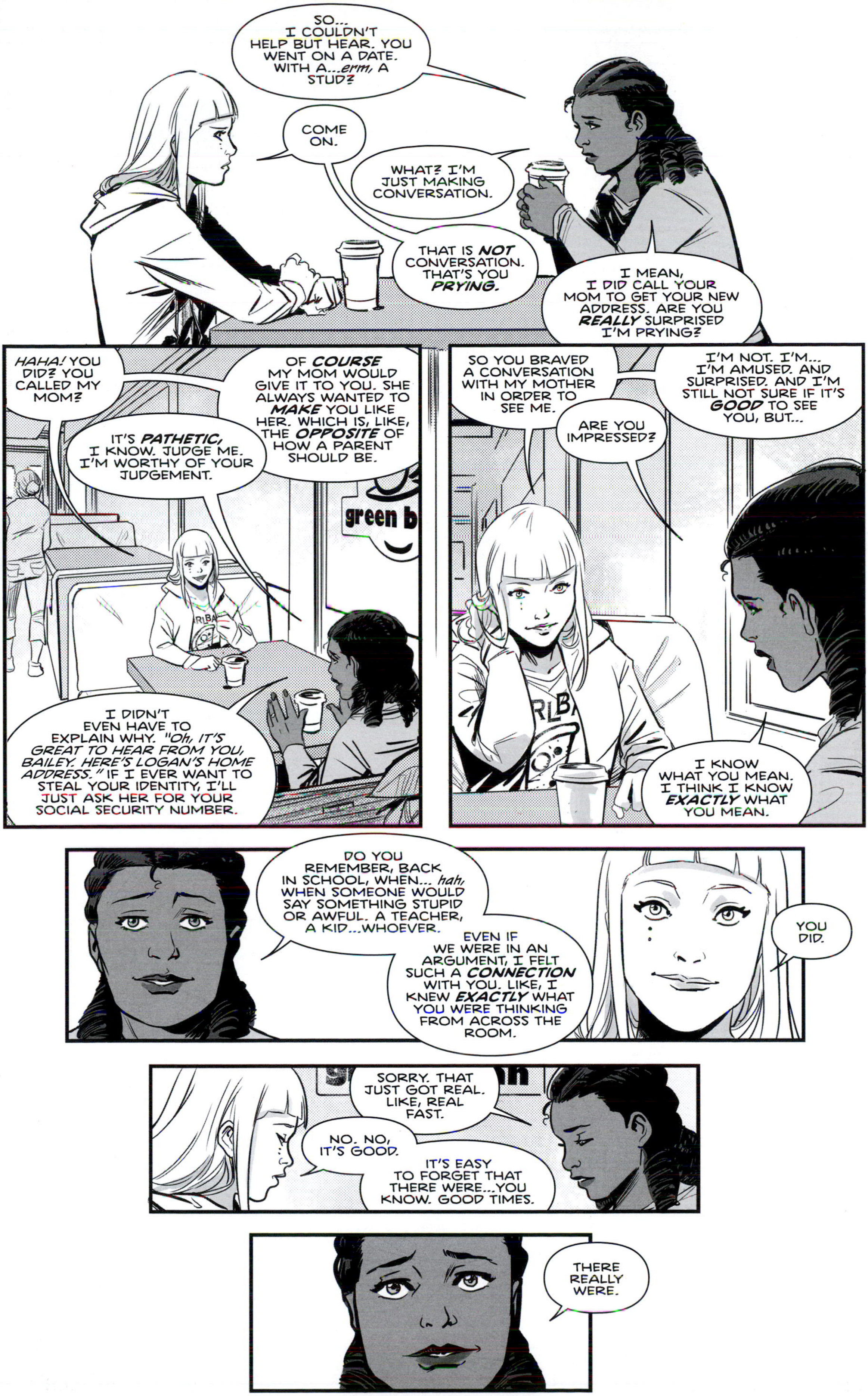
SO... I COULDN'T HELP BUT HEAR. YOU WENT ON A DATE. WITH A...*erm*, A STUD?
COME ON.
WHAT? I'M JUST MAKING CONVERSATION.
THAT IS **NOT** CONVERSATION. THAT'S YOU ***PRYING.***
I MEAN, I DID CALL YOUR MOM TO GET YOUR NEW ADDRESS. ARE YOU ***REALLY*** SURPRISED I'M PRYING?
HAHA! YOU DID? YOU CALLED MY MOM?
IT'S ***PATHETIC,*** I KNOW. JUDGE ME. I'M WORTHY OF YOUR JUDGEMENT.
OF ***COURSE*** MY MOM WOULD GIVE IT TO YOU. SHE ALWAYS WANTED TO ***MAKE*** YOU LIKE HER. WHICH IS, LIKE, THE ***OPPOSITE*** OF HOW A PARENT SHOULD BE.
green b
I DIDN'T EVEN HAVE TO EXPLAIN WHY. *"OH, IT'S GREAT TO HEAR FROM YOU, BAILEY. HERE'S LOGAN'S HOME ADDRESS."* IF I EVER WANT TO STEAL YOUR IDENTITY, I'LL JUST ASK HER FOR YOUR SOCIAL SECURITY NUMBER.
SO YOU BRAVED A CONVERSATION WITH MY MOTHER IN ORDER TO SEE ME.
ARE YOU IMPRESSED?
I'M NOT. I'M... I'M AMUSED. AND SURPRISED. AND I'M STILL NOT SURE IF IT'S ***GOOD*** TO SEE YOU, BUT...
I KNOW WHAT YOU MEAN. I THINK I KNOW ***EXACTLY*** WHAT YOU MEAN.
DO YOU REMEMBER, BACK IN SCHOOL, WHEN... *hah,* WHEN SOMEONE WOULD SAY SOMETHING STUPID OR AWFUL. A TEACHER, A KID...WHOEVER.
EVEN IF WE WERE IN AN ARGUMENT, I FELT SUCH A ***CONNECTION*** WITH YOU. LIKE, I KNEW ***EXACTLY*** WHAT YOU WERE THINKING FROM ACROSS THE ROOM.
YOU DID.
SORRY. THAT JUST GOT REAL. LIKE, REAL FAST.
NO. NO, IT'S GOOD.
IT'S EASY TO FORGET THAT THERE WERE...YOU KNOW. GOOD TIMES.
THERE REALLY WERE.

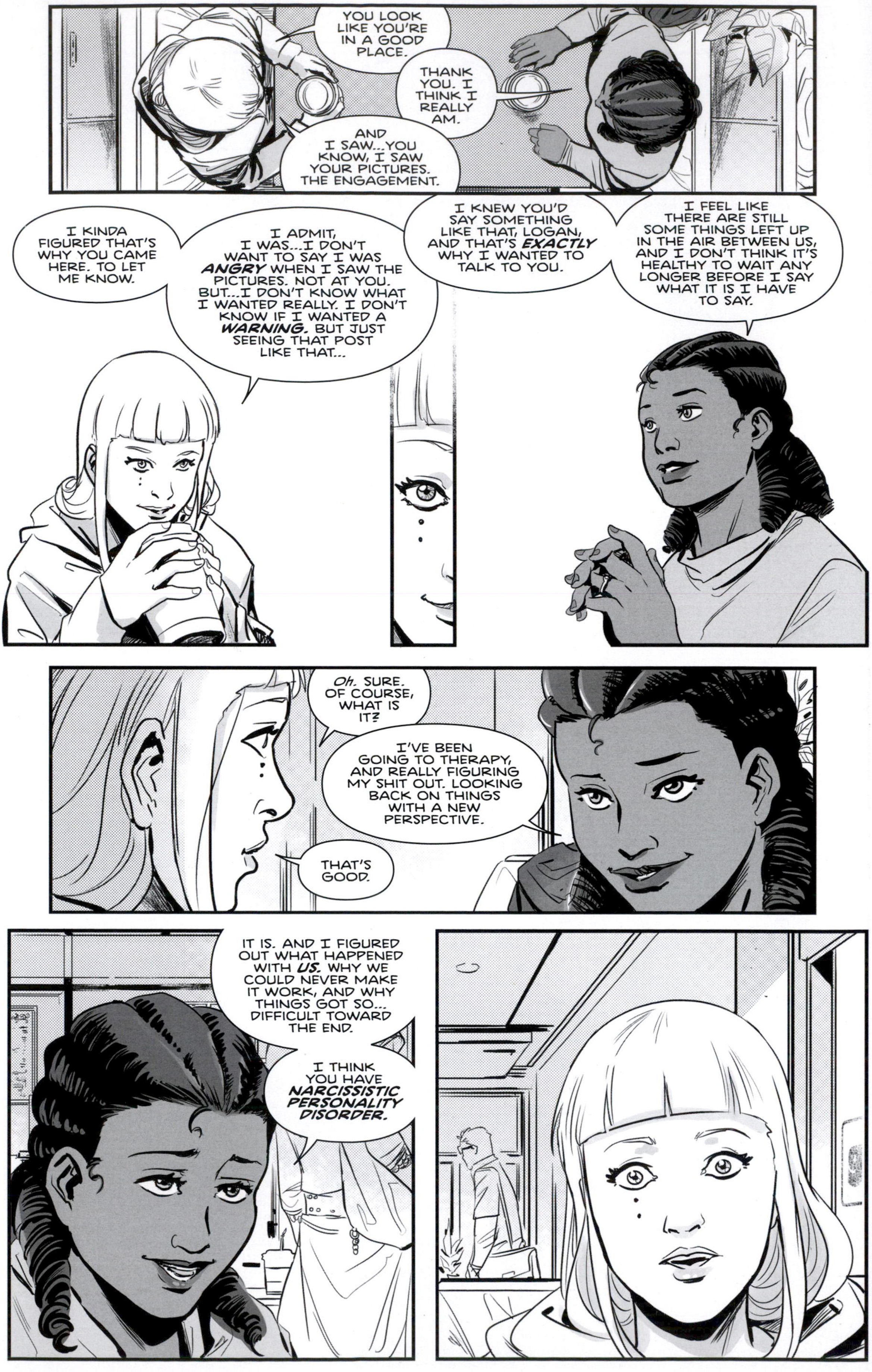
YOU LOOK LIKE YOU'RE IN A GOOD PLACE.
THANK YOU. I THINK I REALLY AM.
AND I SAW...YOU KNOW, I SAW YOUR PICTURES. THE ENGAGEMENT.
I KINDA FIGURED THAT'S WHY YOU CAME HERE. TO LET ME KNOW.
I ADMIT, I WAS...I DON'T WANT TO SAY I WAS ANGRY WHEN I SAW THE PICTURES. NOT AT YOU. BUT...I DON'T KNOW WHAT I WANTED REALLY. I DON'T KNOW IF I WANTED A WARNING. BUT JUST SEEING THAT POST LIKE THAT...
I KNEW YOU'D SAY SOMETHING LIKE THAT, LOGAN, AND THAT'S EXACTLY WHY I WANTED TO TALK TO YOU.
I FEEL LIKE THERE ARE STILL SOME THINGS LEFT UP IN THE AIR BETWEEN US, AND I DON'T THINK IT'S HEALTHY TO WAIT ANY LONGER BEFORE I SAY WHAT IT IS I HAVE TO SAY.
Oh. SURE. OF COURSE, WHAT IS IT?
I'VE BEEN GOING TO THERAPY, AND REALLY FIGURING MY SHIT OUT. LOOKING BACK ON THINGS WITH A NEW PERSPECTIVE.
THAT'S GOOD.
IT IS. AND I FIGURED OUT WHAT HAPPENED WITH US. WHY WE COULD NEVER MAKE IT WORK, AND WHY THINGS GOT SO... DIFFICULT TOWARD THE END.
I THINK YOU HAVE NARCISSISTIC PERSONALITY DISORDER.

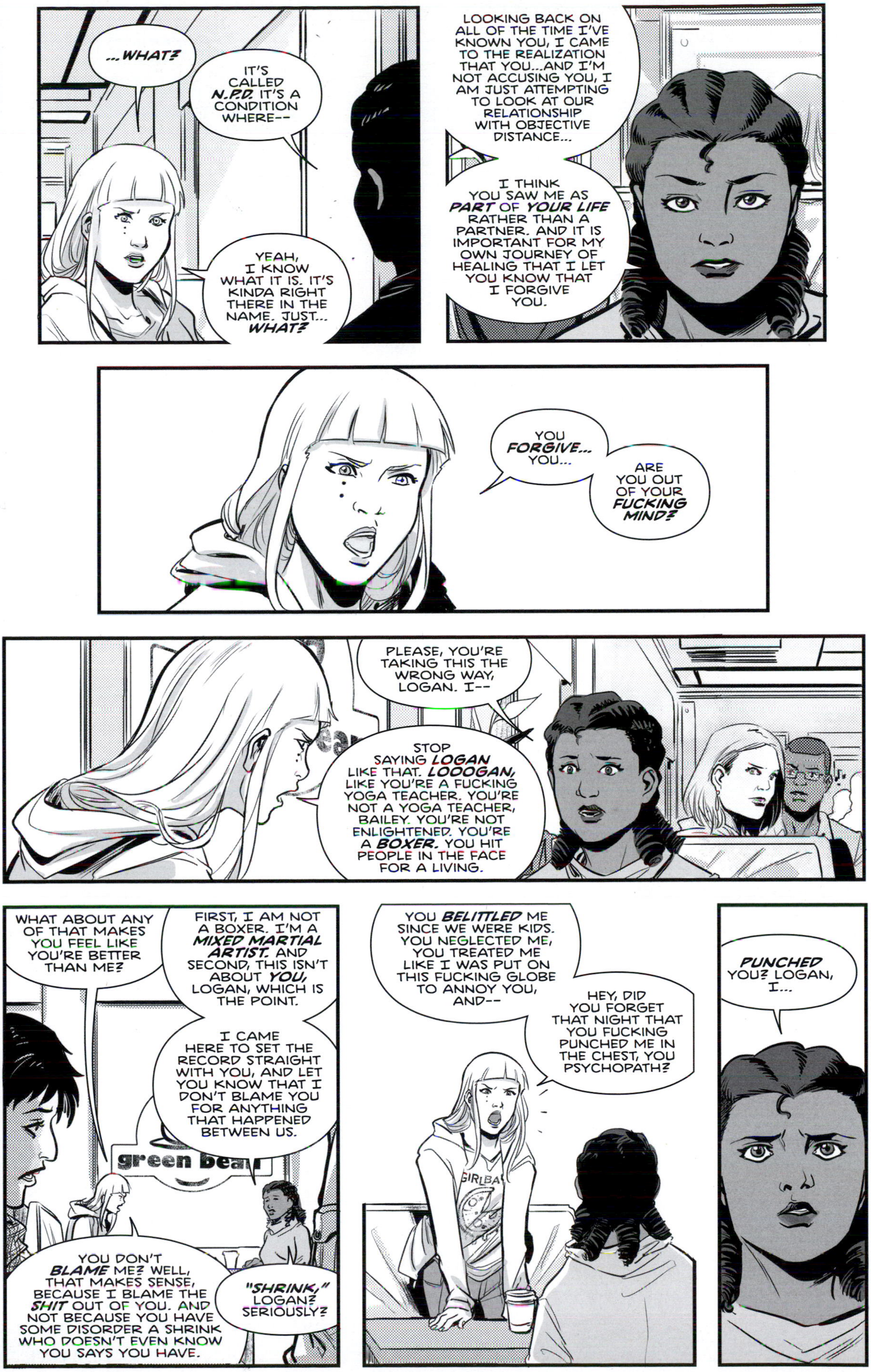
...WHAT?
IT'S CALLED N.P.D. IT'S A CONDITION WHERE--
YEAH, I KNOW WHAT IT IS. IT'S KINDA RIGHT THERE IN THE NAME. JUST... WHAT?
LOOKING BACK ON ALL OF THE TIME I'VE KNOWN YOU, I CAME TO THE REALIZATION THAT YOU...AND I'M NOT ACCUSING YOU, I AM JUST ATTEMPTING TO LOOK AT OUR RELATIONSHIP WITH OBJECTIVE DISTANCE...
I THINK YOU SAW ME AS PART OF YOUR LIFE RATHER THAN A PARTNER. AND IT IS IMPORTANT FOR MY OWN JOURNEY OF HEALING THAT I LET YOU KNOW THAT I FORGIVE YOU.
YOU FORGIVE... YOU...
ARE YOU OUT OF YOUR FUCKING MIND?
PLEASE, YOU'RE TAKING THIS THE WRONG WAY, LOGAN. I--
STOP SAYING LOGAN LIKE THAT. LOOOGAN, LIKE YOU'RE A FUCKING YOGA TEACHER. YOU'RE NOT A YOGA TEACHER, BAILEY. YOU'RE NOT ENLIGHTENED. YOU'RE A BOXER. YOU HIT PEOPLE IN THE FACE FOR A LIVING.
WHAT ABOUT ANY OF THAT MAKES YOU FEEL LIKE YOU'RE BETTER THAN ME?
FIRST, I AM NOT A BOXER. I'M A MIXED MARTIAL ARTIST. AND SECOND, THIS ISN'T ABOUT YOU, LOGAN, WHICH IS THE POINT.
I CAME HERE TO SET THE RECORD STRAIGHT WITH YOU, AND LET YOU KNOW THAT I DON'T BLAME YOU FOR ANYTHING THAT HAPPENED BETWEEN US.
green bea
YOU DON'T BLAME ME? WELL, THAT MAKES SENSE, BECAUSE I BLAME THE SHIT OUT OF YOU. AND NOT BECAUSE YOU HAVE SOME DISORDER A SHRINK WHO DOESN'T EVEN KNOW YOU SAYS YOU HAVE.
"SHRINK," LOGAN? SERIOUSLY?
YOU BELITTLED ME SINCE WE WERE KIDS. YOU NEGLECTED ME, YOU TREATED ME LIKE I WAS PUT ON THIS FUCKING GLOBE TO ANNOY YOU, AND--
HEY, DID YOU FORGET THAT NIGHT THAT YOU FUCKING PUNCHED ME IN THE CHEST, YOU PSYCHOPATH?
PUNCHED YOU? LOGAN, I...

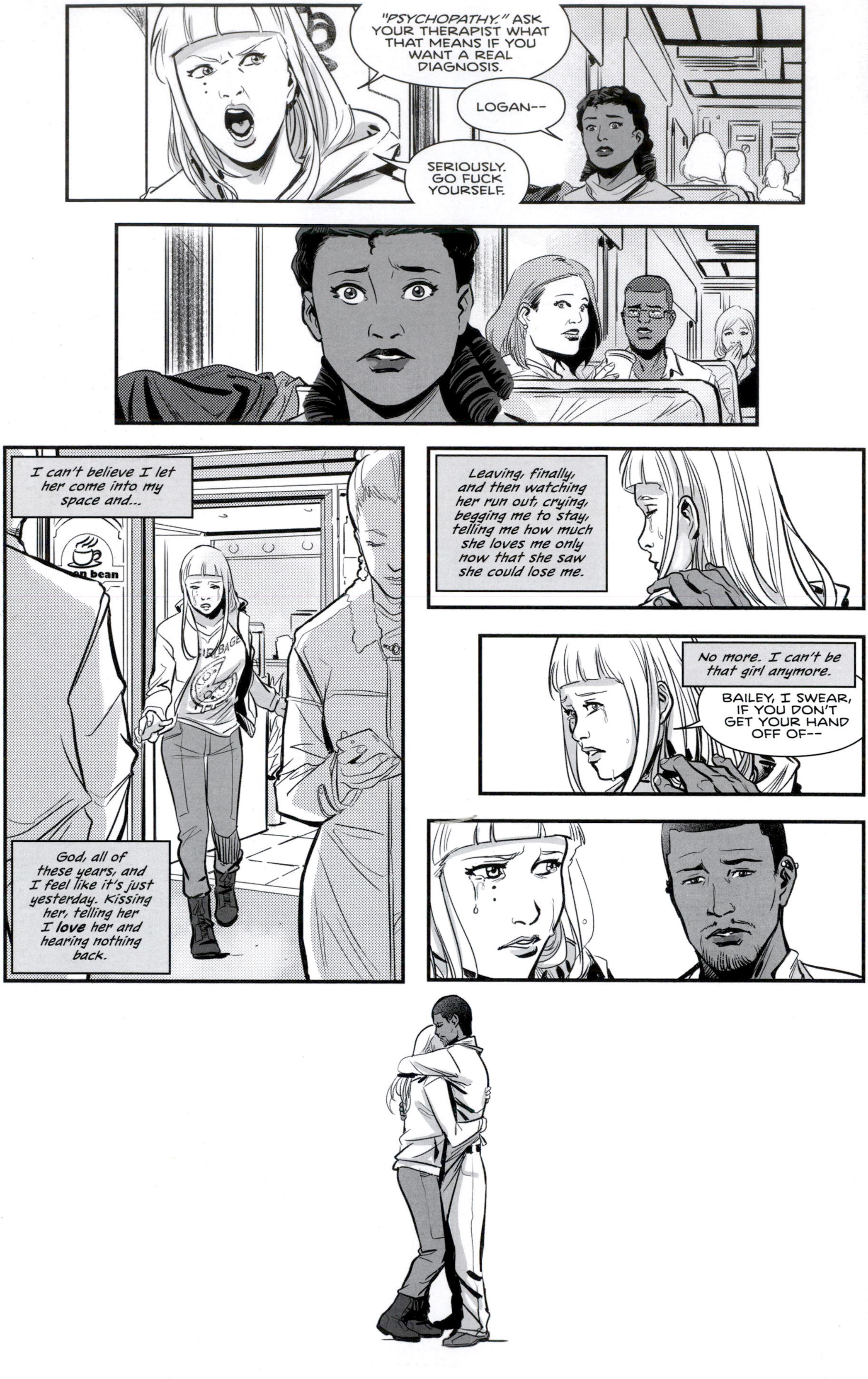
"PSYCHOPATHY." ASK YOUR THERAPIST WHAT THAT MEANS IF YOU WANT A REAL DIAGNOSIS.
LOGAN--
SERIOUSLY. GO FUCK YOURSELF.
I can't believe I let her come into my space and...
God, all of these years, and I feel like it's just yesterday. Kissing her, telling her I **love** her and hearing nothing back.
Leaving, finally, and then watching her run out, crying, begging me to stay, telling me how much she loves me only now that she saw she could lose me.
No more. I can't be that girl anymore.
BAILEY, I SWEAR, IF YOU DON'T GET YOUR HAND OFF OF--

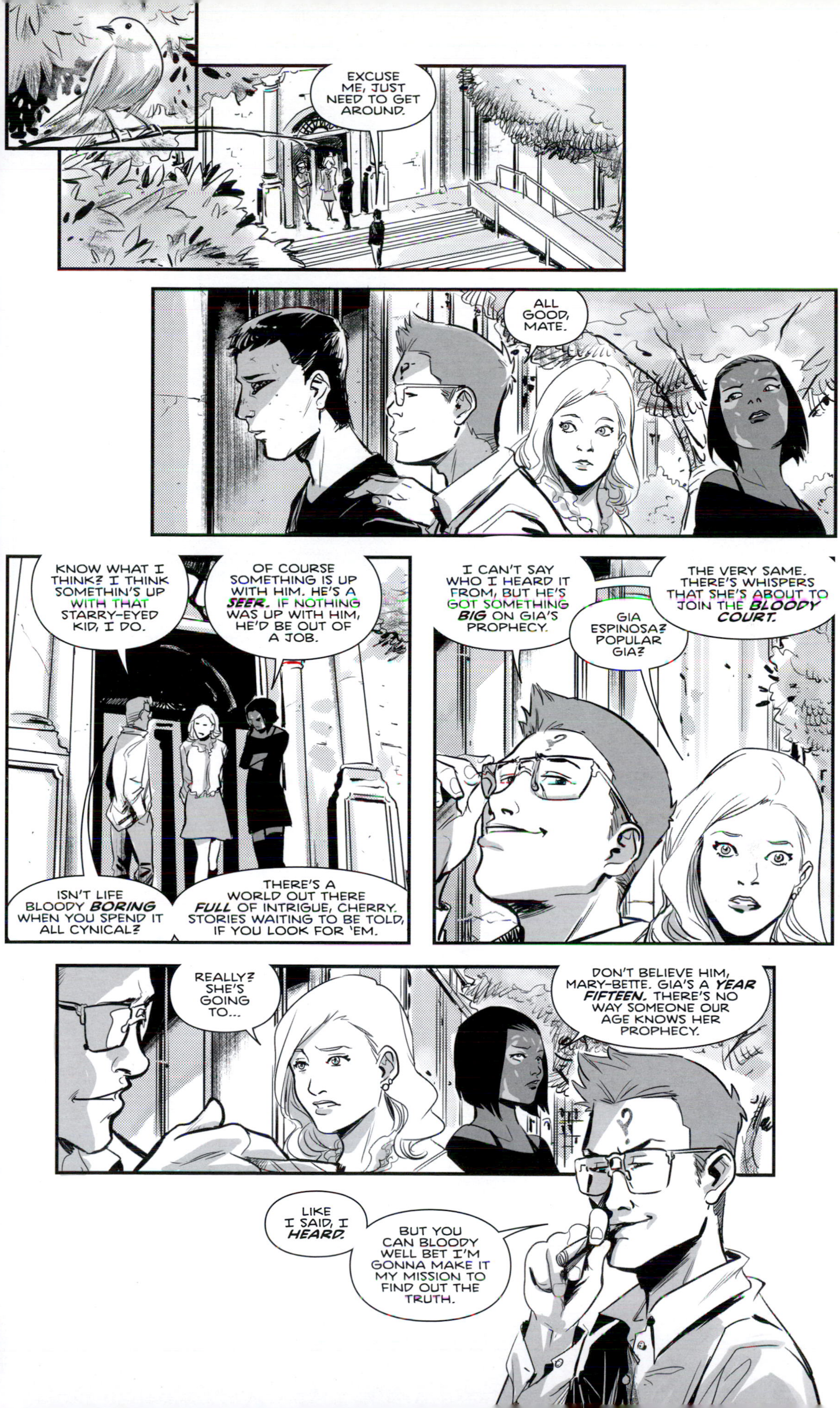
EXCUSE ME, JUST NEED TO GET AROUND.
ALL GOOD, MATE.
KNOW WHAT I THINK? I THINK SOMETHIN'S UP WITH THAT STARRY-EYED KID, I DO.
OF COURSE SOMETHING IS UP WITH HIM. HE'S A SEER. IF NOTHING WAS UP WITH HIM, HE'D BE OUT OF A JOB.
ISN'T LIFE BLOODY BORING WHEN YOU SPEND IT ALL CYNICAL?
THERE'S A WORLD OUT THERE FULL OF INTRIGUE, CHERRY. STORIES WAITING TO BE TOLD, IF YOU LOOK FOR 'EM.
I CAN'T SAY WHO I HEARD IT FROM, BUT HE'S GOT SOMETHING BIG ON GIA'S PROPHECY.
GIA ESPINOSA? POPULAR GIA?
THE VERY SAME. THERE'S WHISPERS THAT SHE'S ABOUT TO JOIN THE BLOODY COURT.
REALLY? SHE'S GOING TO...
DON'T BELIEVE HIM, MARY-BETTE. GIA'S A YEAR FIFTEEN. THERE'S NO WAY SOMEONE OUR AGE KNOWS HER PROPHECY.
LIKE I SAID, I HEARD.
BUT YOU CAN BLOODY WELL BET I'M GONNA MAKE IT MY MISSION TO FIND OUT THE TRUTH.

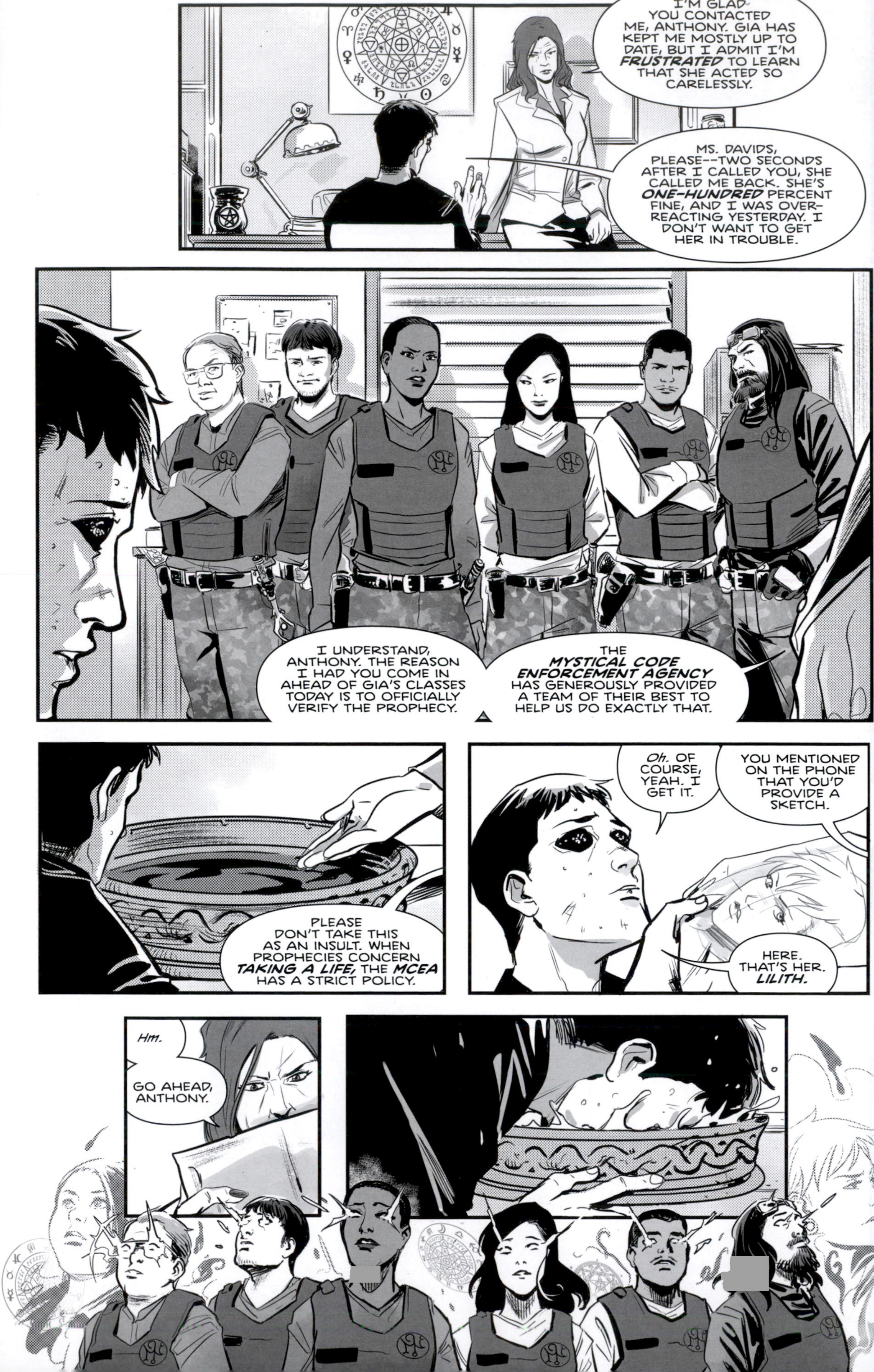
I'M GLAD YOU CONTACTED ME, ANTHONY. GIA HAS KEPT ME MOSTLY UP TO DATE, BUT I ADMIT I'M FRUSTRATED TO LEARN THAT SHE ACTED SO CARELESSLY.
MS. DAVIDS, PLEASE--TWO SECONDS AFTER I CALLED YOU, SHE CALLED ME BACK. SHE'S ONE-HUNDRED PERCENT FINE, AND I WAS OVER-REACTING YESTERDAY. I DON'T WANT TO GET HER IN TROUBLE.
I UNDERSTAND, ANTHONY. THE REASON I HAD YOU COME IN AHEAD OF GIA'S CLASSES TODAY IS TO OFFICIALLY VERIFY THE PROPHECY.
THE MYSTICAL CODE ENFORCEMENT AGENCY HAS GENEROUSLY PROVIDED A TEAM OF THEIR BEST TO HELP US DO EXACTLY THAT.
PLEASE DON'T TAKE THIS AS AN INSULT. WHEN PROPHECIES CONCERN TAKING A LIFE, THE MCEA HAS A STRICT POLICY.
Oh. OF COURSE, YEAH. I GET IT.
YOU MENTIONED ON THE PHONE THAT YOU'D PROVIDE A SKETCH.
HERE. THAT'S HER. LILITH.
Hm.
GO AHEAD, ANTHONY.

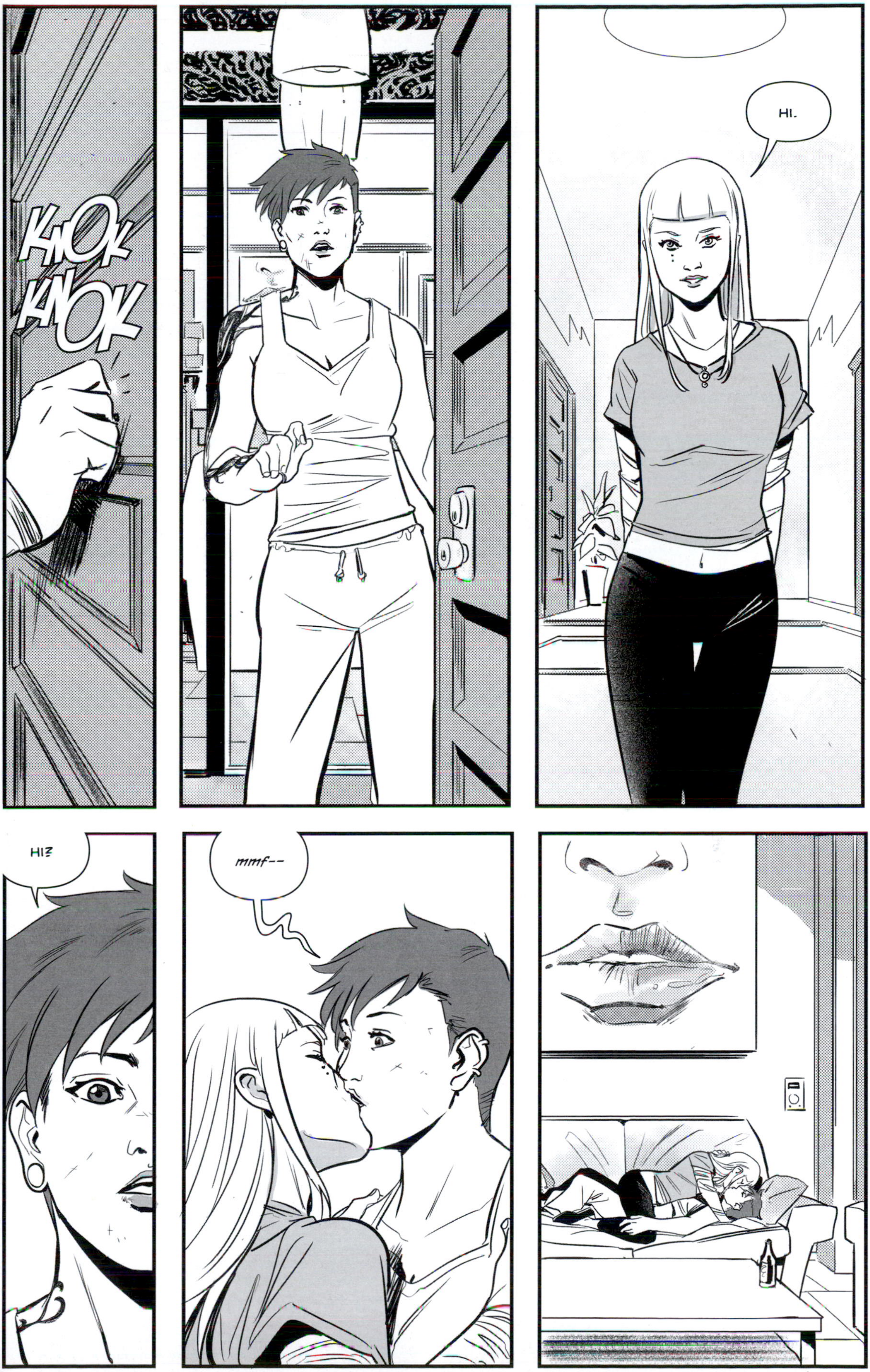
KNOK KNOK
HI.
HI?
mmf--

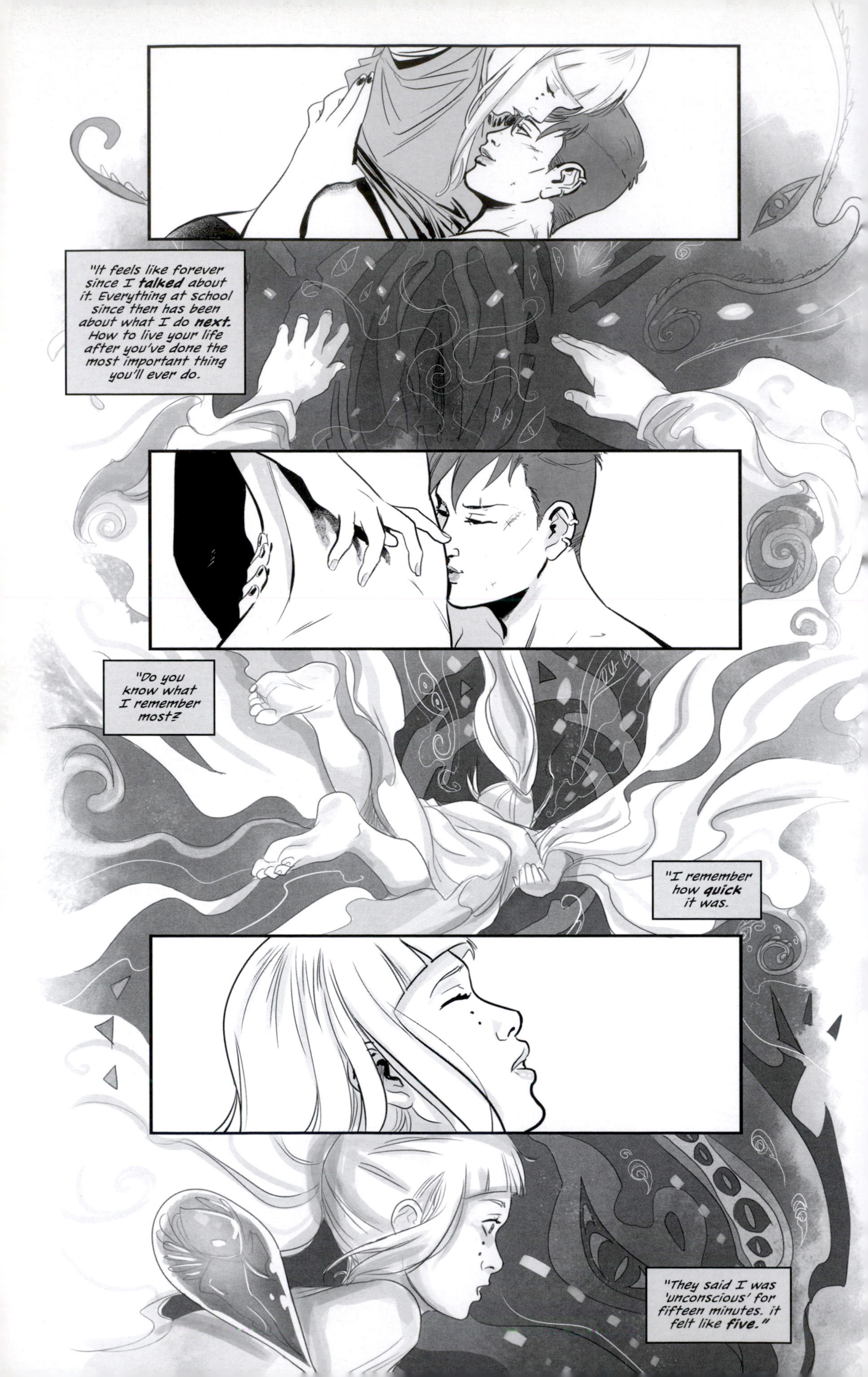
"It feels like forever since I talked about it. Everything at school since then has been about what I do next. How to live your life after you've done the most important thing you'll ever do.
"Do you know what I remember most?
"I remember how quick it was.
"They said I was 'unconscious' for fifteen minutes. it felt like five."

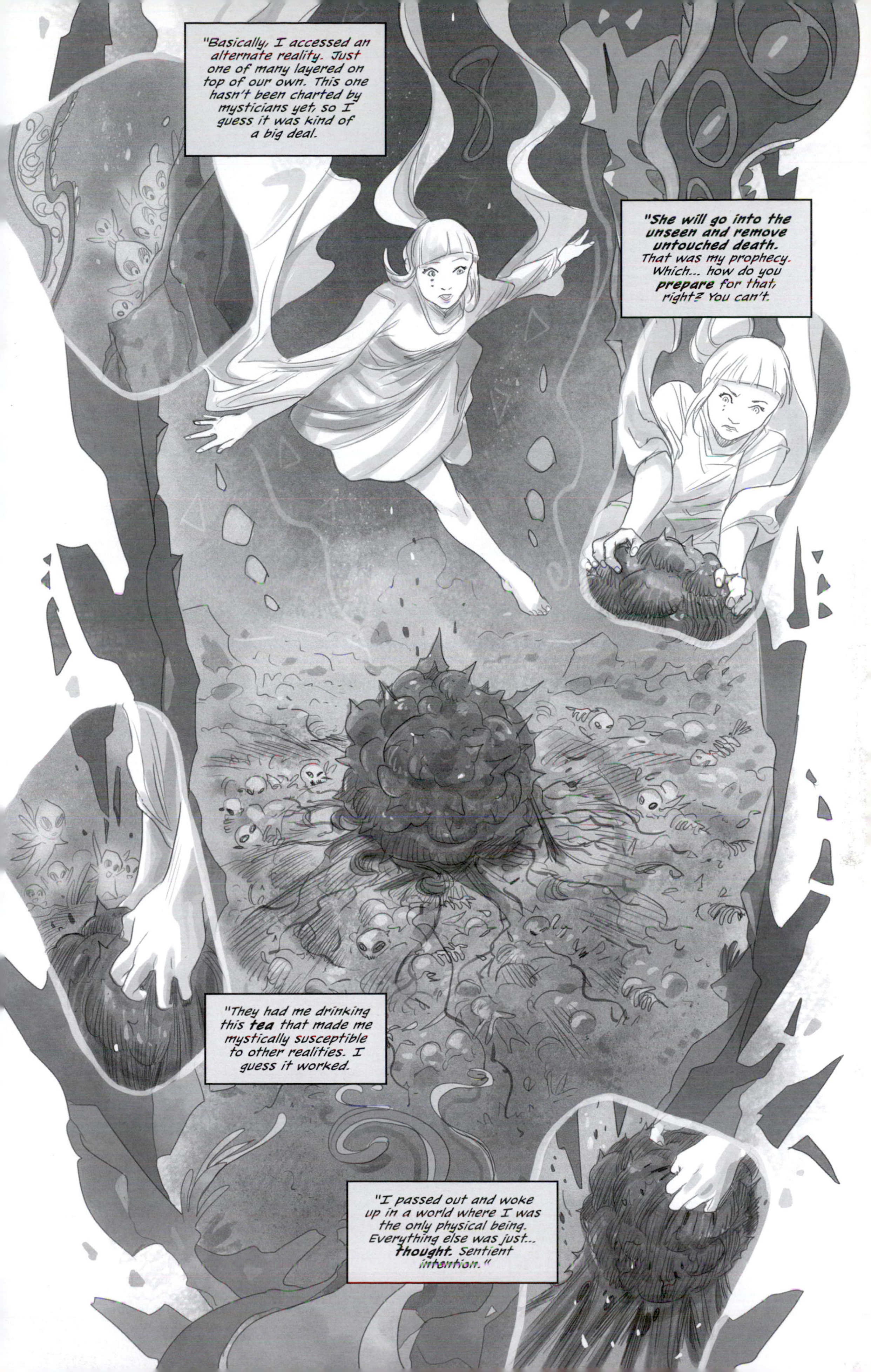
"Basically, I accessed an alternate reality. Just one of many layered on top of our own. This one hasn't been charted by mysticians yet, so I guess it was kind of a big deal.
"She will go into the unseen and remove untouched death. That was my prophecy. Which... how do you prepare for that, right? You can't.
"They had me drinking this tea that made me mystically susceptible to other realities. I guess it worked.
"I passed out and woke up in a world where I was the only physical being. Everything else was just... thought. Sentient intention."

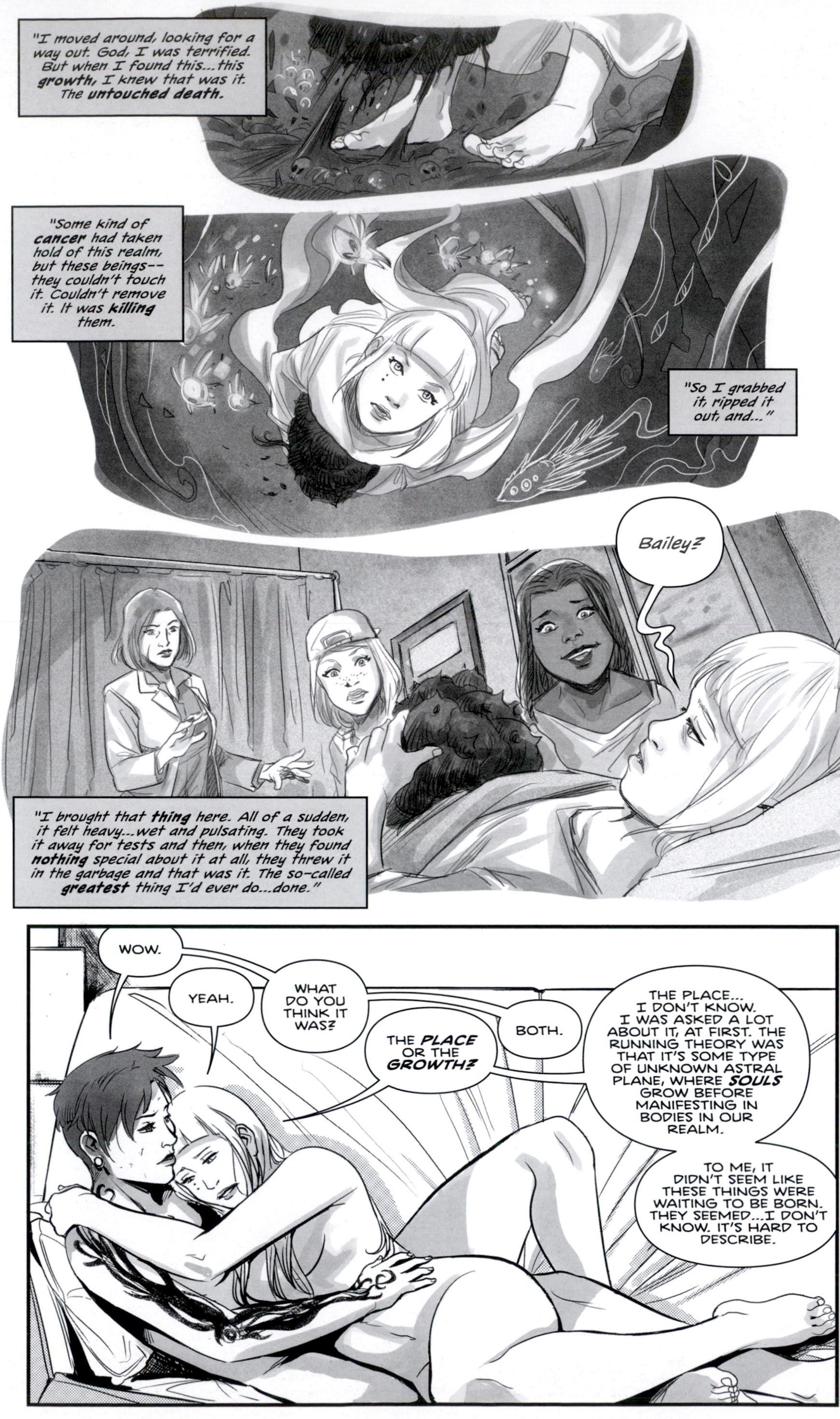
"I moved around, looking for a way out. God, I was terrified. But when I found this... this **growth,** I knew that was it. The **untouched death.**
"Some kind of **cancer** had taken hold of this realm, but these beings-- they couldn't touch it. Couldn't remove it. It was **killing** them.
"So I grabbed it, ripped it out, and..."
Bailey?
"I brought that **thing** here. All of a sudden, it felt heavy... wet and pulsating. They took it away for tests and then, when they found **nothing** special about it at all, they threw it in the garbage and that was it. The so-called **greatest** thing I'd ever do... done."
WOW.
YEAH.
WHAT DO YOU THINK IT WAS?
THE ***PLACE*** OR THE ***GROWTH?***
BOTH.
THE PLACE... I DON'T KNOW. I WAS ASKED A LOT ABOUT IT, AT FIRST. THE RUNNING THEORY WAS THAT IT'S SOME TYPE OF UNKNOWN ASTRAL PLANE, WHERE ***SOULS*** GROW BEFORE MANIFESTING IN BODIES IN OUR REALM.
TO ME, IT DIDN'T SEEM LIKE THESE THINGS WERE WAITING TO BE BORN. THEY SEEMED... I DON'T KNOW. IT'S HARD TO DESCRIBE.

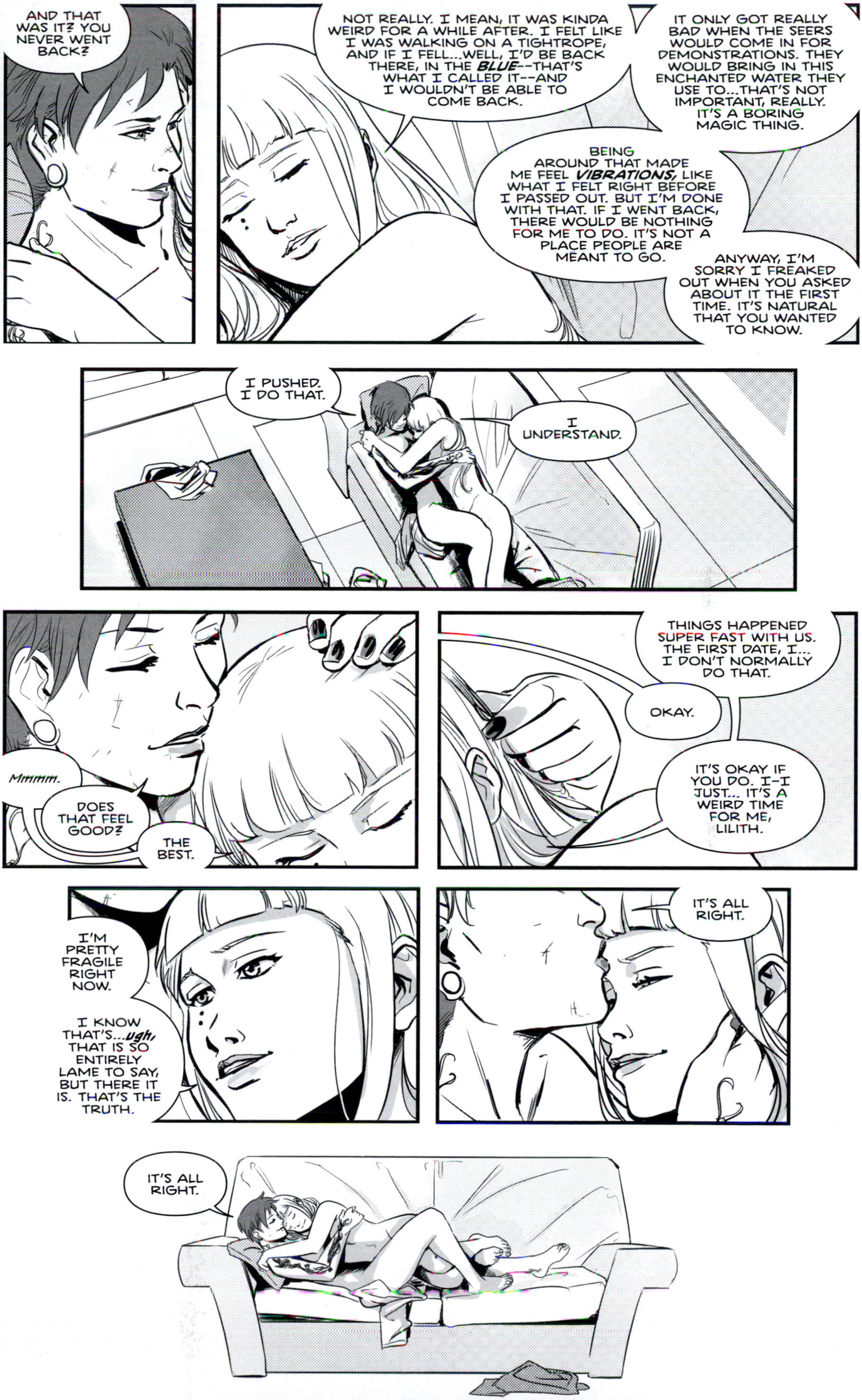
AND THAT WAS IT? YOU NEVER WENT BACK?
NOT REALLY. I MEAN, IT WAS KINDA WEIRD FOR A WHILE AFTER. I FELT LIKE I WAS WALKING ON A TIGHTROPE, AND IF I FELL...WELL, I'D BE BACK THERE, IN THE *BLUE*--THAT'S WHAT I CALLED IT--AND I WOULDN'T BE ABLE TO COME BACK.
IT ONLY GOT REALLY BAD WHEN THE SEERS WOULD COME IN FOR DEMONSTRATIONS. THEY WOULD BRING IN THIS ENCHANTED WATER THEY USE TO...THAT'S NOT IMPORTANT, REALLY. IT'S A BORING MAGIC THING.
BEING AROUND THAT MADE ME FEEL ***VIBRATIONS,*** LIKE WHAT I FELT RIGHT BEFORE I PASSED OUT. BUT I'M DONE WITH THAT. IF I WENT BACK, THERE WOULD BE NOTHING FOR ME TO DO. IT'S NOT A PLACE PEOPLE ARE MEANT TO GO.
ANYWAY, I'M SORRY I FREAKED OUT WHEN YOU ASKED ABOUT IT THE FIRST TIME. IT'S NATURAL THAT YOU WANTED TO KNOW.
I PUSHED. I DO THAT.
I UNDERSTAND.
Mmmm.
DOES THAT FEEL GOOD?
THE BEST.
THINGS HAPPENED SUPER FAST WITH US. THE FIRST DATE, I... I DON'T NORMALLY DO THAT.
OKAY.
IT'S OKAY IF YOU DO. I-I JUST... IT'S A WEIRD TIME FOR ME, LILITH.
I'M PRETTY FRAGILE RIGHT NOW.
I KNOW THAT'S...*ugh,* THAT IS SO ENTIRELY LAME TO SAY, BUT THERE IT IS. THAT'S THE TRUTH.
IT'S ALL RIGHT.
IT'S ALL RIGHT.

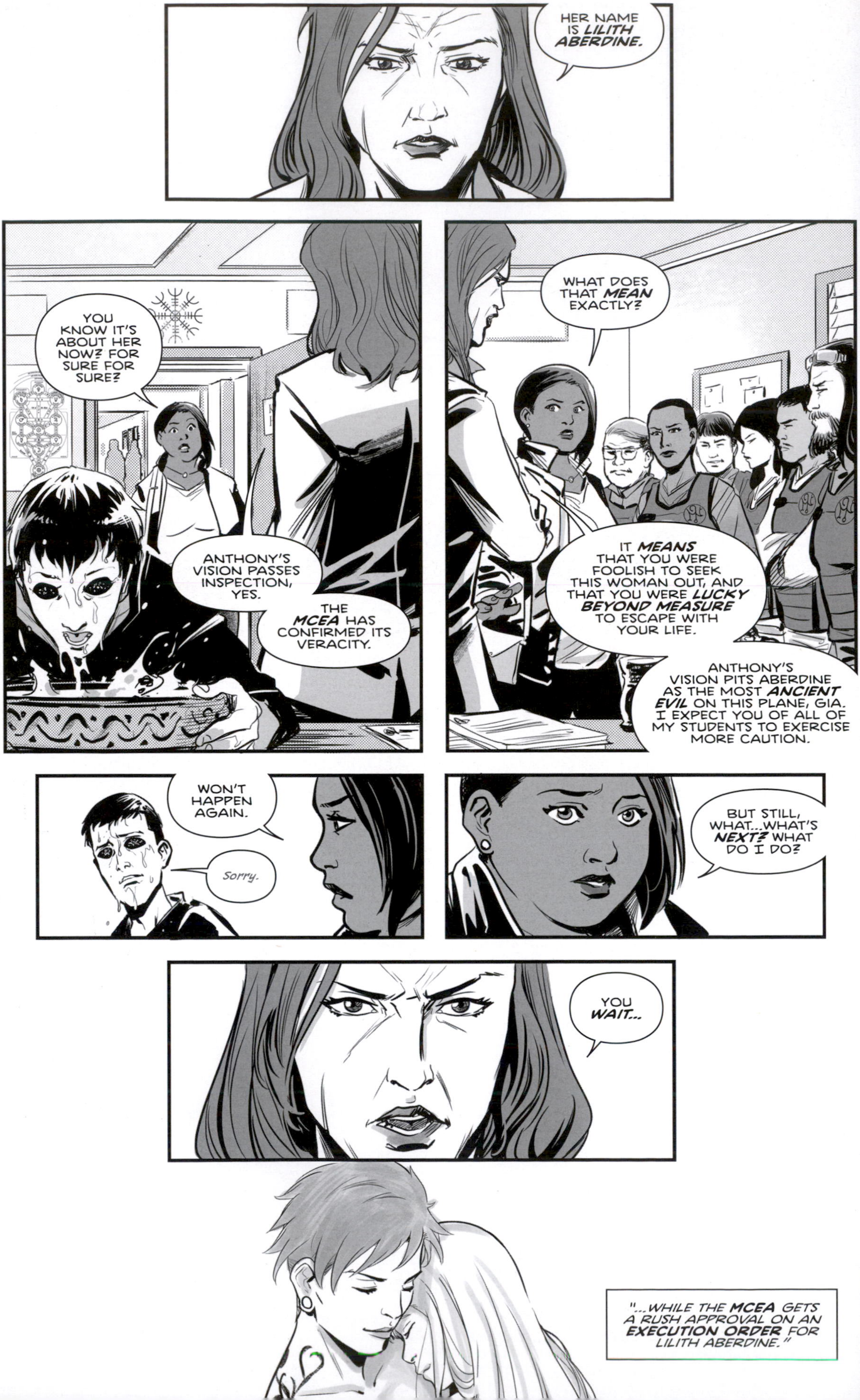
HER NAME IS LILITH ABERDINE.
YOU KNOW IT'S ABOUT HER NOW? FOR SURE FOR SURE?
ANTHONY'S VISION PASSES INSPECTION, YES.
THE MCEA HAS CONFIRMED ITS VERACITY.
WHAT DOES THAT MEAN EXACTLY?
IT MEANS THAT YOU WERE FOOLISH TO SEEK THIS WOMAN OUT, AND THAT YOU WERE LUCKY BEYOND MEASURE TO ESCAPE WITH YOUR LIFE.
ANTHONY'S VISION PITS ABERDINE AS THE MOST ANCIENT EVIL ON THIS PLANE, GIA. I EXPECT YOU OF ALL OF MY STUDENTS TO EXERCISE MORE CAUTION.
WON'T HAPPEN AGAIN.
Sorry.
BUT STILL, WHAT...WHAT'S NEXT? WHAT DO I DO?
YOU WAIT...
"...WHILE THE MCEA GETS A RUSH APPROVAL ON AN EXECUTION ORDER FOR LILITH ABERDINE."

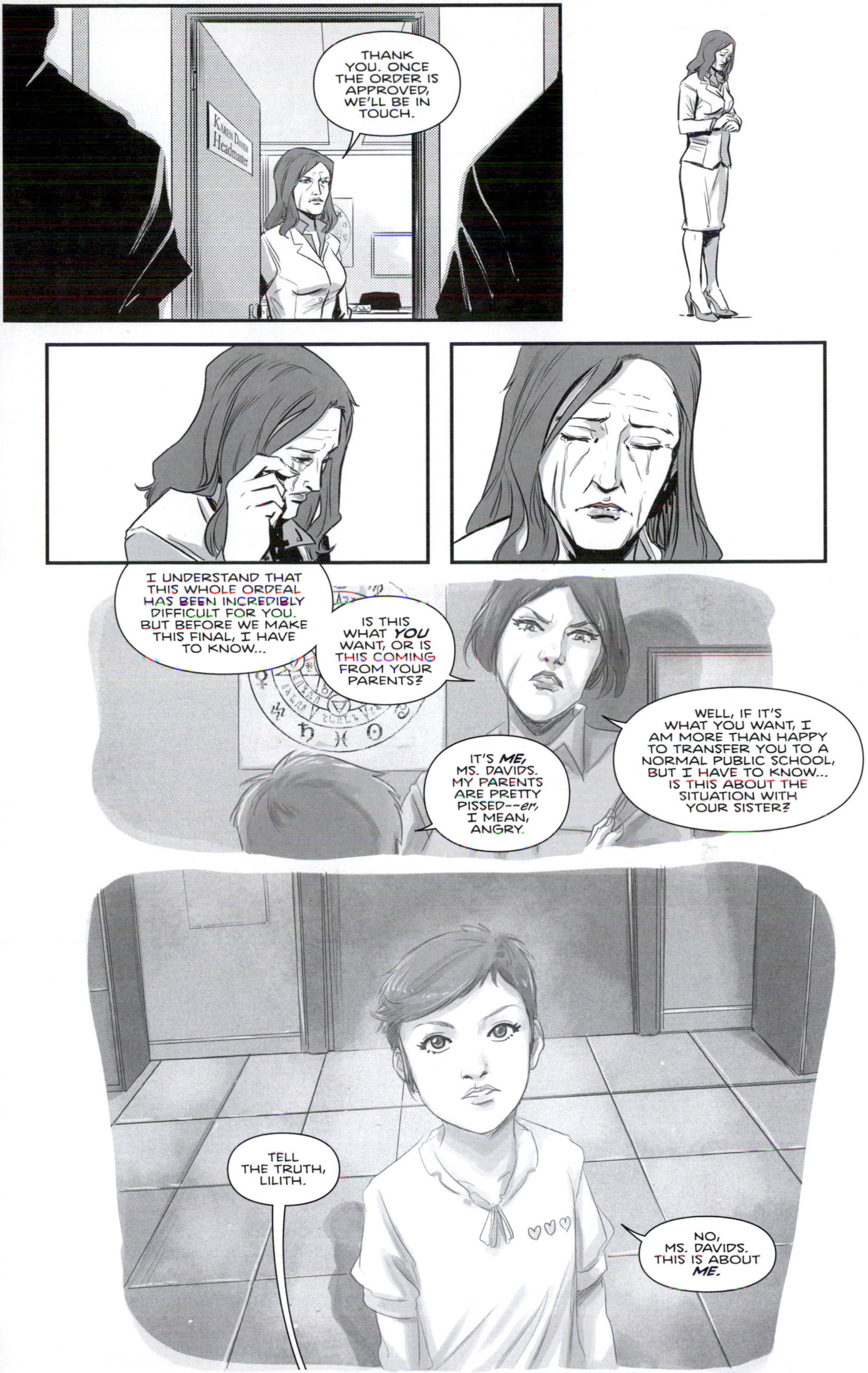
THANK YOU. ONCE THE ORDER IS APPROVED, WE'LL BE IN TOUCH.
KAREN DAVIDS Headmaster
I UNDERSTAND THAT THIS WHOLE ORDEAL HAS BEEN INCREDIBLY DIFFICULT FOR YOU. BUT BEFORE WE MAKE THIS FINAL, I HAVE TO KNOW...
IS THIS WHAT *YOU* WANT, OR IS THIS COMING FROM YOUR PARENTS?
IT'S *ME,* MS. DAVIDS. MY PARENTS ARE PRETTY PISSED--*er,* I MEAN, ANGRY.
WELL, IF IT'S WHAT YOU WANT, I AM MORE THAN HAPPY TO TRANSFER YOU TO A NORMAL PUBLIC SCHOOL, BUT I HAVE TO KNOW... IS THIS ABOUT THE SITUATION WITH YOUR SISTER?
TELL THE TRUTH, LILITH.
NO, MS. DAVIDS. THIS IS ABOUT *ME.*

CHAPTER FOUR

The Narcissist and the Killer

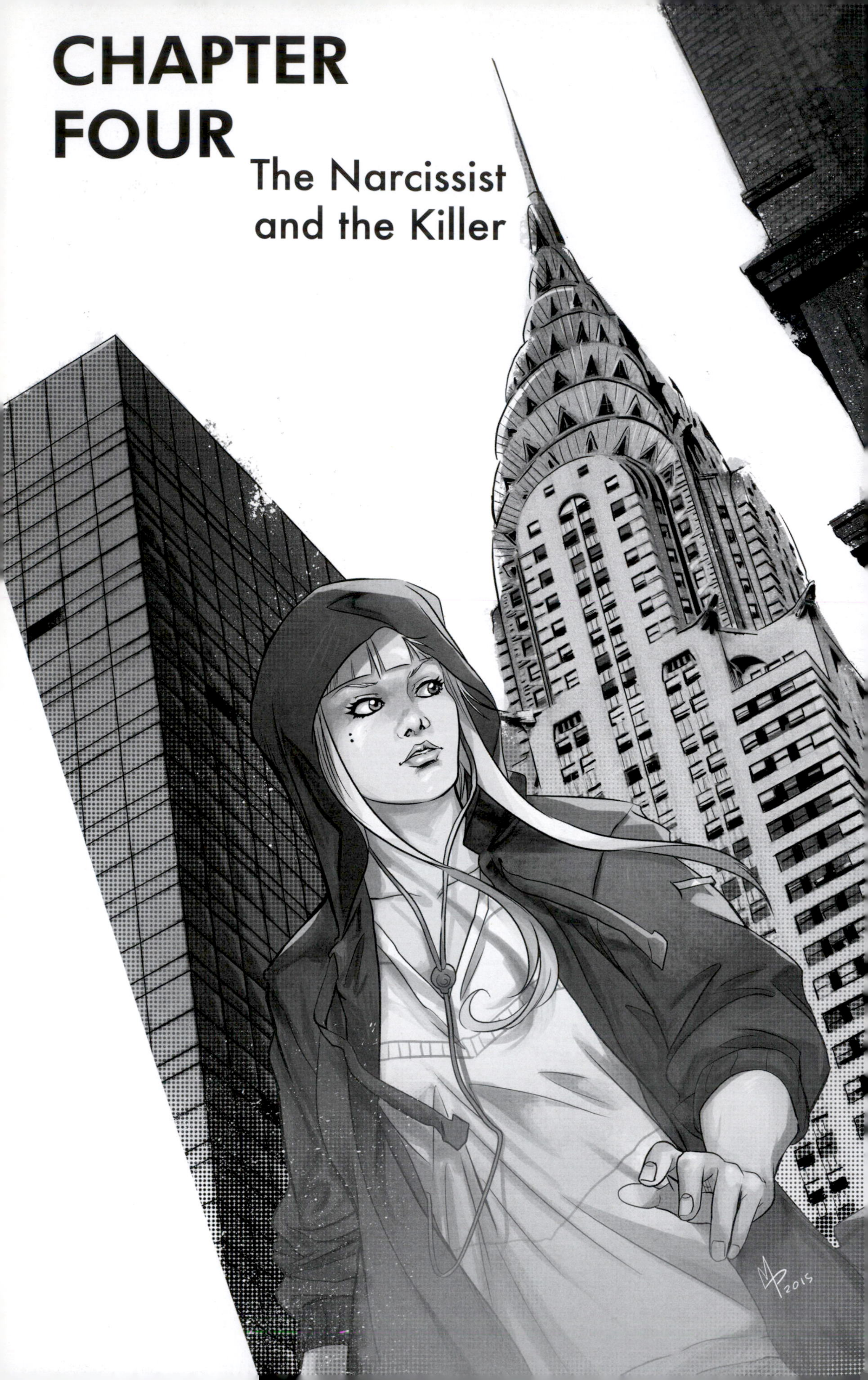

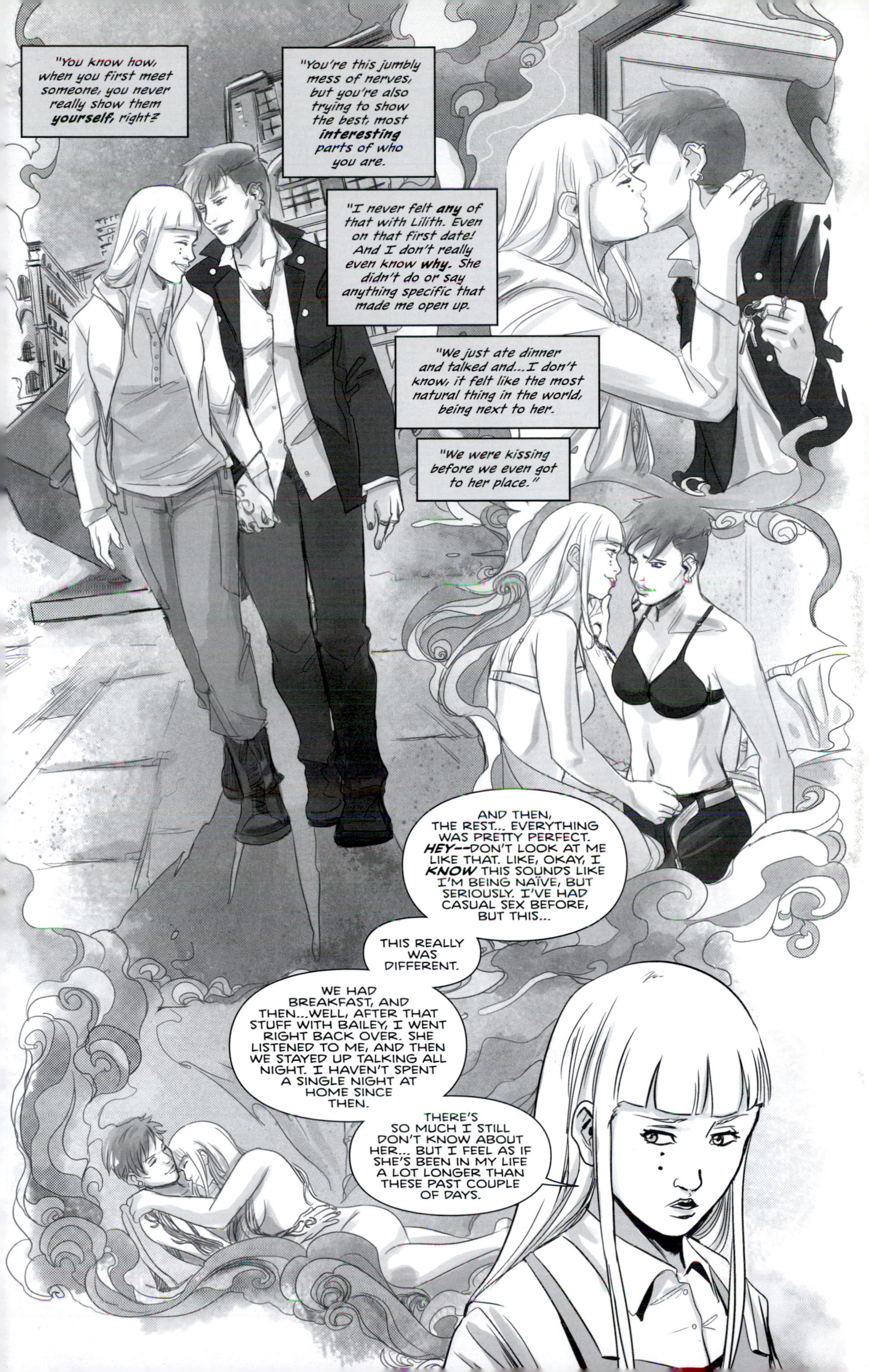
"You know how, when you first meet someone, you never really show them yourself, right?
"You're this jumbly mess of nerves, but you're also trying to show the best, most interesting parts of who you are.
"I never felt any of that with Lilith. Even on that first date! And I don't really even know why. She didn't do or say anything specific that made me open up.
"We just ate dinner and talked and...I don't know, it felt like the most natural thing in the world, being next to her.
"We were kissing before we even got to her place."
AND THEN, THE REST... EVERYTHING WAS PRETTY PERFECT. HEY--DON'T LOOK AT ME LIKE THAT. LIKE, OKAY, I KNOW THIS SOUNDS LIKE I'M BEING NAÏVE, BUT SERIOUSLY. I'VE HAD CASUAL SEX BEFORE, BUT THIS...
THIS REALLY WAS DIFFERENT.
WE HAD BREAKFAST, AND THEN...WELL, AFTER THAT STUFF WITH BAILEY, I WENT RIGHT BACK OVER. SHE LISTENED TO ME, AND THEN WE STAYED UP TALKING ALL NIGHT. I HAVEN'T SPENT A SINGLE NIGHT AT HOME SINCE THEN.
THERE'S SO MUCH I STILL DON'T KNOW ABOUT HER... BUT I FEEL AS IF SHE'S BEEN IN MY LIFE A LOT LONGER THAN THESE PAST COUPLE OF DAYS.

RIGHT, SO YOU'RE MOVING *WAY* TOO FUCKING FAST.

AW, COME ON, AUGUSTEN. *THAT'S* WHAT YOU GOT FROM ALL OF THAT?

Uh, YES? BECAUSE I KNOW YOU? BECAUSE I KNOW YOUR LIFE?

NOOOO, DON'T MAKE IT SOUND LIKE THAT. THIS IS DIFFERENT.

Mmmmhm.

PLEASE DON'T TALK TO ME LIKE I'M CRAZY. I'VE BEEN ACCUSED OF PERSONALITY DISORDERS ENOUGH THIS WEEK, THANKS.

YOU KNOW I'VE SLEPT WITH GIRLS BEFORE AND DIDN'T GET ATTACHED.

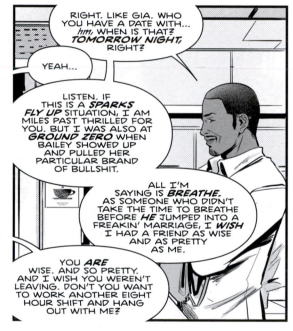

RIGHT. LIKE GIA. WHO YOU HAVE A DATE WITH... *hm,* WHEN IS THAT? *TOMORROW NIGHT,* RIGHT?

YEAH...

LISTEN. IF THIS IS A *SPARKS FLY UP* SITUATION, I AM MILES PAST THRILLED FOR YOU. BUT I WAS ALSO AT *GROUND ZERO* WHEN BAILEY SHOWED UP AND PULLED HER PARTICULAR BRAND OF BULLSHIT.

ALL I'M SAYING IS *BREATHE.* AS SOMEONE WHO DIDN'T TAKE THE TIME TO BREATHE BEFORE *HE* JUMPED INTO A FREAKIN' MARRIAGE, I *WISH* I HAD A FRIEND AS WISE AND AS PRETTY AS ME.

YOU *ARE* WISE. AND SO PRETTY. AND I WISH YOU WEREN'T LEAVING. DON'T YOU WANT TO WORK ANOTHER EIGHT HOUR SHIFT AND HANG OUT WITH ME?

I'D RATHER SWIM IN A VOLCANO. CIAO!

"OKAY, LOVELY. TELL ANDRE I SAY HI."

"YEAH... WILL DO."

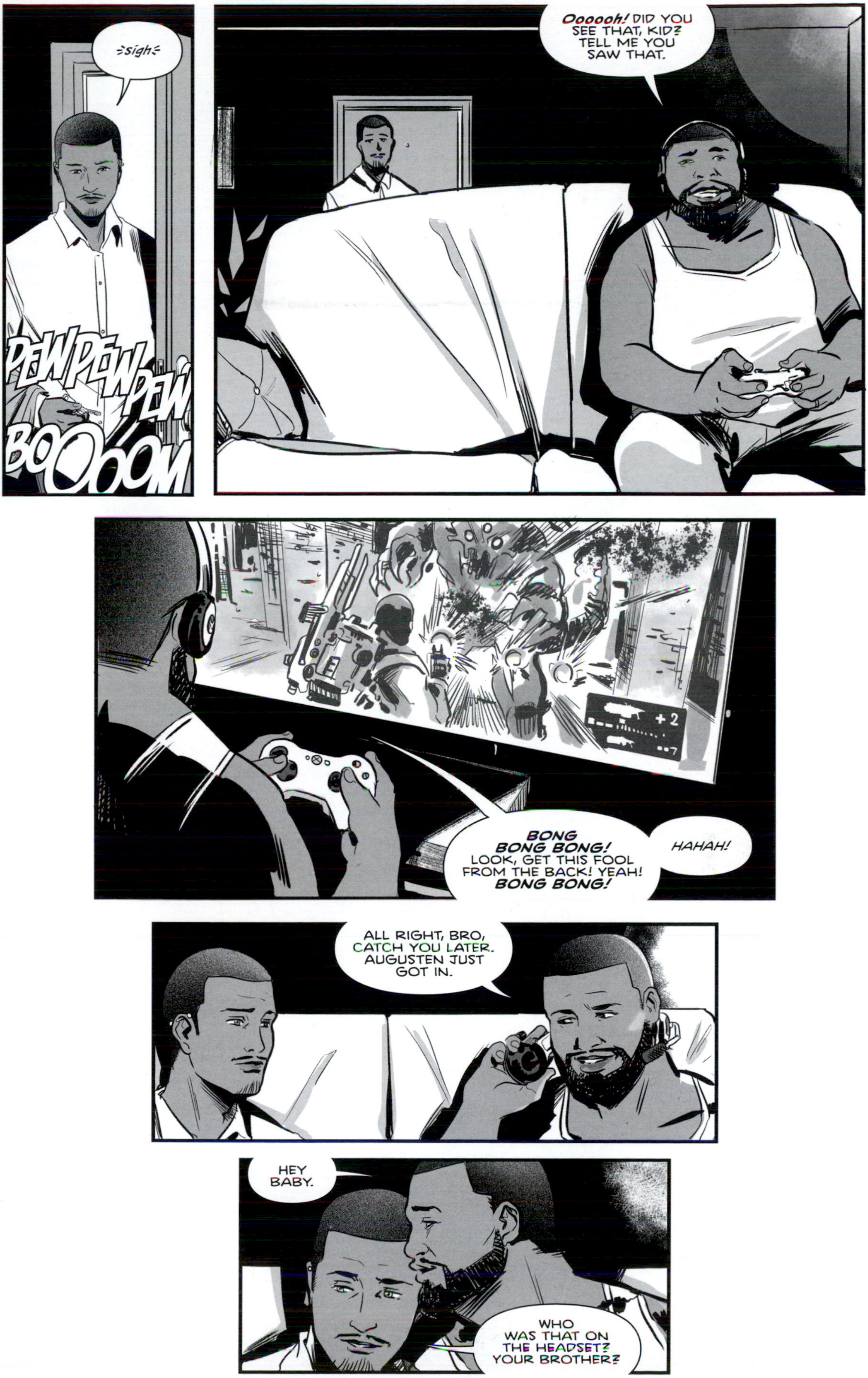

sigh
PEW PEW PEW PEW
BOOOOOM
Oooooh! DID YOU SEE THAT, KID? TELL ME YOU SAW THAT.
BONG BONG BONG! LOOK, GET THIS FOOL FROM THE BACK! YEAH! BONG BONG!
HAHAH!
ALL RIGHT, BRO, CATCH YOU LATER. AUGUSTEN JUST GOT IN.
HEY BABY.
WHO WAS THAT ON THE HEADSET? YOUR BROTHER?

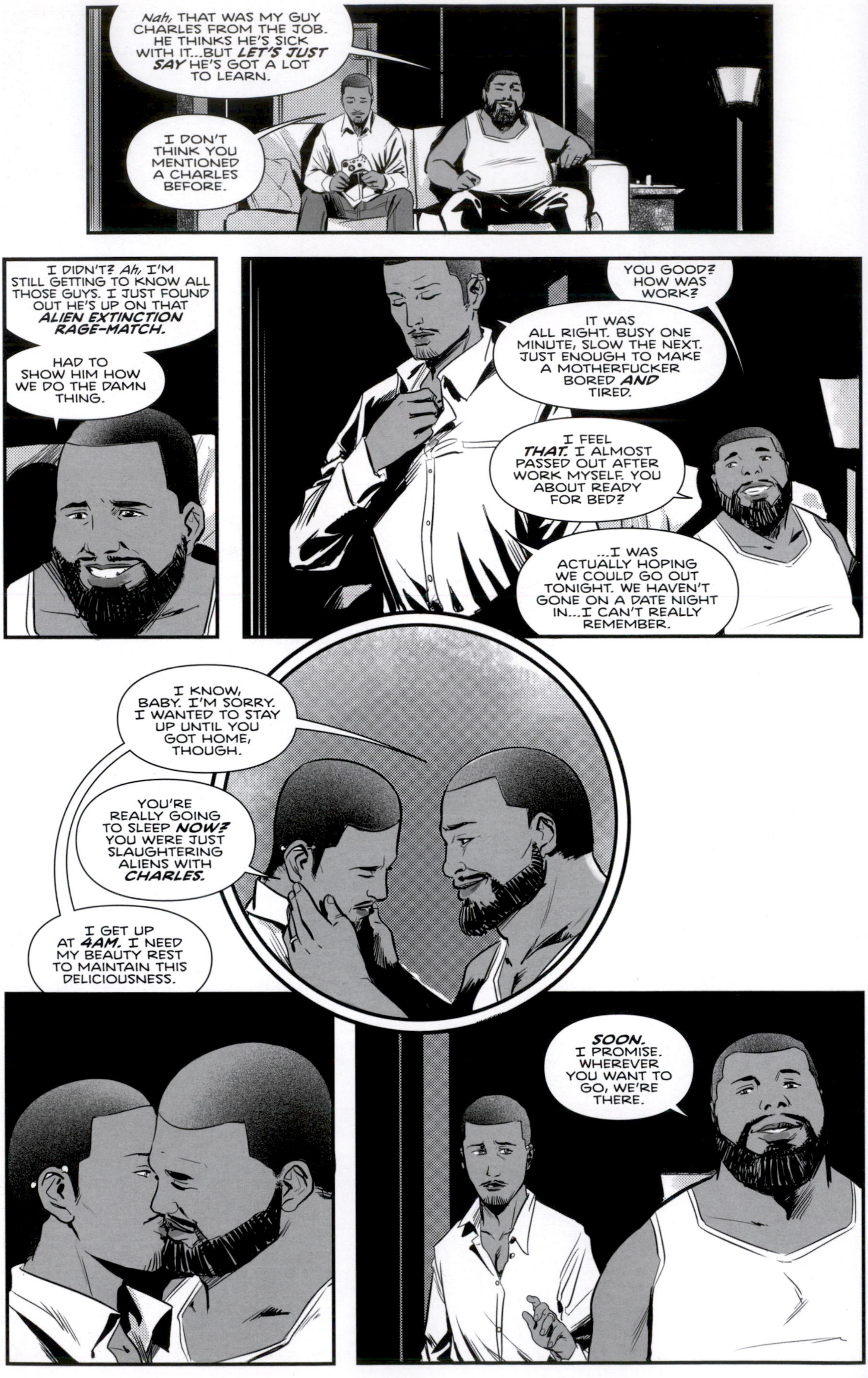
Nah, THAT WAS MY GUY CHARLES FROM THE JOB. HE THINKS HE'S SICK WITH IT...BUT ***LET'S JUST SAY*** HE'S GOT A LOT TO LEARN.
I DON'T THINK YOU MENTIONED A CHARLES BEFORE.
I DIDN'T? *Ah,* I'M STILL GETTING TO KNOW ALL THOSE GUYS. I JUST FOUND OUT HE'S UP ON THAT ***ALIEN EXTINCTION RAGE-MATCH.***
HAD TO SHOW HIM HOW WE DO THE DAMN THING.
YOU GOOD? HOW WAS WORK?
IT WAS ALL RIGHT. BUSY ONE MINUTE, SLOW THE NEXT. JUST ENOUGH TO MAKE A MOTHERFUCKER BORED ***AND*** TIRED.
I FEEL ***THAT.*** I ALMOST PASSED OUT AFTER WORK MYSELF. YOU ABOUT READY FOR BED?
...I WAS ACTUALLY HOPING WE COULD GO OUT TONIGHT. WE HAVEN'T GONE ON A DATE NIGHT IN...I CAN'T REALLY REMEMBER.
I KNOW, BABY. I'M SORRY. I WANTED TO STAY UP UNTIL YOU GOT HOME, THOUGH.
YOU'RE REALLY GOING TO SLEEP ***NOW?*** YOU WERE JUST SLAUGHTERING ALIENS WITH ***CHARLES.***
I GET UP AT ***4AM.*** I NEED MY BEAUTY REST TO MAINTAIN THIS DELICIOUSNESS.
SOON. I PROMISE. WHEREVER YOU WANT TO GO, WE'RE THERE.

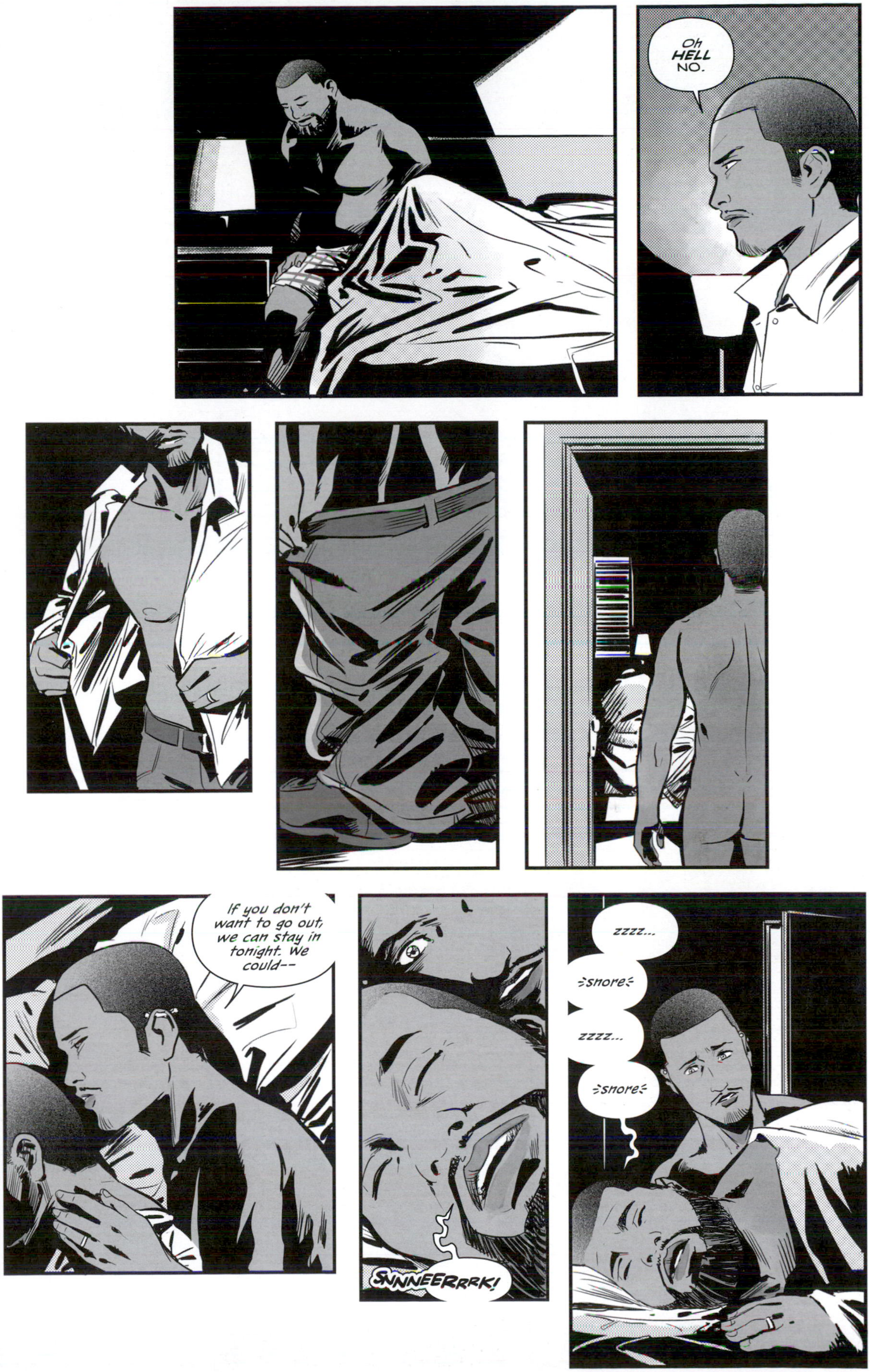
Oh HELL NO.
If you don't want to go out, we can stay in tonight. We could--
SNNNEERRRK!
zzzz...
snore
zzzz...
snore

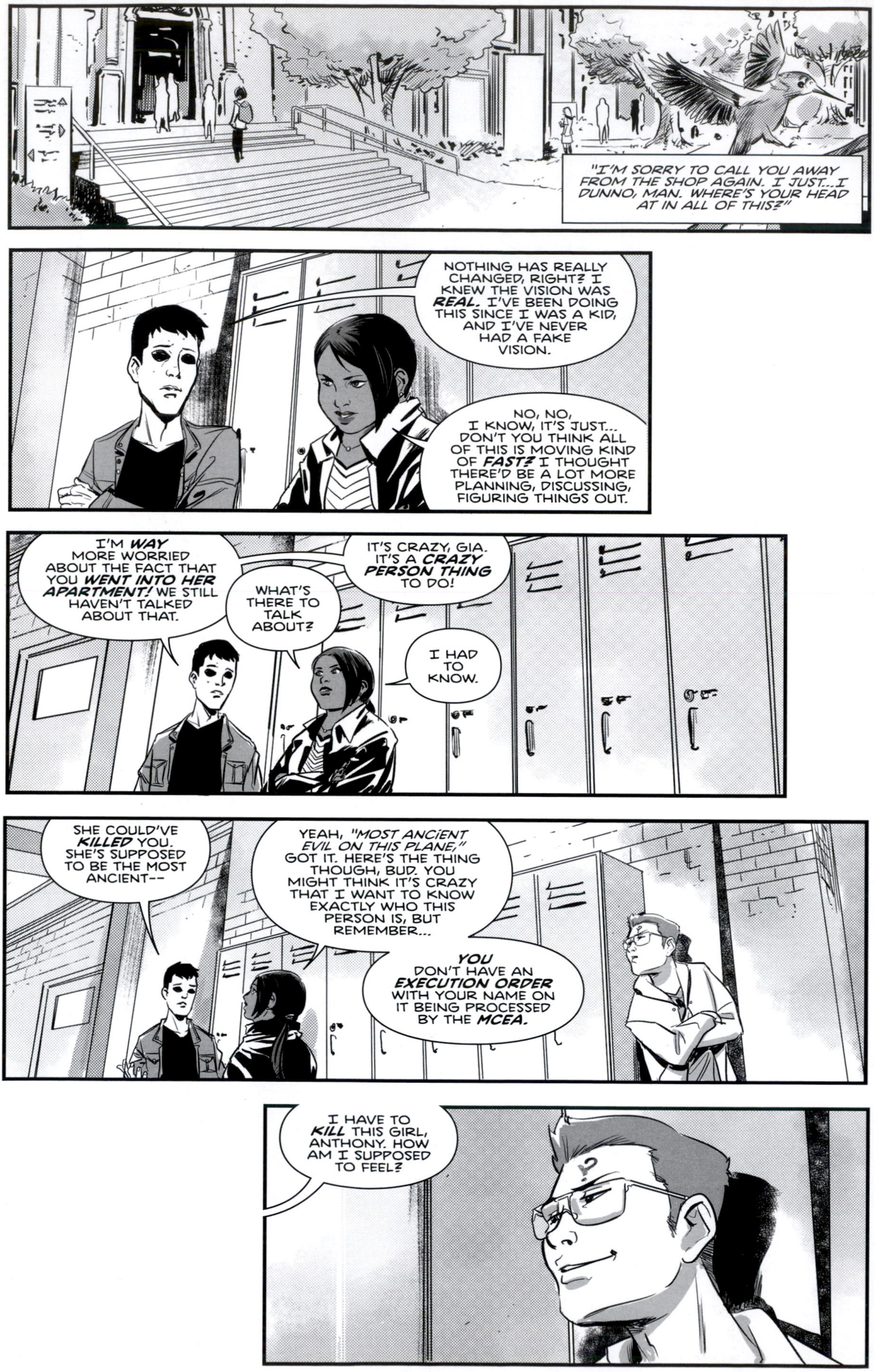

"I'M SORRY TO CALL YOU AWAY FROM THE SHOP AGAIN. I JUST...I DUNNO, MAN. WHERE'S YOUR HEAD AT IN ALL OF THIS?"
NOTHING HAS REALLY CHANGED, RIGHT? I KNEW THE VISION WAS REAL. I'VE BEEN DOING THIS SINCE I WAS A KID, AND I'VE NEVER HAD A FAKE VISION.
NO, NO, I KNOW, IT'S JUST... DON'T YOU THINK ALL OF THIS IS MOVING KIND OF FAST? I THOUGHT THERE'D BE A LOT MORE PLANNING, DISCUSSING, FIGURING THINGS OUT.
I'M WAY MORE WORRIED ABOUT THE FACT THAT YOU WENT INTO HER APARTMENT! WE STILL HAVEN'T TALKED ABOUT THAT.
WHAT'S THERE TO TALK ABOUT?
IT'S CRAZY, GIA. IT'S A CRAZY PERSON THING TO DO!
I HAD TO KNOW.
SHE COULD'VE KILLED YOU. SHE'S SUPPOSED TO BE THE MOST ANCIENT--
YEAH, "MOST ANCIENT EVIL ON THIS PLANE," GOT IT. HERE'S THE THING THOUGH, BUD. YOU MIGHT THINK IT'S CRAZY THAT I WANT TO KNOW EXACTLY WHO THIS PERSON IS, BUT REMEMBER...
YOU DON'T HAVE AN EXECUTION ORDER WITH YOUR NAME ON IT BEING PROCESSED BY THE MCEA.
I HAVE TO KILL THIS GIRL, ANTHONY. HOW AM I SUPPOSED TO FEEL?

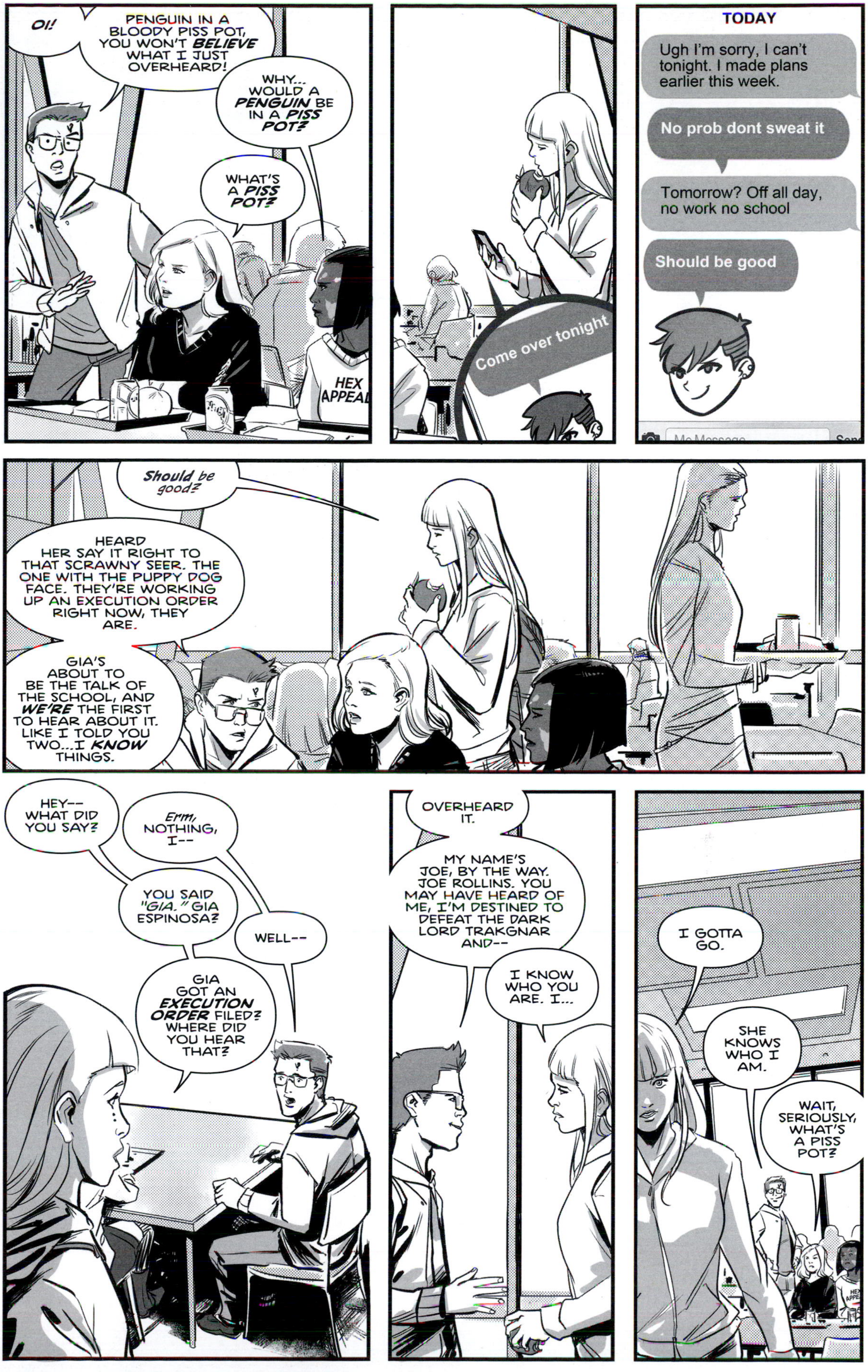

OI!
PENGUIN IN A BLOODY PISS POT, YOU WON'T BELIEVE WHAT I JUST OVERHEARD!
WHY... WOULD A PENGUIN BE IN A PISS POT?
WHAT'S A PISS POT?
HEX APPEAL
Come over tonight
TODAY
Ugh I'm sorry, I can't tonight. I made plans earlier this week.
No prob dont sweat it
Tomorrow? Off all day, no work no school
Should be good
Should be good?
HEARD HER SAY IT RIGHT TO THAT SCRAWNY SEER. THE ONE WITH THE PUPPY DOG FACE. THEY'RE WORKING UP AN EXECUTION ORDER RIGHT NOW, THEY ARE.
GIA'S ABOUT TO BE THE TALK OF THE SCHOOL, AND WE'RE THE FIRST TO HEAR ABOUT IT. LIKE I TOLD YOU TWO...I KNOW THINGS.
HEY-- WHAT DID YOU SAY?
Erm, NOTHING, I--
YOU SAID "GIA." GIA ESPINOSA?
WELL--
GIA GOT AN EXECUTION ORDER FILED? WHERE DID YOU HEAR THAT?
OVERHEARD IT.
MY NAME'S JOE, BY THE WAY. JOE ROLLINS. YOU MAY HAVE HEARD OF ME, I'M DESTINED TO DEFEAT THE DARK LORD TRAKGNAR AND--
I KNOW WHO YOU ARE. I...
I GOTTA GO.
SHE KNOWS WHO I AM.
WAIT, SERIOUSLY, WHAT'S A PISS POT?

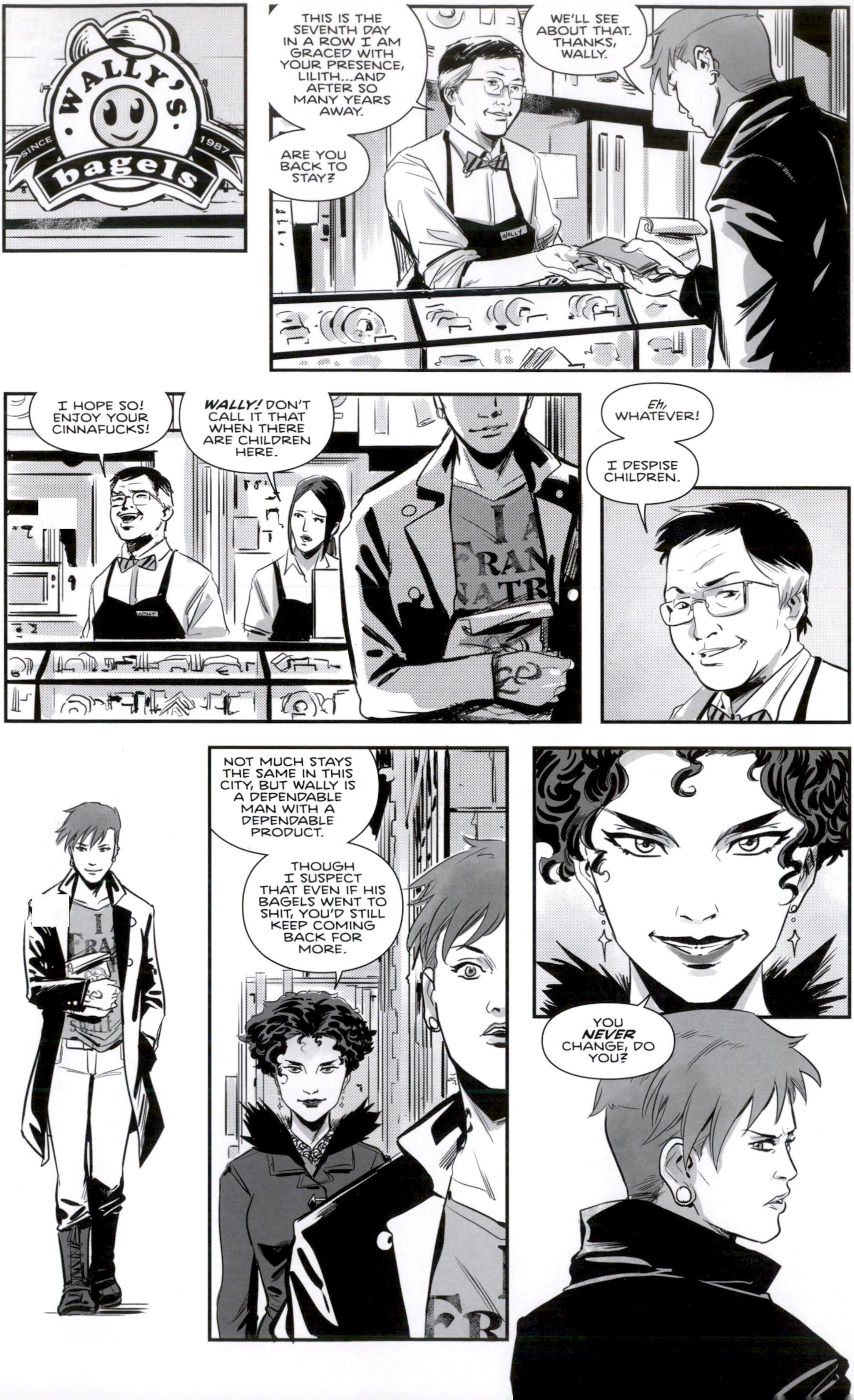
WALLY'S
SINCE 1987
bagels
THIS IS THE SEVENTH DAY IN A ROW I AM GRACED WITH YOUR PRESENCE, LILITH...AND AFTER SO MANY YEARS AWAY.
ARE YOU BACK TO STAY?
WE'LL SEE ABOUT THAT. THANKS, WALLY.
I HOPE SO! ENJOY YOUR CINNAFUCKS!
WALLY! DON'T CALL IT THAT WHEN THERE ARE CHILDREN HERE.
Eh, WHATEVER!
I DESPISE CHILDREN.
NOT MUCH STAYS THE SAME IN THIS CITY, BUT WALLY IS A DEPENDABLE MAN WITH A DEPENDABLE PRODUCT.
THOUGH I SUSPECT THAT EVEN IF HIS BAGELS WENT TO SHIT, YOU'D STILL KEEP COMING BACK FOR MORE.
YOU NEVER CHANGE, DO YOU?

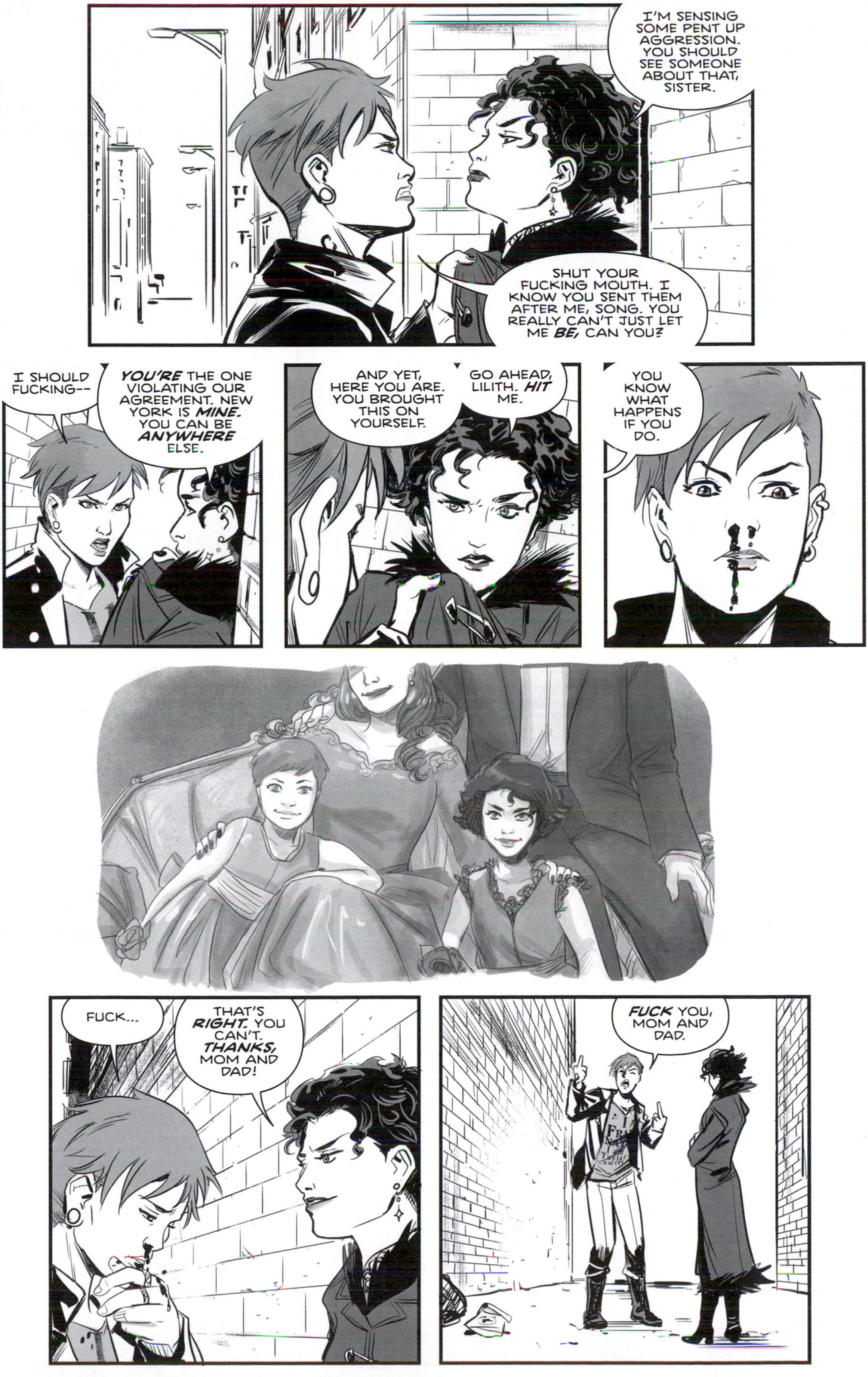
I'M SENSING SOME PENT UP AGGRESSION. YOU SHOULD SEE SOMEONE ABOUT THAT, SISTER.
SHUT YOUR FUCKING MOUTH. I KNOW YOU SENT THEM AFTER ME, SONG. YOU REALLY CAN'T JUST LET ME BE, CAN YOU?
I SHOULD FUCKING--
YOU'RE THE ONE VIOLATING OUR AGREEMENT. NEW YORK IS MINE. YOU CAN BE ANYWHERE ELSE.
AND YET, HERE YOU ARE. YOU BROUGHT THIS ON YOURSELF.
GO AHEAD, LILITH. HIT ME.
YOU KNOW WHAT HAPPENS IF YOU DO.
FUCK...
THAT'S RIGHT. YOU CAN'T. THANKS, MOM AND DAD!
FUCK YOU, MOM AND DAD.

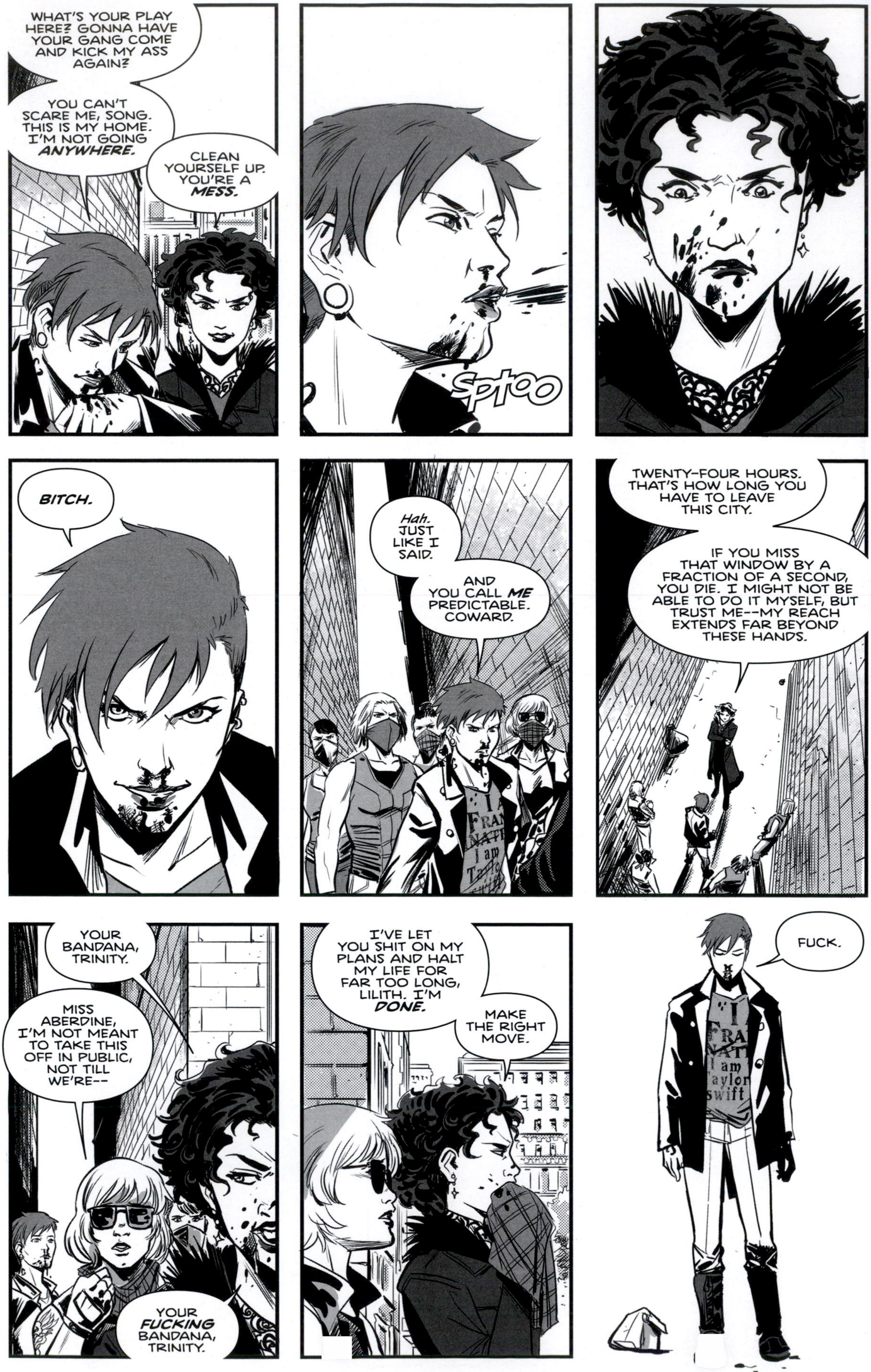
WHAT'S YOUR PLAY HERE? GONNA HAVE YOUR GANG COME AND KICK MY ASS AGAIN?
YOU CAN'T SCARE ME, SONG. THIS IS MY HOME. I'M NOT GOING *ANYWHERE.*
CLEAN YOURSELF UP. YOU'RE A *MESS.*
SPTOO
BITCH.
Hah. JUST LIKE I SAID.
AND YOU CALL *ME* PREDICTABLE. COWARD.
TWENTY-FOUR HOURS. THAT'S HOW LONG YOU HAVE TO LEAVE THIS CITY.
IF YOU MISS THAT WINDOW BY A FRACTION OF A SECOND, YOU DIE. I MIGHT NOT BE ABLE TO DO IT MYSELF, BUT TRUST ME--MY REACH EXTENDS FAR BEYOND THESE HANDS.
YOUR BANDANA, TRINITY.
MISS ABERDINE, I'M NOT MEANT TO TAKE THIS OFF IN PUBLIC, NOT TILL WE'RE--
YOUR *FUCKING* BANDANA, TRINITY.
I'VE LET YOU SHIT ON MY PLANS AND HALT MY LIFE FOR FAR TOO LONG, LILITH. I'M *DONE.*
MAKE THE RIGHT MOVE.
FUCK.

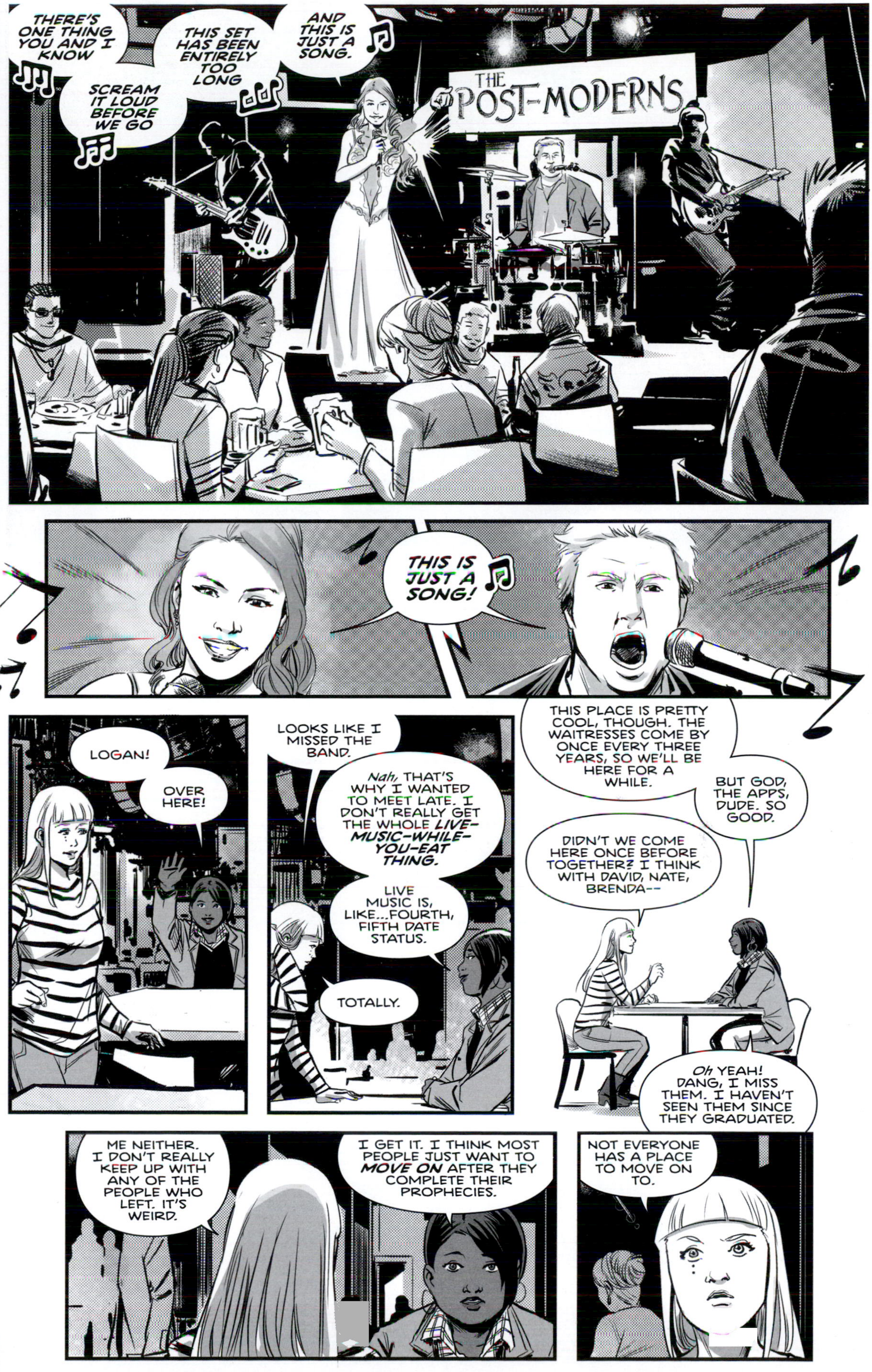
THERE'S ONE THING YOU AND I KNOW
SCREAM IT LOUD BEFORE WE GO
THIS SET HAS BEEN ENTIRELY TOO LONG
AND THIS IS JUST A SONG.
THE POST-MODERNS
THIS IS JUST A SONG!
LOGAN!
OVER HERE!
LOOKS LIKE I MISSED THE BAND.
Nah, THAT'S WHY I WANTED TO MEET LATE. I DON'T REALLY GET THE WHOLE ***LIVE-MUSIC-WHILE-YOU-EAT THING.***
LIVE MUSIC IS, LIKE...FOURTH, FIFTH DATE STATUS.
TOTALLY.
THIS PLACE IS PRETTY COOL, THOUGH. THE WAITRESSES COME BY ONCE EVERY THREE YEARS, SO WE'LL BE HERE FOR A WHILE.
BUT GOD, THE APPS, DUDE. SO GOOD.
DIDN'T WE COME HERE ONCE BEFORE TOGETHER? I THINK WITH DAVID, NATE, BRENDA--
Oh YEAH! DANG, I MISS THEM. I HAVEN'T SEEN THEM SINCE THEY GRADUATED.
ME NEITHER. I DON'T REALLY KEEP UP WITH ANY OF THE PEOPLE WHO LEFT. IT'S WEIRD.
I GET IT. I THINK MOST PEOPLE JUST WANT TO ***MOVE ON*** AFTER THEY COMPLETE THEIR PROPHECIES.
NOT EVERYONE HAS A PLACE TO MOVE ON TO.

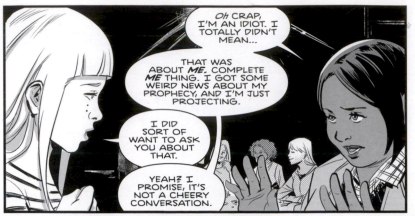

Oh CRAP, I'M AN IDIOT. I TOTALLY DIDN'T MEAN...

THAT WAS ABOUT *ME.* COMPLETE *ME* THING. I GOT SOME WEIRD NEWS ABOUT MY PROPHECY, AND I'M JUST PROJECTING.

I DID SORT OF WANT TO ASK YOU ABOUT THAT.

YEAH? I PROMISE, IT'S NOT A CHEERY CONVERSATION.

I HEARD THAT YOU GOT AN *EXECUTION ORDER* APPROVED.

YOU *HEARD?* FROM WHO?!

JOE ROLLINS.

HOW THE--

OKAY, YOU KNOW WHAT...NEVER MIND. I'LL MAKE A MENTAL NOTE TO SLAP THAT FOOL THE NEXT TIME I SEE HIM. LITTLE PUNK.

IS IT TRUE?

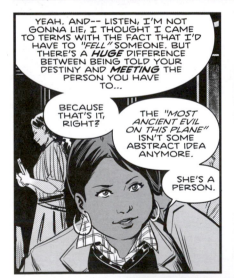

YEAH. AND-- LISTEN, I'M NOT GONNA LIE, I THOUGHT I CAME TO TERMS WITH THE FACT THAT I'D HAVE TO *"FELL"* SOMEONE. BUT THERE'S A *HUGE* DIFFERENCE BETWEEN BEING TOLD YOUR DESTINY AND *MEETING* THE PERSON YOU HAVE TO...

BECAUSE THAT'S IT, RIGHT?

THE *"MOST ANCIENT EVIL ON THIS PLANE"* ISN'T SOME ABSTRACT IDEA ANYMORE.

SHE'S A PERSON.

AND MY *DESTINY--* THE REASON I'M *HERE,* APPARENTLY...IS TO KILL HER. THAT'S A LOT.

YOU MET HER?

I DID. AND SHE SEEMS... *GAAAAH,* SORRY, IS IT OKAY IF WE TALK ABOUT LITERALLY ANYTHING ELSE IN THE WORLD? MOVIES? WHERE OUR WAITRESS IS? MAYBE THE POLITICAL SITUATION IN NEPAL?

WHERE *IS* OUR WAITRESS ANYWAY?

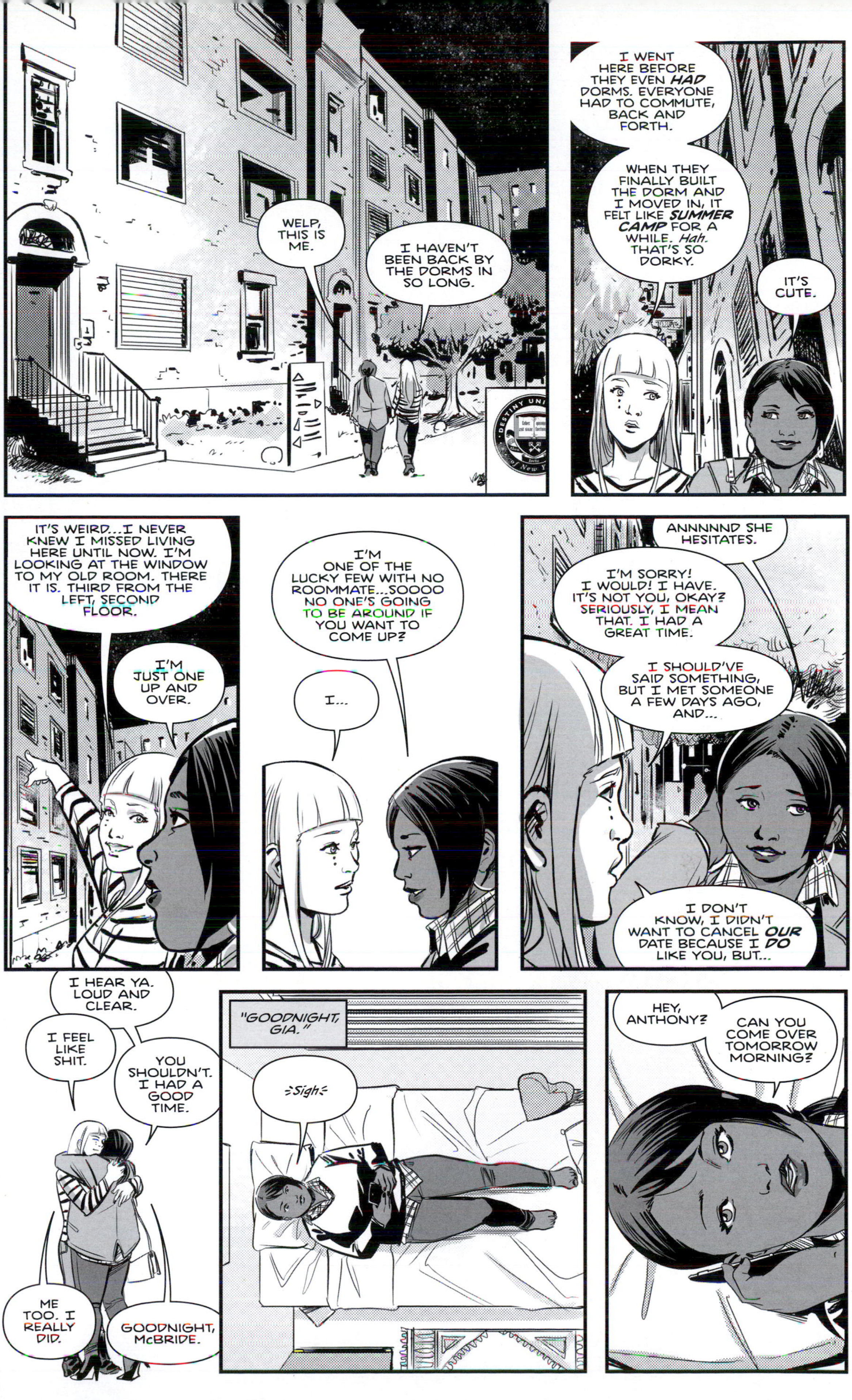
WELP, THIS IS ME.
I HAVEN'T BEEN BACK BY THE DORMS IN SO LONG.
I WENT HERE BEFORE THEY EVEN HAD DORMS. EVERYONE HAD TO COMMUTE, BACK AND FORTH.
WHEN THEY FINALLY BUILT THE DORM AND I MOVED IN, IT FELT LIKE SUMMER CAMP FOR A WHILE. Hah. THAT'S SO DORKY.
IT'S CUTE.
IT'S WEIRD...I NEVER KNEW I MISSED LIVING HERE UNTIL NOW. I'M LOOKING AT THE WINDOW TO MY OLD ROOM. THERE IT IS. THIRD FROM THE LEFT, SECOND FLOOR.
I'M JUST ONE UP AND OVER.
I'M ONE OF THE LUCKY FEW WITH NO ROOMMATE...SOOOO NO ONE'S GOING TO BE AROUND IF YOU WANT TO COME UP?
I...
ANNNNND SHE HESITATES.
I'M SORRY! I WOULD! I HAVE. IT'S NOT YOU, OKAY? SERIOUSLY, I MEAN THAT. I HAD A GREAT TIME.
I SHOULD'VE SAID SOMETHING, BUT I MET SOMEONE A FEW DAYS AGO, AND...
I DON'T KNOW, I DIDN'T WANT TO CANCEL OUR DATE BECAUSE I DO LIKE YOU, BUT...
I HEAR YA. LOUD AND CLEAR.
I FEEL LIKE SHIT.
YOU SHOULDN'T. I HAD A GOOD TIME.
ME TOO. I REALLY DID.
GOODNIGHT, McBRIDE.
"GOODNIGHT, GIA."
Sigh
HEY, ANTHONY?
CAN YOU COME OVER TOMORROW MORNING?

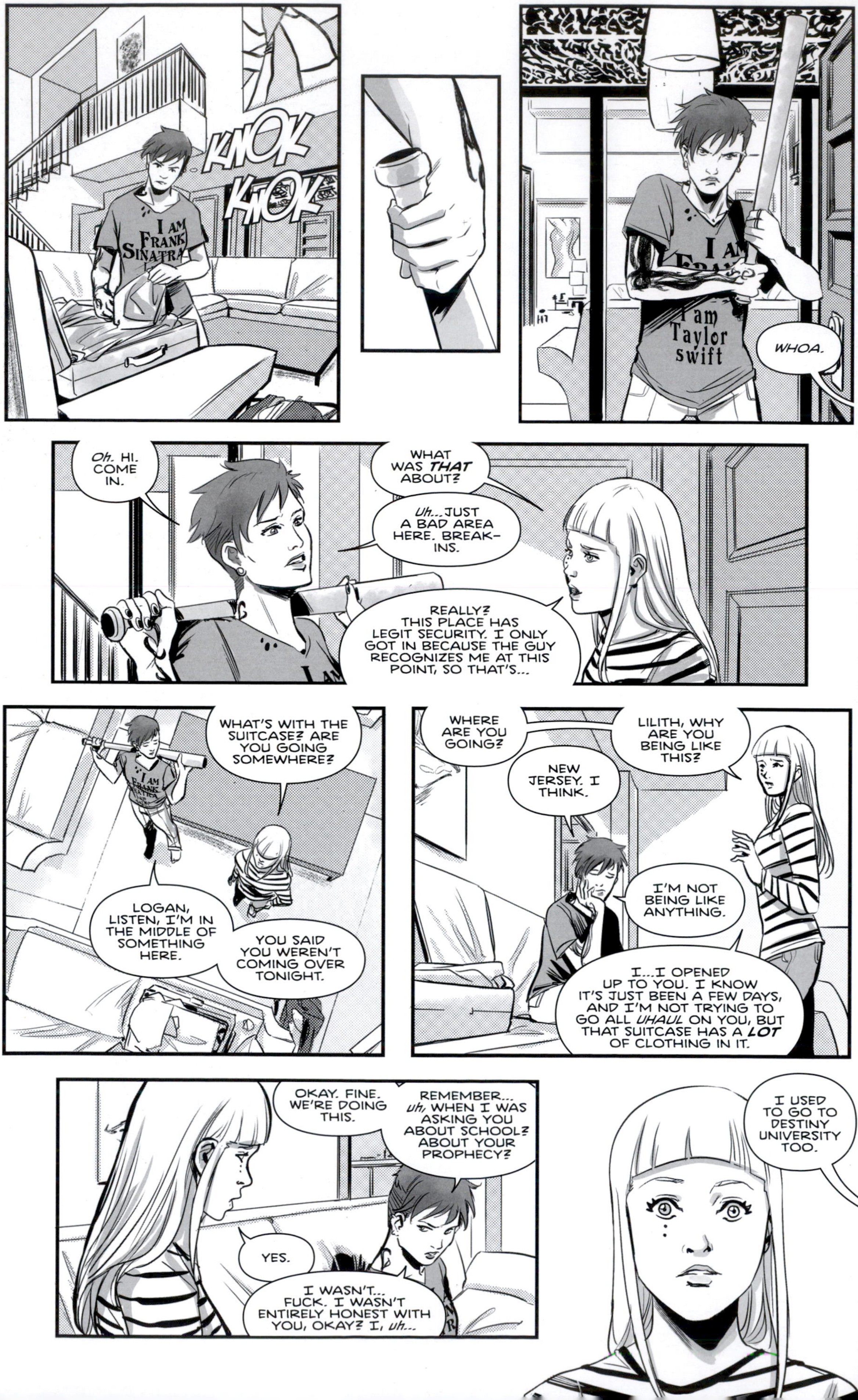
I AM FRANK SINATRA
KNOK
KNOK
I AM FRANK
I am Taylor swift
WHOA.
Oh. HI. COME IN.
WHAT WAS THAT ABOUT?
Uh... JUST A BAD AREA HERE. BREAK-INS.
REALLY? THIS PLACE HAS LEGIT SECURITY. I ONLY GOT IN BECAUSE THE GUY RECOGNIZES ME AT THIS POINT, SO THAT'S...
WHAT'S WITH THE SUITCASE? ARE YOU GOING SOMEWHERE?
LOGAN, LISTEN, I'M IN THE MIDDLE OF SOMETHING HERE.
YOU SAID YOU WEREN'T COMING OVER TONIGHT.
WHERE ARE YOU GOING?
NEW JERSEY. I THINK.
LILITH, WHY ARE YOU BEING LIKE THIS?
I'M NOT BEING LIKE ANYTHING.
I... I OPENED UP TO YOU. I KNOW IT'S JUST BEEN A FEW DAYS, AND I'M NOT TRYING TO GO ALL UHAUL ON YOU, BUT THAT SUITCASE HAS A LOT OF CLOTHING IN IT.
OKAY. FINE. WE'RE DOING THIS.
REMEMBER... uh, WHEN I WAS ASKING YOU ABOUT SCHOOL? ABOUT YOUR PROPHECY?
YES.
I WASN'T... FUCK. I WASN'T ENTIRELY HONEST WITH YOU, OKAY? I, uh...
I USED TO GO TO DESTINY UNIVERSITY TOO.

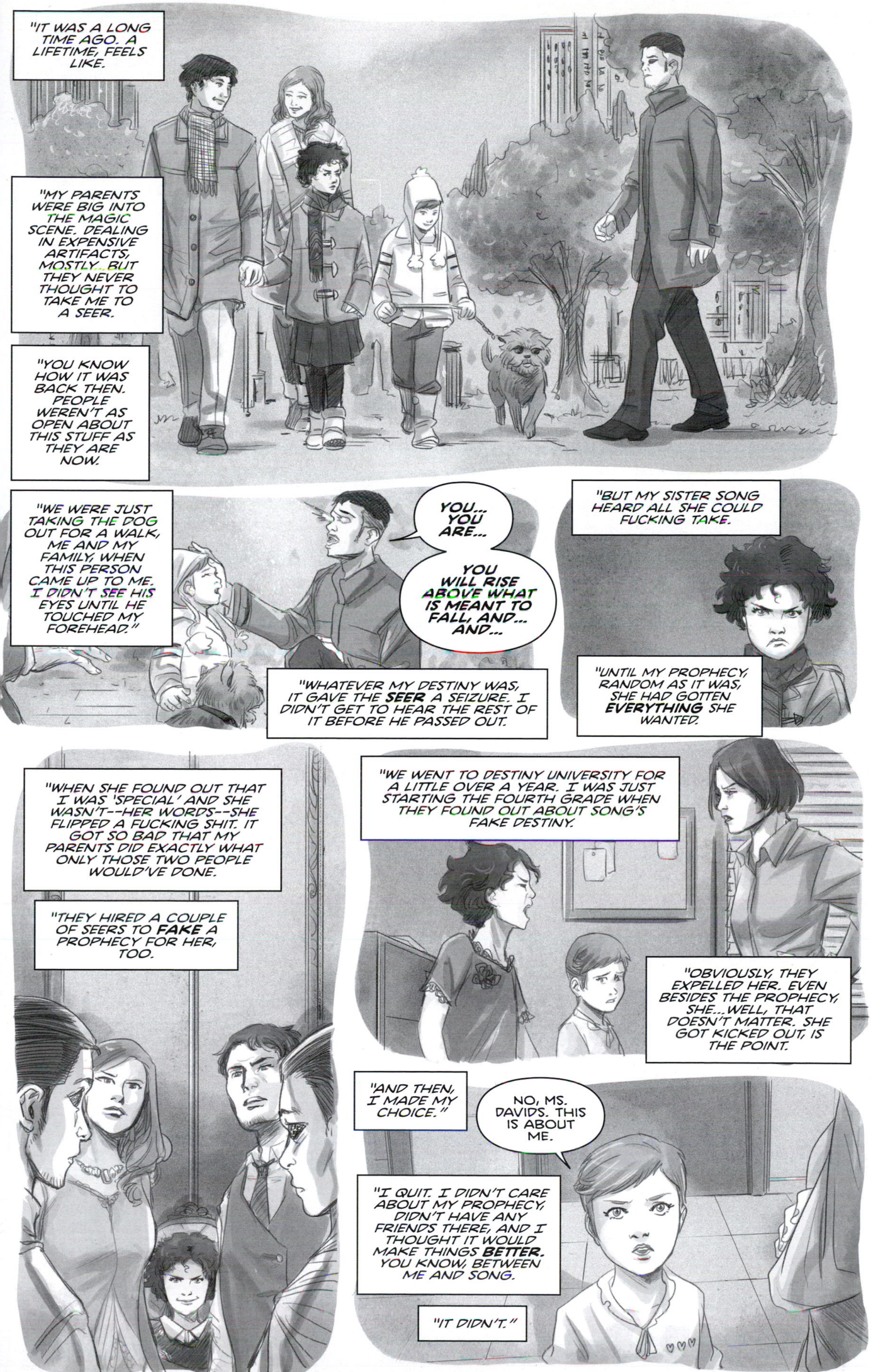
"IT WAS A LONG TIME AGO. A LIFETIME, FEELS LIKE.
"MY PARENTS WERE BIG INTO THE MAGIC SCENE. DEALING IN EXPENSIVE ARTIFACTS, MOSTLY...BUT THEY NEVER THOUGHT TO TAKE ME TO A SEER.
"YOU KNOW HOW IT WAS BACK THEN. PEOPLE WEREN'T AS OPEN ABOUT THIS STUFF AS THEY ARE NOW.
"WE WERE JUST TAKING THE DOG OUT FOR A WALK, ME AND MY FAMILY, WHEN THIS PERSON CAME UP TO ME. I DIDN'T SEE HIS EYES UNTIL HE TOUCHED MY FOREHEAD."
YOU... YOU ARE...
YOU WILL RISE ABOVE WHAT IS MEANT TO FALL, AND... AND...
"WHATEVER MY DESTINY WAS, IT GAVE THE SEER A SEIZURE. I DIDN'T GET TO HEAR THE REST OF IT BEFORE HE PASSED OUT.
"BUT MY SISTER SONG HEARD ALL SHE COULD FUCKING TAKE.
"UNTIL MY PROPHECY, RANDOM AS IT WAS, SHE HAD GOTTEN EVERYTHING SHE WANTED.
"WHEN SHE FOUND OUT THAT I WAS 'SPECIAL' AND SHE WASN'T--HER WORDS--SHE FLIPPED A FUCKING SHIT. IT GOT SO BAD THAT MY PARENTS DID EXACTLY WHAT ONLY THOSE TWO PEOPLE WOULD'VE DONE.
"THEY HIRED A COUPLE OF SEERS TO FAKE A PROPHECY FOR HER, TOO.
"WE WENT TO DESTINY UNIVERSITY FOR A LITTLE OVER A YEAR. I WAS JUST STARTING THE FOURTH GRADE WHEN THEY FOUND OUT ABOUT SONG'S FAKE DESTINY.
"OBVIOUSLY, THEY EXPELLED HER. EVEN BESIDES THE PROPHECY, SHE...WELL, THAT DOESN'T MATTER. SHE GOT KICKED OUT, IS THE POINT.
"AND THEN, I MADE MY CHOICE."
NO, MS. DAVIDS. THIS IS ABOUT ME.
"I QUIT. I DIDN'T CARE ABOUT MY PROPHECY, DIDN'T HAVE ANY FRIENDS THERE, AND I THOUGHT IT WOULD MAKE THINGS BETTER. YOU KNOW, BETWEEN ME AND SONG.
"IT DIDN'T."

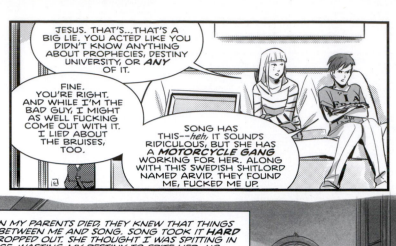

JESUS. THAT'S...THAT'S A BIG LIE. YOU ACTED LIKE YOU DIDN'T KNOW ANYTHING ABOUT PROPHECIES, DESTINY UNIVERSITY, OR *ANY* OF IT.

FINE. YOU'RE RIGHT. AND WHILE I'M THE BAD GUY, I MIGHT AS WELL FUCKING COME OUT WITH IT. I LIED ABOUT THE BRUISES, TOO.

SONG HAS THIS--*heh*, IT SOUNDS RIDICULOUS, BUT SHE HAS A *MOTORCYCLE GANG* WORKING FOR HER. ALONG WITH THIS SWEDISH SHITLORD NAMED ARVID. THEY FOUND ME, FUCKED ME UP.

"SEE, WHEN MY PARENTS DIED, THEY KNEW THAT THINGS WERE BAD BETWEEN ME AND SONG. SONG TOOK IT *HARD* WHEN I DROPPED OUT. SHE THOUGHT I WAS SPITTING IN HER FACE, WASTING MY DESTINY TO SPITE HER. NO MATTER WHAT I DID, SHE WOULD'VE HATED ME.

"SOOOO THEY PUT IT IN THEIR WILL-- THAT, ALONG WITH OUR INHERITANCES, WE'RE MAGICALLY BOUND TO NOT HARM EACH OTHER.

"IF I SO MUCH AS SLAPPED HER, IT'D FEEL AS IF I GOT STABBED IN THE TEMPLE WITH AN ICE PICK. SAME FOR HER TO ME.

"BUT IT DOESN'T STOP HER FROM HAVING OTHER PEOPLE DO IT FOR HER. SHE THINKS I'M OUT TO *RUIN* HER, FOR WHATEVER REASON. AND MAYBE, AFTER ALL THESE YEARS, I *AM*.

"AFTER ALL, SHE TOLD ME TO LEAVE NEW YORK CITY, AND I DID. I CAME BACK A MONTH AGO. OF ALL THE PLACES I COULD BE, HERE I AM."

A GANG BEAT YOU UP. A MOTORCYCLE GANG.

YEAH. AND THEY'RE GONNA DO WORSE IF I'M NOT OUT OF HERE BY TOMORROW AFTERNOON.

LILITH...

I KNOW.

THIS IS *INSANE*. SONG IS...WHAT, SHE'S DOING ALL OF THIS OVER A PROPHECY FROM WHEN YOU WERE A *KID*?

IT'S MORE COMPLICATED THAN THAT. SHE'S A TRIP.

LOGAN, LISTEN TO ME. SONG IS A BIG PLAYER IN THIS CITY. SHE HAS POLITICAL CONNECTS OUT THE ASS, AND SHE'S PLANNING--PLANNING *SOMETHING*. WHATEVER IT IS, YOU DO *NOT* WANT TO BE INVOLVED.

WHY *DID* YOU COME BACK, THEN? YOU DON'T SEEM AT ALL SURPRISED THAT SHE'S AFTER YOU, SO WHY DID YOU EVEN--

ANSWER ME. WHY DID YOU COME BACK?

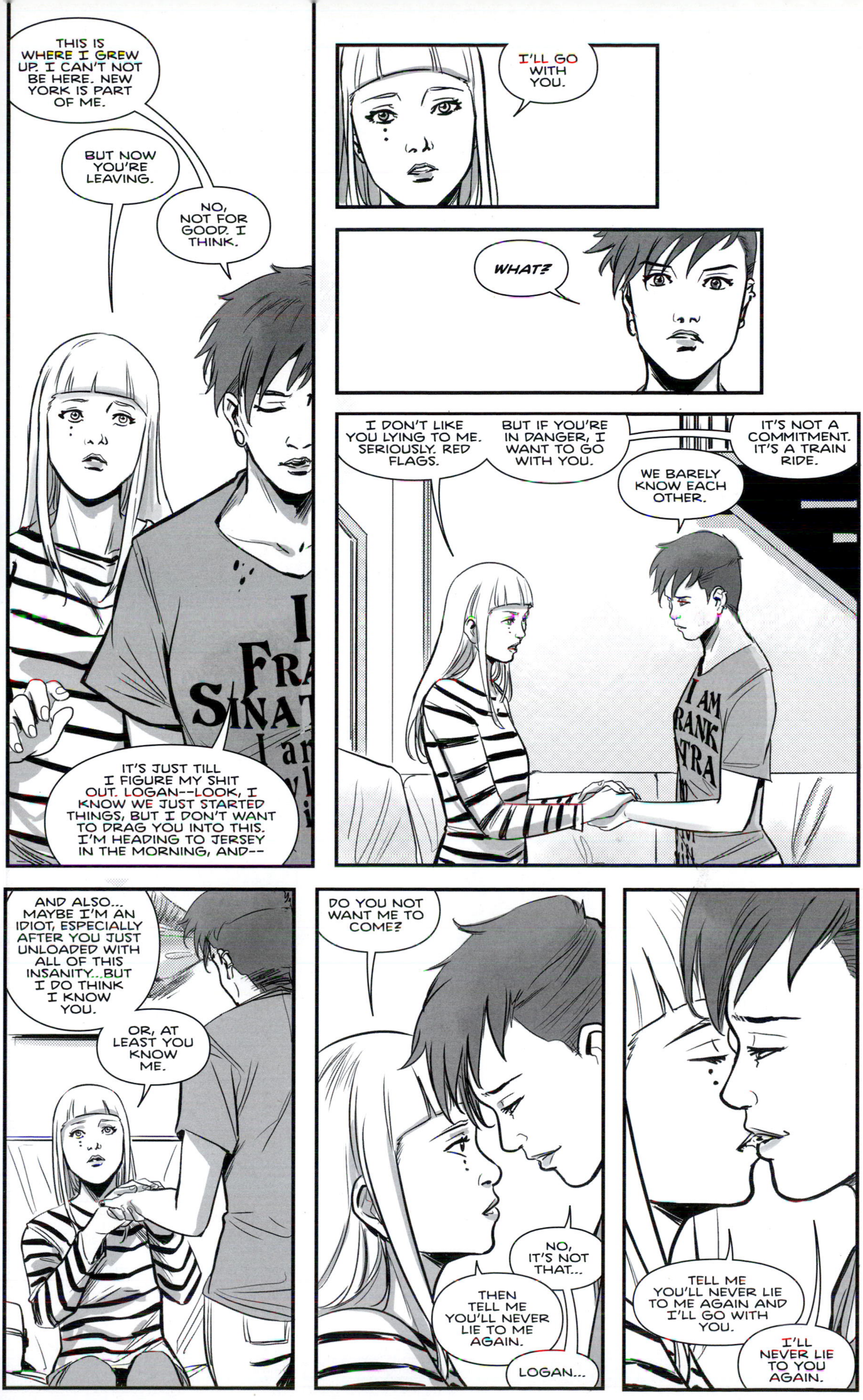
THIS IS WHERE I GREW UP. I CAN'T NOT BE HERE. NEW YORK IS PART OF ME.
BUT NOW YOU'RE LEAVING.
NO, NOT FOR GOOD. I THINK.
IT'S JUST TILL I FIGURE MY SHIT OUT. LOGAN--LOOK, I KNOW WE JUST STARTED THINGS, BUT I DON'T WANT TO DRAG YOU INTO THIS. I'M HEADING TO JERSEY IN THE MORNING, AND--
I'LL GO WITH YOU.
WHAT?
I DON'T LIKE YOU LYING TO ME. SERIOUSLY. RED FLAGS.
BUT IF YOU'RE IN DANGER, I WANT TO GO WITH YOU.
IT'S NOT A COMMITMENT. IT'S A TRAIN RIDE.
WE BARELY KNOW EACH OTHER.
AND ALSO... MAYBE I'M AN IDIOT, ESPECIALLY AFTER YOU JUST UNLOADED WITH ALL OF THIS INSANITY...BUT I DO THINK I KNOW YOU.
OR, AT LEAST YOU KNOW ME.
DO YOU NOT WANT ME TO COME?
NO, IT'S NOT THAT...
THEN TELL ME YOU'LL NEVER LIE TO ME AGAIN.
LOGAN...
TELL ME YOU'LL NEVER LIE TO ME AGAIN AND I'LL GO WITH YOU.
I'LL NEVER LIE TO YOU AGAIN.

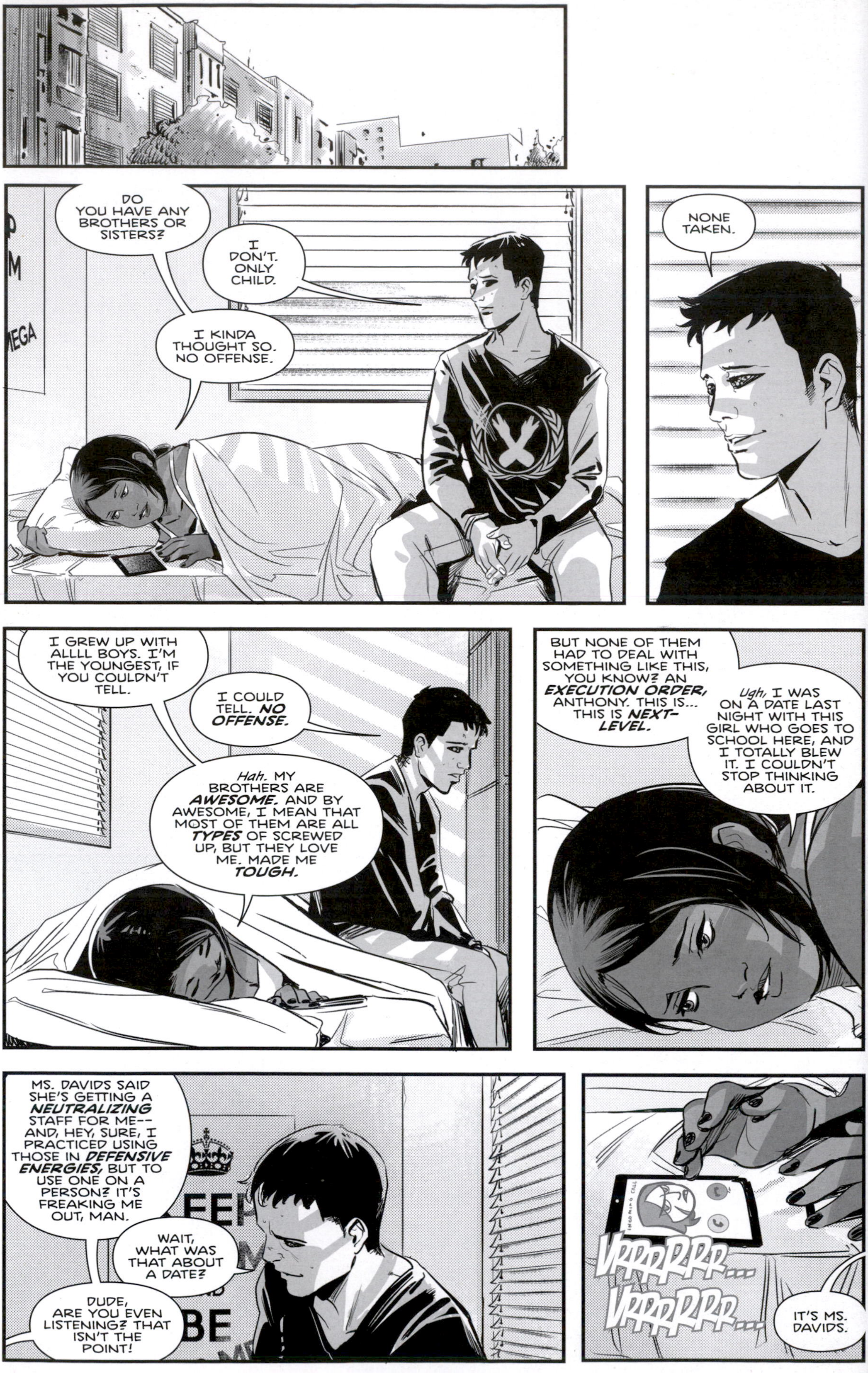

DO YOU HAVE ANY BROTHERS OR SISTERS?
I DON'T. ONLY CHILD.
I KINDA THOUGHT SO. NO OFFENSE.
NONE TAKEN.
I GREW UP WITH ALLLL BOYS. I'M THE YOUNGEST, IF YOU COULDN'T TELL.
I COULD TELL. NO OFFENSE.
Hah. MY BROTHERS ARE AWESOME. AND BY AWESOME, I MEAN THAT MOST OF THEM ARE ALL TYPES OF SCREWED UP, BUT THEY LOVE ME. MADE ME TOUGH.
BUT NONE OF THEM HAD TO DEAL WITH SOMETHING LIKE THIS, YOU KNOW? AN EXECUTION ORDER, ANTHONY. THIS IS... THIS IS NEXT-LEVEL.
Ugh, I WAS ON A DATE LAST NIGHT WITH THIS GIRL WHO GOES TO SCHOOL HERE, AND I TOTALLY BLEW IT. I COULDN'T STOP THINKING ABOUT IT.
MS. DAVIDS SAID SHE'S GETTING A NEUTRALIZING STAFF FOR ME--AND, HEY, SURE, I PRACTICED USING THOSE IN DEFENSIVE ENERGIES, BUT TO USE ONE ON A PERSON? IT'S FREAKING ME OUT, MAN.
WAIT, WHAT WAS THAT ABOUT A DATE?
DUDE, ARE YOU EVEN LISTENING? THAT ISN'T THE POINT!
VRRRRRRR...
VRRRRRRR...
IT'S MS. DAVIDS.

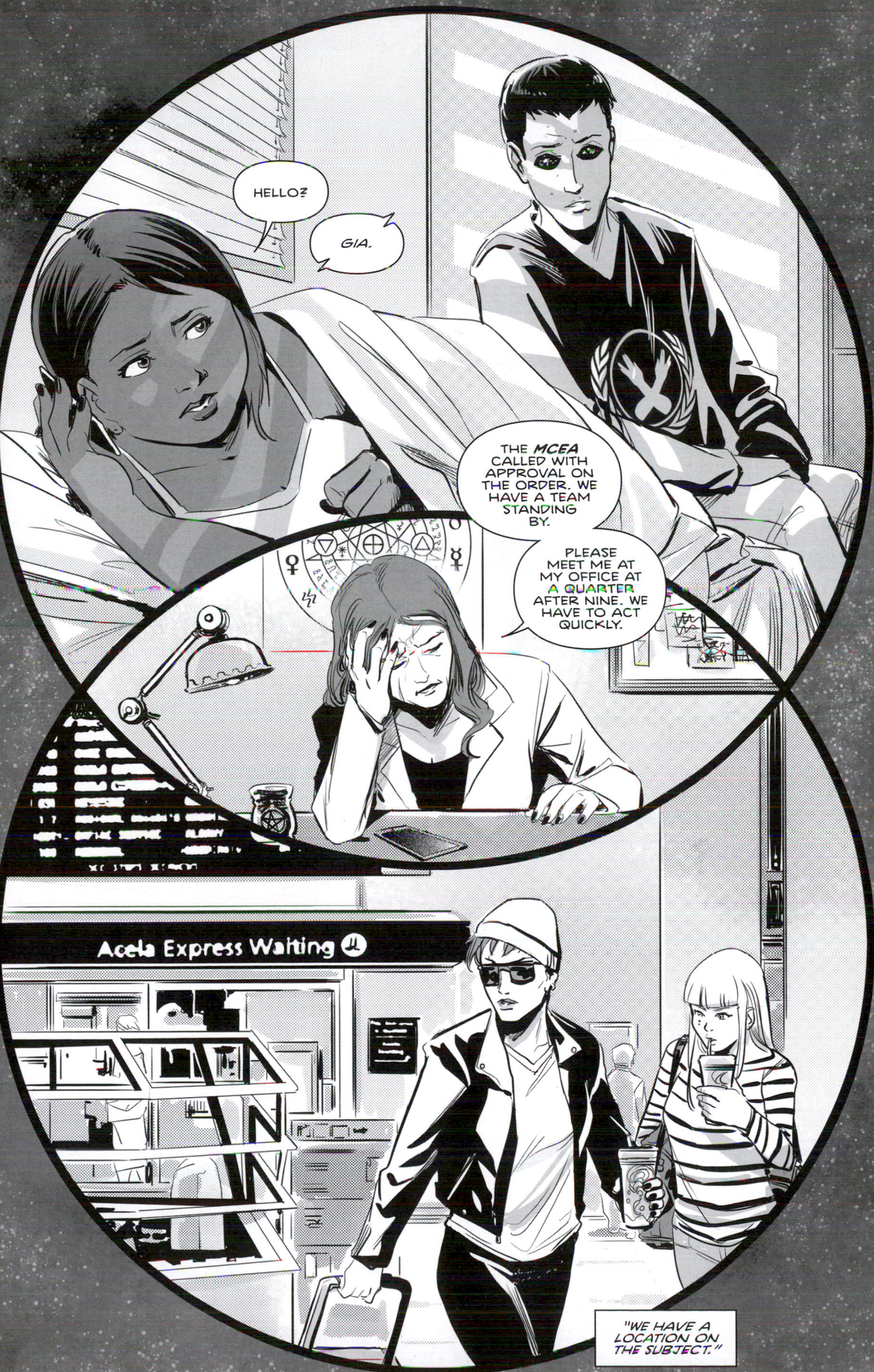
HELLO?
GIA.
THE MCEA CALLED WITH APPROVAL ON THE ORDER. WE HAVE A TEAM STANDING BY.
PLEASE MEET ME AT MY OFFICE AT A QUARTER AFTER NINE. WE HAVE TO ACT QUICKLY.
Acela Express Waiting
"WE HAVE A LOCATION ON THE SUBJECT."

HEY, WATCH THE BAGS FOR A SEC. I'M GONNA GO GRAB THE TICKETS.

SURE.

07:20

< Back(2)   Aug   Contac

TODAY

Okay so don't freak out but can you cover for me for the next maybe three days?

Is everything ok????

Yes don't worry. Something crazy came up and I'm about to get on an Amtrak with Lilith

Bitch WHAT

I know it sounds insane but I can explain. Grace owes me, she can probably cover

Me Message   Send

TODAY

I swear i could kill you

Ur doing that BIG epic throw everything away for the moment thing again and it is NOT CUTE

I swear it will make sense. Please just help me.

Me Message   Send

GRACE, YOU KNOW HOW I ALWAYS MAKE FUN OF YOU FOR BEING THE *ONLY* PERSON I KNOW IN THIS CITY WITH A CAR?

YES. IT'S CONSTANT.

IS THERE ANY CHANCE THAT I CAN MAYBE *BORROW* SAID CAR?

Hm, ODD.

WHAT?

IT SEEMS THAT THERE WAS A PROBLEM WITH THE PAYMENT. GIVE ME A MOMENT. I'LL HAVE TO GET TO MY SUPERVISOR.

NOT TO BE THAT GUY, BUT I CAN *PROMISE* THERE'S NOTHING WRONG WITH THE PAYMENT.

SORRY. THERE'S NOTHING I CAN DO FROM MY STATION. BE RIGHT BACK.

WHAT'S GOING ON?

SHOULDN'T HAVE ORDERED THE TICKETS ONLINE. THERE'S ALWAYS A PROBLEM WITH PICK-UP. I--

VEEEEERP

VEEEEEERP

WHOA. IS THAT THE FIRE ALARM?

THIS IS *AGENT GUTIERREZ* WITH THE *MCEA!*

WE NEED THIS AREA CLEAR, NOW! PLEASE MAKE YOUR WAY OUT OF THE STATION!

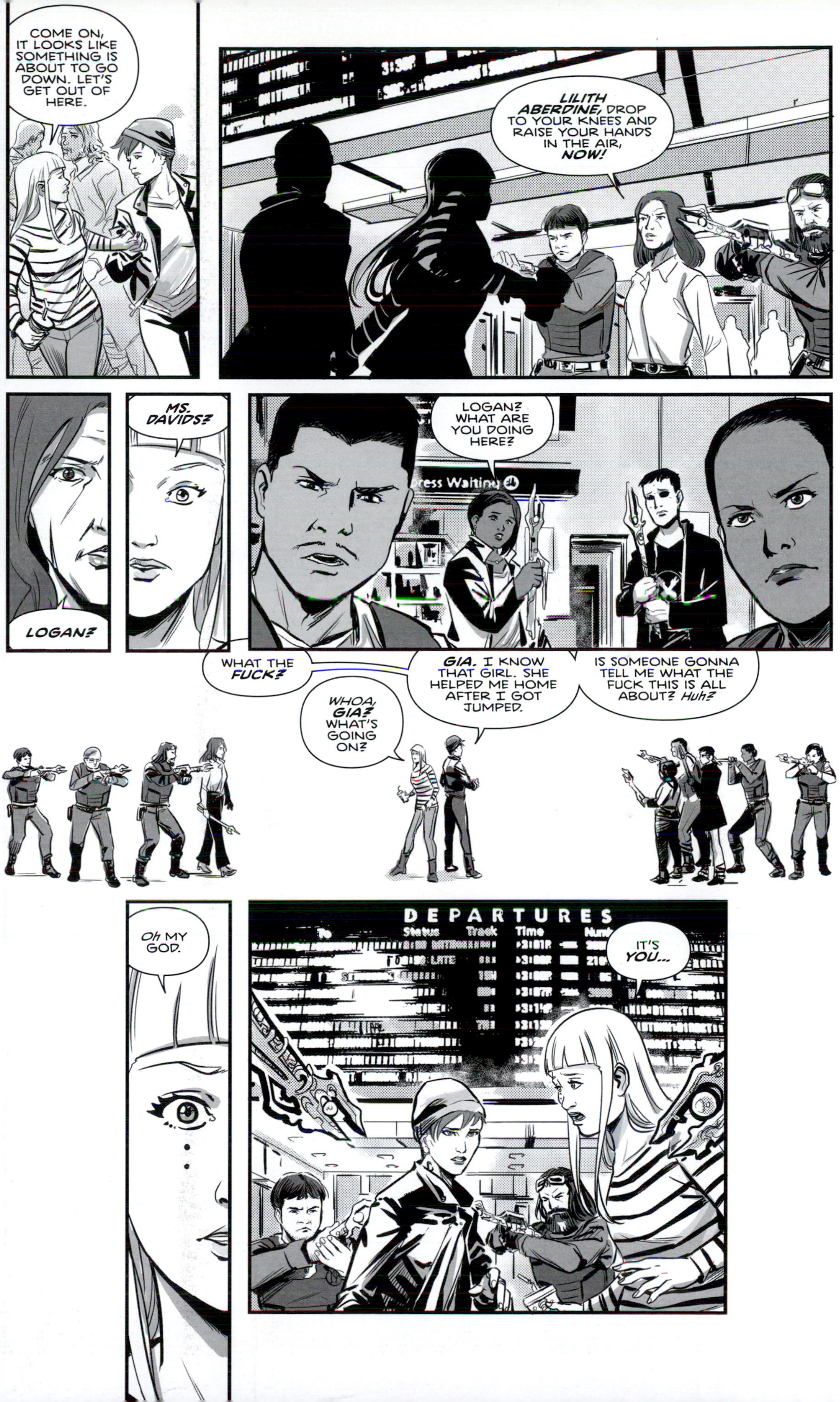
COME ON, IT LOOKS LIKE SOMETHING IS ABOUT TO GO DOWN. LET'S GET OUT OF HERE.
LILITH ABERDINE, DROP TO YOUR KNEES AND RAISE YOUR HANDS IN THE AIR, NOW!
LOGAN?
MS. DAVIDS?
LOGAN? WHAT ARE YOU DOING HERE?
Press Waiting
WHAT THE FUCK?
GIA. I KNOW THAT GIRL. SHE HELPED ME HOME AFTER I GOT JUMPED.
IS SOMEONE GONNA TELL ME WHAT THE FUCK THIS IS ALL ABOUT? Huh?
WHOA, GIA? WHAT'S GOING ON?
Oh MY GOD.
DEPARTURES
Status
Track
Time
IT'S YOU...

CHAPTER FIVE

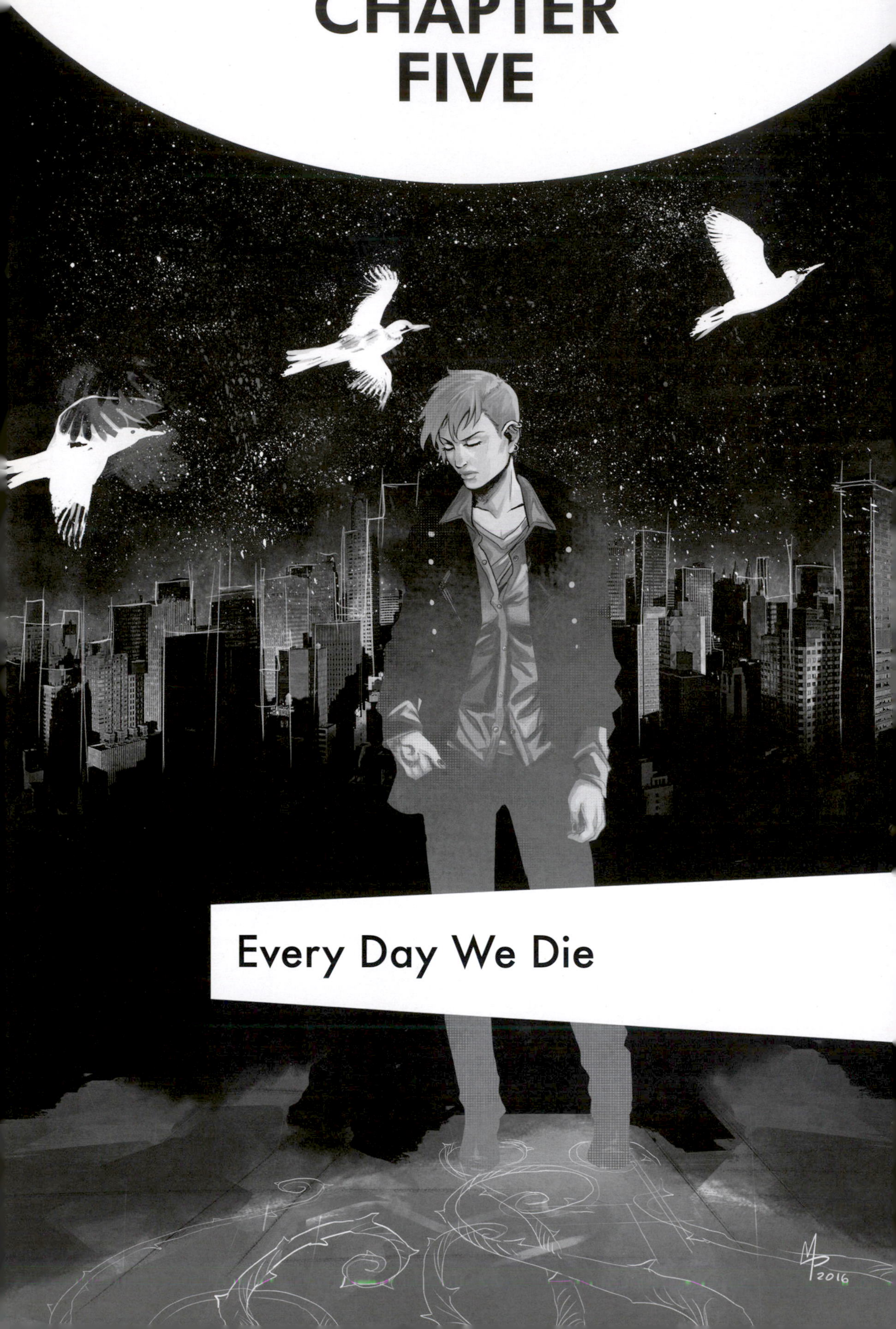

Every Day We Die

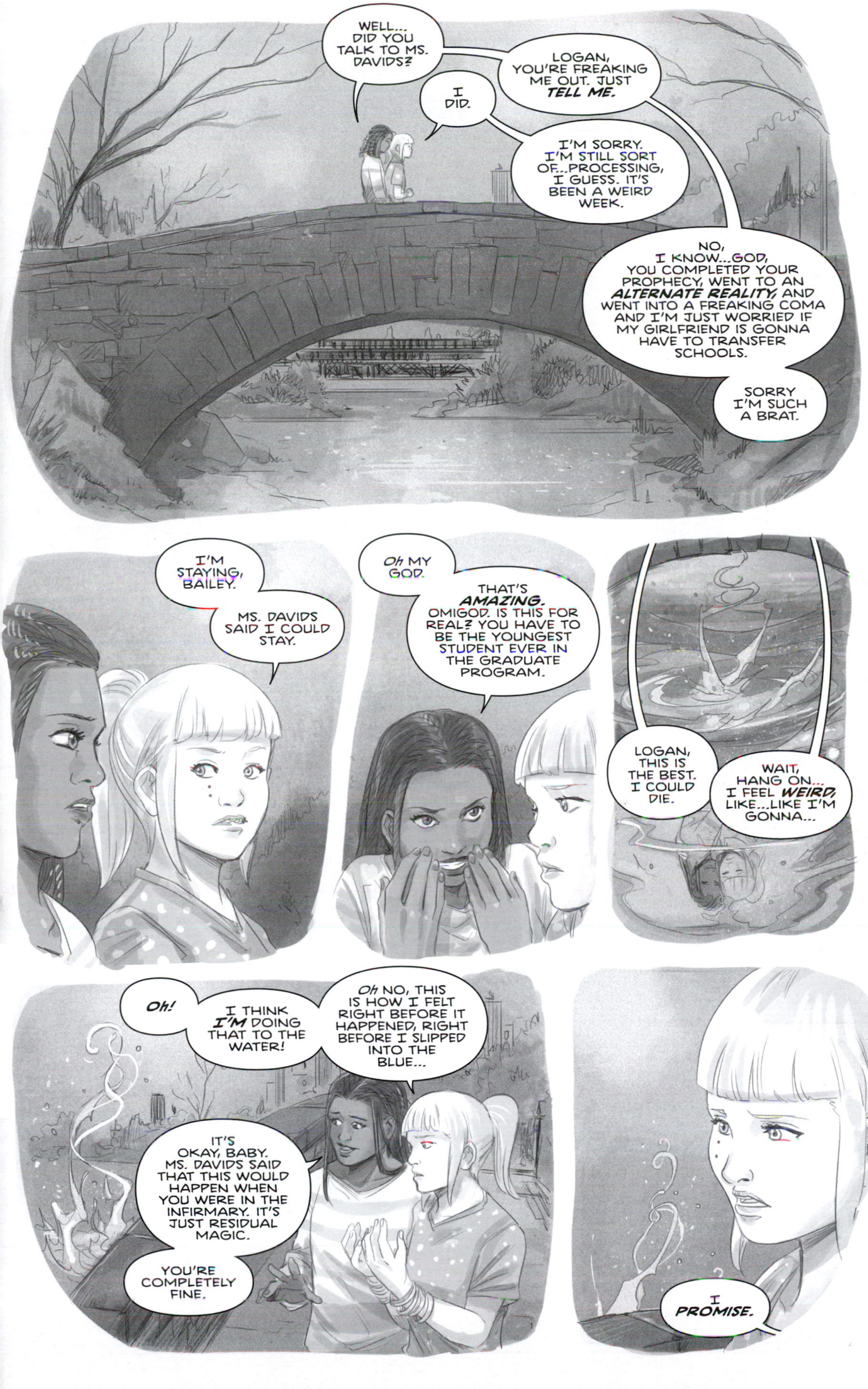
WELL... DID YOU TALK TO MS. DAVIDS?
I DID.
LOGAN, YOU'RE FREAKING ME OUT. JUST TELL ME.
I'M SORRY. I'M STILL SORT OF...PROCESSING, I GUESS. IT'S BEEN A WEIRD WEEK.
NO, I KNOW...GOD, YOU COMPLETED YOUR PROPHECY, WENT TO AN ALTERNATE REALITY, AND WENT INTO A FREAKING COMA AND I'M JUST WORRIED IF MY GIRLFRIEND IS GONNA HAVE TO TRANSFER SCHOOLS.
SORRY I'M SUCH A BRAT.
I'M STAYING, BAILEY.
MS. DAVIDS SAID I COULD STAY.
OH MY GOD.
THAT'S AMAZING. OMIGOD. IS THIS FOR REAL? YOU HAVE TO BE THE YOUNGEST STUDENT EVER IN THE GRADUATE PROGRAM.
LOGAN, THIS IS THE BEST. I COULD DIE.
WAIT, HANG ON... I FEEL WEIRD, LIKE...LIKE I'M GONNA...
OH!
I THINK I'M DOING THAT TO THE WATER!
OH NO, THIS IS HOW I FELT RIGHT BEFORE IT HAPPENED, RIGHT BEFORE I SLIPPED INTO THE BLUE...
IT'S OKAY, BABY. MS. DAVIDS SAID THAT THIS WOULD HAPPEN WHEN YOU WERE IN THE INFIRMARY. IT'S JUST RESIDUAL MAGIC.
YOU'RE COMPLETELY FINE.
I PROMISE.

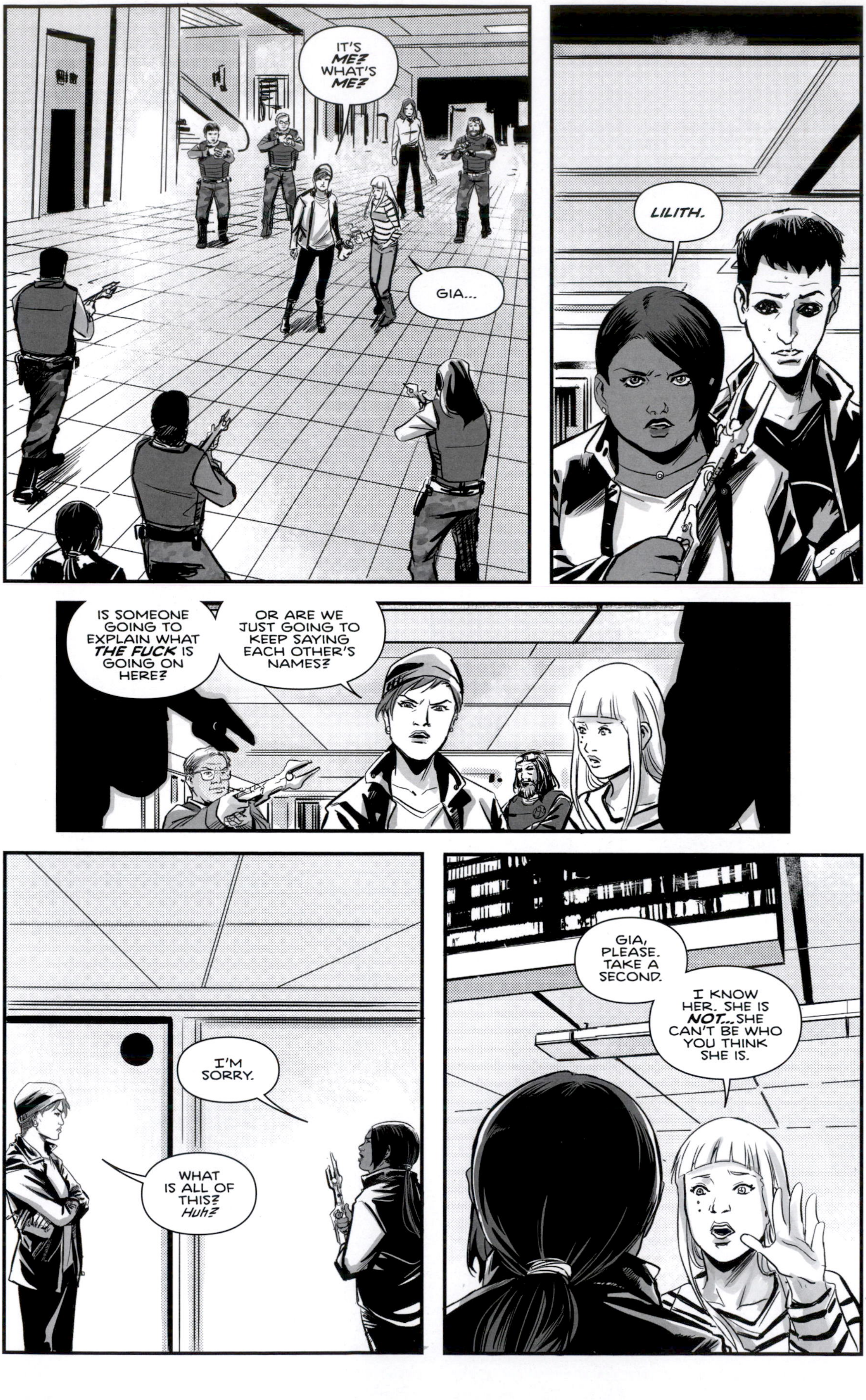
IT'S ME? WHAT'S ME?
GIA...
LILITH.
IS SOMEONE GOING TO EXPLAIN WHAT THE FUCK IS GOING ON HERE?
OR ARE WE JUST GOING TO KEEP SAYING EACH OTHER'S NAMES?
I'M SORRY.
WHAT IS ALL OF THIS? Huh?
GIA, PLEASE. TAKE A SECOND.
I KNOW HER. SHE IS NOT... SHE CAN'T BE WHO YOU THINK SHE IS.

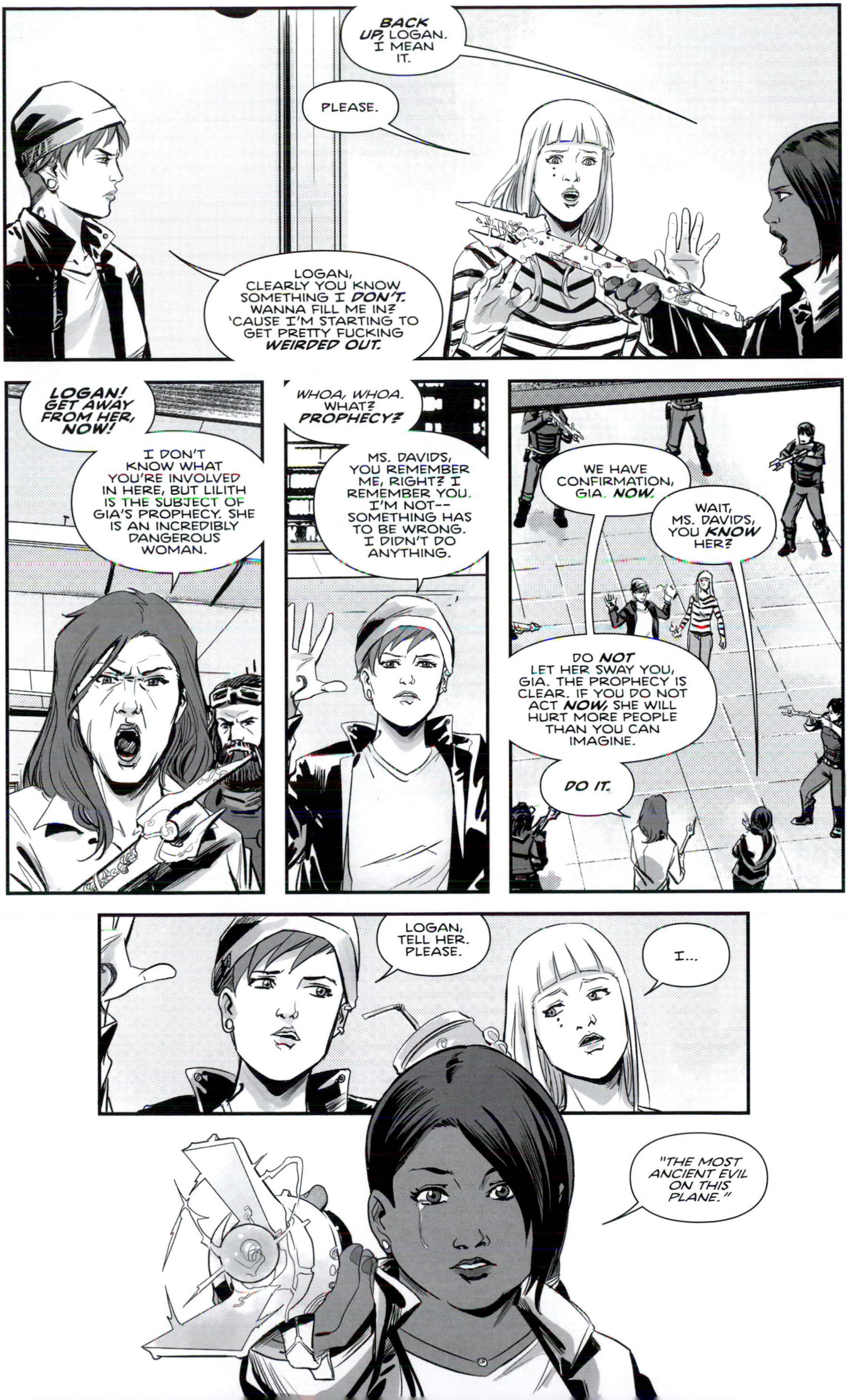
BACK UP, LOGAN. I MEAN IT.
PLEASE.
LOGAN, CLEARLY YOU KNOW SOMETHING I DON'T. WANNA FILL ME IN? 'CAUSE I'M STARTING TO GET PRETTY FUCKING WEIRDED OUT.
LOGAN! GET AWAY FROM HER, NOW!
I DON'T KNOW WHAT YOU'RE INVOLVED IN HERE, BUT LILITH IS THE SUBJECT OF GIA'S PROPHECY. SHE IS AN INCREDIBLY DANGEROUS WOMAN.
WHOA, WHOA. WHAT? PROPHECY?
MS. DAVIDS, YOU REMEMBER ME, RIGHT? I REMEMBER YOU. I'M NOT-- SOMETHING HAS TO BE WRONG. I DIDN'T DO ANYTHING.
WE HAVE CONFIRMATION, GIA. NOW.
WAIT, MS. DAVIDS, YOU KNOW HER?
DO NOT LET HER SWAY YOU, GIA. THE PROPHECY IS CLEAR. IF YOU DO NOT ACT NOW, SHE WILL HURT MORE PEOPLE THAN YOU CAN IMAGINE.
DO IT.
LOGAN, TELL HER. PLEASE.
I...
"THE MOST ANCIENT EVIL ON THIS PLANE."

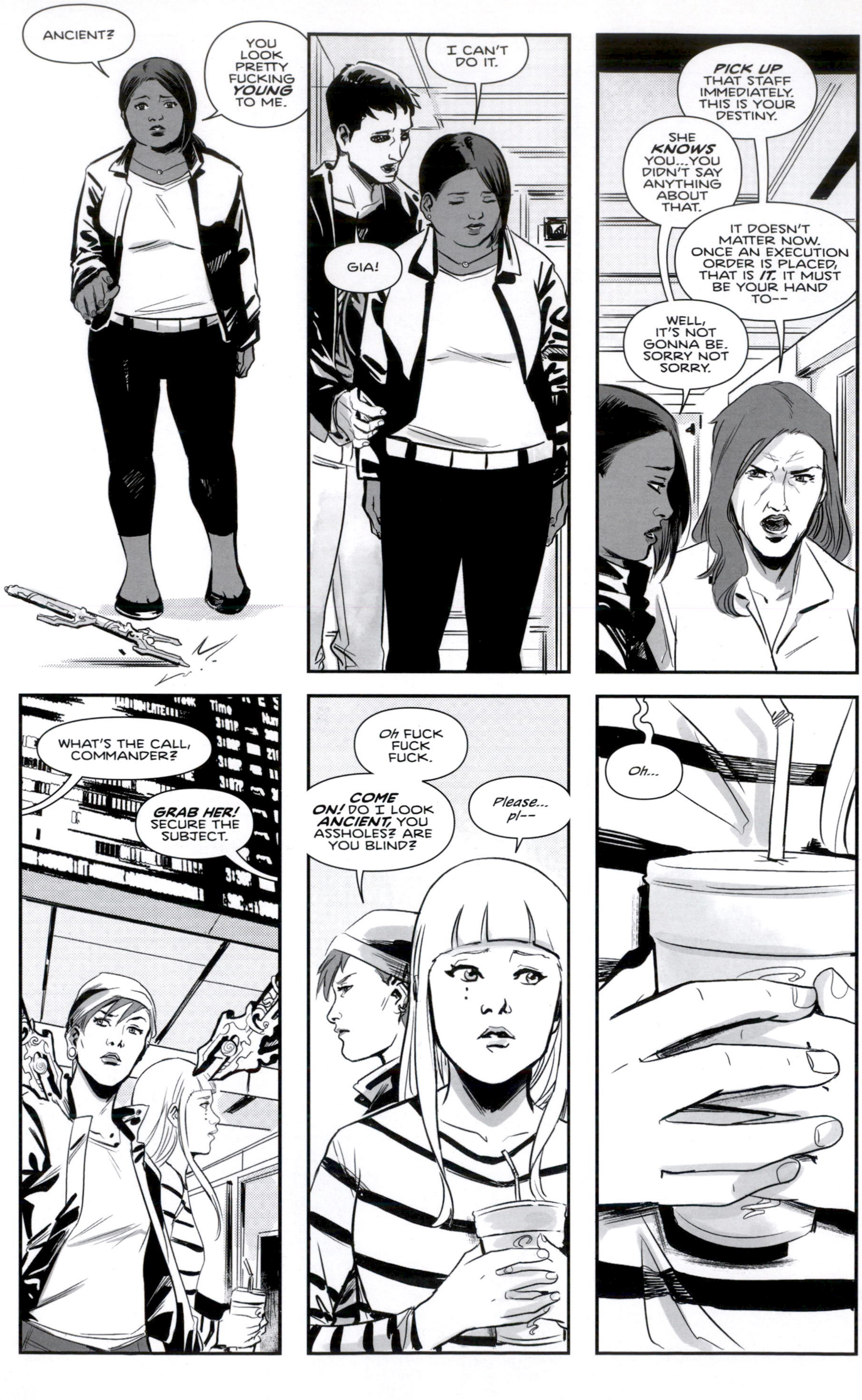
ANCIENT?
YOU LOOK PRETTY FUCKING YOUNG TO ME.
I CAN'T DO IT.
GIA!
PICK UP THAT STAFF IMMEDIATELY. THIS IS YOUR DESTINY.
SHE KNOWS YOU...YOU DIDN'T SAY ANYTHING ABOUT THAT.
IT DOESN'T MATTER NOW. ONCE AN EXECUTION ORDER IS PLACED, THAT IS IT. IT MUST BE YOUR HAND TO--
WELL, IT'S NOT GONNA BE. SORRY NOT SORRY.
WHAT'S THE CALL, COMMANDER?
GRAB HER! SECURE THE SUBJECT.
Oh FUCK FUCK FUCK.
COME ON! DO I LOOK ANCIENT, YOU ASSHOLES? ARE YOU BLIND?
Please... pl--
Oh...

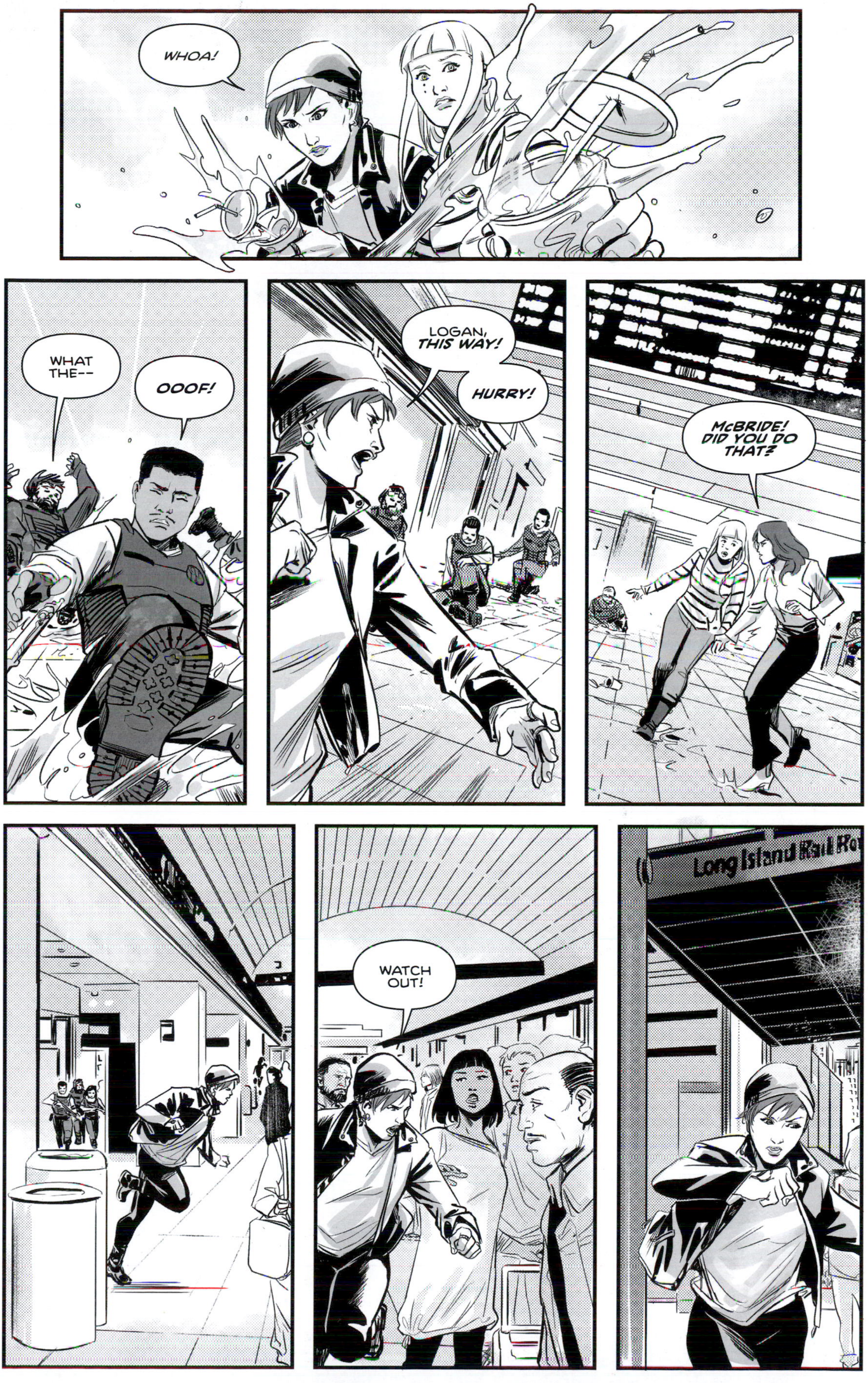
WHOA!
WHAT THE--
OOOF!
LOGAN, THIS WAY!
HURRY!
McBRIDE! DID YOU DO THAT?
WATCH OUT!
Long Island Rail Ro

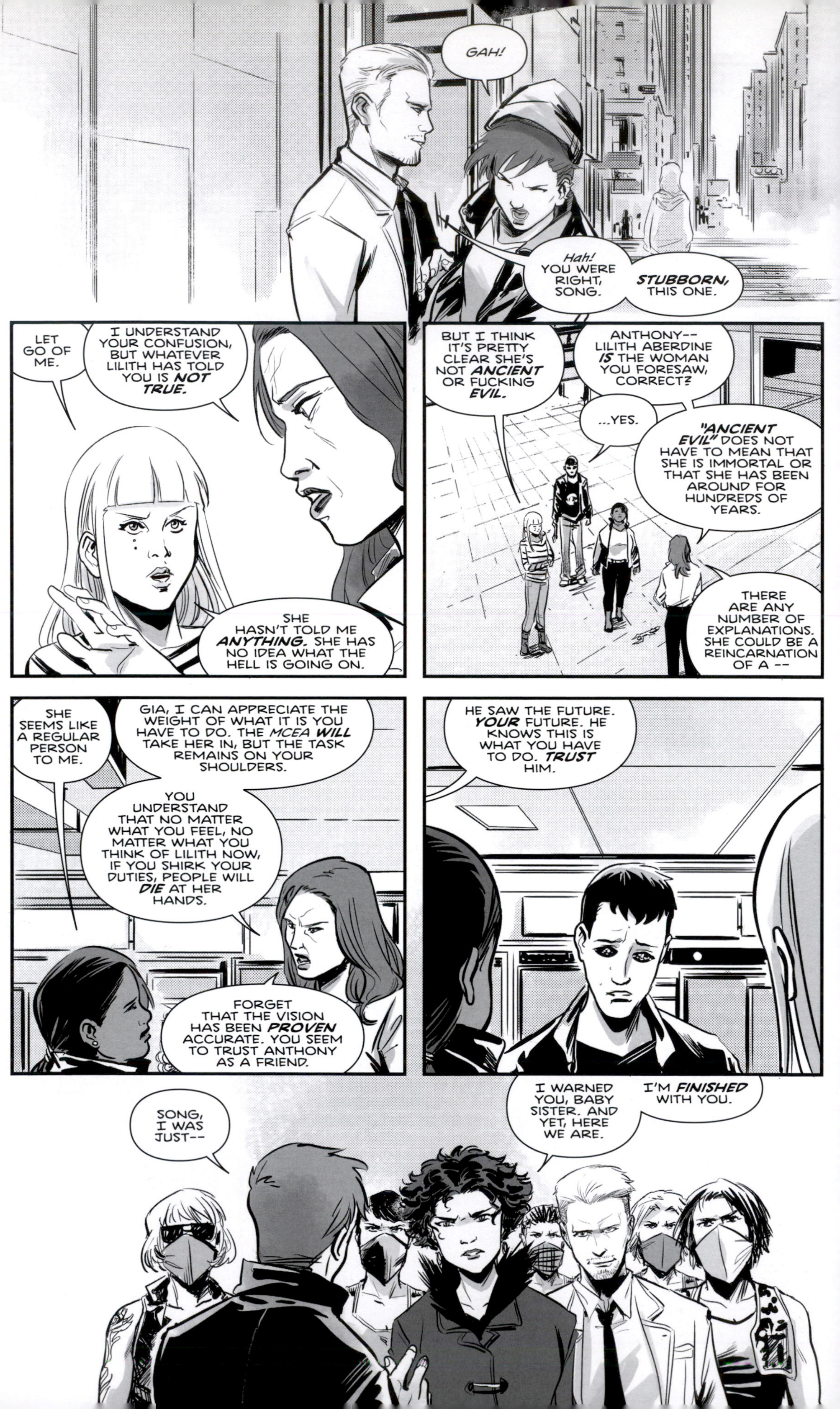
GAH!
Hah! YOU WERE RIGHT, SONG.
STUBBORN, THIS ONE.
LET GO OF ME.
I UNDERSTAND YOUR CONFUSION, BUT WHATEVER LILITH HAS TOLD YOU IS NOT TRUE.
SHE HASN'T TOLD ME ANYTHING. SHE HAS NO IDEA WHAT THE HELL IS GOING ON.
BUT I THINK IT'S PRETTY CLEAR SHE'S NOT ANCIENT OR FUCKING EVIL.
ANTHONY-- LILITH ABERDINE IS THE WOMAN YOU FORESAW, CORRECT?
...YES.
"ANCIENT EVIL" DOES NOT HAVE TO MEAN THAT SHE IS IMMORTAL OR THAT SHE HAS BEEN AROUND FOR HUNDREDS OF YEARS.
THERE ARE ANY NUMBER OF EXPLANATIONS. SHE COULD BE A REINCARNATION OF A --
SHE SEEMS LIKE A REGULAR PERSON TO ME.
GIA, I CAN APPRECIATE THE WEIGHT OF WHAT IT IS YOU HAVE TO DO. THE MCEA WILL TAKE HER IN, BUT THE TASK REMAINS ON YOUR SHOULDERS.
YOU UNDERSTAND THAT NO MATTER WHAT YOU FEEL, NO MATTER WHAT YOU THINK OF LILITH NOW, IF YOU SHIRK YOUR DUTIES, PEOPLE WILL DIE AT HER HANDS.
FORGET THAT THE VISION HAS BEEN PROVEN ACCURATE. YOU SEEM TO TRUST ANTHONY AS A FRIEND.
HE SAW THE FUTURE. YOUR FUTURE. HE KNOWS THIS IS WHAT YOU HAVE TO DO. TRUST HIM.
SONG, I WAS JUST--
I WARNED YOU, BABY SISTER. AND YET, HERE WE ARE.
I'M FINISHED WITH YOU.

FORGET THIS. I'M GOING AFTER HER.

DON'T DO THIS.

YOU WITH ME, ANTHONY?

ANTHONY!

Uhhhh, yes?

YES! WITH YOU!

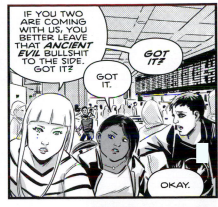

IF YOU TWO ARE COMING WITH US, YOU BETTER LEAVE THAT *ANCIENT EVIL* BULLSHIT TO THE SIDE. GOT IT?

GOT IT?

GOT IT.

OKAY.

HEY! YOU'RE IN VIOLATION--

G-G-GO *VIOLATE* YOURSELF!

YOU DID NOT JUST SAY THAT.

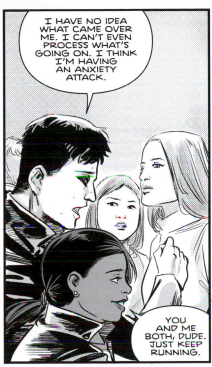

I HAVE NO IDEA WHAT CAME OVER ME. I CAN'T EVEN PROCESS WHAT'S GOING ON. I THINK I'M HAVING AN ANXIETY ATTACK.

YOU AND ME BOTH, DUDE. JUST KEEP RUNNING.

LILITH!

LILITH, ARE YOU...

Oh GOD.

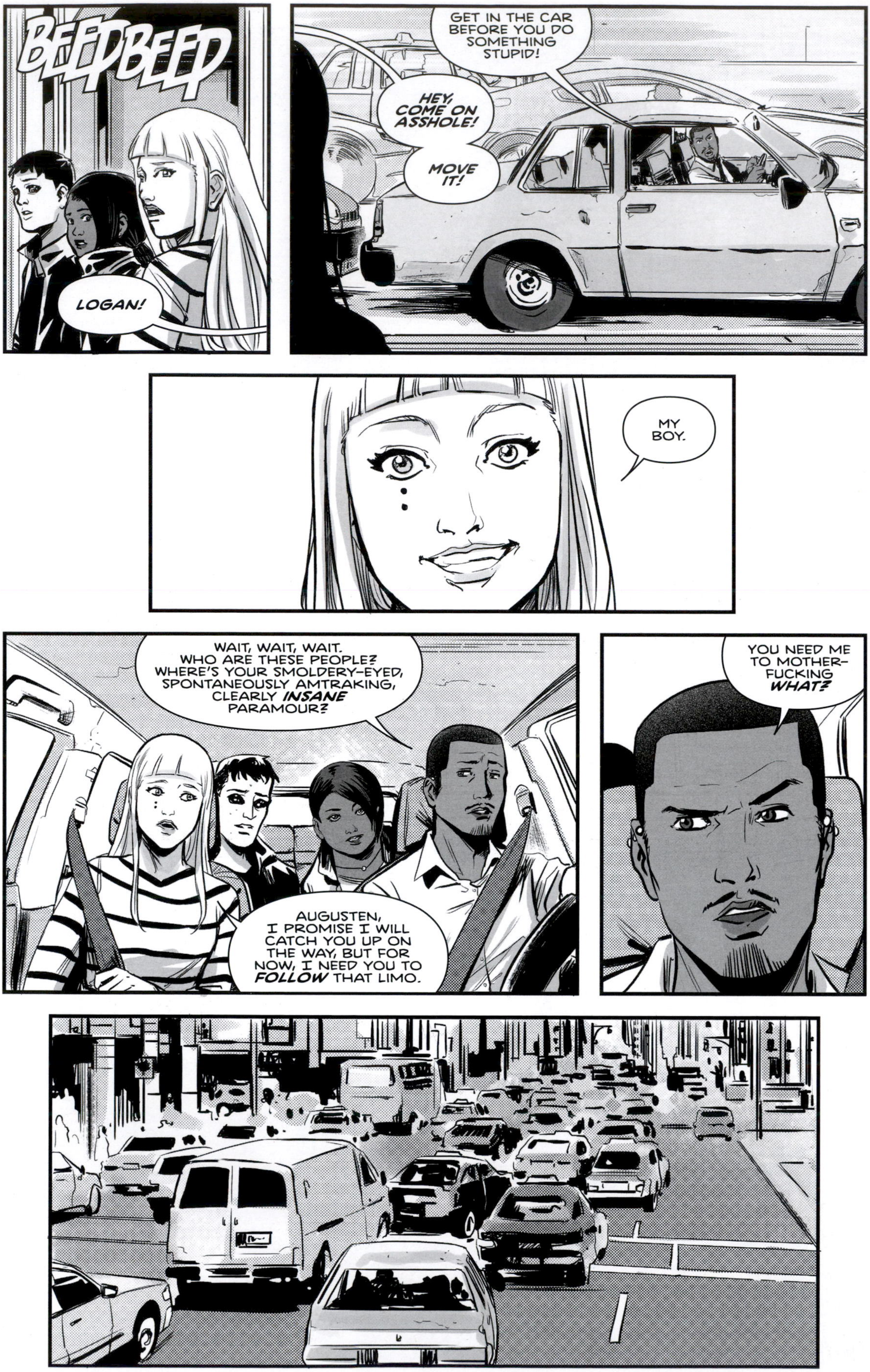
BEEPBEEP
LOGAN!
GET IN THE CAR BEFORE YOU DO SOMETHING STUPID!
HEY, COME ON ASSHOLE!
MOVE IT!
MY BOY.
WAIT, WAIT, WAIT. WHO ARE THESE PEOPLE? WHERE'S YOUR SMOLDERY-EYED, SPONTANEOUSLY AMTRAKING, CLEARLY INSANE PARAMOUR?
AUGUSTEN, I PROMISE I WILL CATCH YOU UP ON THE WAY, BUT FOR NOW, I NEED YOU TO FOLLOW THAT LIMO.
YOU NEED ME TO MOTHER-FUCKING WHAT?

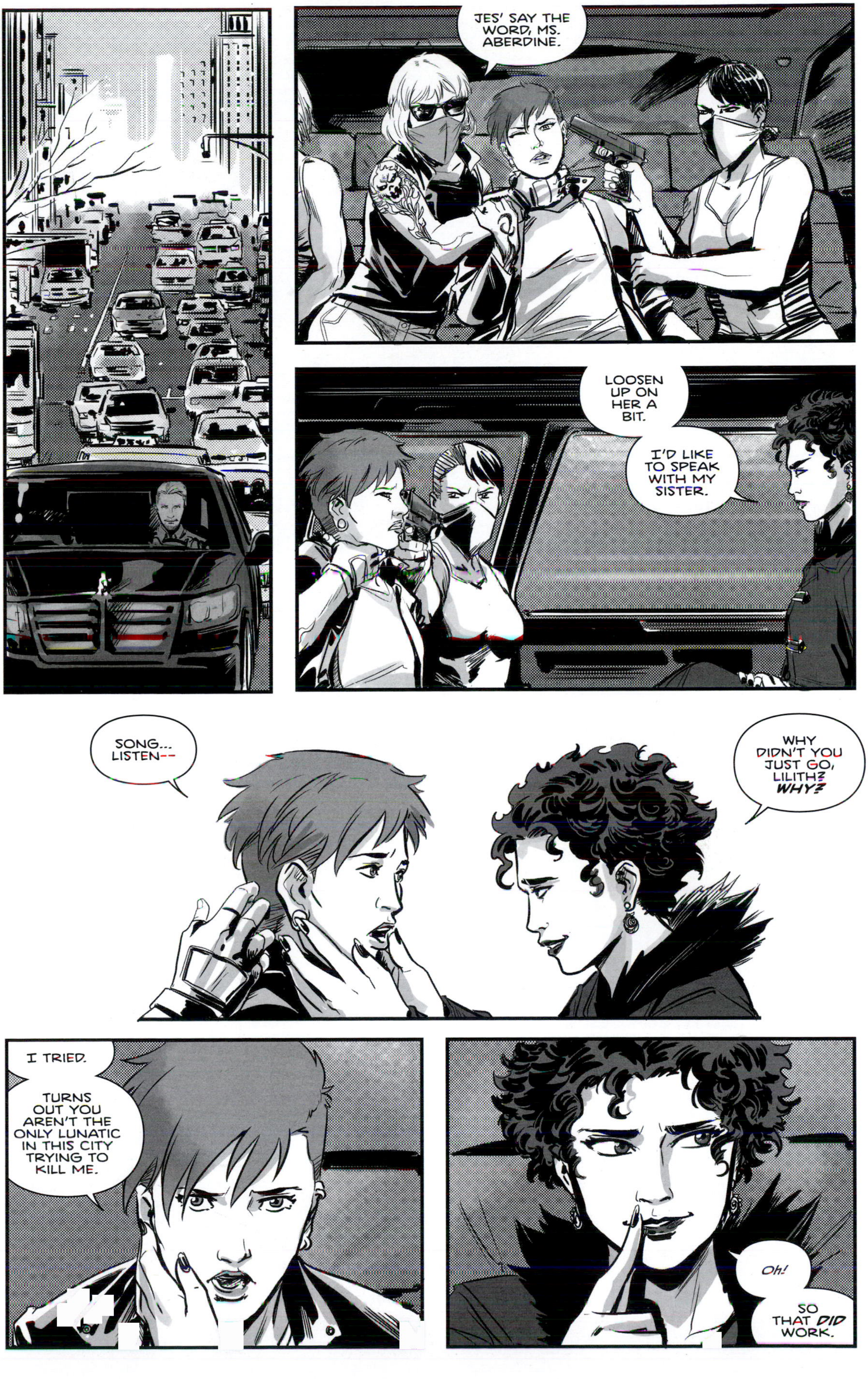
JES' SAY THE WORD, MS. ABERDINE.
LOOSEN UP ON HER A BIT.
I'D LIKE TO SPEAK WITH MY SISTER.
SONG... LISTEN--
WHY DIDN'T YOU JUST GO, LILITH? WHY?
I TRIED.
TURNS OUT YOU AREN'T THE ONLY LUNATIC IN THIS CITY TRYING TO KILL ME.
Oh!
SO THAT DID WORK.

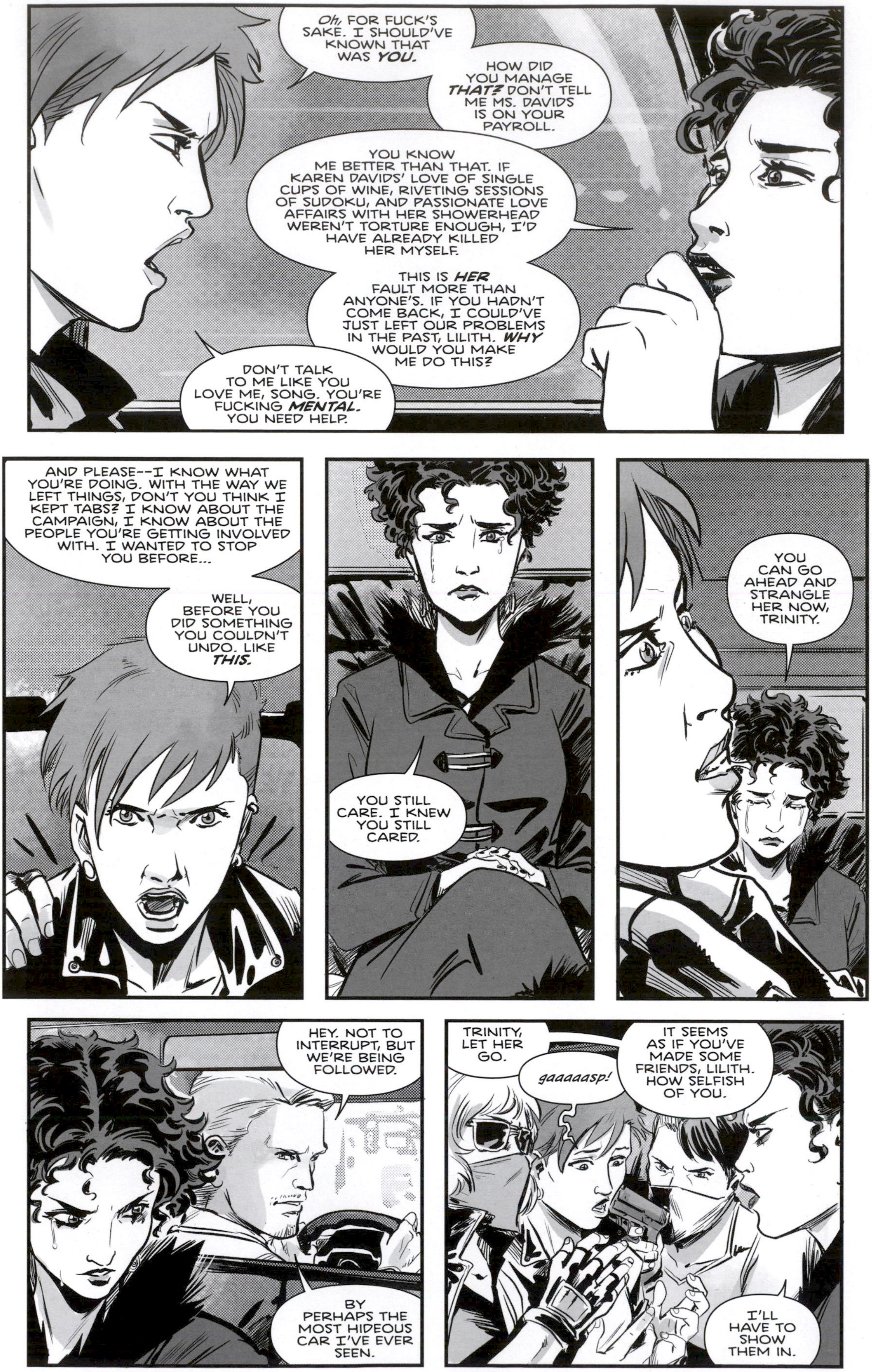

Oh, FOR FUCK'S SAKE. I SHOULD'VE KNOWN THAT WAS YOU.
HOW DID YOU MANAGE THAT? DON'T TELL ME MS. DAVIDS IS ON YOUR PAYROLL.
YOU KNOW ME BETTER THAN THAT. IF KAREN DAVIDS' LOVE OF SINGLE CUPS OF WINE, RIVETING SESSIONS OF SUDOKU, AND PASSIONATE LOVE AFFAIRS WITH HER SHOWERHEAD WEREN'T TORTURE ENOUGH, I'D HAVE ALREADY KILLED HER MYSELF.
THIS IS HER FAULT MORE THAN ANYONE'S. IF YOU HADN'T COME BACK, I COULD'VE JUST LEFT OUR PROBLEMS IN THE PAST, LILITH. WHY WOULD YOU MAKE ME DO THIS?
DON'T TALK TO ME LIKE YOU LOVE ME, SONG. YOU'RE FUCKING MENTAL. YOU NEED HELP.
AND PLEASE--I KNOW WHAT YOU'RE DOING. WITH THE WAY WE LEFT THINGS, DON'T YOU THINK I KEPT TABS? I KNOW ABOUT THE CAMPAIGN, I KNOW ABOUT THE PEOPLE YOU'RE GETTING INVOLVED WITH. I WANTED TO STOP YOU BEFORE...
WELL, BEFORE YOU DID SOMETHING YOU COULDN'T UNDO. LIKE THIS.
YOU STILL CARE. I KNEW YOU STILL CARED.
YOU CAN GO AHEAD AND STRANGLE HER NOW, TRINITY.
HEY. NOT TO INTERRUPT, BUT WE'RE BEING FOLLOWED.
BY PERHAPS THE MOST HIDEOUS CAR I'VE EVER SEEN.
TRINITY, LET HER GO.
gaaaaasp!
IT SEEMS AS IF YOU'VE MADE SOME FRIENDS, LILITH. HOW SELFISH OF YOU.
I'LL HAVE TO SHOW THEM IN.

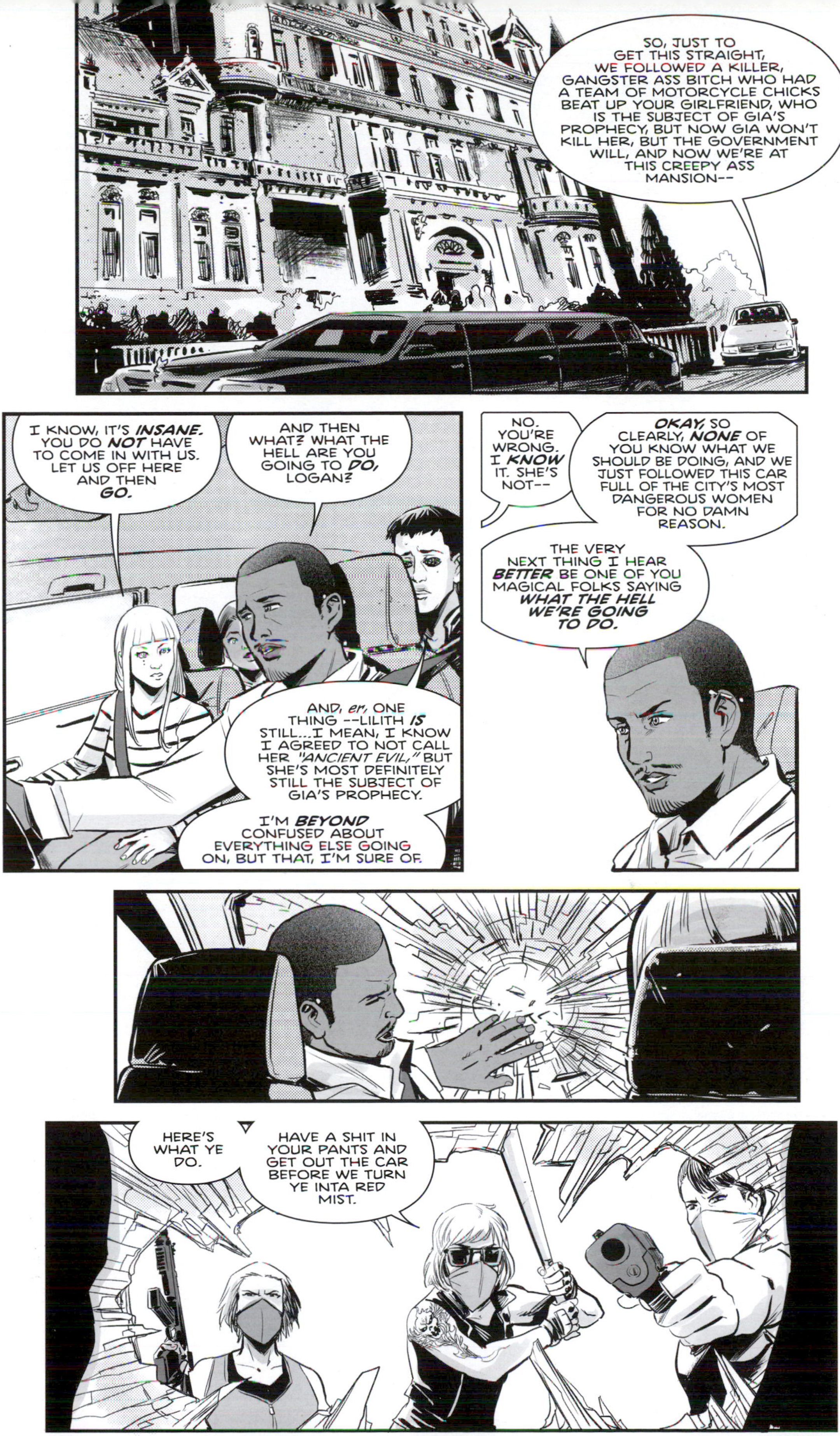
SO, JUST TO GET THIS STRAIGHT, WE FOLLOWED A KILLER, GANGSTER ASS BITCH WHO HAD A TEAM OF MOTORCYCLE CHICKS BEAT UP YOUR GIRLFRIEND, WHO IS THE SUBJECT OF GIA'S PROPHECY, BUT NOW GIA WON'T KILL HER, BUT THE GOVERNMENT WILL, AND NOW WE'RE AT THIS CREEPY ASS MANSION--
I KNOW, IT'S INSANE. YOU DO NOT HAVE TO COME IN WITH US. LET US OFF HERE AND THEN GO.
AND THEN WHAT? WHAT THE HELL ARE YOU GOING TO DO, LOGAN?
AND, er, ONE THING --LILITH IS STILL...I MEAN, I KNOW I AGREED TO NOT CALL HER "ANCIENT EVIL," BUT SHE'S MOST DEFINITELY STILL THE SUBJECT OF GIA'S PROPHECY.
I'M BEYOND CONFUSED ABOUT EVERYTHING ELSE GOING ON, BUT THAT, I'M SURE OF.
NO. YOU'RE WRONG. I KNOW IT. SHE'S NOT--
OKAY, SO CLEARLY, NONE OF YOU KNOW WHAT WE SHOULD BE DOING, AND WE JUST FOLLOWED THIS CAR FULL OF THE CITY'S MOST DANGEROUS WOMEN FOR NO DAMN REASON.
THE VERY NEXT THING I HEAR BETTER BE ONE OF YOU MAGICAL FOLKS SAYING WHAT THE HELL WE'RE GOING TO DO.
HERE'S WHAT YE DO.
HAVE A SHIT IN YOUR PANTS AND GET OUT THE CAR BEFORE WE TURN YE INTA RED MIST.

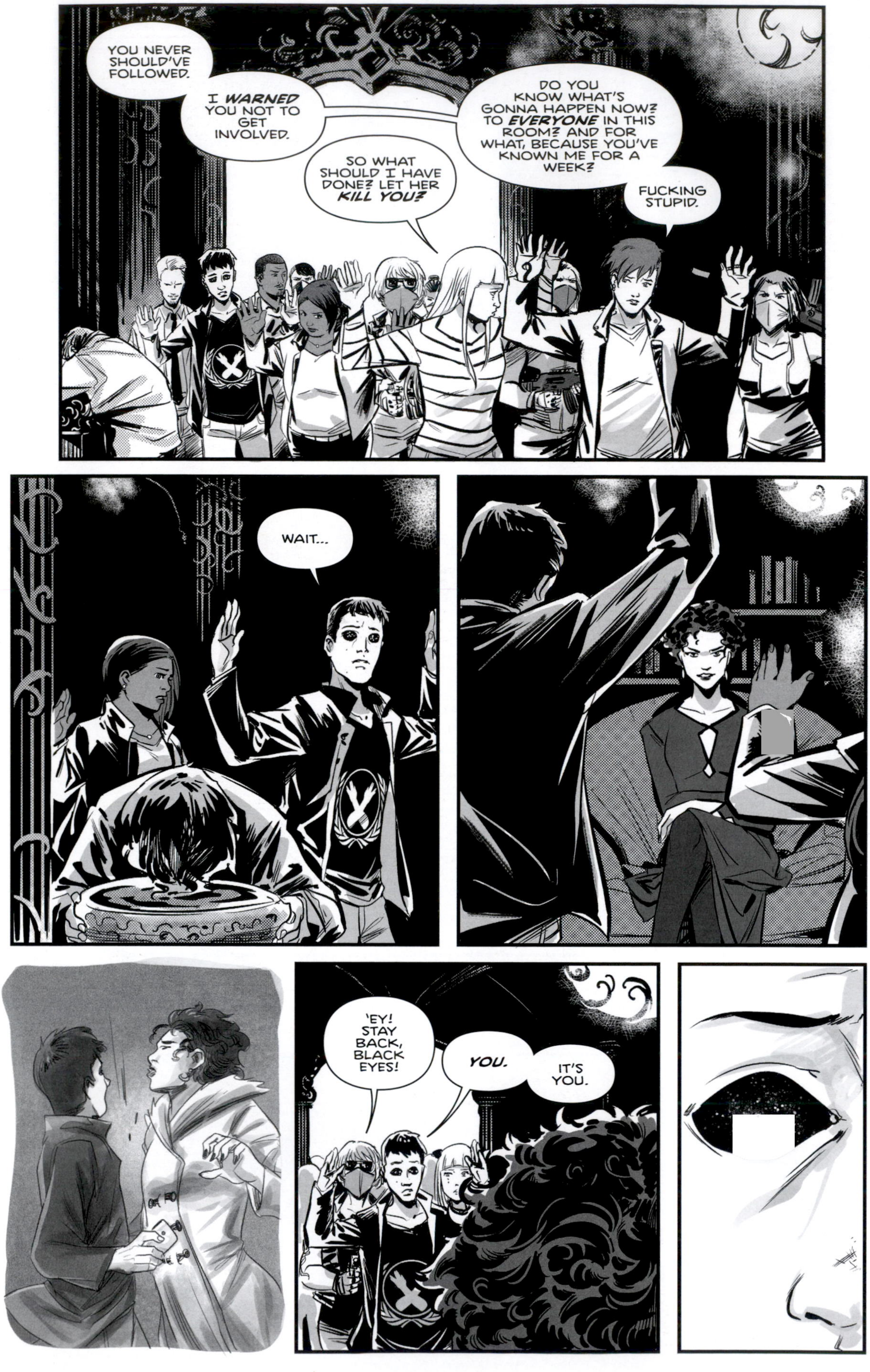

YOU NEVER SHOULD'VE FOLLOWED.
I WARNED YOU NOT TO GET INVOLVED.
DO YOU KNOW WHAT'S GONNA HAPPEN NOW? TO EVERYONE IN THIS ROOM? AND FOR WHAT, BECAUSE YOU'VE KNOWN ME FOR A WEEK?
SO WHAT SHOULD I HAVE DONE? LET HER KILL YOU?
FUCKING STUPID.
WAIT...
'EY! STAY BACK, BLACK EYES!
YOU.
IT'S YOU.

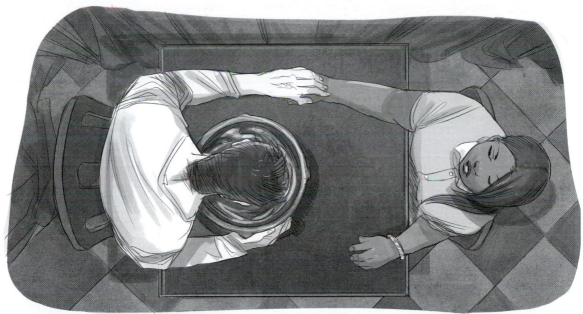

YOU WILL *FELL THE MOST* *ANCIENT EVIL* *ON THIS* *PLANE.*

WOW.

THAT'S *MAJOR.*

HEY, QUESTION. WHAT'S WITH THE *WATER?*

I'VE ALWAYS WONDERED THAT ABOUT SEERS. LIKE, WHY DO YOU NEED TO DUNK YOUR FACE IN THAT THING TO GET A CLEAR READING? AND DOES IT EVER GO UP YOUR NOSE?

IT'S A POWERFUL CONDUIT. I'VE NEVER HAD TO PUT IT INTO WORDS, SO IT MIGHT NOT MAKE SENSE...

BUT IT ACTS AS A BRIDGE BETWEEN THE *PHYSICAL BODY* AND THE *METAPHYSICAL SOUL.*

I...JUST TOLD YOU YOUR *DESTINY.* YOU'VE WAITED FOR YOUR ENTIRE LIFE TO KNOW THAT, AND YOU WANT TO KNOW WHY SEERS USE *WATER?*

HEY, I'M JUST KEEPING IT LIGHT, MAN. I'M AWARE THAT WHAT YOU JUST SAID IS *INTENSE* AND, YOU KNOW, *LIFE CHANGING...* BUT IT DOESN'T SEEM REAL, YOU KNOW?

I DO. THAT'S KIND OF HOW I FELT THE FIRST TIME I HAD A VISION.

SO...THE WATER?

WITHOUT IT, I CAN HAVE A VISION, BUT WITH IT--I CAN *SEE.*

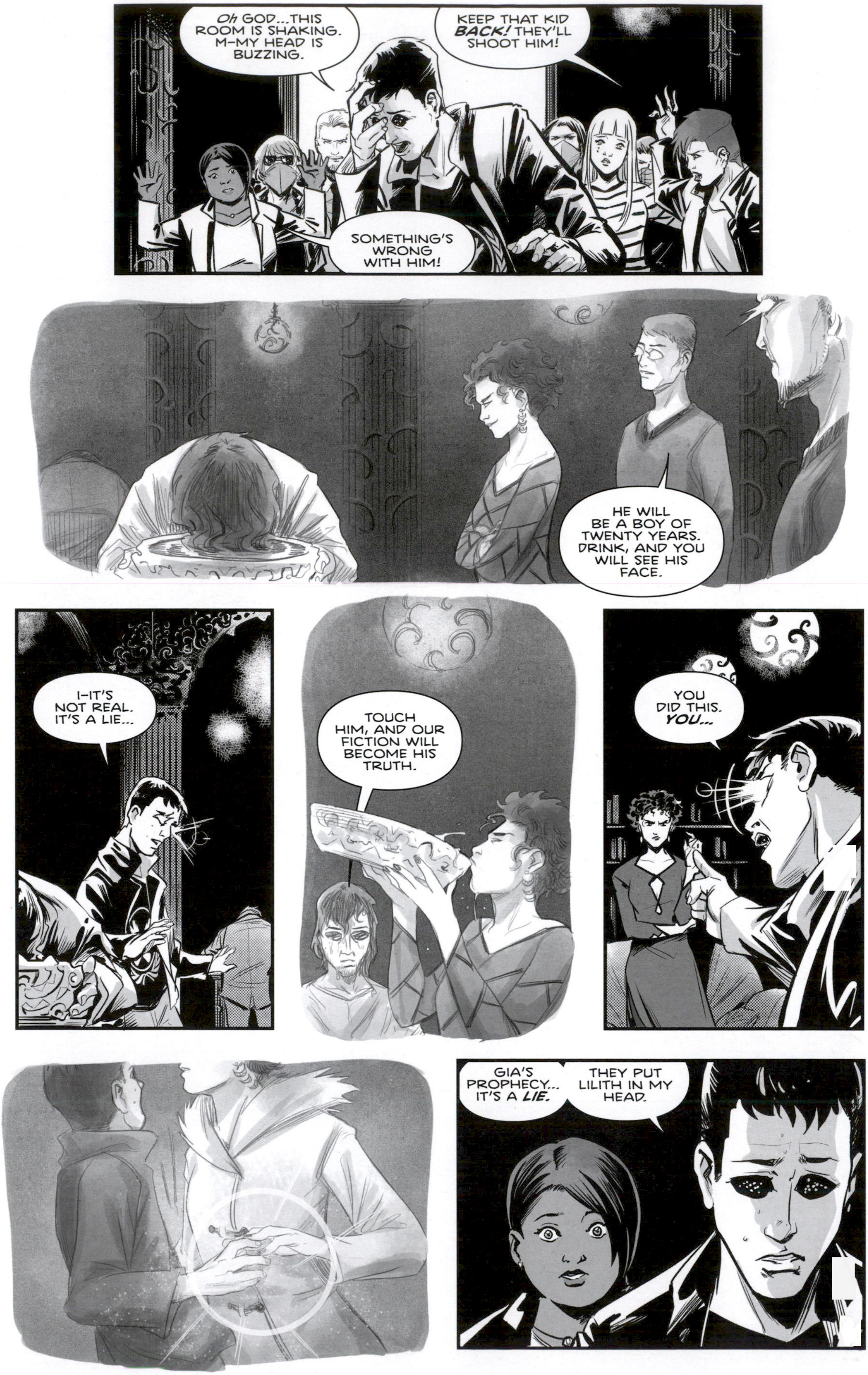
Oh GOD...THIS ROOM IS SHAKING. M-MY HEAD IS BUZZING.
KEEP THAT KID BACK! THEY'LL SHOOT HIM!
SOMETHING'S WRONG WITH HIM!
HE WILL BE A BOY OF TWENTY YEARS. DRINK, AND YOU WILL SEE HIS FACE.
I-IT'S NOT REAL. IT'S A LIE...
TOUCH HIM, AND OUR FICTION WILL BECOME HIS TRUTH.
YOU DID THIS. YOU...
GIA'S PROPHECY... IT'S A LIE.
THEY PUT LILITH IN MY HEAD.

S'ENOUGH OF THAT.

=GNN=

ANTHONY!

THANK YOU, TRINITY. I'M NOT SURE WHY HE THOUGHT THAT WAS WORTH SHARING.

I'M GONNA MAKE A RUN FOR SONG. IT'LL PROBABLY GIVE ME AN ANEURISM, BUT IT'LL GET THE ATTENTION OFF YOU TWO FOR A MINUTE.

WHEN I DO IT...YOU RUN. YOU FUCKING RUN AND YOU DO NOT LOOK BACK. OKAY?

MS. ABERDINE, SOMETHING'S WRONG WITH THE WATER BASINS.

SHUT UP. I WANT EVERY SEER EXCEPT THE BOY OUT OF THIS ROOM. NOW.

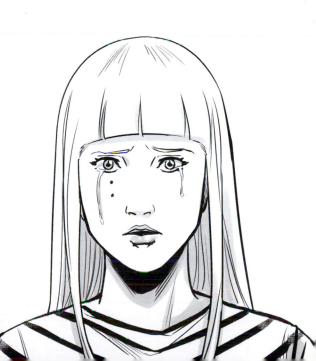

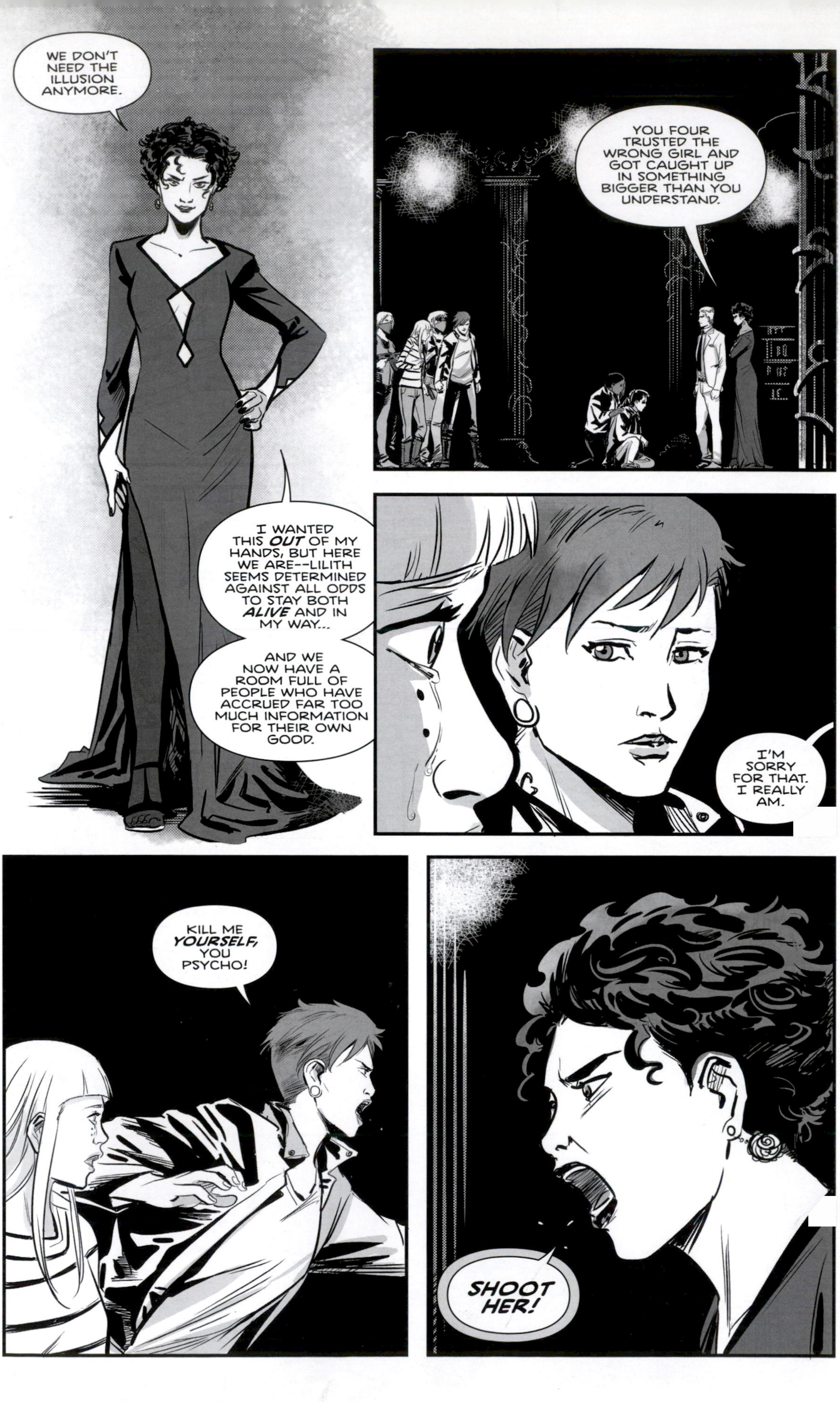
WE DON'T NEED THE ILLUSION ANYMORE.
YOU FOUR TRUSTED THE WRONG GIRL AND GOT CAUGHT UP IN SOMETHING BIGGER THAN YOU UNDERSTAND.
I WANTED THIS *OUT* OF MY HANDS, BUT HERE WE ARE--LILITH SEEMS DETERMINED AGAINST ALL ODDS TO STAY BOTH *ALIVE* AND IN MY WAY...
AND WE NOW HAVE A ROOM FULL OF PEOPLE WHO HAVE ACCRUED FAR TOO MUCH INFORMATION FOR THEIR OWN GOOD.
I'M SORRY FOR THAT. I REALLY AM.
KILL ME *YOURSELF,* YOU PSYCHO!
SHOOT HER!

You know that feeling when you see a home video from when you were a kid?

I can't think of anything else that feels that way. Even the happy memories ache.

BRATATATATATA

There's this one from the day I turned **three**. My parents filmed the entire day. They wrote LOGAN'S BIRTHDAY on a sticker, which stuck to the side of the tape until it eventually peeled off.

They still play that tape **every time** I go to visit them in California.

When I was younger, I would groan and stomp out of the room when they put it on.

But ever since they moved away...ever since I left Bailey... I watch it and I feel something **familiar** deep in my chest.

I watch myself, young and wide-eyed and squealing with laughter, and I feel as if I'm that little girl again. Like I never stopped being her.

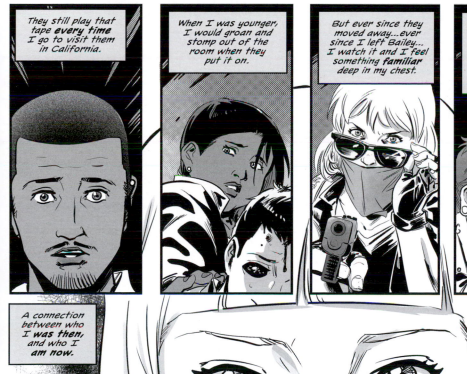

A connection between who I **was then**, and who I **am now**.

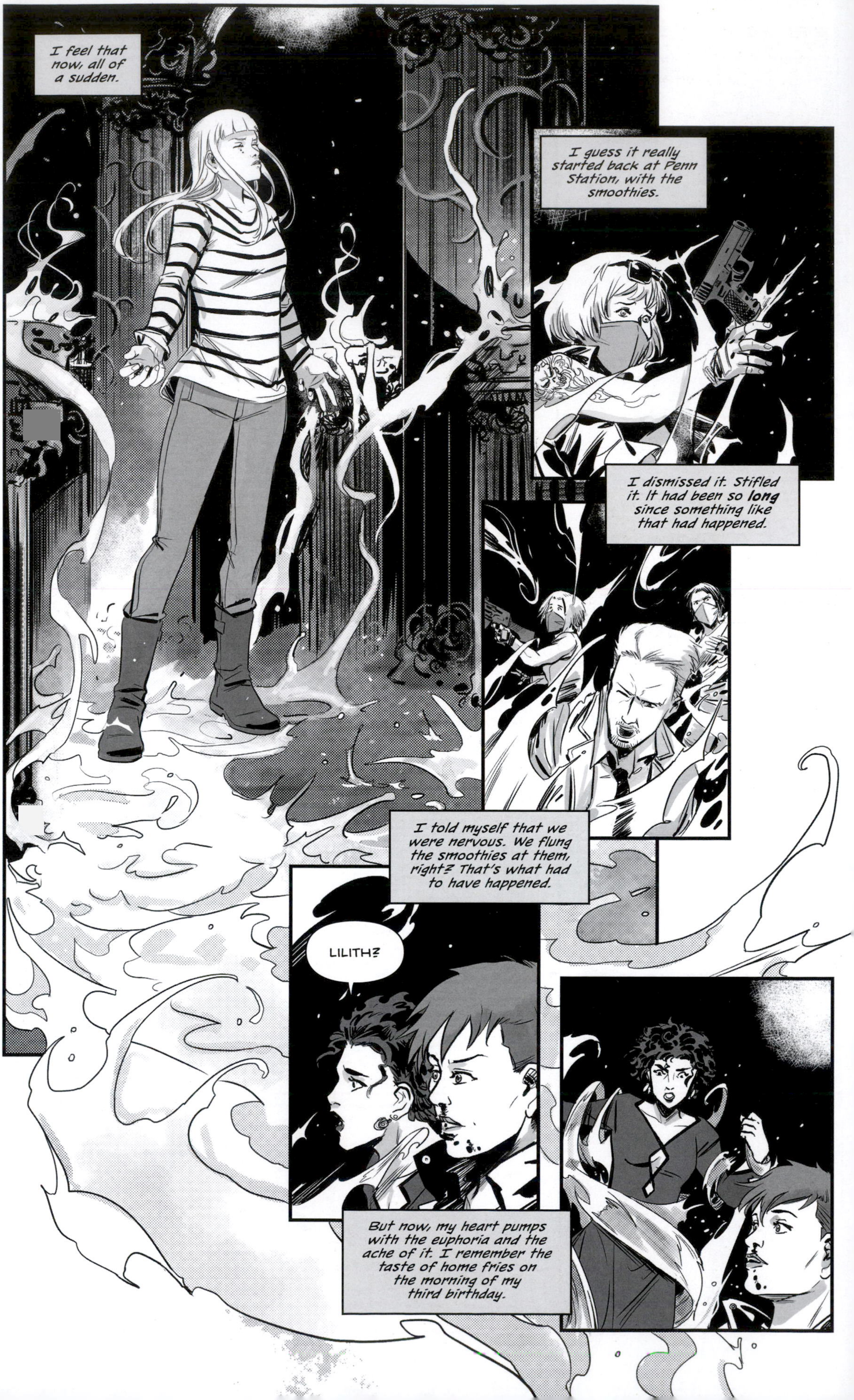
I feel that now, all of a sudden.
I guess it really started back at Penn Station, with the smoothies.
I dismissed it. Stifled it. It had been so **long** since something like that had happened.
I told myself that we were nervous. We flung the smoothies at them, right? That's what had to have happened.
LILITH?
But now, my heart pumps with the euphoria and the ache of it. I remember the taste of home fries on the morning of my third birthday.

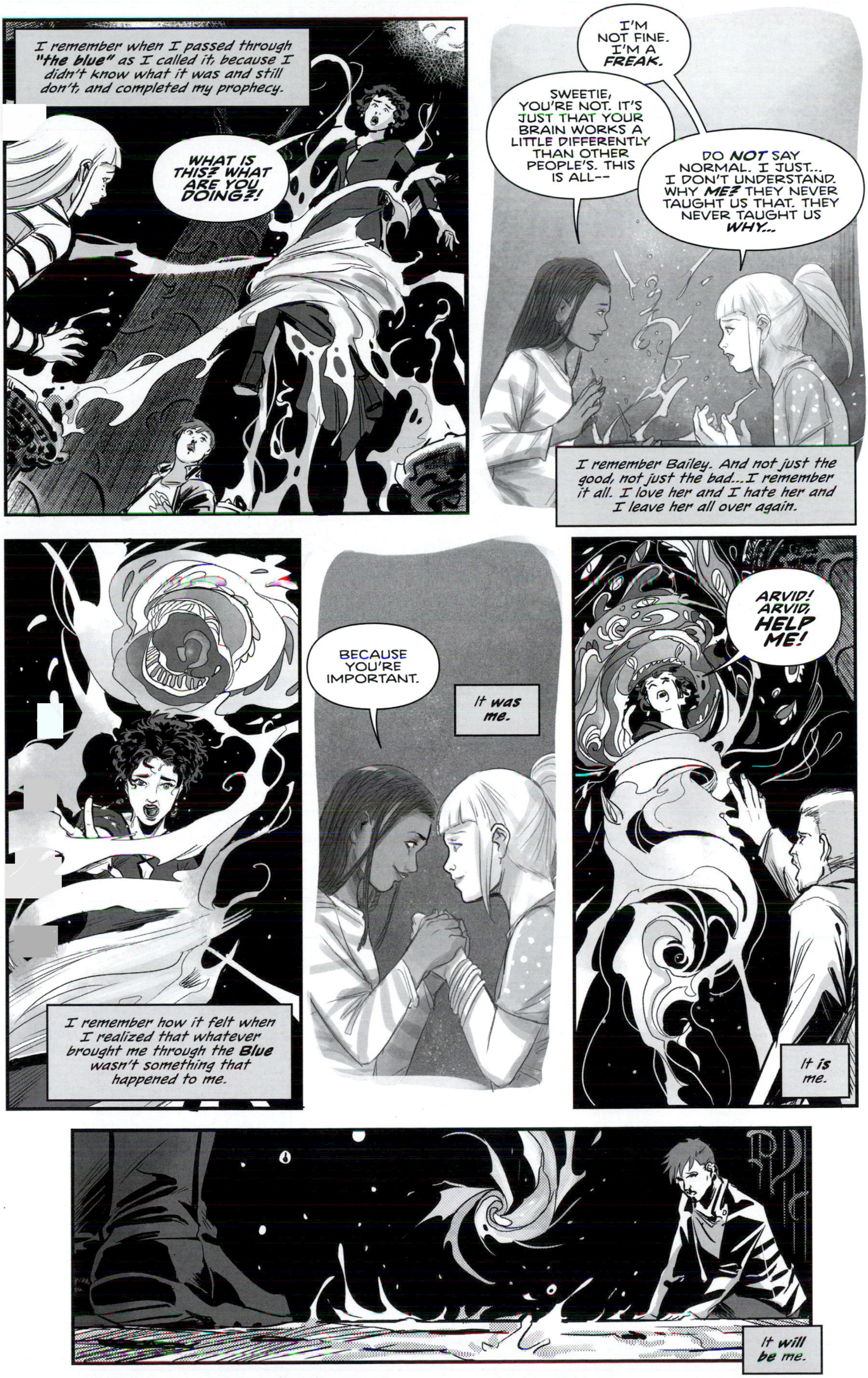
I remember when I passed through "the blue" as I called it, because I didn't know what it was and still don't, and completed my prophecy.
WHAT IS THIS?! WHAT ARE YOU DOING?!
I'M NOT FINE. I'M A FREAK.
SWEETIE, YOU'RE NOT. IT'S JUST THAT YOUR BRAIN WORKS A LITTLE DIFFERENTLY THAN OTHER PEOPLE'S. THIS IS ALL--
DO NOT SAY NORMAL. I JUST... I DON'T UNDERSTAND. WHY ME? THEY NEVER TAUGHT US THAT. THEY NEVER TAUGHT US WHY...
I remember Bailey. And not just the good, not just the bad... I remember it all. I love her and I hate her and I leave her all over again.
I remember how it felt when I realized that whatever brought me through the Blue wasn't something that happened to me.
BECAUSE YOU'RE IMPORTANT.
It was me.
ARVID! ARVID, HELP ME!
It is me.
It will be me.

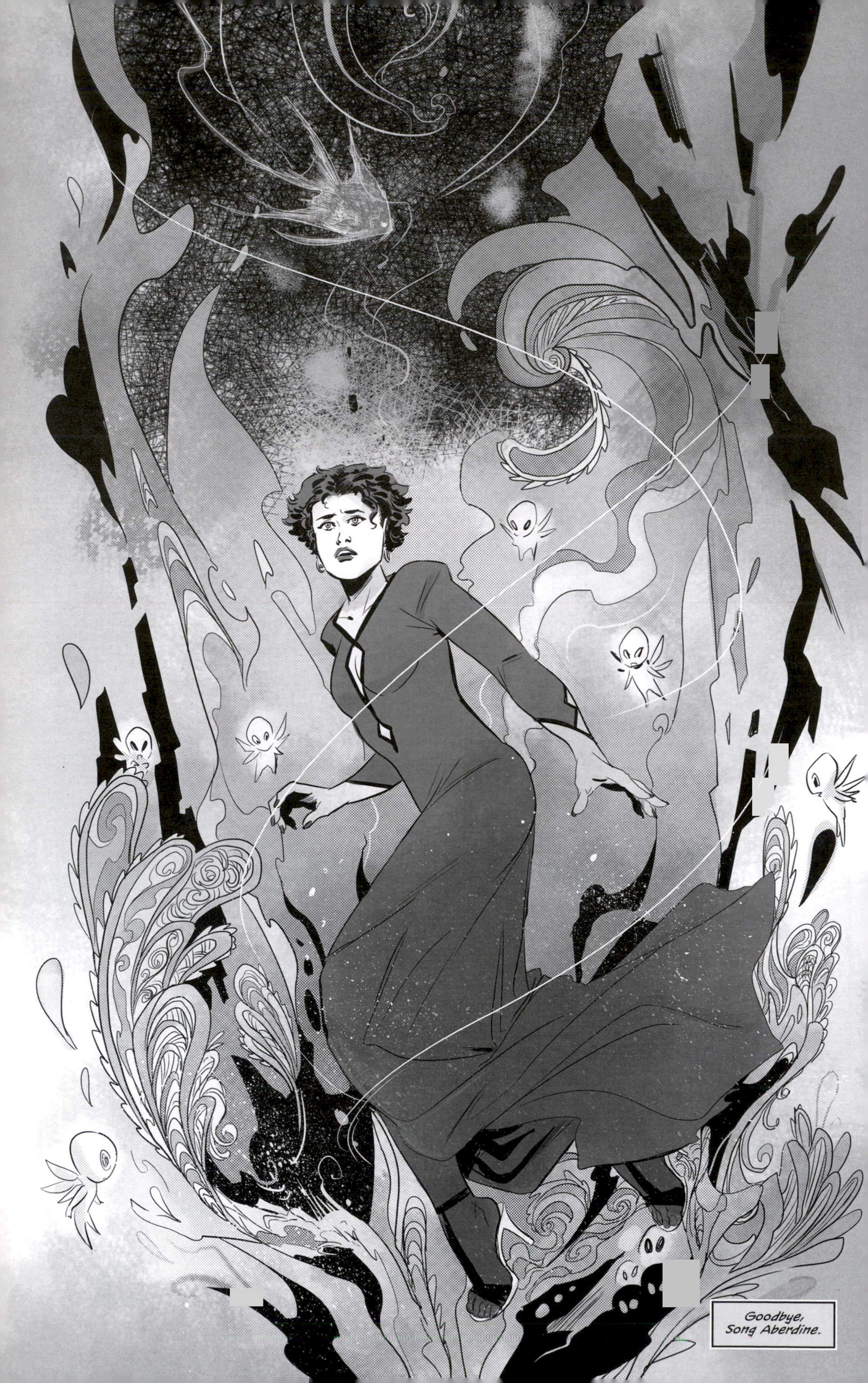
Goodbye, Song Aberdine.

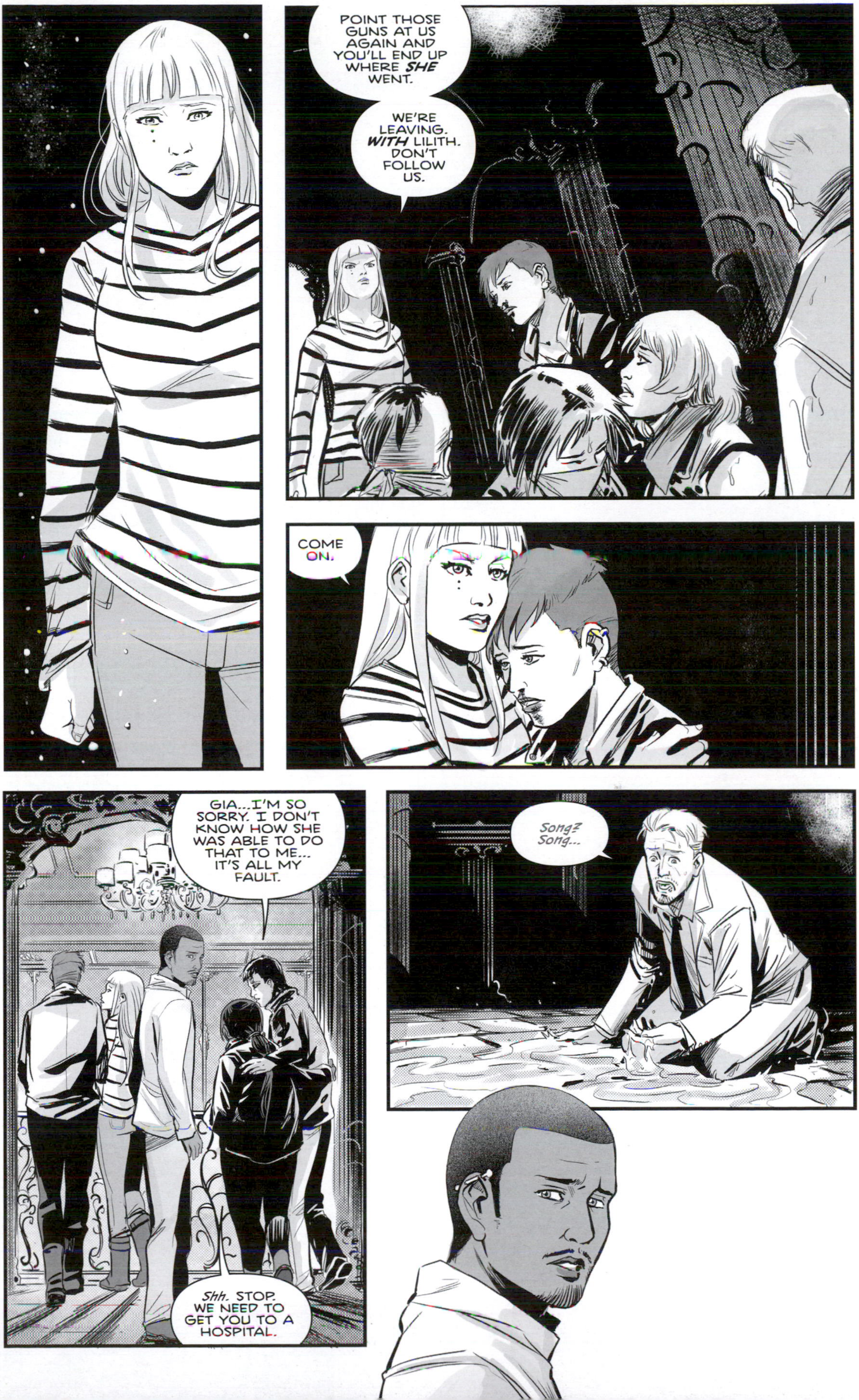

POINT THOSE GUNS AT US AGAIN AND YOU'LL END UP WHERE SHE WENT.
WE'RE LEAVING. WITH LILITH. DON'T FOLLOW US.
COME ON.
GIA...I'M SO SORRY. I DON'T KNOW HOW SHE WAS ABLE TO DO THAT TO ME... IT'S ALL MY FAULT.
Shh. STOP. WE NEED TO GET YOU TO A HOSPITAL.
Song? Song...

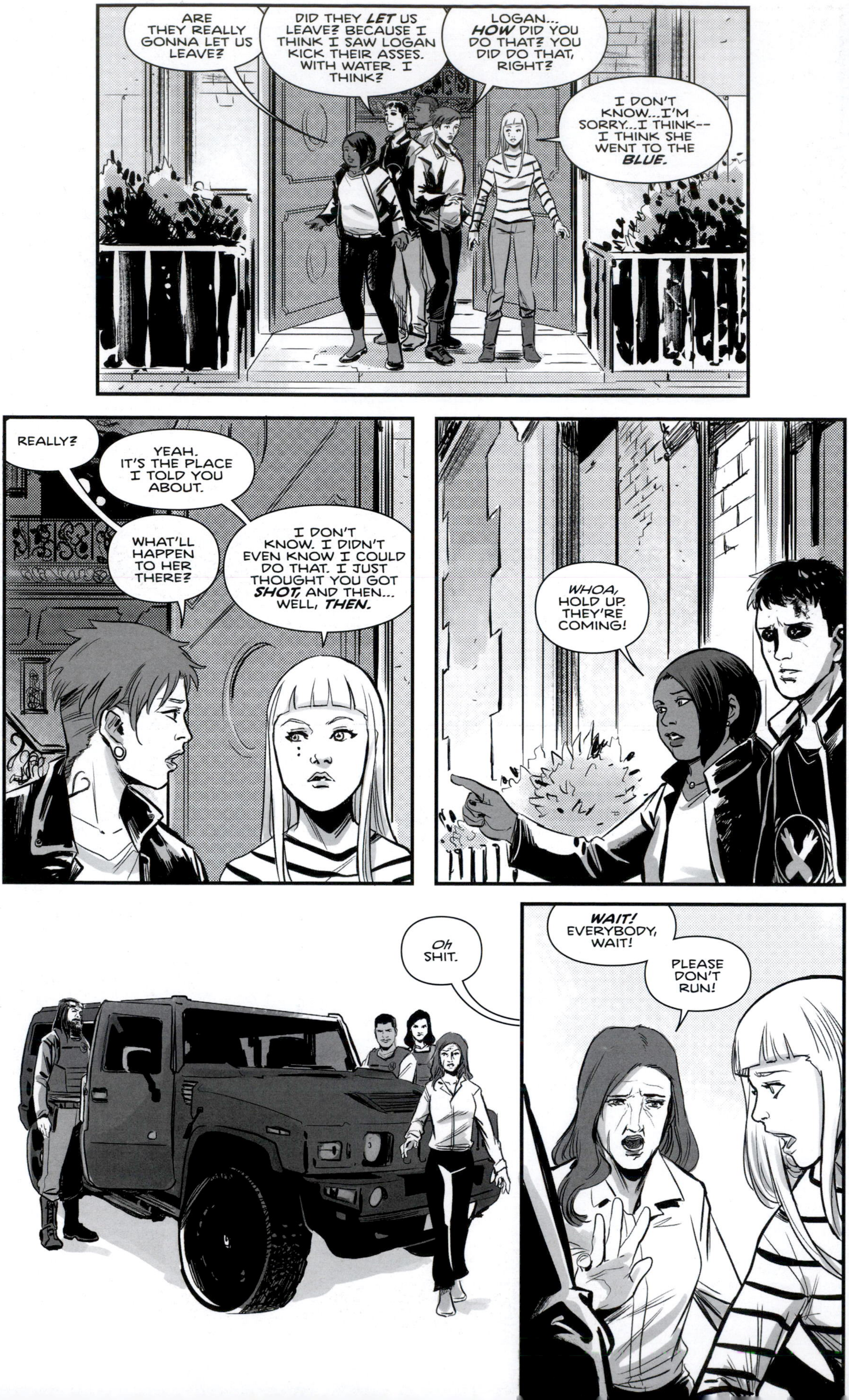
ARE THEY REALLY GONNA LET US LEAVE?
DID THEY LET US LEAVE? BECAUSE I THINK I SAW LOGAN KICK THEIR ASSES. WITH WATER. I THINK?
LOGAN... HOW DID YOU DO THAT? YOU DID DO THAT, RIGHT?
I DON'T KNOW...I'M SORRY...I THINK-- I THINK SHE WENT TO THE BLUE.
REALLY?
YEAH. IT'S THE PLACE I TOLD YOU ABOUT.
WHAT'LL HAPPEN TO HER THERE?
I DON'T KNOW. I DIDN'T EVEN KNOW I COULD DO THAT. I JUST THOUGHT YOU GOT SHOT, AND THEN... WELL, THEN.
WHOA, HOLD UP. THEY'RE COMING!
Oh SHIT.
WAIT! EVERYBODY, WAIT!
PLEASE DON'T RUN!

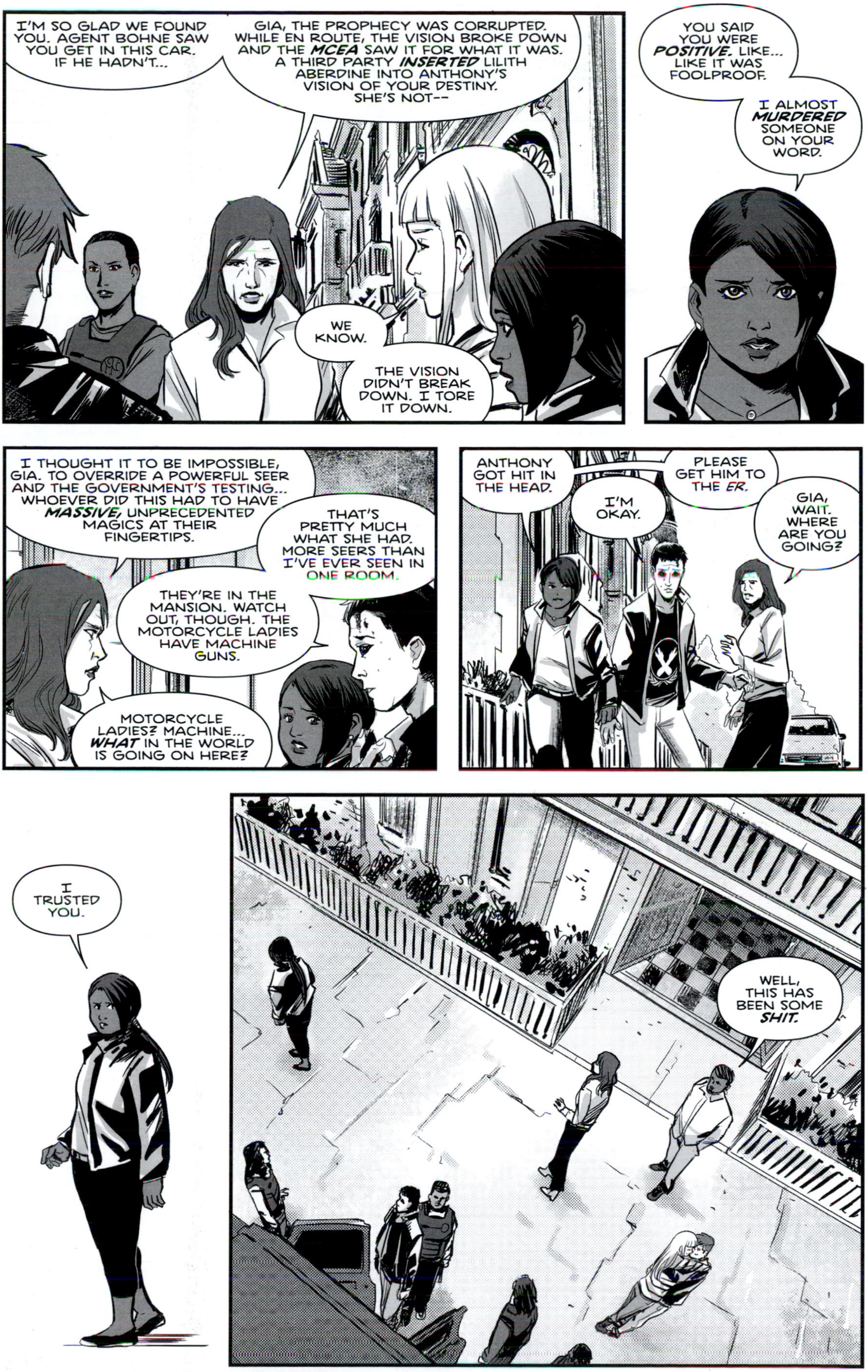
I'M SO GLAD WE FOUND YOU. AGENT BOHNE SAW YOU GET IN THIS CAR. IF HE HADN'T...
GIA, THE PROPHECY WAS CORRUPTED. WHILE EN ROUTE, THE VISION BROKE DOWN AND THE MCEA SAW IT FOR WHAT IT WAS. A THIRD PARTY INSERTED LILITH ABERDINE INTO ANTHONY'S VISION OF YOUR DESTINY. SHE'S NOT--
WE KNOW.
THE VISION DIDN'T BREAK DOWN. I TORE IT DOWN.
YOU SAID YOU WERE POSITIVE. LIKE... LIKE IT WAS FOOLPROOF.
I ALMOST MURDERED SOMEONE ON YOUR WORD.
I THOUGHT IT TO BE IMPOSSIBLE, GIA. TO OVERRIDE A POWERFUL SEER AND THE GOVERNMENT'S TESTING... WHOEVER DID THIS HAD TO HAVE MASSIVE, UNPRECEDENTED MAGICS AT THEIR FINGERTIPS.
THAT'S PRETTY MUCH WHAT SHE HAD. MORE SEERS THAN I'VE EVER SEEN IN ONE ROOM.
THEY'RE IN THE MANSION. WATCH OUT, THOUGH. THE MOTORCYCLE LADIES HAVE MACHINE GUNS.
MOTORCYCLE LADIES? MACHINE... WHAT IN THE WORLD IS GOING ON HERE?
ANTHONY GOT HIT IN THE HEAD.
PLEASE GET HIM TO THE ER.
I'M OKAY.
GIA, WAIT. WHERE ARE YOU GOING?
I TRUSTED YOU.
WELL, THIS HAS BEEN SOME SHIT.

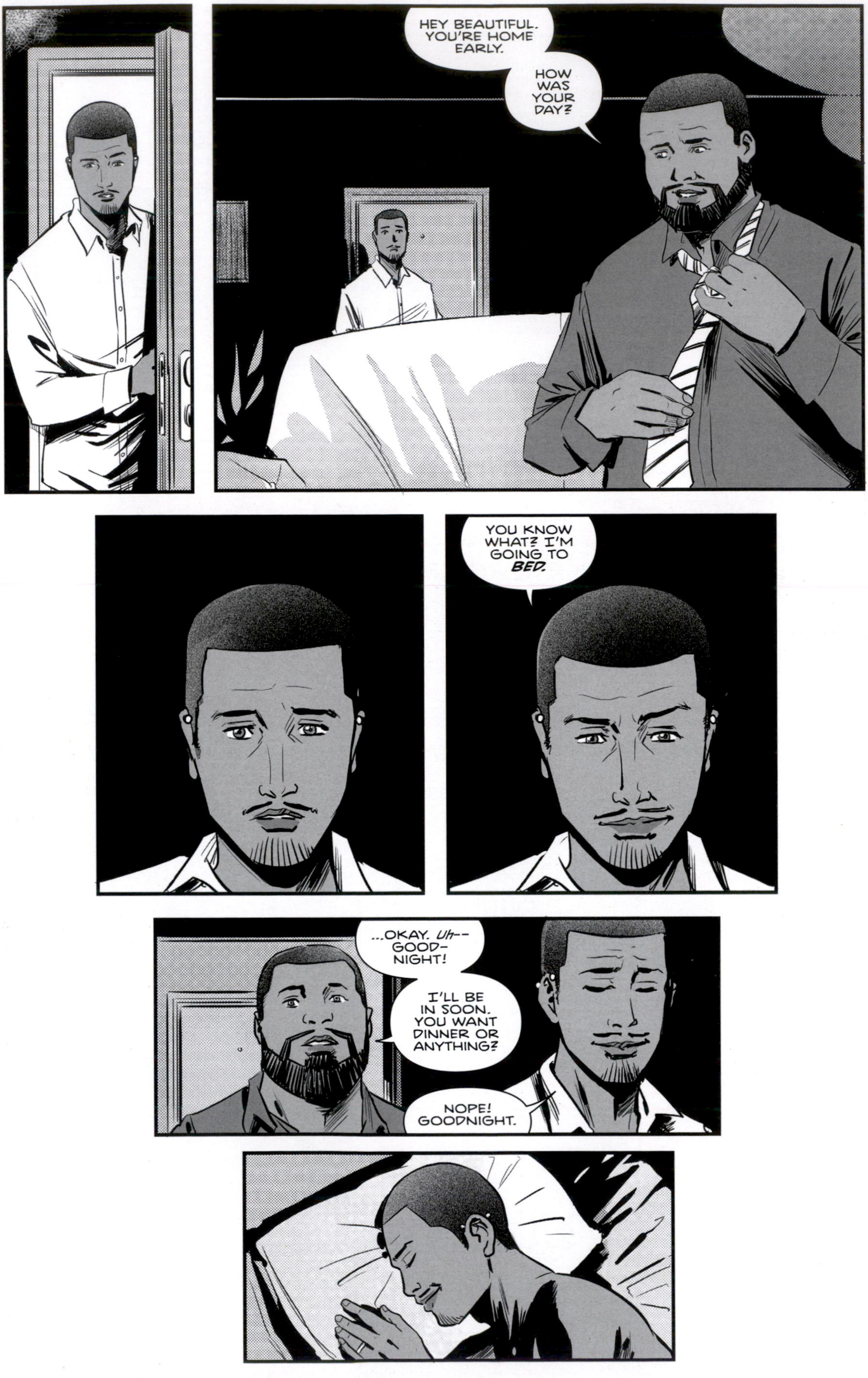
HEY BEAUTIFUL. YOU'RE HOME EARLY.
HOW WAS YOUR DAY?
YOU KNOW WHAT? I'M GOING TO *BED.*
...OKAY. *Uh--* GOOD-NIGHT!
I'LL BE IN SOON. YOU WANT DINNER OR ANYTHING?
NOPE! GOODNIGHT.

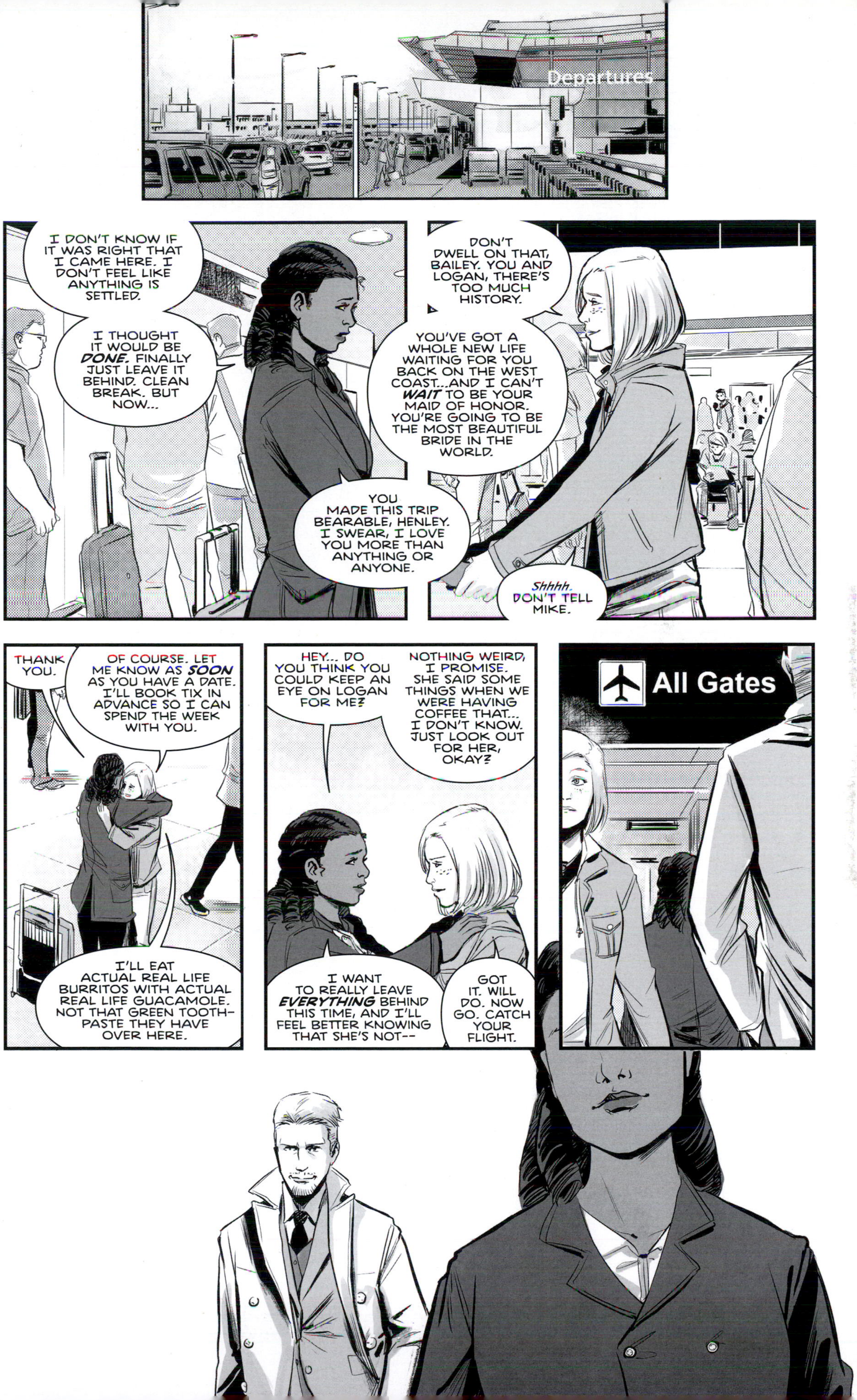
Departures
I DON'T KNOW IF IT WAS RIGHT THAT I CAME HERE. I DON'T FEEL LIKE ANYTHING IS SETTLED.
I THOUGHT IT WOULD BE DONE. FINALLY JUST LEAVE IT BEHIND. CLEAN BREAK. BUT NOW...
DON'T DWELL ON THAT, BAILEY. YOU AND LOGAN, THERE'S TOO MUCH HISTORY.
YOU'VE GOT A WHOLE NEW LIFE WAITING FOR YOU BACK ON THE WEST COAST...AND I CAN'T WAIT TO BE YOUR MAID OF HONOR. YOU'RE GOING TO BE THE MOST BEAUTIFUL BRIDE IN THE WORLD.
YOU MADE THIS TRIP BEARABLE, HENLEY. I SWEAR, I LOVE YOU MORE THAN ANYTHING OR ANYONE.
Shhhh. DON'T TELL MIKE.
THANK YOU.
OF COURSE. LET ME KNOW AS SOON AS YOU HAVE A DATE. I'LL BOOK TIX IN ADVANCE SO I CAN SPEND THE WEEK WITH YOU.
I'LL EAT ACTUAL REAL LIFE BURRITOS WITH ACTUAL REAL LIFE GUACAMOLE. NOT THAT GREEN TOOTH-PASTE THEY HAVE OVER HERE.
HEY... DO YOU THINK YOU COULD KEEP AN EYE ON LOGAN FOR ME?
NOTHING WEIRD, I PROMISE. SHE SAID SOME THINGS WHEN WE WERE HAVING COFFEE THAT... I DON'T KNOW. JUST LOOK OUT FOR HER, OKAY?
I WANT TO REALLY LEAVE EVERYTHING BEHIND THIS TIME, AND I'LL FEEL BETTER KNOWING THAT SHE'S NOT--
GOT IT. WILL DO. NOW GO. CATCH YOUR FLIGHT.
All Gates

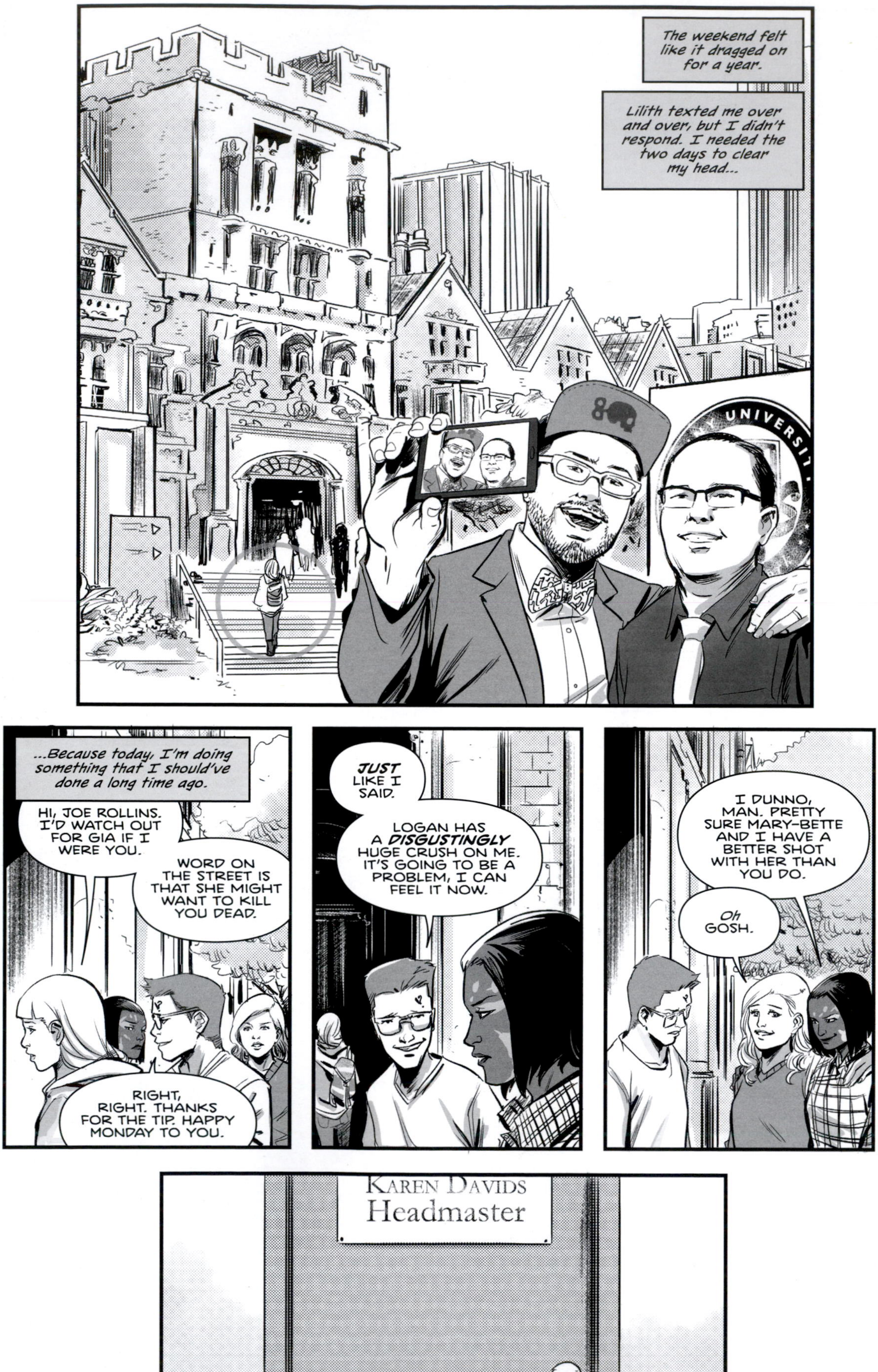

The weekend felt like it dragged on for a year.
Lilith texted me over and over, but I didn't respond. I needed the two days to clear my head...
UNIVERSIT
...Because today, I'm doing something that I should've done a long time ago.
HI, JOE ROLLINS. I'D WATCH OUT FOR GIA IF I WERE YOU.
WORD ON THE STREET IS THAT SHE MIGHT WANT TO KILL YOU DEAD.
RIGHT, RIGHT. THANKS FOR THE TIP. HAPPY MONDAY TO YOU.
JUST LIKE I SAID.
LOGAN HAS A DISGUSTINGLY HUGE CRUSH ON ME. IT'S GOING TO BE A PROBLEM, I CAN FEEL IT NOW.
I DUNNO, MAN. PRETTY SURE MARY-BETTE AND I HAVE A BETTER SHOT WITH HER THAN YOU DO.
Oh GOSH.
KAREN DAVIDS
Headmaster

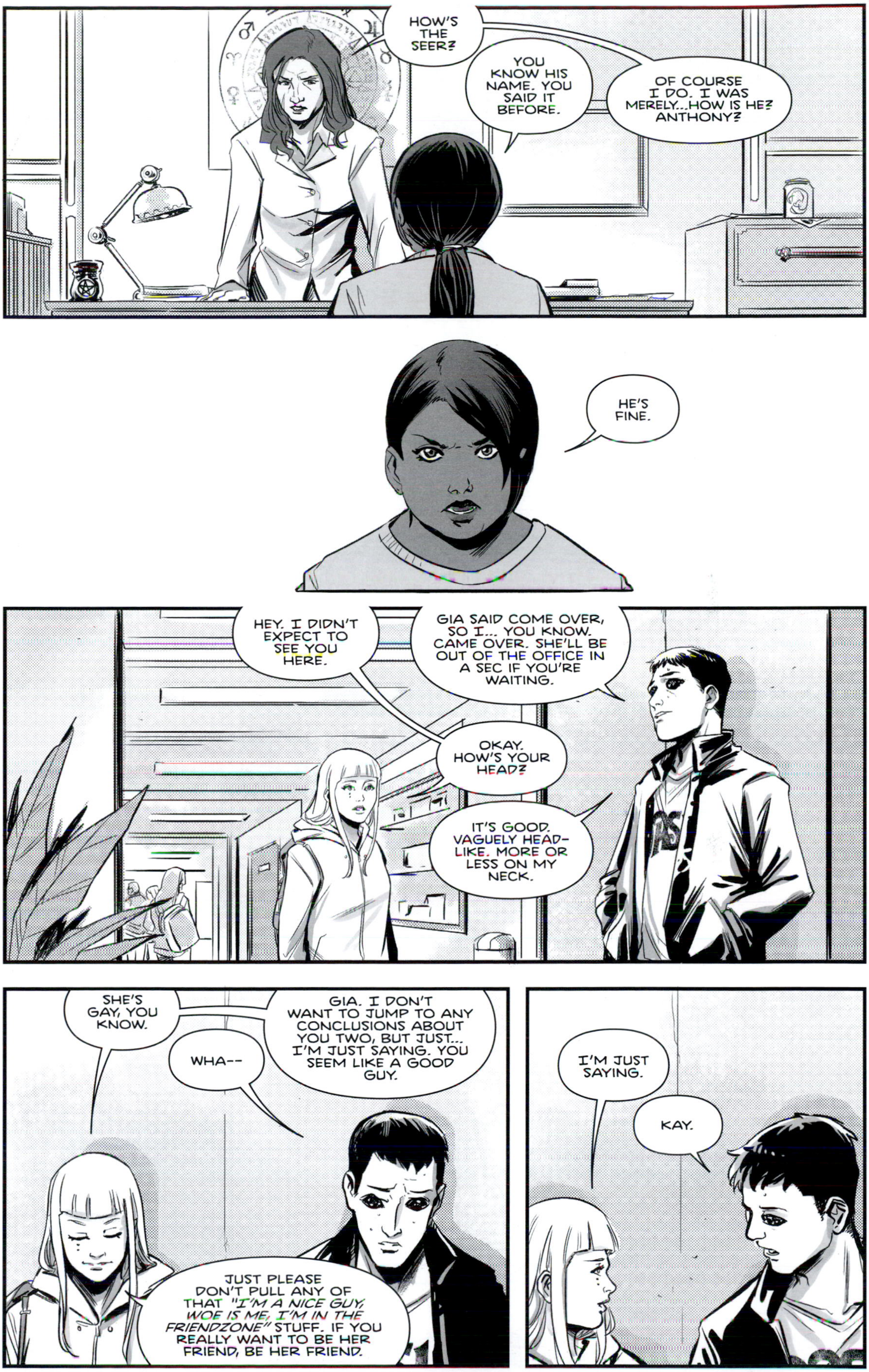
HOW'S THE SEER?
YOU KNOW HIS NAME. YOU SAID IT BEFORE.
OF COURSE I DO. I WAS MERELY...HOW IS HE? ANTHONY?
HE'S FINE.
HEY. I DIDN'T EXPECT TO SEE YOU HERE.
GIA SAID COME OVER, SO I... YOU KNOW. CAME OVER. SHE'LL BE OUT OF THE OFFICE IN A SEC IF YOU'RE WAITING.
OKAY. HOW'S YOUR HEAD?
IT'S GOOD. VAGUELY HEAD-LIKE. MORE OR LESS ON MY NECK.
SHE'S GAY, YOU KNOW.
WHA--
GIA. I DON'T WANT TO JUMP TO ANY CONCLUSIONS ABOUT YOU TWO, BUT JUST... I'M JUST SAYING. YOU SEEM LIKE A GOOD GUY.
JUST PLEASE DON'T PULL ANY OF THAT *"I'M A NICE GUY, WOE IS ME, I'M IN THE FRIENDZONE"* STUFF. IF YOU REALLY WANT TO BE HER FRIEND, BE HER FRIEND.
I'M JUST SAYING.
KAY.

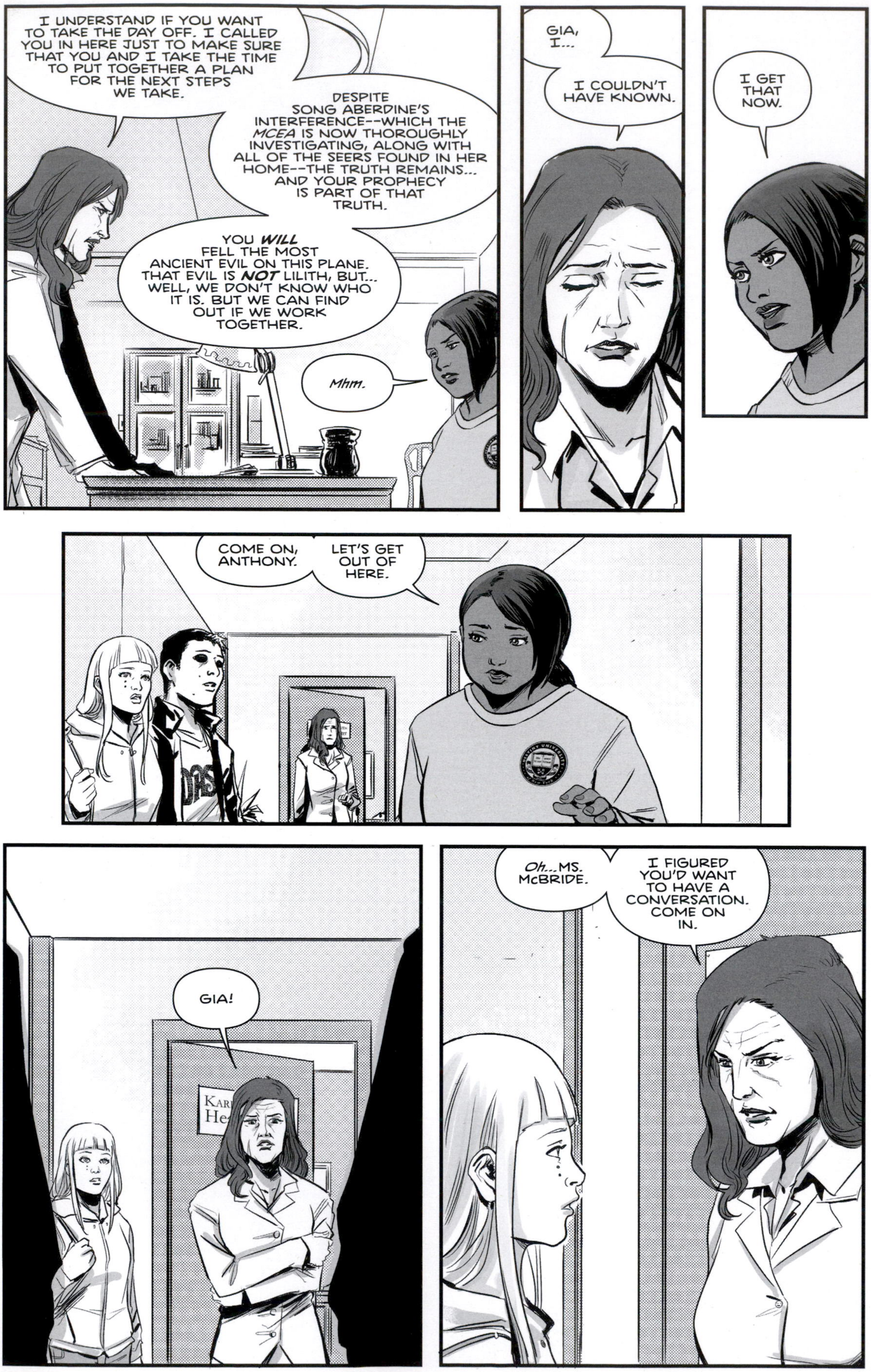
I UNDERSTAND IF YOU WANT TO TAKE THE DAY OFF. I CALLED YOU IN HERE JUST TO MAKE SURE THAT YOU AND I TAKE THE TIME TO PUT TOGETHER A PLAN FOR THE NEXT STEPS WE TAKE.
DESPITE SONG ABERDINE'S INTERFERENCE--WHICH THE *MCEA* IS NOW THOROUGHLY INVESTIGATING, ALONG WITH ALL OF THE SEERS FOUND IN HER HOME--THE TRUTH REMAINS... AND YOUR PROPHECY IS PART OF THAT TRUTH.
YOU ***WILL*** FELL THE MOST ANCIENT EVIL ON THIS PLANE. THAT EVIL IS ***NOT*** LILITH, BUT... WELL, WE DON'T KNOW WHO IT IS. BUT WE CAN FIND OUT IF WE WORK TOGETHER.
Mhm.
GIA, I...
I COULDN'T HAVE KNOWN.
I GET THAT NOW.
COME ON, ANTHONY.
LET'S GET OUT OF HERE.
GIA!
Oh... MS. McBRIDE.
I FIGURED YOU'D WANT TO HAVE A CONVERSATION. COME ON IN.

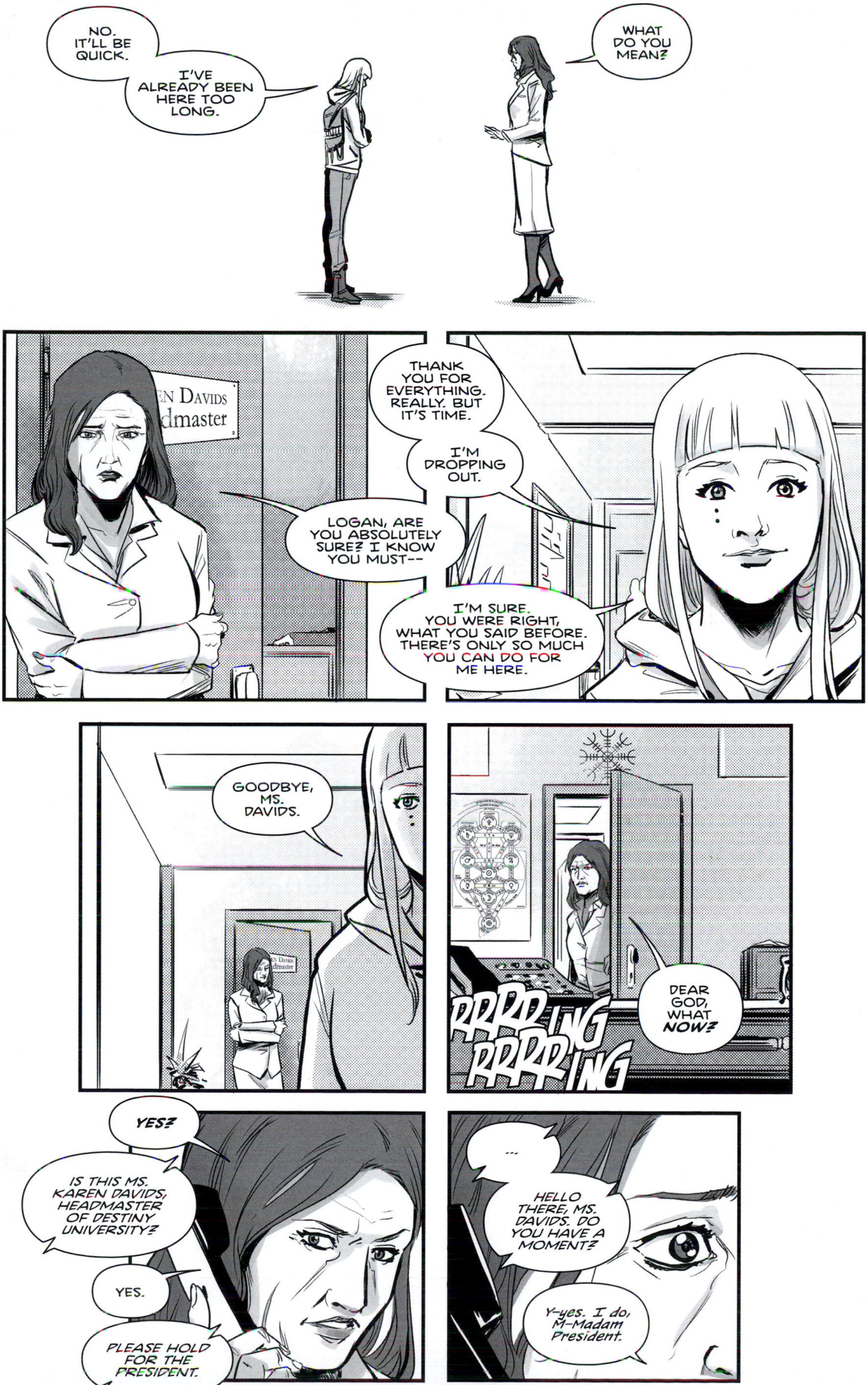
NO. IT'LL BE QUICK.
I'VE ALREADY BEEN HERE TOO LONG.
WHAT DO YOU MEAN?
EN DAVIDS
dmaster
THANK YOU FOR EVERYTHING. REALLY. BUT IT'S TIME.
I'M DROPPING OUT.
LOGAN, ARE YOU ABSOLUTELY SURE? I KNOW YOU MUST--
I'M SURE. YOU WERE RIGHT, WHAT YOU SAID BEFORE. THERE'S ONLY SO MUCH YOU CAN DO FOR ME HERE.
GOODBYE, MS. DAVIDS.
RRRRING
RRRRING
DEAR GOD, WHAT NOW?
YES?
IS THIS MS. KAREN DAVIDS, HEADMASTER OF DESTINY UNIVERSITY?
YES.
PLEASE HOLD FOR THE PRESIDENT.
...
HELLO THERE, MS. DAVIDS. DO YOU HAVE A MOMENT?
Y-yes. I do, M-Madam President.

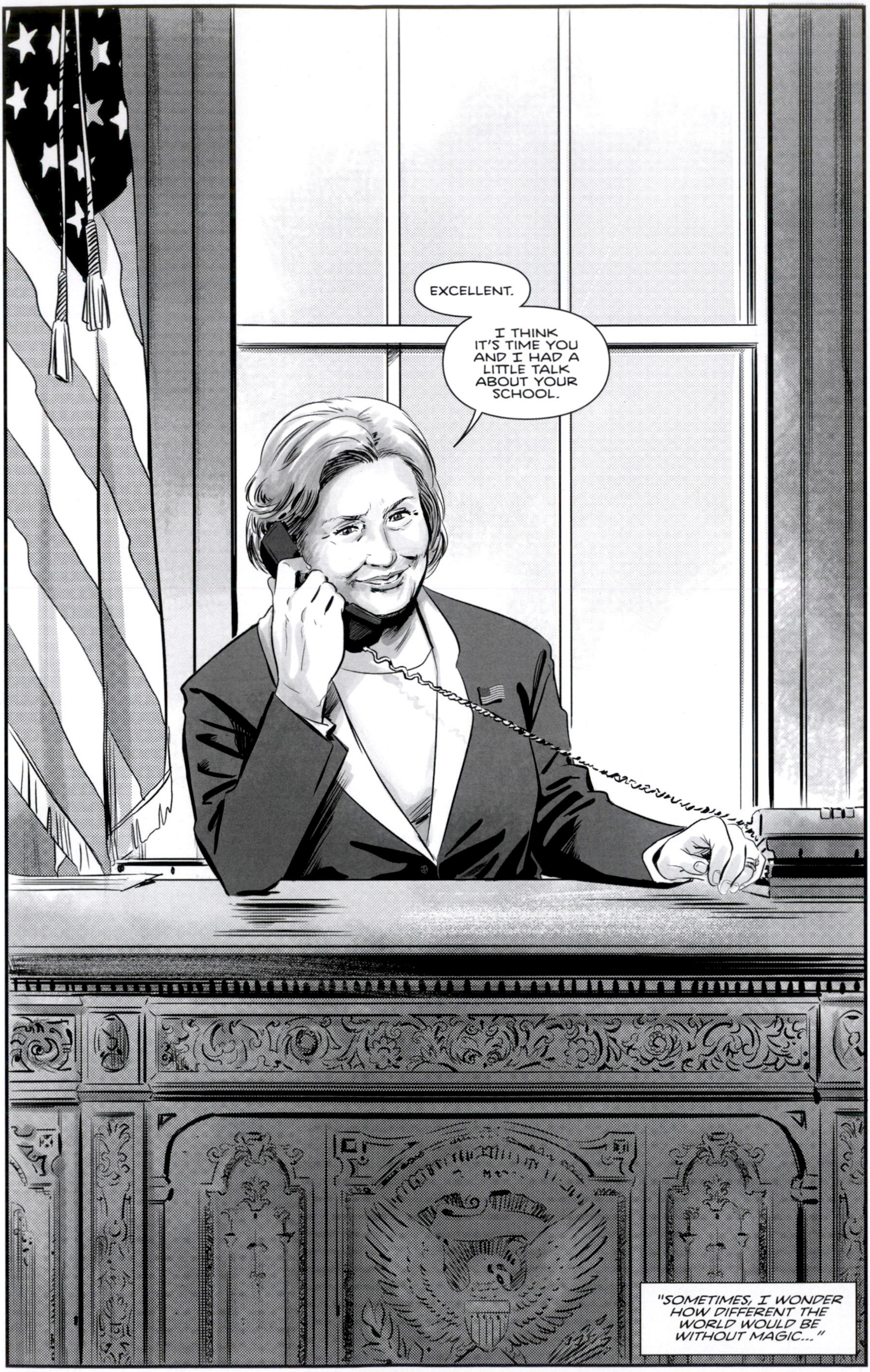
EXCELLENT.
I THINK IT'S TIME YOU AND I HAD A LITTLE TALK ABOUT YOUR SCHOOL.
"SOMETIMES, I WONDER HOW DIFFERENT THE WORLD WOULD BE WITHOUT MAGIC..."

"IF THINGS WOULD BE ANY BETTER FOR US...

"PROBABLY NOT, THOUGH."

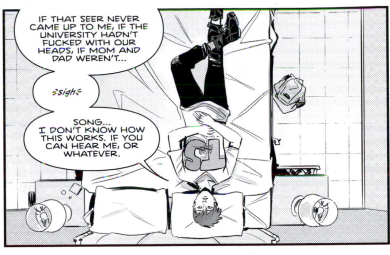

IF THAT SEER NEVER CAME UP TO ME, IF THE UNIVERSITY HADN'T FUCKED WITH OUR HEADS, IF MOM AND DAD WEREN'T...

≷sigh≷

SONG... I DON'T KNOW HOW THIS WORKS. IF YOU CAN HEAR ME, OR WHATEVER.

I CAN'T EVEN BEGIN TO UNDERSTAND IT, AND I'M PRETTY SURE LOGAN'S DONE WITH ME, SOOOO THERE GOES AN EXPLANATION. BUT IF YOU CAN HEAR ME, I HOPE THAT--

KNOK KNOK

HOLD THAT THOUGHT.

NO BAT THIS TIME.

NO BAT.

I TEXTED YOU A BUNCH. WASN'T SURE IF YOU'D COME BACK.

I'M SORRY I DIDN'T GET BACK TO YOU. I JUST NEEDED TO... JUST BE ME FOR A LITTLE BIT.

HOW'D THAT GO?

DEPENDS. ARE YOU STAYING IN NEW YORK?

YEAH. I'M STAYING.

CAN I GET YOU ANYTHING? DRINK OR SOMETHING?

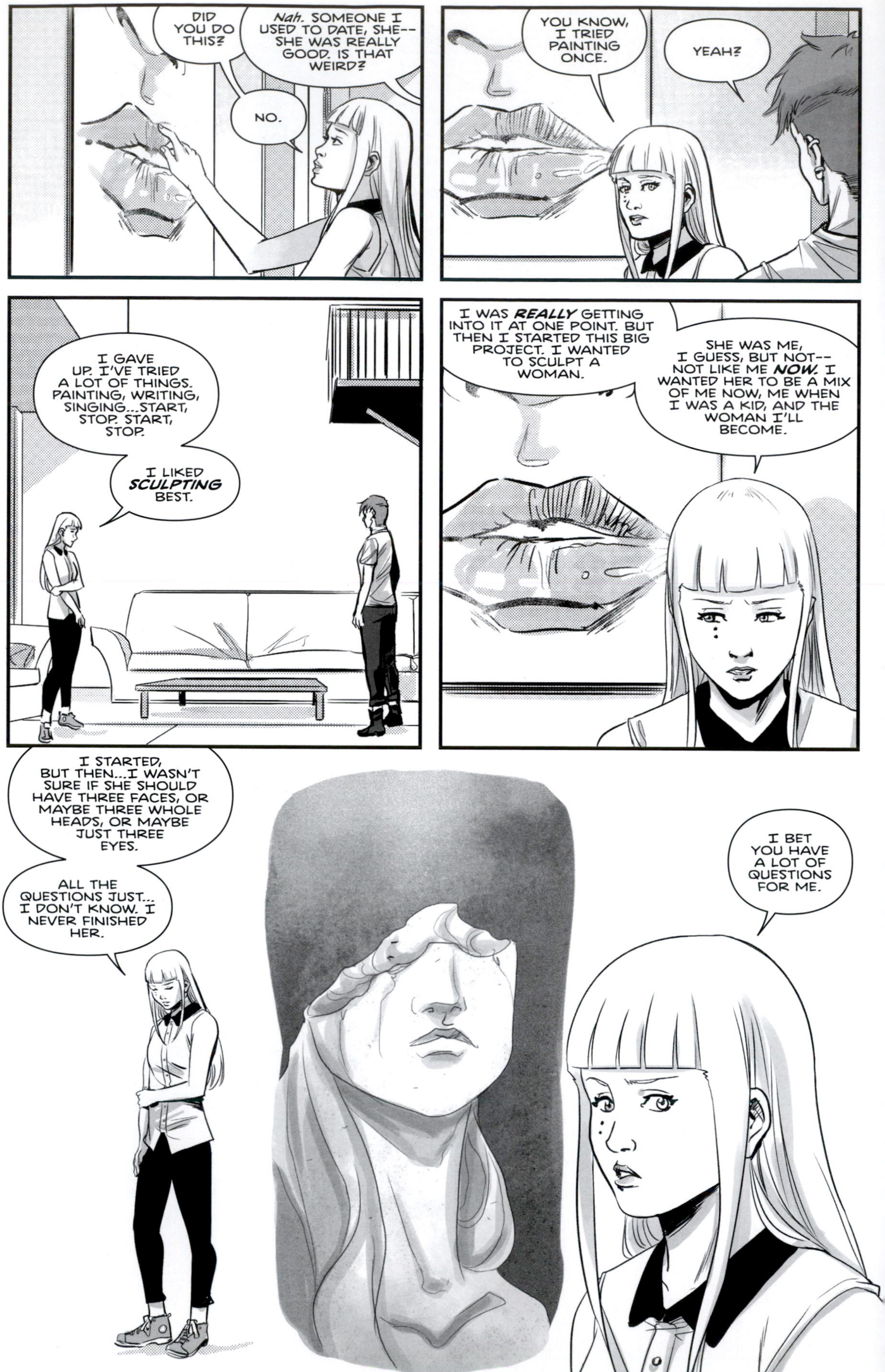
DID YOU DO THIS?
Nah. SOMEONE I USED TO DATE, SHE-- SHE WAS REALLY GOOD. IS THAT WEIRD?
NO.
YOU KNOW, I TRIED PAINTING ONCE.
YEAH?
I GAVE UP. I'VE TRIED A LOT OF THINGS. PAINTING, WRITING, SINGING... START, STOP. START, STOP.
I LIKED SCULPTING BEST.
I WAS REALLY GETTING INTO IT AT ONE POINT. BUT THEN I STARTED THIS BIG PROJECT. I WANTED TO SCULPT A WOMAN.
SHE WAS ME, I GUESS, BUT NOT-- NOT LIKE ME NOW. I WANTED HER TO BE A MIX OF ME NOW, ME WHEN I WAS A KID, AND THE WOMAN I'LL BECOME.
I STARTED, BUT THEN... I WASN'T SURE IF SHE SHOULD HAVE THREE FACES, OR MAYBE THREE WHOLE HEADS, OR MAYBE JUST THREE EYES.
ALL THE QUESTIONS JUST... I DON'T KNOW. I NEVER FINISHED HER.
I BET YOU HAVE A LOT OF QUESTIONS FOR ME.

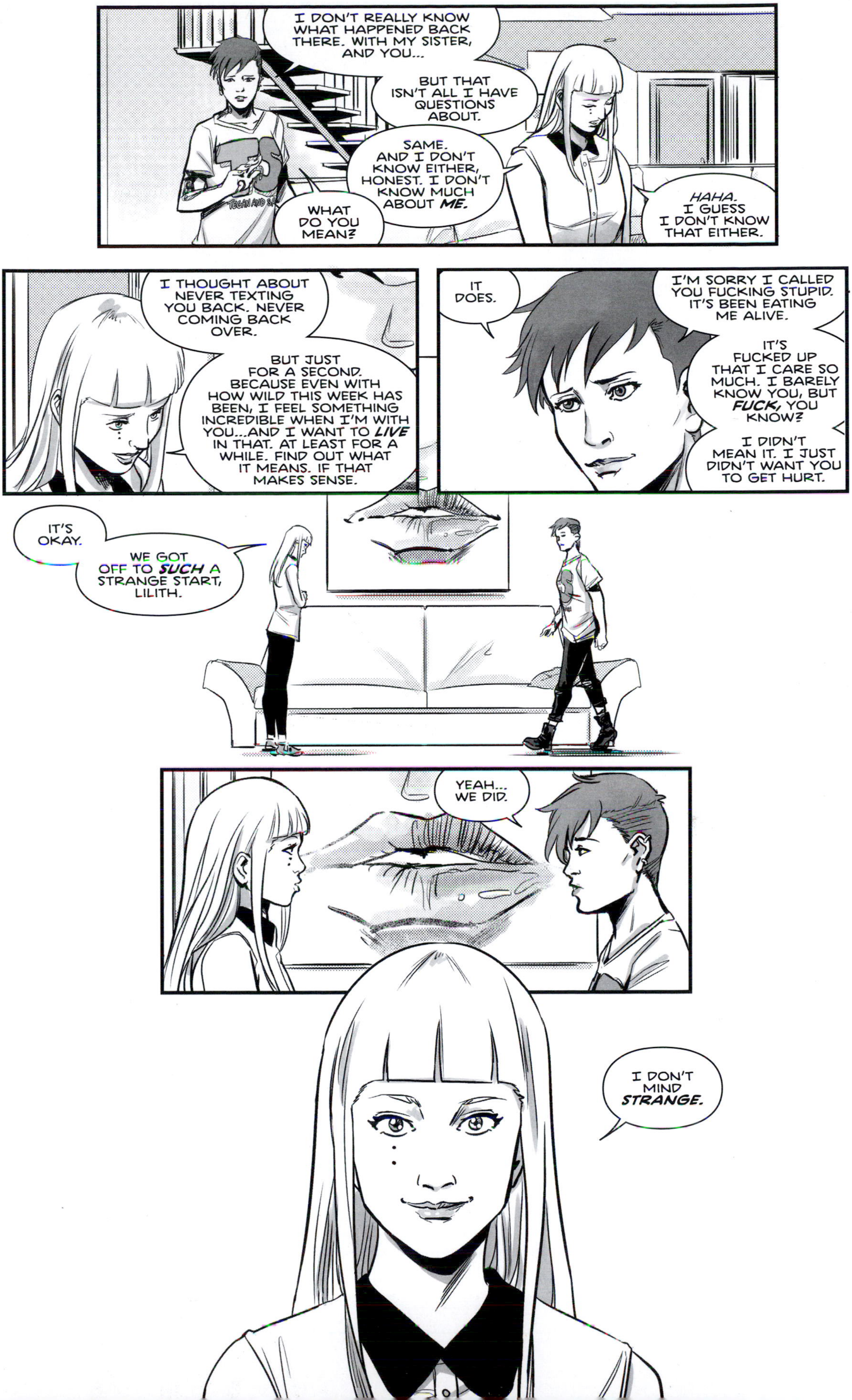
I DON'T REALLY KNOW WHAT HAPPENED BACK THERE. WITH MY SISTER, AND YOU...
BUT THAT ISN'T ALL I HAVE QUESTIONS ABOUT.
SAME. AND I DON'T KNOW EITHER, HONEST. I DON'T KNOW MUCH ABOUT ME.
WHAT DO YOU MEAN?
HAHA. I GUESS I DON'T KNOW THAT EITHER.
I THOUGHT ABOUT NEVER TEXTING YOU BACK. NEVER COMING BACK OVER.
BUT JUST FOR A SECOND. BECAUSE EVEN WITH HOW WILD THIS WEEK HAS BEEN, I FEEL SOMETHING INCREDIBLE WHEN I'M WITH YOU...AND I WANT TO LIVE IN THAT. AT LEAST FOR A WHILE. FIND OUT WHAT IT MEANS. IF THAT MAKES SENSE.
IT DOES.
I'M SORRY I CALLED YOU FUCKING STUPID. IT'S BEEN EATING ME ALIVE.
IT'S FUCKED UP THAT I CARE SO MUCH. I BARELY KNOW YOU, BUT FUCK, YOU KNOW?
I DIDN'T MEAN IT. I JUST DIDN'T WANT YOU TO GET HURT.
IT'S OKAY.
WE GOT OFF TO SUCH A STRANGE START, LILITH.
YEAH... WE DID.
I DON'T MIND STRANGE.
TEGAN AND SA

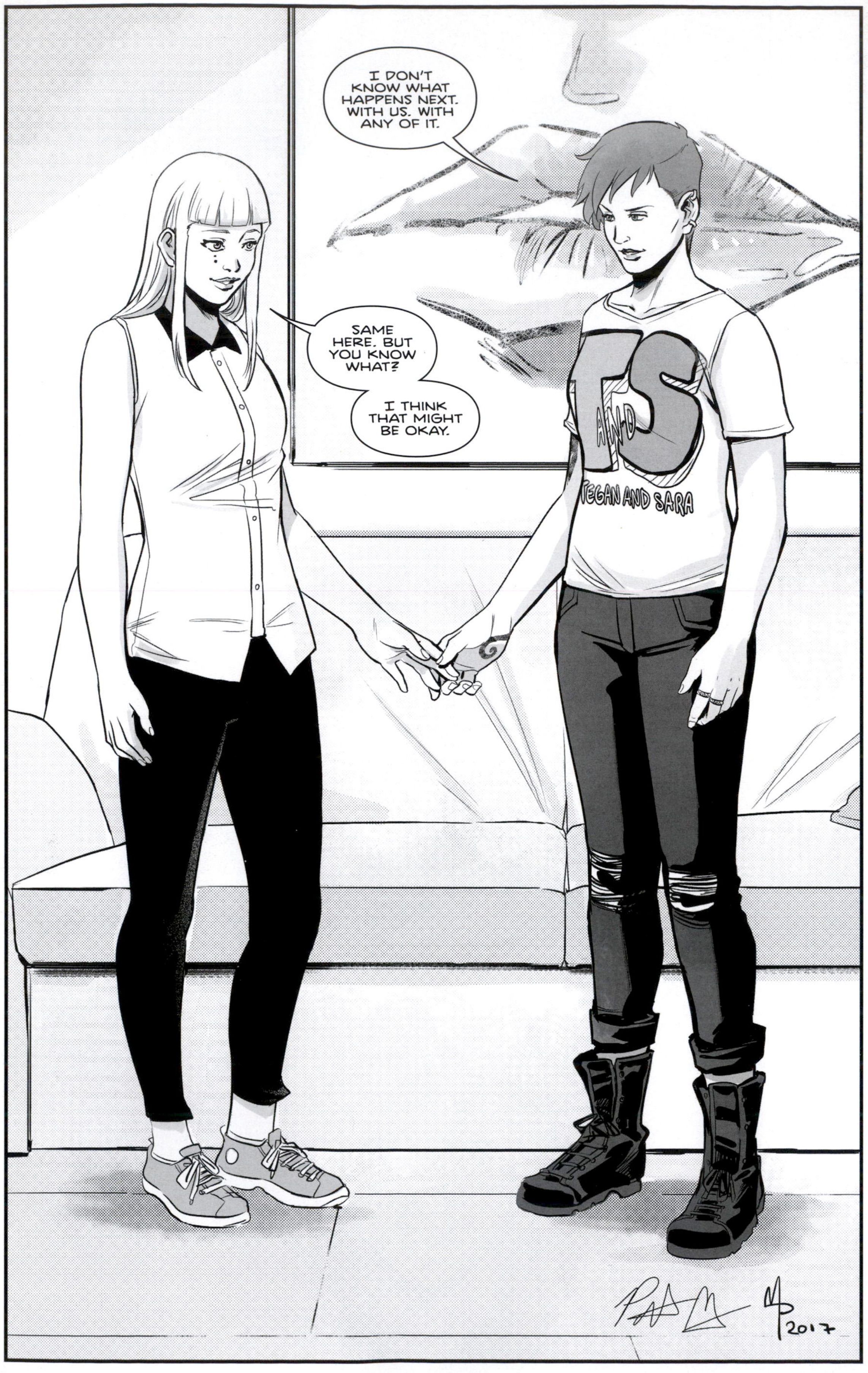
I DON'T KNOW WHAT HAPPENS NEXT. WITH US. WITH ANY OF IT.
SAME HERE. BUT YOU KNOW WHAT?
I THINK THAT MIGHT BE OKAY.
TS AND
TEGAN AND SARA
2017

CHAPTER SIX

A Little Closer

Short stories from the world of Destiny, NY...

Lilith Aberdine in...
CAIRN

Story by
Katie KUFFEL & Pat SHAND
Words by Katie KUFFEL
Artwork by Rosi KÄMPE

Joe Rollins in...
JOE'S EPIC WEEKEND

Story by
Ryan FASSETT & Pat SHAND
Artwork by
Roberta INGRANATA

Gia Espinosa in...
HALF WAY

Story by
Tanya EVERETT & Pat SHAND
Artwork by
Andrea KENDRICK

Logan McBride in...
RELENT

Story by Pat SHAND
Artwork by Phillip SEVY
Shading by Manuel PREITANO

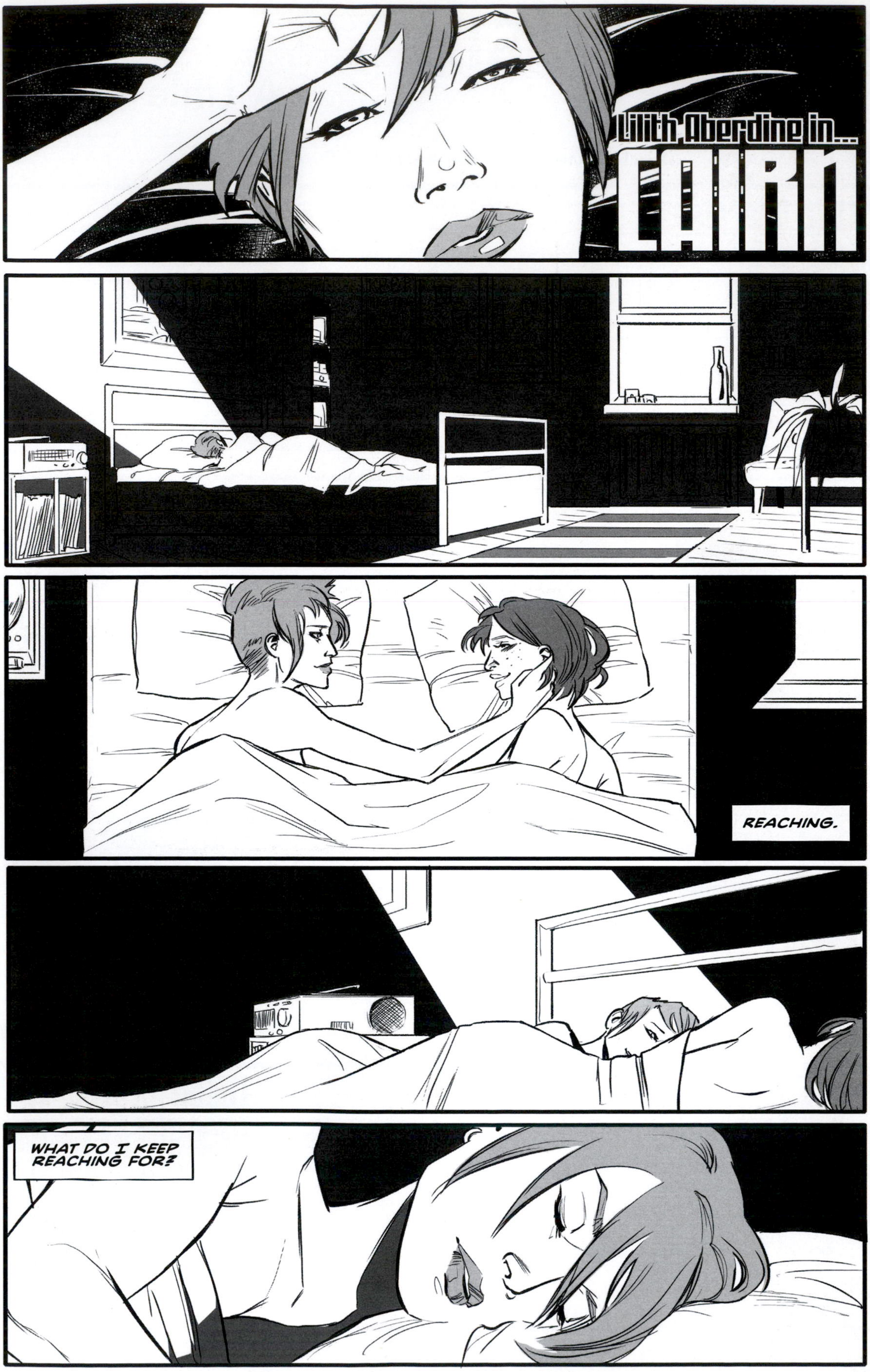
Lilith Aberdine in...
CAIRN
REACHING.
WHAT DO I KEEP REACHING FOR?

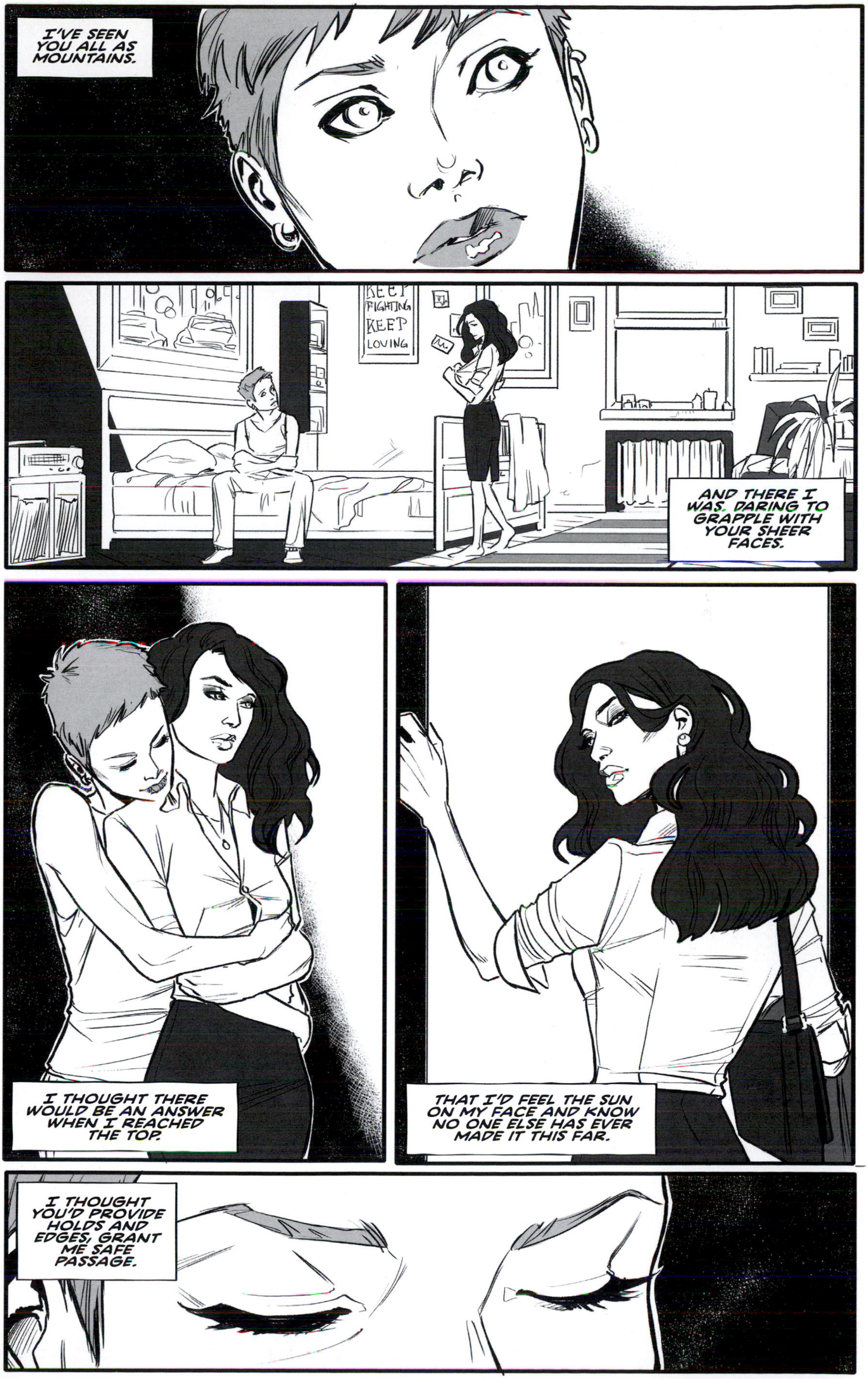
I'VE SEEN YOU ALL AS MOUNTAINS.
KEEP FIGHTING KEEP LOVING
AND THERE I WAS. DARING TO GRAPPLE WITH YOUR SHEER FACES.
I THOUGHT THERE WOULD BE AN ANSWER WHEN I REACHED THE TOP.
THAT I'D FEEL THE SUN ON MY FACE AND KNOW NO ONE ELSE HAS EVER MADE IT THIS FAR.
I THOUGHT YOU'D PROVIDE HOLDS AND EDGES, GRANT ME SAFE PASSAGE.

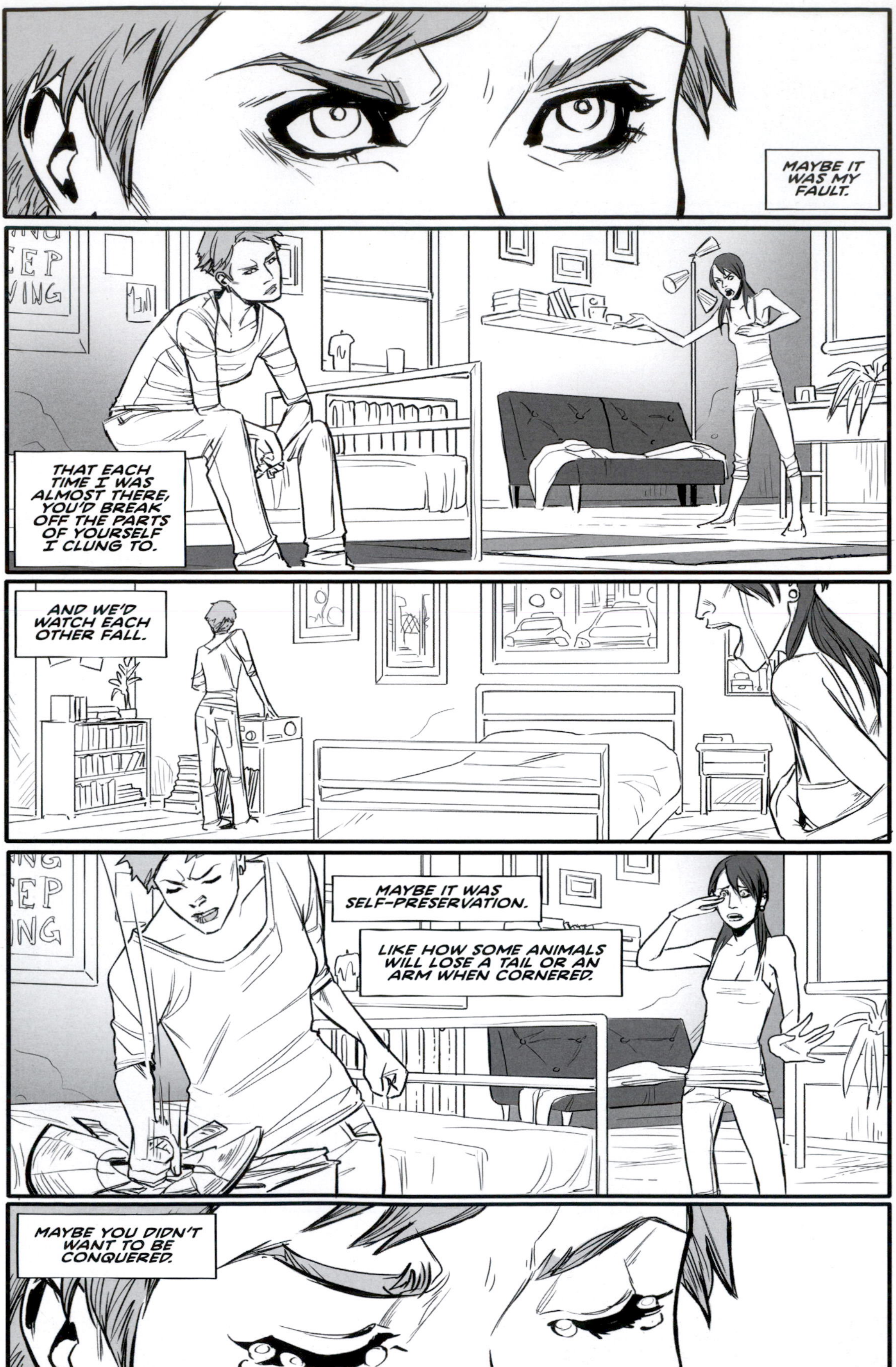
MAYBE IT WAS MY FAULT.
THAT EACH TIME I WAS ALMOST THERE, YOU'D BREAK OFF THE PARTS OF YOURSELF I CLUNG TO.
AND WE'D WATCH EACH OTHER FALL.
MAYBE IT WAS SELF-PRESERVATION.
LIKE HOW SOME ANIMALS WILL LOSE A TAIL OR AN ARM WHEN CORNERED.
MAYBE YOU DIDN'T WANT TO BE CONQUERED.

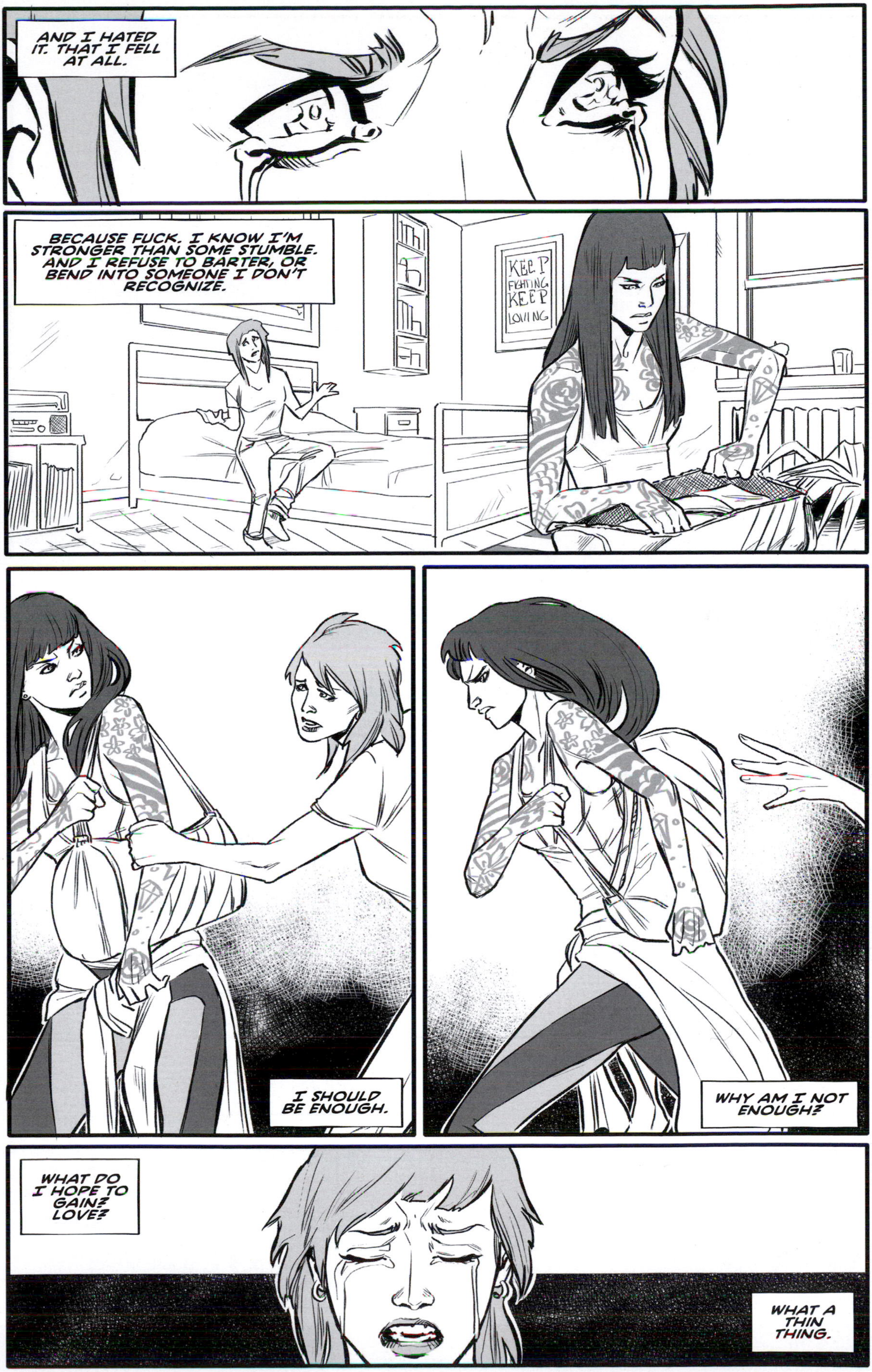
AND I HATED IT. THAT I FELL AT ALL.
BECAUSE FUCK. I KNOW I'M STRONGER THAN SOME STUMBLE. AND I REFUSE TO BARTER, OR BEND INTO SOMEONE I DON'T RECOGNIZE.
KEEP FIGHTING KEEP LOVING
I SHOULD BE ENOUGH.
WHY AM I NOT ENOUGH?
WHAT DO I HOPE TO GAIN? LOVE?
WHAT A THIN THING.

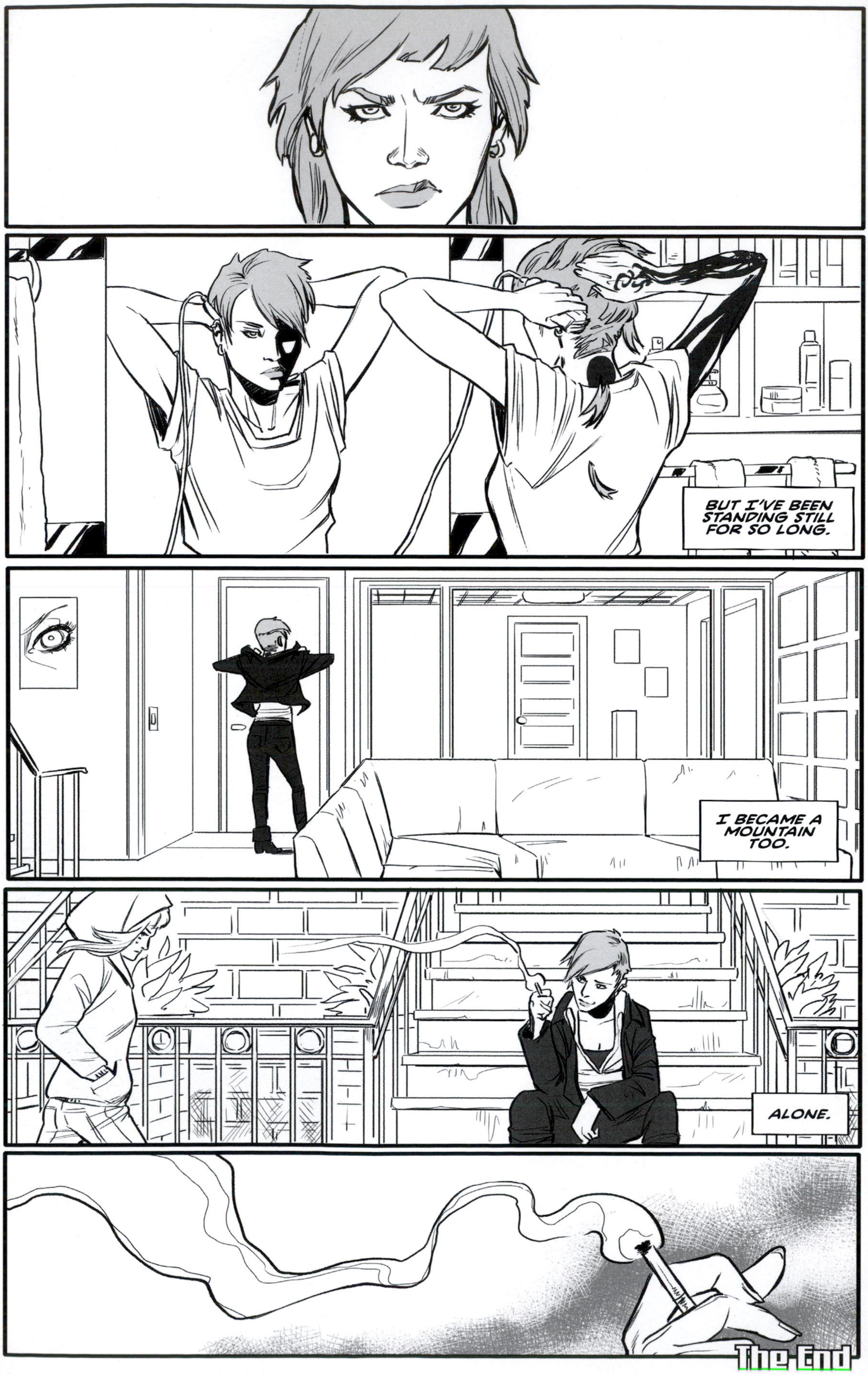
BUT I'VE BEEN STANDING STILL FOR SO LONG.
I BECAME A MOUNTAIN TOO.
ALONE.
The End

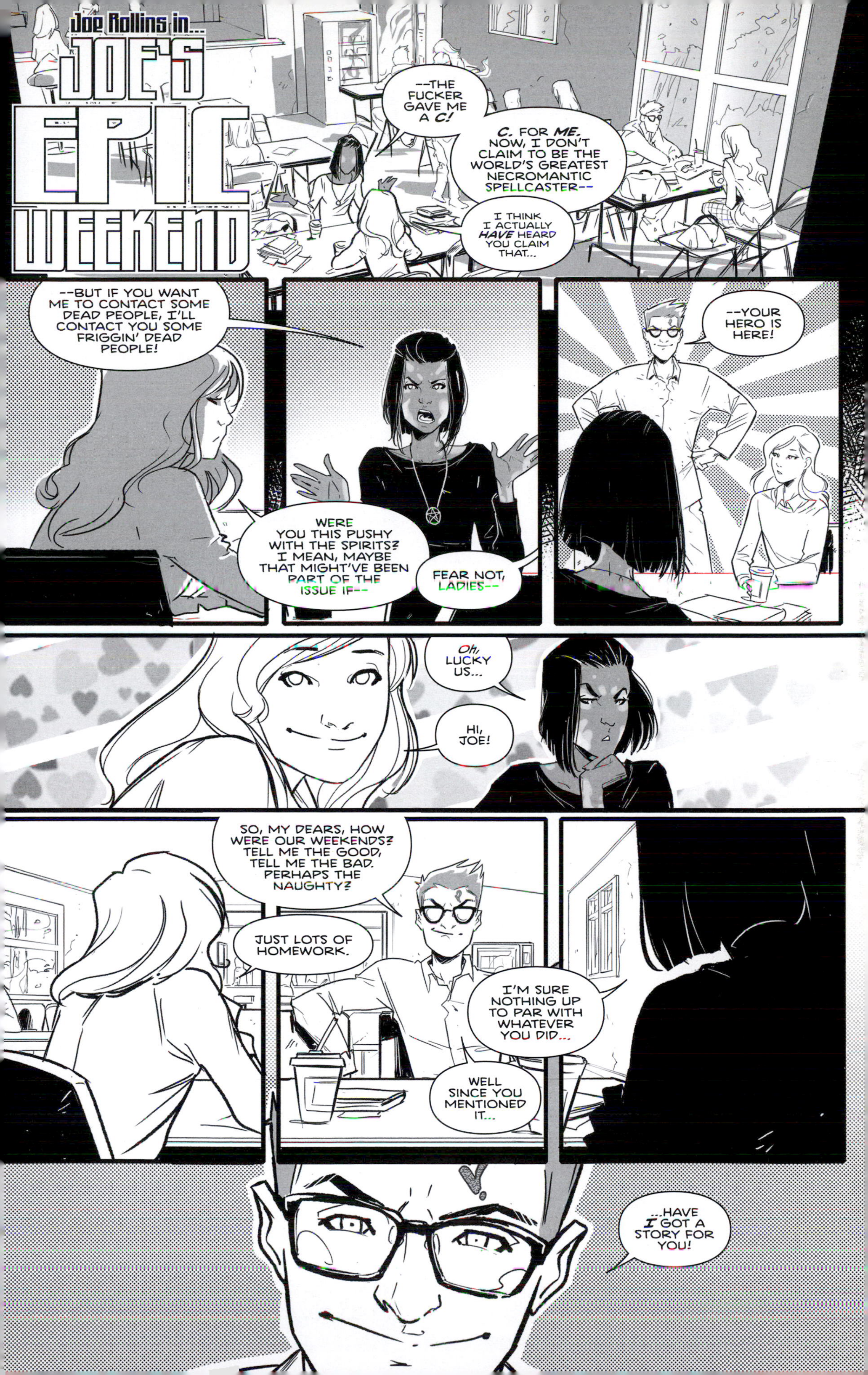
Joe Rollins in...
JOE'S EPIC WEEKEND
--THE FUCKER GAVE ME A C!
C. FOR ME. NOW, I DON'T CLAIM TO BE THE WORLD'S GREATEST NECROMANTIC SPELLCASTER--
I THINK I ACTUALLY HAVE HEARD YOU CLAIM THAT...
--BUT IF YOU WANT ME TO CONTACT SOME DEAD PEOPLE, I'LL CONTACT YOU SOME FRIGGIN' DEAD PEOPLE!
WERE YOU THIS PUSHY WITH THE SPIRITS? I MEAN, MAYBE THAT MIGHT'VE BEEN PART OF THE ISSUE IF--
FEAR NOT, LADIES--
--YOUR HERO IS HERE!
Oh, LUCKY US...
HI, JOE!
SO, MY DEARS, HOW WERE OUR WEEKENDS? TELL ME THE GOOD, TELL ME THE BAD. PERHAPS THE NAUGHTY?
JUST LOTS OF HOMEWORK.
I'M SURE NOTHING UP TO PAR WITH WHATEVER YOU DID...
WELL SINCE YOU MENTIONED IT...
...HAVE I GOT A STORY FOR YOU!

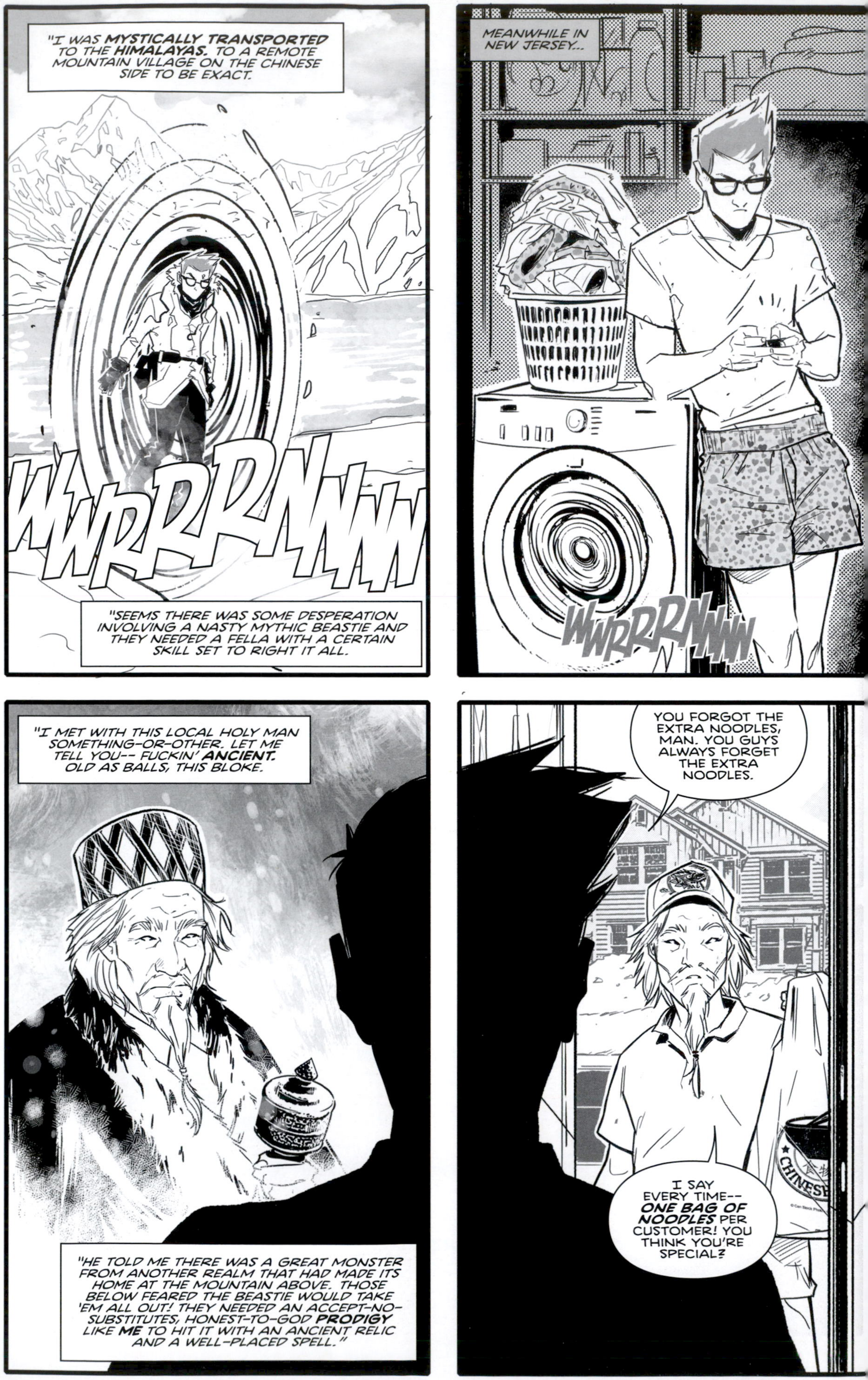
"I WAS MYSTICALLY TRANSPORTED TO THE HIMALAYAS. TO A REMOTE MOUNTAIN VILLAGE ON THE CHINESE SIDE TO BE EXACT.
WWRRRNNNN
"SEEMS THERE WAS SOME DESPERATION INVOLVING A NASTY MYTHIC BEASTIE AND THEY NEEDED A FELLA WITH A CERTAIN SKILL SET TO RIGHT IT ALL.
MEANWHILE IN NEW JERSEY...
WWRRRNNNN
"I MET WITH THIS LOCAL HOLY MAN SOMETHING-OR-OTHER. LET ME TELL YOU-- FUCKIN' ANCIENT. OLD AS BALLS, THIS BLOKE.
"HE TOLD ME THERE WAS A GREAT MONSTER FROM ANOTHER REALM THAT HAD MADE ITS HOME AT THE MOUNTAIN ABOVE. THOSE BELOW FEARED THE BEASTIE WOULD TAKE 'EM ALL OUT! THEY NEEDED AN ACCEPT-NO-SUBSTITUTES, HONEST-TO-GOD PRODIGY LIKE ME TO HIT IT WITH AN ANCIENT RELIC AND A WELL-PLACED SPELL."
YOU FORGOT THE EXTRA NOODLES, MAN. YOU GUYS ALWAYS FORGET THE EXTRA NOODLES.
I SAY EVERY TIME-- ONE BAG OF NOODLES PER CUSTOMER! YOU THINK YOU'RE SPECIAL?

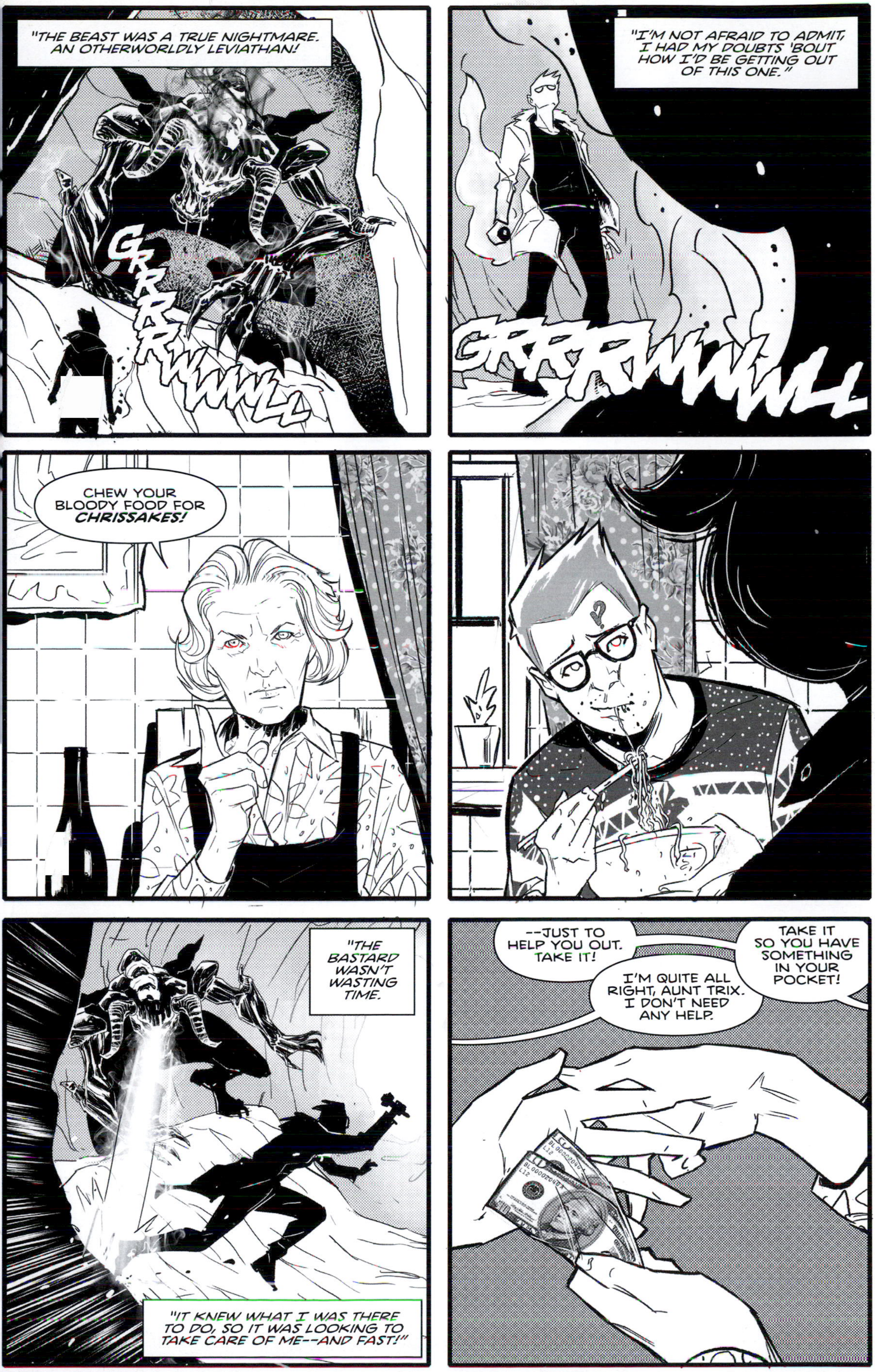
"THE BEAST WAS A TRUE NIGHTMARE. AN OTHERWORLDLY LEVIATHAN!
GRRRWWWLL
"I'M NOT AFRAID TO ADMIT, I HAD MY DOUBTS 'BOUT HOW I'D BE GETTING OUT OF THIS ONE."
GRRRWWWLL
CHEW YOUR BLOODY FOOD FOR CHRISSAKES!
"THE BASTARD WASN'T WASTING TIME.
"IT KNEW WHAT I WAS THERE TO DO, SO IT WAS LOOKING TO TAKE CARE OF ME--AND FAST!"
--JUST TO HELP YOU OUT. TAKE IT!
TAKE IT SO YOU HAVE SOMETHING IN YOUR POCKET!
I'M QUITE ALL RIGHT, AUNT TRIX. I DON'T NEED ANY HELP.

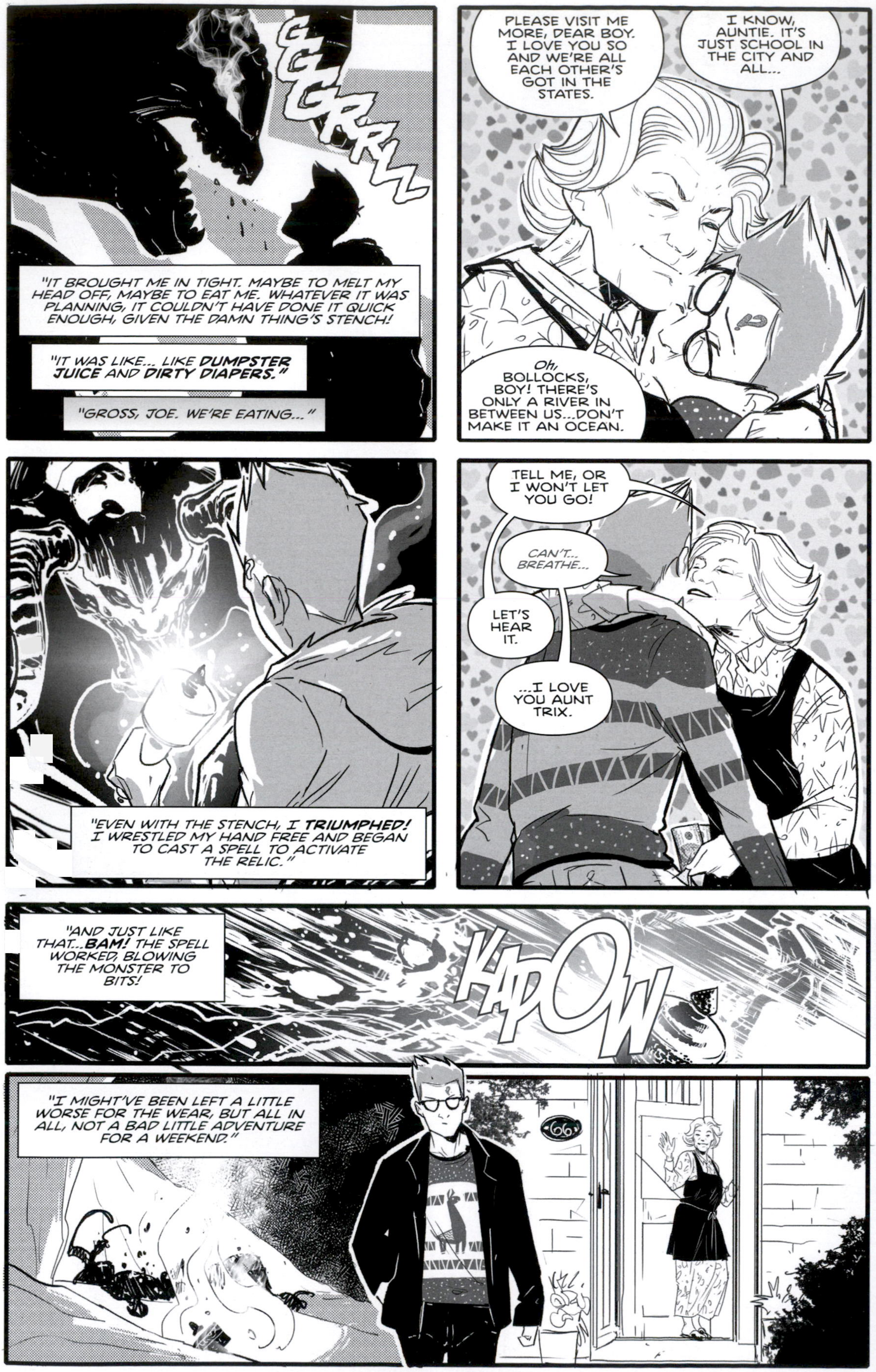
GGGRRRLLL
"IT BROUGHT ME IN TIGHT. MAYBE TO MELT MY HEAD OFF, MAYBE TO EAT ME. WHATEVER IT WAS PLANNING, IT COULDN'T HAVE DONE IT QUICK ENOUGH, GIVEN THE DAMN THING'S STENCH!
"IT WAS LIKE... LIKE DUMPSTER JUICE AND DIRTY DIAPERS."
"GROSS, JOE. WE'RE EATING..."
PLEASE VISIT ME MORE, DEAR BOY. I LOVE YOU SO AND WE'RE ALL EACH OTHER'S GOT IN THE STATES.
I KNOW, AUNTIE. IT'S JUST SCHOOL IN THE CITY AND ALL...
Oh, BOLLOCKS, BOY! THERE'S ONLY A RIVER IN BETWEEN US...DON'T MAKE IT AN OCEAN.
"EVEN WITH THE STENCH, I TRIUMPHED! I WRESTLED MY HAND FREE AND BEGAN TO CAST A SPELL TO ACTIVATE THE RELIC."
TELL ME, OR I WON'T LET YOU GO!
CAN'T... BREATHE...
LET'S HEAR IT.
...I LOVE YOU AUNT TRIX.
"AND JUST LIKE THAT...BAM! THE SPELL WORKED, BLOWING THE MONSTER TO BITS!
KADOW
"I MIGHT'VE BEEN LEFT A LITTLE WORSE FOR THE WEAR, BUT ALL IN ALL, NOT A BAD LITTLE ADVENTURE FOR A WEEKEND."
66

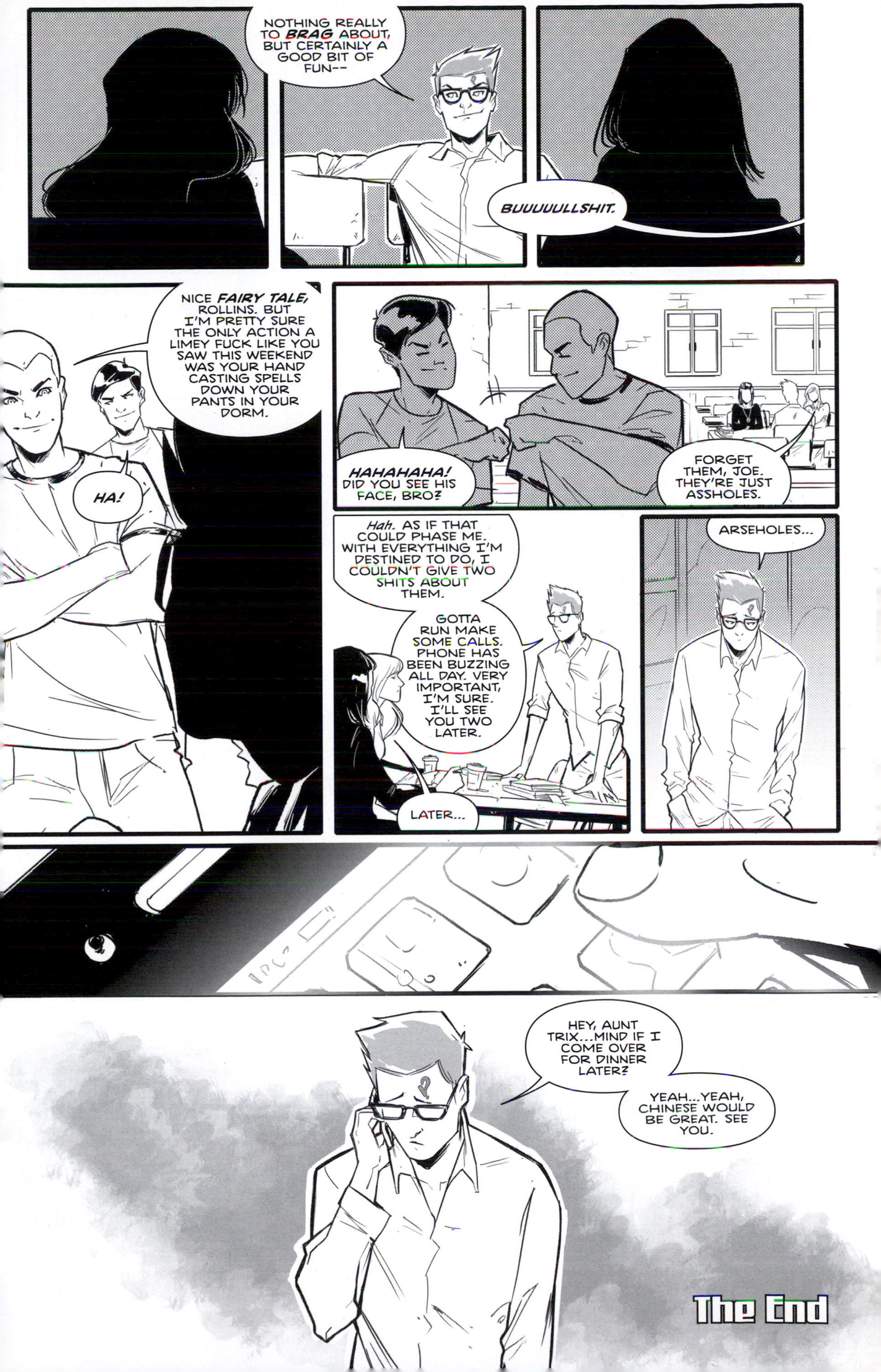
NOTHING REALLY TO BRAG ABOUT, BUT CERTAINLY A GOOD BIT OF FUN--
BUUUUULLSHIT.
NICE FAIRY TALE, ROLLINS. BUT I'M PRETTY SURE THE ONLY ACTION A LIMEY FUCK LIKE YOU SAW THIS WEEKEND WAS YOUR HAND CASTING SPELLS DOWN YOUR PANTS IN YOUR DORM.
HA!
HAHAHAHA! DID YOU SEE HIS FACE, BRO?
FORGET THEM, JOE. THEY'RE JUST ASSHOLES.
Hah. AS IF THAT COULD PHASE ME. WITH EVERYTHING I'M DESTINED TO DO, I COULDN'T GIVE TWO SHITS ABOUT THEM.
GOTTA RUN MAKE SOME CALLS. PHONE HAS BEEN BUZZING ALL DAY. VERY IMPORTANT, I'M SURE. I'LL SEE YOU TWO LATER.
LATER...
ARSEHOLES...
HEY, AUNT TRIX...MIND IF I COME OVER FOR DINNER LATER?
YEAH...YEAH, CHINESE WOULD BE GREAT. SEE YOU.
The End

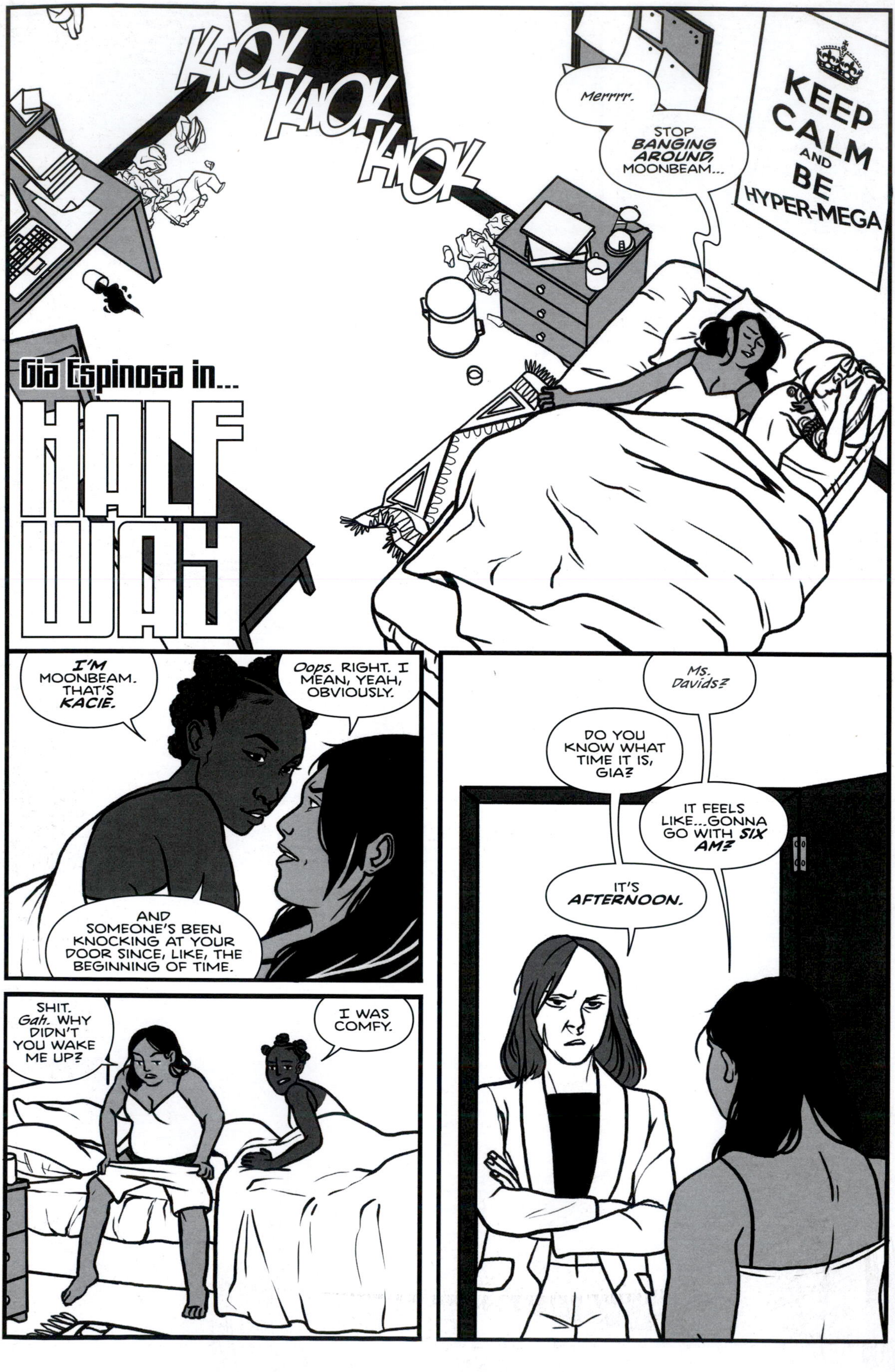
KNOK KNOK KNOK
Merrrr.
STOP BANGING AROUND, MOONBEAM...
KEEP CALM AND BE HYPER-MEGA
Gia Espinosa in...
HALF WAY
I'M MOONBEAM. THAT'S KACIE.
Oops. RIGHT. I MEAN, YEAH, OBVIOUSLY.
AND SOMEONE'S BEEN KNOCKING AT YOUR DOOR SINCE, LIKE, THE BEGINNING OF TIME.
SHIT. Gah. WHY DIDN'T YOU WAKE ME UP?
I WAS COMFY.
Ms. Davids?
DO YOU KNOW WHAT TIME IT IS, GIA?
IT FEELS LIKE...GONNA GO WITH SIX AM?
IT'S AFTERNOON.

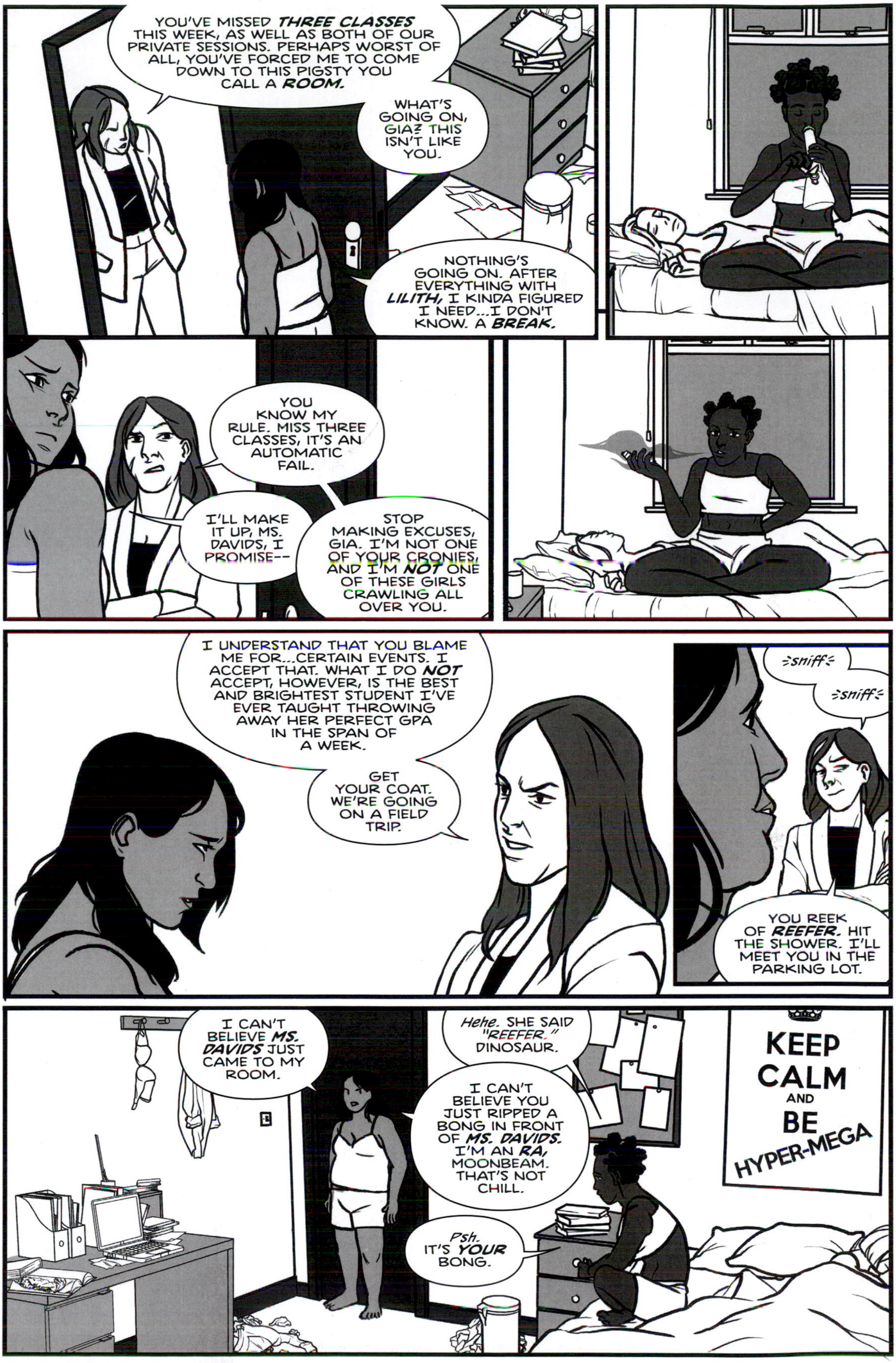
YOU'VE MISSED THREE CLASSES THIS WEEK, AS WELL AS BOTH OF OUR PRIVATE SESSIONS. PERHAPS WORST OF ALL, YOU'VE FORCED ME TO COME DOWN TO THIS PIGSTY YOU CALL A ROOM.
WHAT'S GOING ON, GIA? THIS ISN'T LIKE YOU.
NOTHING'S GOING ON. AFTER EVERYTHING WITH LILITH, I KINDA FIGURED I NEED... I DON'T KNOW. A BREAK.
YOU KNOW MY RULE. MISS THREE CLASSES, IT'S AN AUTOMATIC FAIL.
I'LL MAKE IT UP, MS. DAVIDS, I PROMISE--
STOP MAKING EXCUSES, GIA. I'M NOT ONE OF YOUR CRONIES, AND I'M NOT ONE OF THESE GIRLS CRAWLING ALL OVER YOU.
I UNDERSTAND THAT YOU BLAME ME FOR... CERTAIN EVENTS. I ACCEPT THAT. WHAT I DO NOT ACCEPT, HOWEVER, IS THE BEST AND BRIGHTEST STUDENT I'VE EVER TAUGHT THROWING AWAY HER PERFECT GPA IN THE SPAN OF A WEEK.
GET YOUR COAT. WE'RE GOING ON A FIELD TRIP.
sniff
sniff
YOU REEK OF REEFER. HIT THE SHOWER. I'LL MEET YOU IN THE PARKING LOT.
I CAN'T BELIEVE MS. DAVIDS JUST CAME TO MY ROOM.
Hehe. SHE SAID "REEFER." DINOSAUR.
I CAN'T BELIEVE YOU JUST RIPPED A BONG IN FRONT OF MS. DAVIDS. I'M AN RA, MOONBEAM. THAT'S NOT CHILL.
Psh. IT'S YOUR BONG.
KEEP CALM AND BE HYPER-MEGA

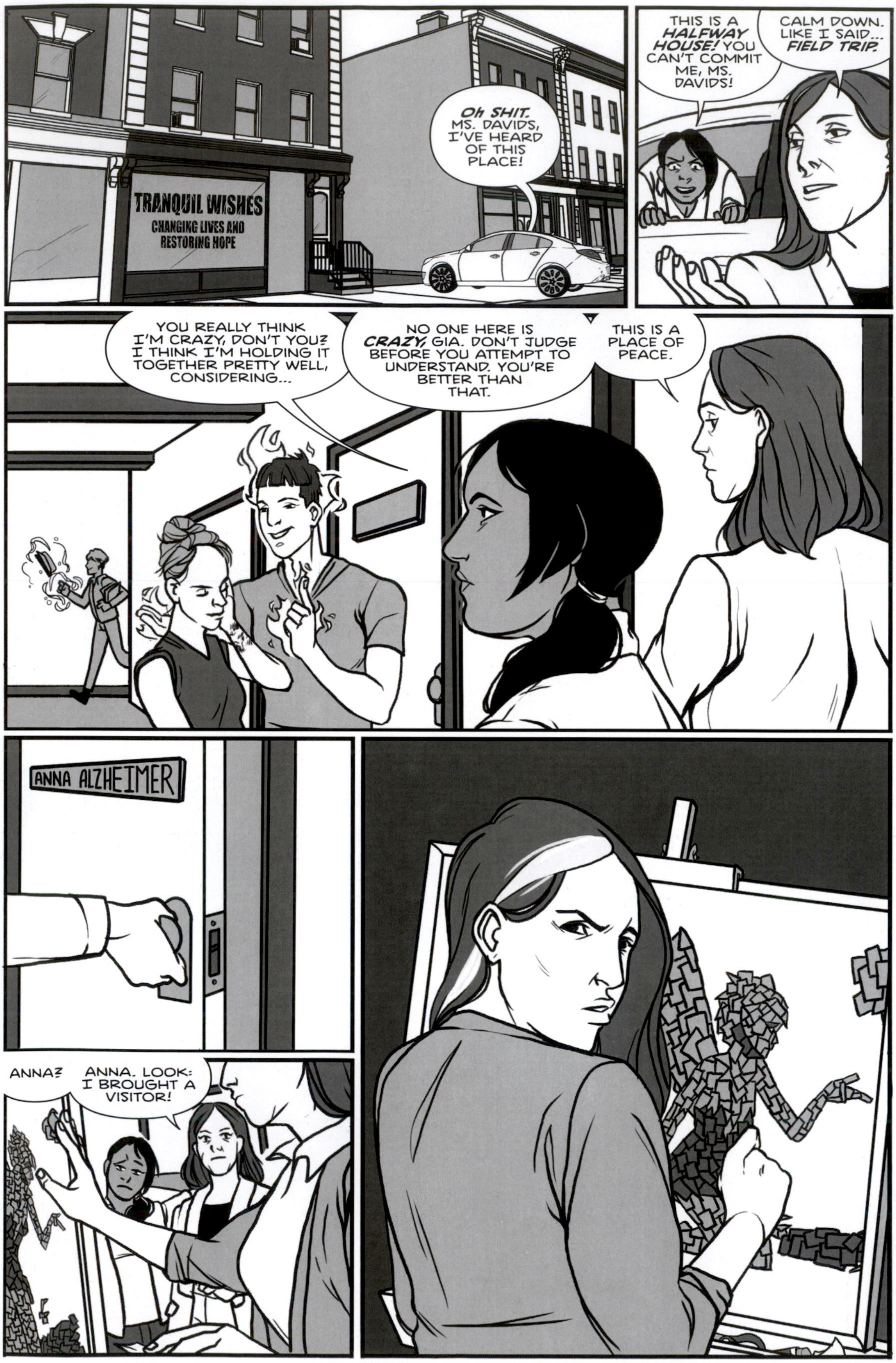
TRANQUIL WISHES
CHANGING LIVES AND RESTORING HOPE
Oh SHIT. MS. DAVIDS, I'VE HEARD OF THIS PLACE!
THIS IS A HALFWAY HOUSE! YOU CAN'T COMMIT ME, MS. DAVIDS!
CALM DOWN. LIKE I SAID... FIELD TRIP.
YOU REALLY THINK I'M CRAZY, DON'T YOU? I THINK I'M HOLDING IT TOGETHER PRETTY WELL, CONSIDERING...
NO ONE HERE IS CRAZY, GIA. DON'T JUDGE BEFORE YOU ATTEMPT TO UNDERSTAND. YOU'RE BETTER THAN THAT.
THIS IS A PLACE OF PEACE.
ANNA ALZHEIMER
ANNA?
ANNA. LOOK: I BROUGHT A VISITOR!

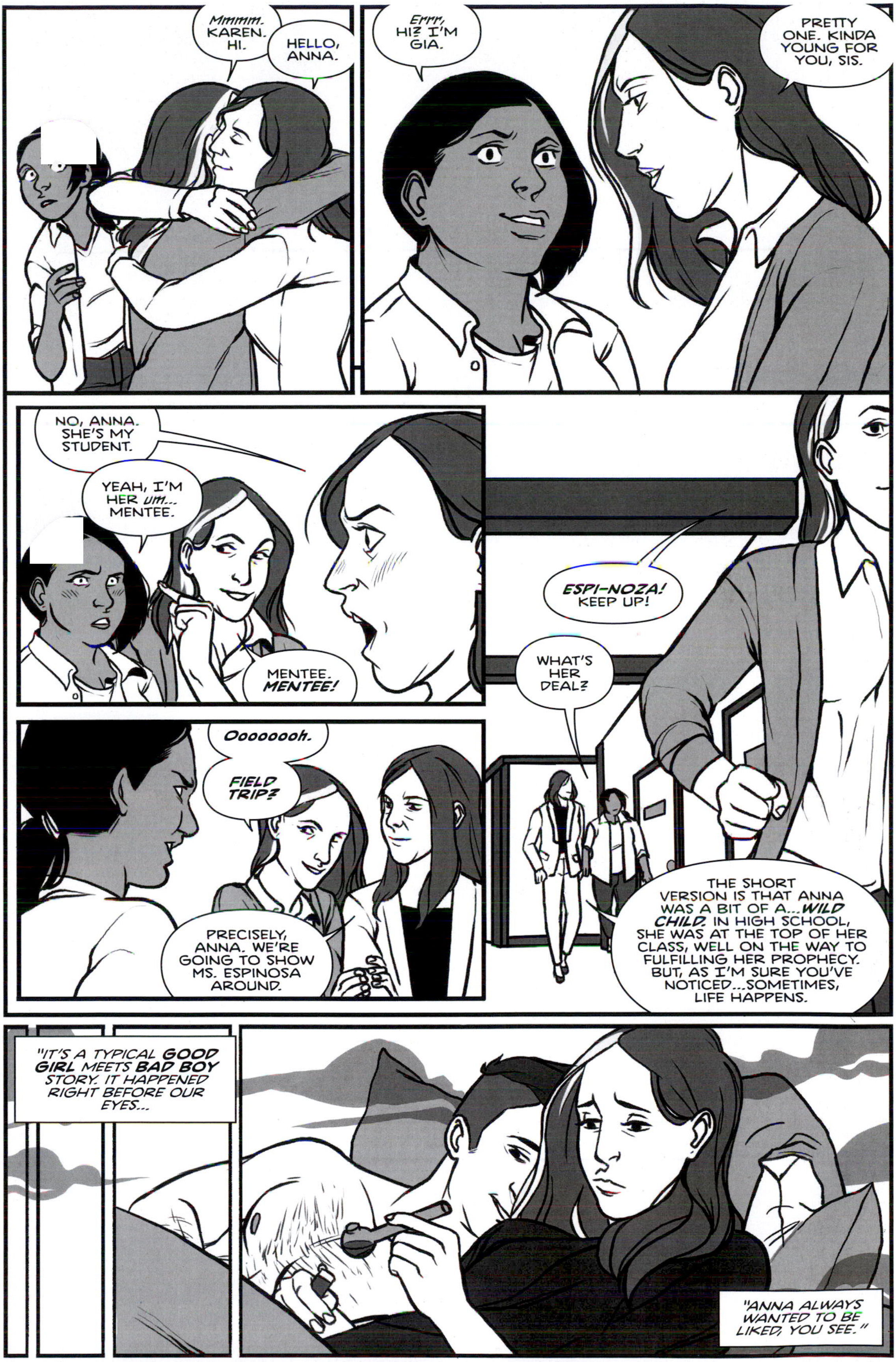

Mmmm. KAREN. HI.
HELLO, ANNA.
Errr, HI? I'M GIA.
PRETTY ONE. KINDA YOUNG FOR YOU, SIS.
NO, ANNA. SHE'S MY STUDENT.
YEAH, I'M HER um... MENTEE.
MENTEE. MENTEE!
Ooooooh.
FIELD TRIP?
PRECISELY, ANNA. WE'RE GOING TO SHOW MS. ESPINOSA AROUND.
ESPI-NOZA! KEEP UP!
WHAT'S HER DEAL?
THE SHORT VERSION IS THAT ANNA WAS A BIT OF A...WILD CHILD, IN HIGH SCHOOL, SHE WAS AT THE TOP OF HER CLASS, WELL ON THE WAY TO FULFILLING HER PROPHECY. BUT, AS I'M SURE YOU'VE NOTICED...SOMETIMES, LIFE HAPPENS.
"IT'S A TYPICAL GOOD GIRL MEETS BAD BOY STORY. IT HAPPENED RIGHT BEFORE OUR EYES...
"ANNA ALWAYS WANTED TO BE LIKED, YOU SEE."

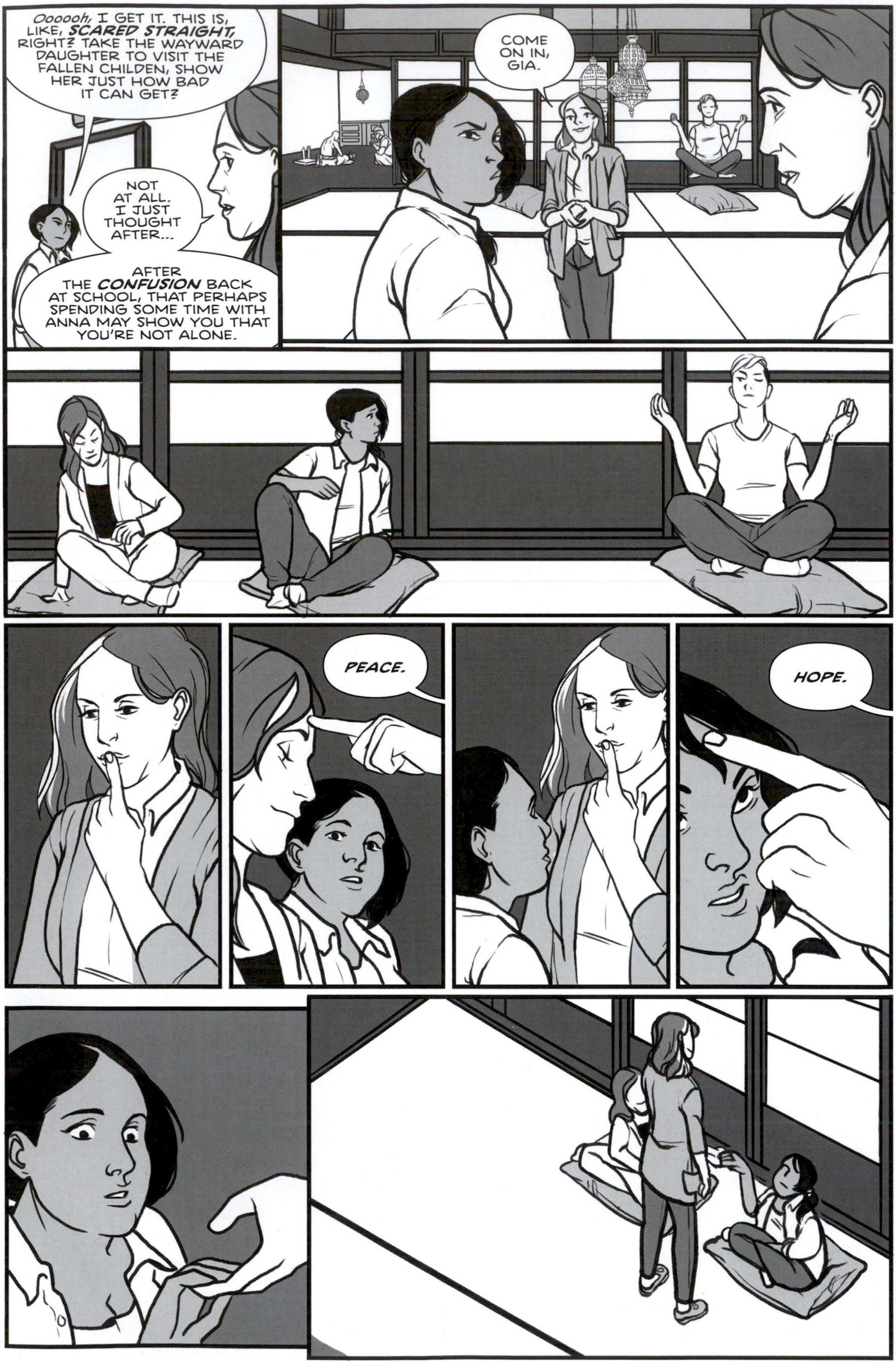
Oooooh, I GET IT. THIS IS, LIKE, SCARED STRAIGHT, RIGHT? TAKE THE WAYWARD DAUGHTER TO VISIT THE FALLEN CHILDEN, SHOW HER JUST HOW BAD IT CAN GET?
NOT AT ALL. I JUST THOUGHT AFTER...
AFTER THE CONFUSION BACK AT SCHOOL, THAT PERHAPS SPENDING SOME TIME WITH ANNA MAY SHOW YOU THAT YOU'RE NOT ALONE.
COME ON IN, GIA.
PEACE.
HOPE.

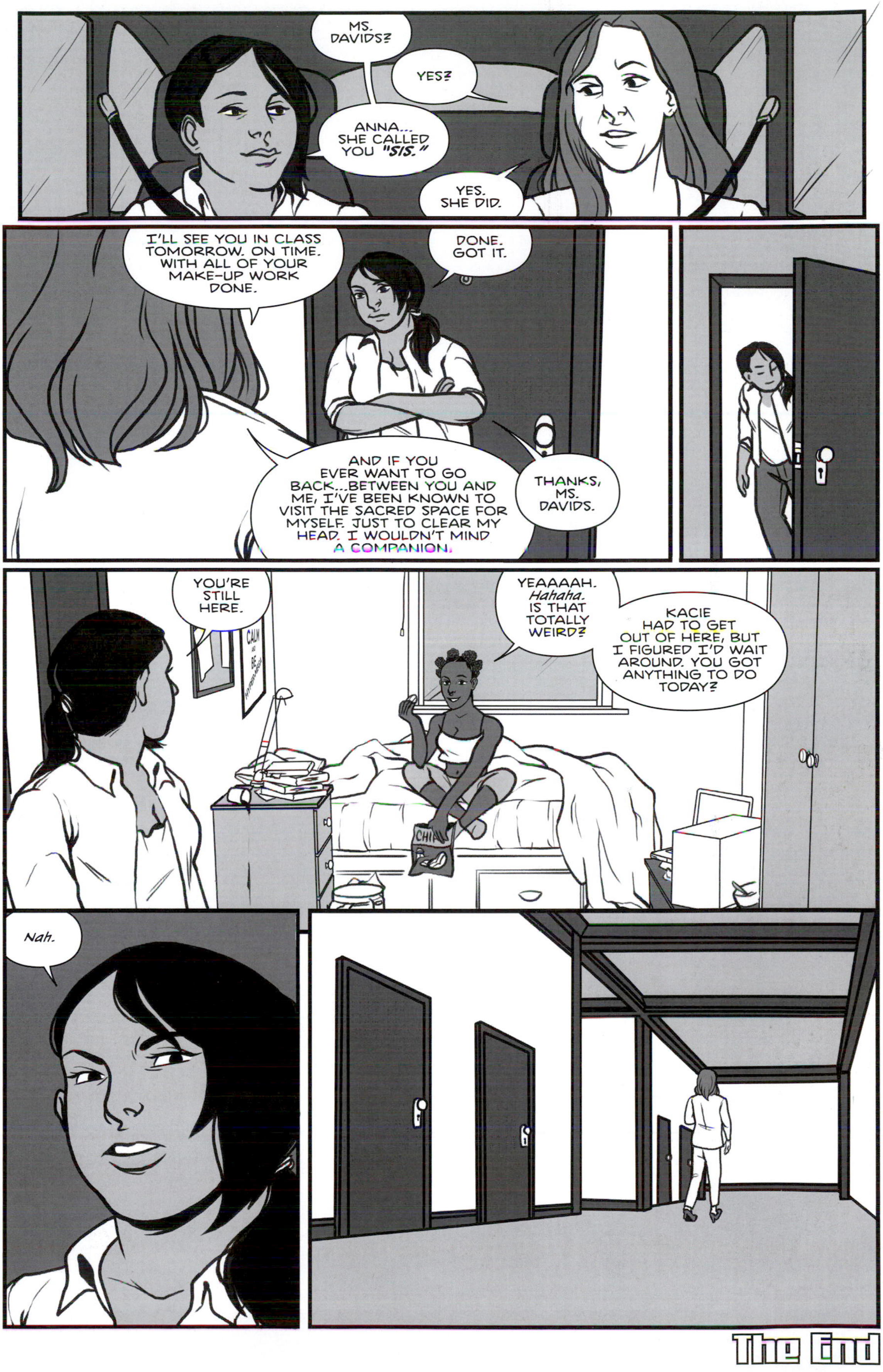
MS. DAVIDS?
YES?
ANNA... SHE CALLED YOU "SIS."
YES. SHE DID.
I'LL SEE YOU IN CLASS TOMORROW. ON TIME. WITH ALL OF YOUR MAKE-UP WORK DONE.
DONE. GOT IT.
AND IF YOU EVER WANT TO GO BACK...BETWEEN YOU AND ME, I'VE BEEN KNOWN TO VISIT THE SACRED SPACE FOR MYSELF. JUST TO CLEAR MY HEAD. I WOULDN'T MIND A COMPANION.
THANKS, MS. DAVIDS.
YOU'RE STILL HERE.
YEAAAAH. *Hahaha.* IS THAT TOTALLY WEIRD?
KACIE HAD TO GET OUT OF HERE, BUT I FIGURED I'D WAIT AROUND. YOU GOT ANYTHING TO DO TODAY?
Nah.
The End

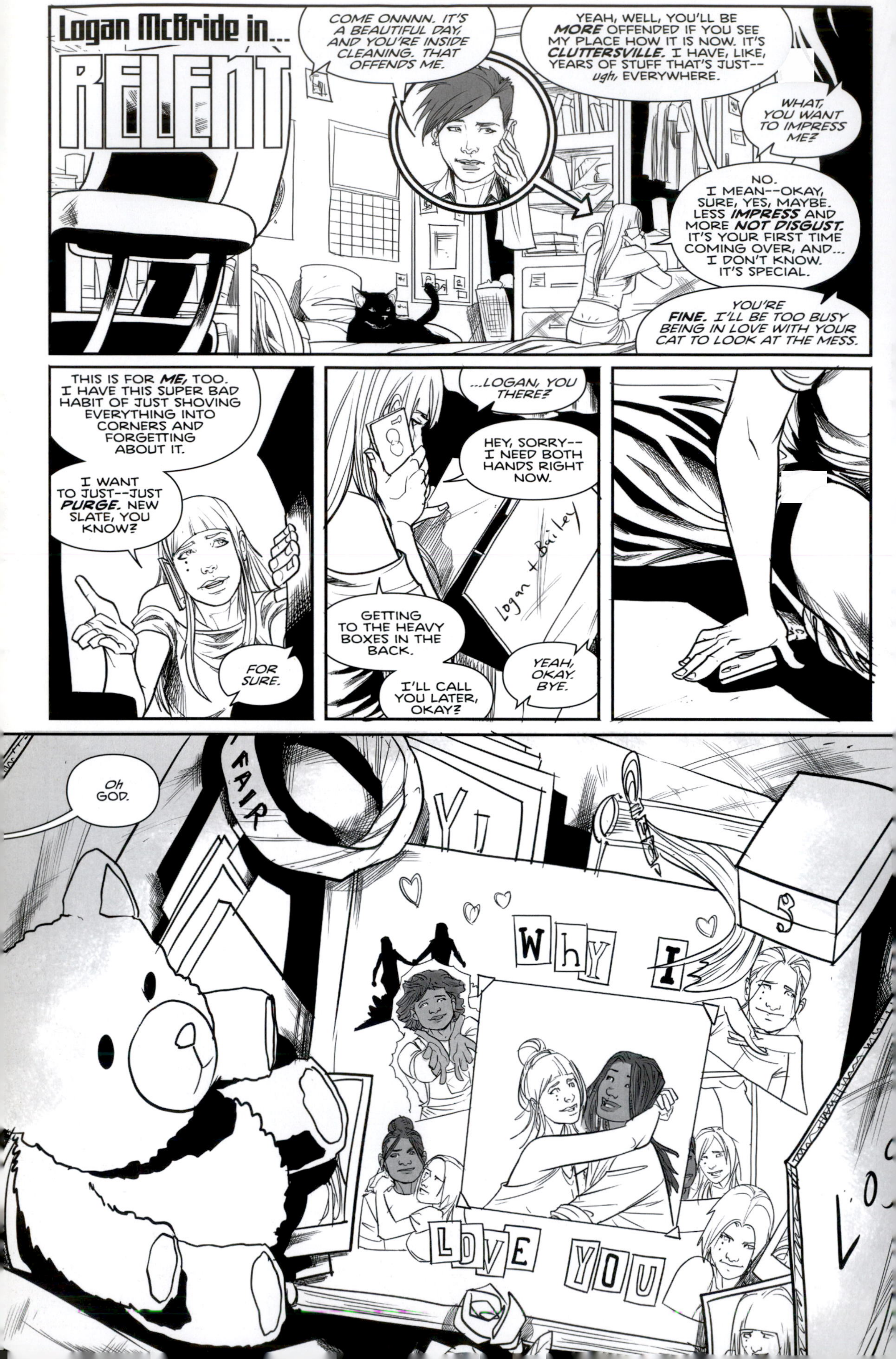
Logan McBride in...
RELENT
COME ONNNN. IT'S A BEAUTIFUL DAY, AND YOU'RE INSIDE CLEANING. THAT OFFENDS ME.
YEAH, WELL, YOU'LL BE MORE OFFENDED IF YOU SEE MY PLACE HOW IT IS NOW. IT'S CLUTTERSVILLE. I HAVE, LIKE, YEARS OF STUFF THAT'S JUST-- ugh, EVERYWHERE.
WHAT, YOU WANT TO IMPRESS ME?
NO. I MEAN--OKAY, SURE, YES, MAYBE. LESS IMPRESS AND MORE NOT DISGUST. IT'S YOUR FIRST TIME COMING OVER, AND... I DON'T KNOW. IT'S SPECIAL.
YOU'RE FINE. I'LL BE TOO BUSY BEING IN LOVE WITH YOUR CAT TO LOOK AT THE MESS.
THIS IS FOR ME, TOO. I HAVE THIS SUPER BAD HABIT OF JUST SHOVING EVERYTHING INTO CORNERS AND FORGETTING ABOUT IT.
I WANT TO JUST--JUST PURGE. NEW SLATE, YOU KNOW?
FOR SURE.
...LOGAN, YOU THERE?
HEY, SORRY-- I NEED BOTH HANDS RIGHT NOW.
Logan + Bailey
GETTING TO THE HEAVY BOXES IN THE BACK.
I'LL CALL YOU LATER, OKAY?
YEAH, OKAY. BYE.
Oh GOD.
FAIR
Why I
LOVE YOU

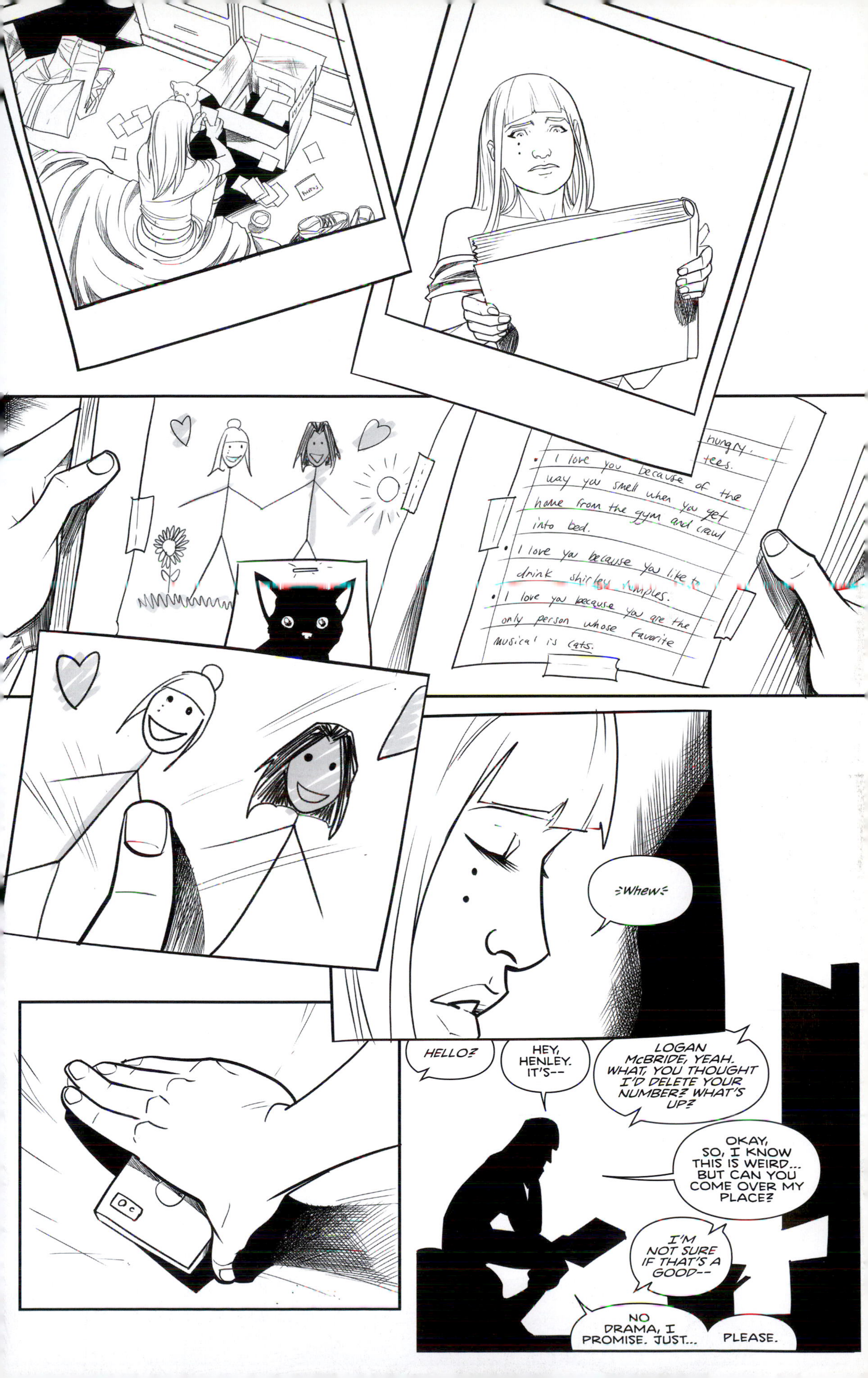

PHOTOS
hungry.
tees.
• I love you because of the way you smell when you get home from the gym and crawl into bed.
• I love you because you like to drink shirley temples.
• I love you because you are the only person whose favorite musical is cats.
:Whew:
HELLO?
HEY, HENLEY. IT'S--
LOGAN MCBRIDE, YEAH. WHAT, YOU THOUGHT I'D DELETE YOUR NUMBER? WHAT'S UP?
OKAY, SO, I KNOW THIS IS WEIRD... BUT CAN YOU COME OVER MY PLACE?
I'M NOT SURE IF THAT'S A GOOD--
NO DRAMA, I PROMISE. JUST...
PLEASE.

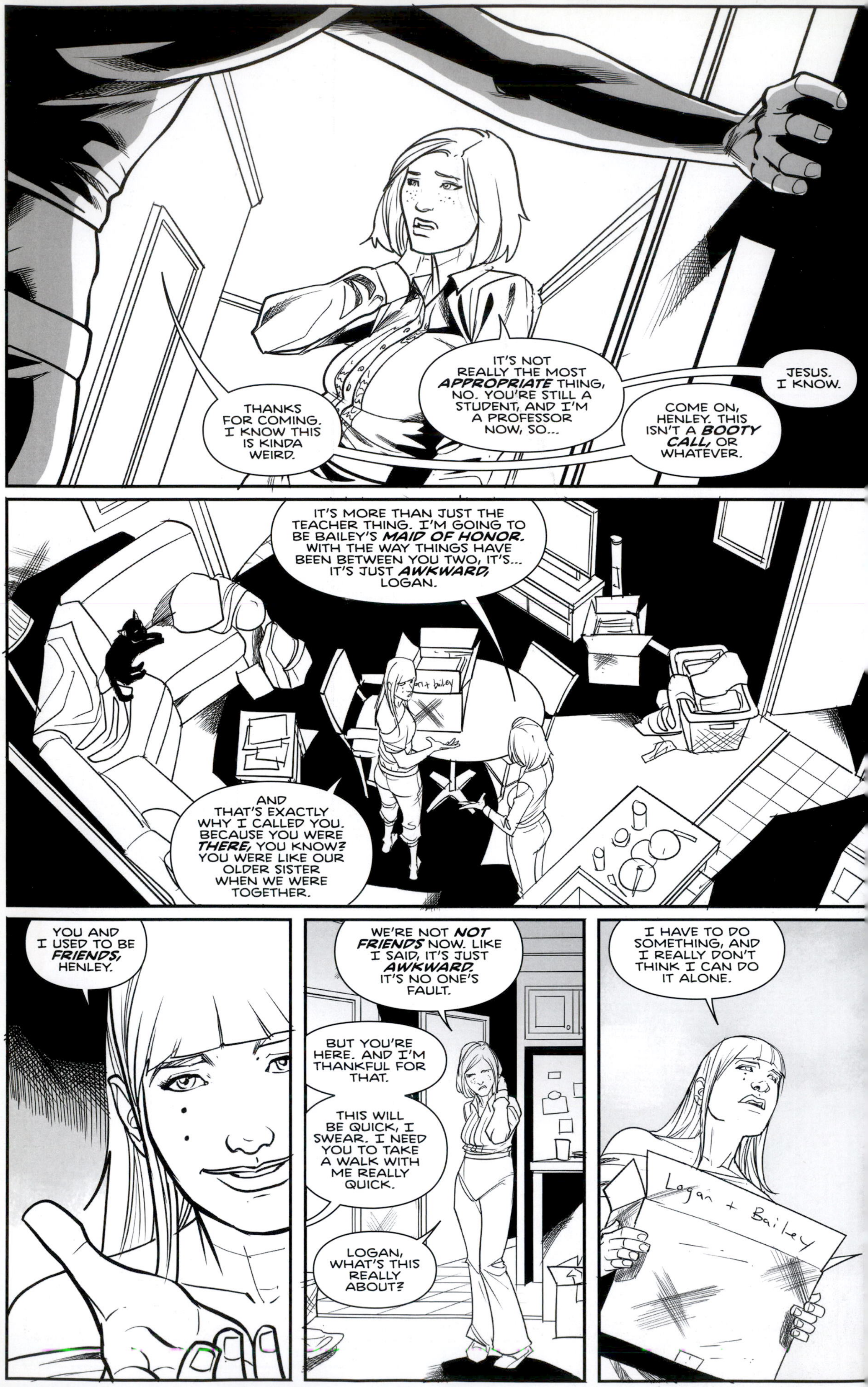
THANKS FOR COMING. I KNOW THIS IS KINDA WEIRD.
COME ON, HENLEY. THIS ISN'T A BOOTY CALL, OR WHATEVER.
IT'S NOT REALLY THE MOST APPROPRIATE THING, NO. YOU'RE STILL A STUDENT, AND I'M A PROFESSOR NOW, SO...
JESUS. I KNOW.
IT'S MORE THAN JUST THE TEACHER THING. I'M GOING TO BE BAILEY'S MAID OF HONOR. WITH THE WAY THINGS HAVE BEEN BETWEEN YOU TWO, IT'S... IT'S JUST AWKWARD, LOGAN.
AND THAT'S EXACTLY WHY I CALLED YOU. BECAUSE YOU WERE THERE, YOU KNOW? YOU WERE LIKE OUR OLDER SISTER WHEN WE WERE TOGETHER.
YOU AND I USED TO BE FRIENDS, HENLEY.
WE'RE NOT NOT FRIENDS NOW. LIKE I SAID, IT'S JUST AWKWARD. IT'S NO ONE'S FAULT.
BUT YOU'RE HERE. AND I'M THANKFUL FOR THAT.
THIS WILL BE QUICK, I SWEAR. I NEED YOU TO TAKE A WALK WITH ME REALLY QUICK.
LOGAN, WHAT'S THIS REALLY ABOUT?
I HAVE TO DO SOMETHING, AND I REALLY DON'T THINK I CAN DO IT ALONE.
Logan + Bailey

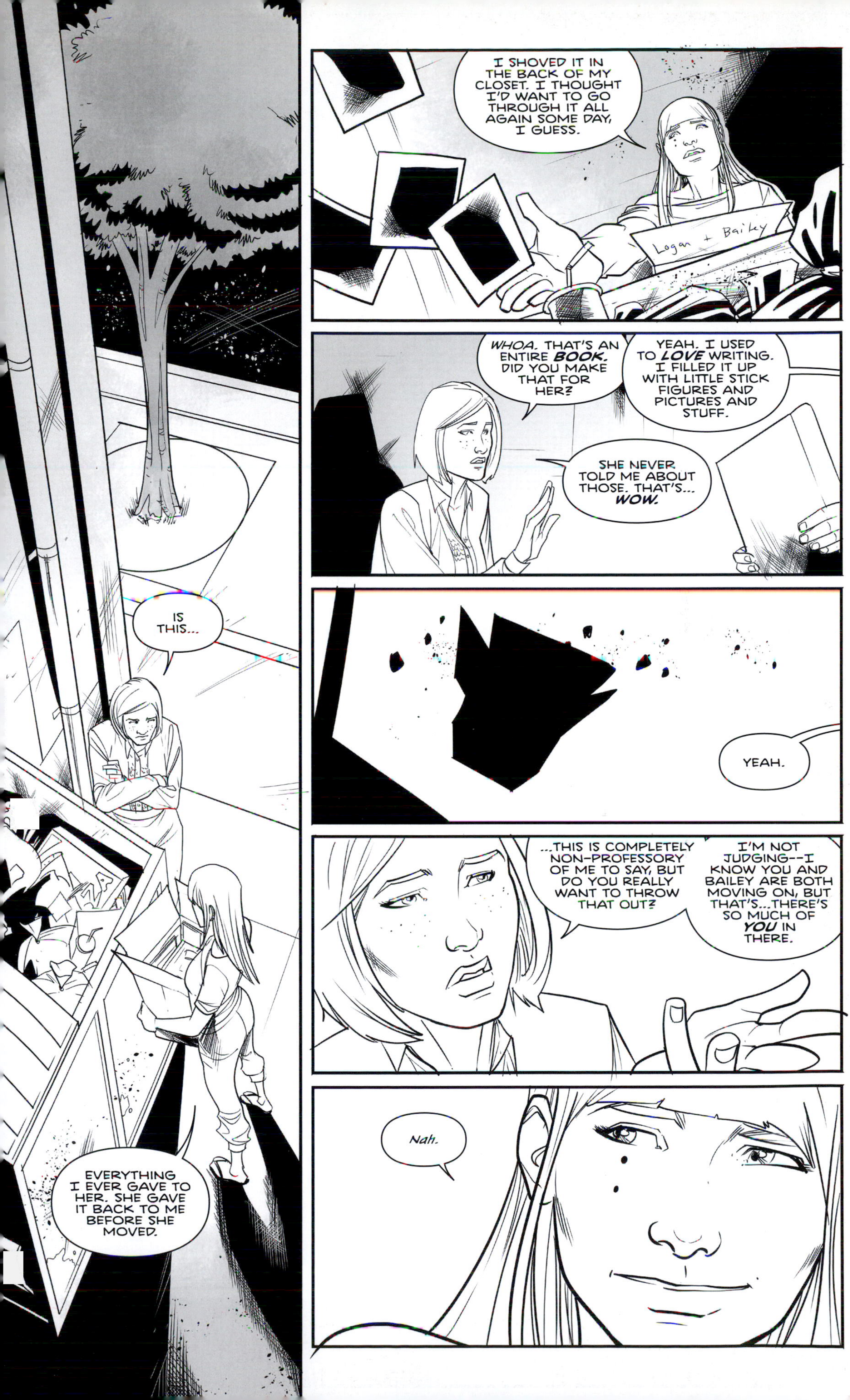
IS THIS...
EVERYTHING I EVER GAVE TO HER. SHE GAVE IT BACK TO ME BEFORE SHE MOVED.
I SHOVED IT IN THE BACK OF MY CLOSET. I THOUGHT I'D WANT TO GO THROUGH IT ALL AGAIN SOME DAY, I GUESS.
Logan + Bailey
WHOA. THAT'S AN ENTIRE BOOK. DID YOU MAKE THAT FOR HER?
YEAH. I USED TO LOVE WRITING. I FILLED IT UP WITH LITTLE STICK FIGURES AND PICTURES AND STUFF.
SHE NEVER TOLD ME ABOUT THOSE. THAT'S... WOW.
YEAH.
...THIS IS COMPLETELY NON-PROFESSORY OF ME TO SAY, BUT DO YOU REALLY WANT TO THROW THAT OUT?
I'M NOT JUDGING--I KNOW YOU AND BAILEY ARE BOTH MOVING ON, BUT THAT'S...THERE'S SO MUCH OF YOU IN THERE.
Nah.

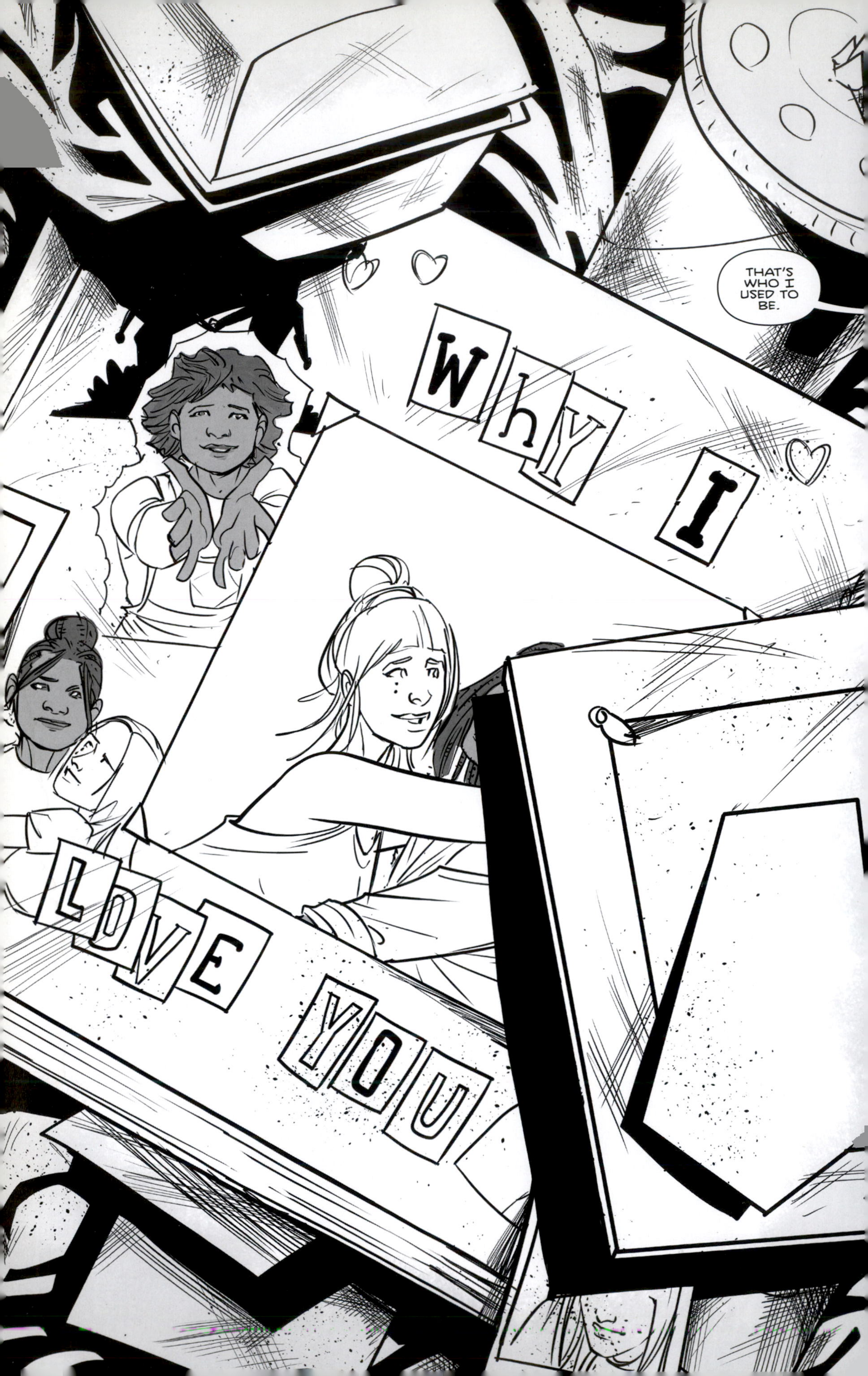

THAT'S WHO I USED TO BE.
WHY I
LOVE YOU

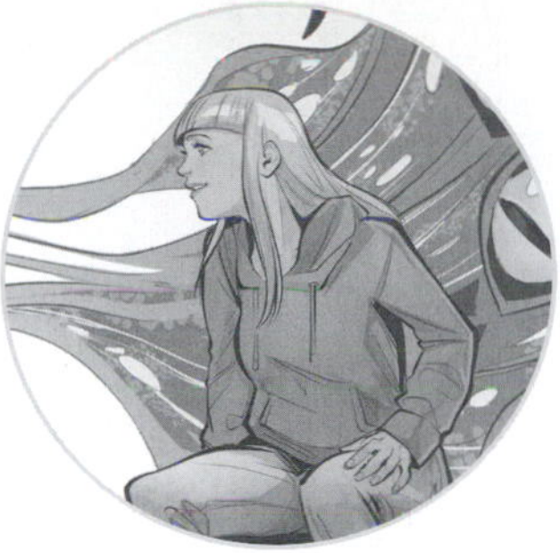

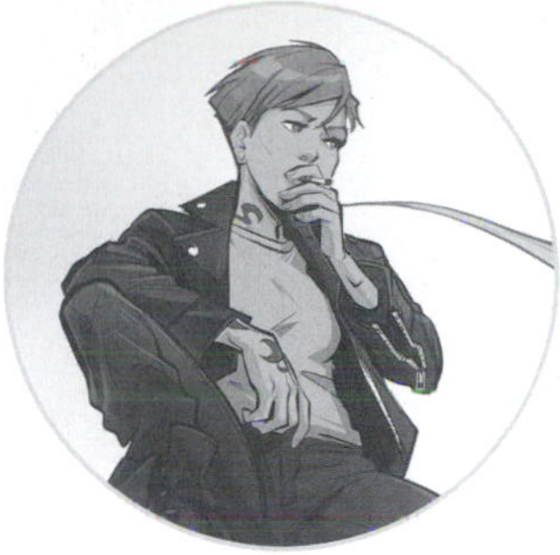

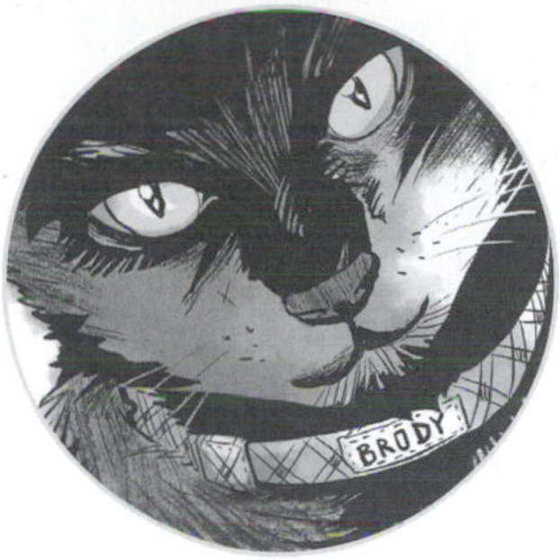
BRODY

AUTHOR'S NOTE

Longform storytelling made me fall in love with comics. I miss it.

Y: The Last Man, Ex Machina, Preacher, Strangers in Paradise, all of these titles showed me as a hungry reader and aspiring writer that comics was a beautiful medium with which to study character and dig for human emotion. The thing is, comics are incredibly difficult and expensive to make. Pitch a series the size of *Y: The Last Man* to a publisher in person and a convention and watch the light fade from their expression. Go ask Matt Pizzolo from Black Mask next time you see him. Pitch him exclusively ongoing series. That'd be hilarious to me.

For real, though, it's a wild ask in the current market. That's why most of the comics you've seen me create go as far as #4 or #6 if I'm wildly lucky. To be able to have six issues to tell my story? Dude! That's like the equivalent of having a 40-issue run in 2010. If a publisher tells me we've got six issues to work with, I'm heading to the jeweler to put a ring on their finger. Six issues? Come on, we're married.

Which is why, with Destiny, NY, I did it myself first.

This is the beginning of a long journey. I've been writing and funding *Destiny, NY* thanks to support on Kickstarter I'll be forever grateful for now for five years as of writing this letter. I've worked on this series with some of my favorite artists in the industry and great friends as well. This book right here is the kind of story – the exact story – I dreamed of telling when I saw what my favorite creators could do when passion, love of character, and years of hard work overlapped. I *love* telling this story. If you enjoy reading it, all I can say for now is that I'm so glad you're with us. If things go my way, it's going to be a rocky relationship with me and you, reader. I want to make you cry a little, I can't lie. I do. More, though, I want to make you laugh and care and feel. If this book made anyone feel how I felt after experiencing the stories that inspired me, then... well, then fuck, maybe I'll cry too.

Logan and Lilith have miles to go. See you next time.

- **Pat SHAND**, July 14th, 2021

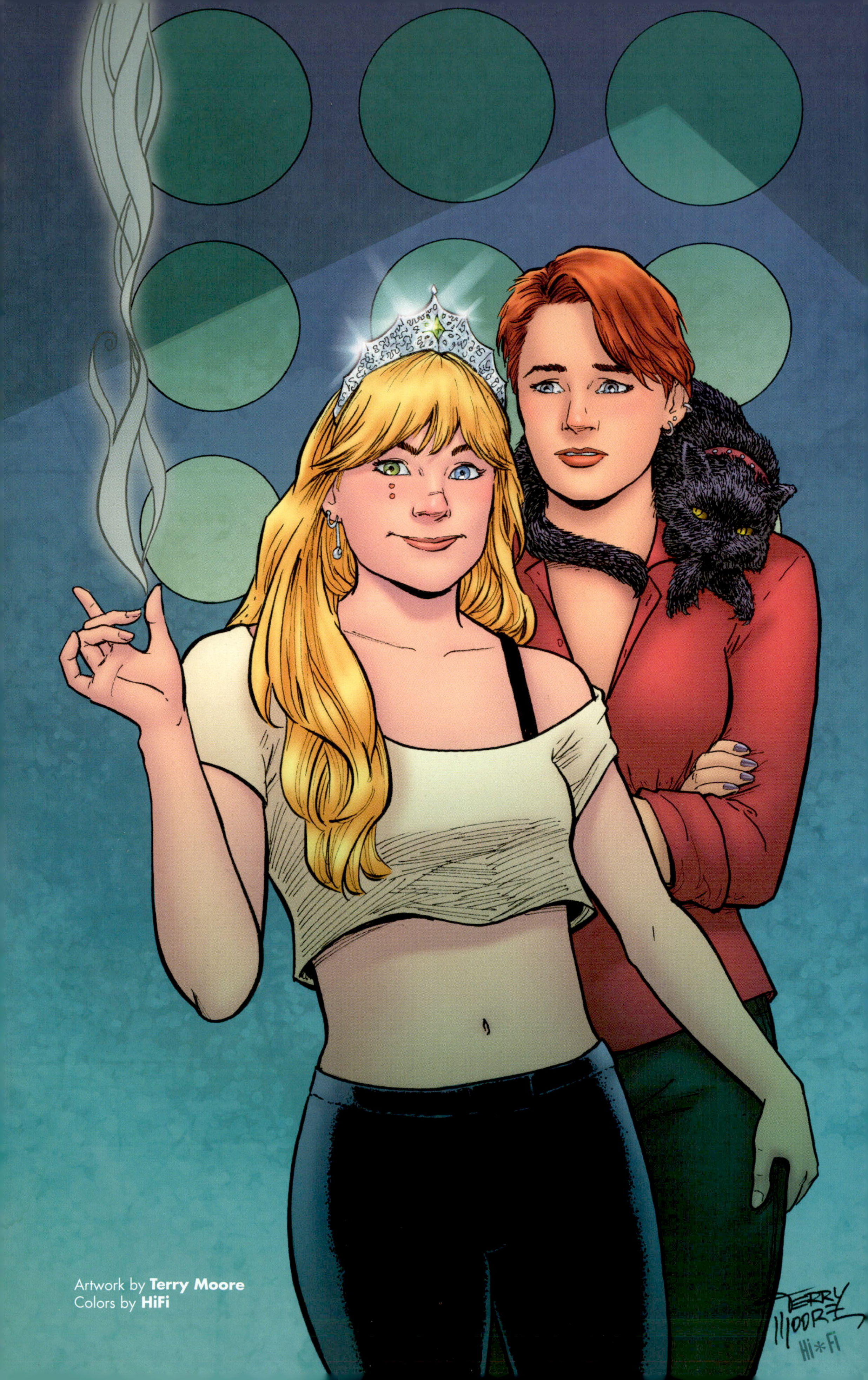
TERRY MOORE
Hi*Fi

Artwork by **Terry Moore**
Colors by **HiFi**

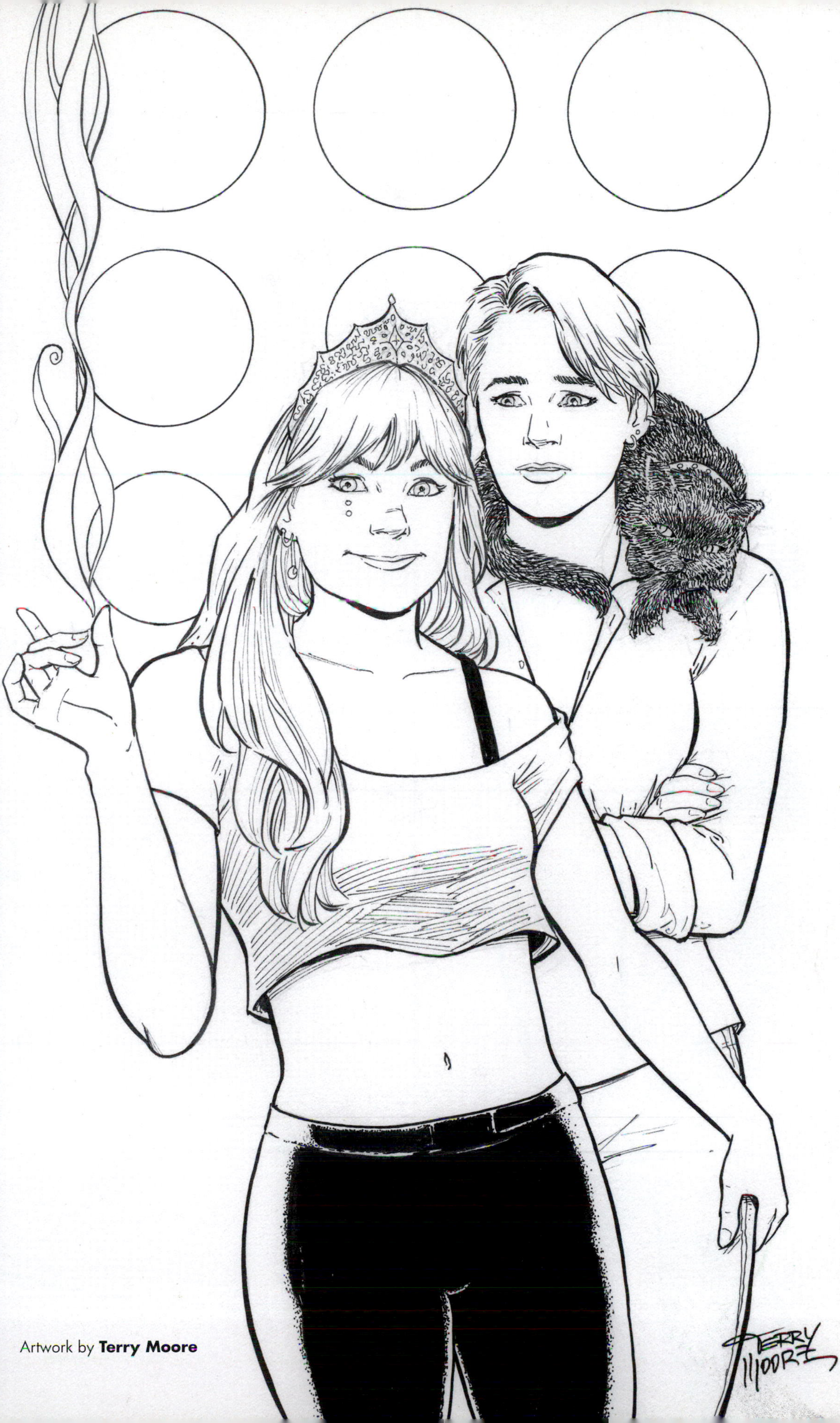
TERRY MOORE

Artwork by **Terry Moore**

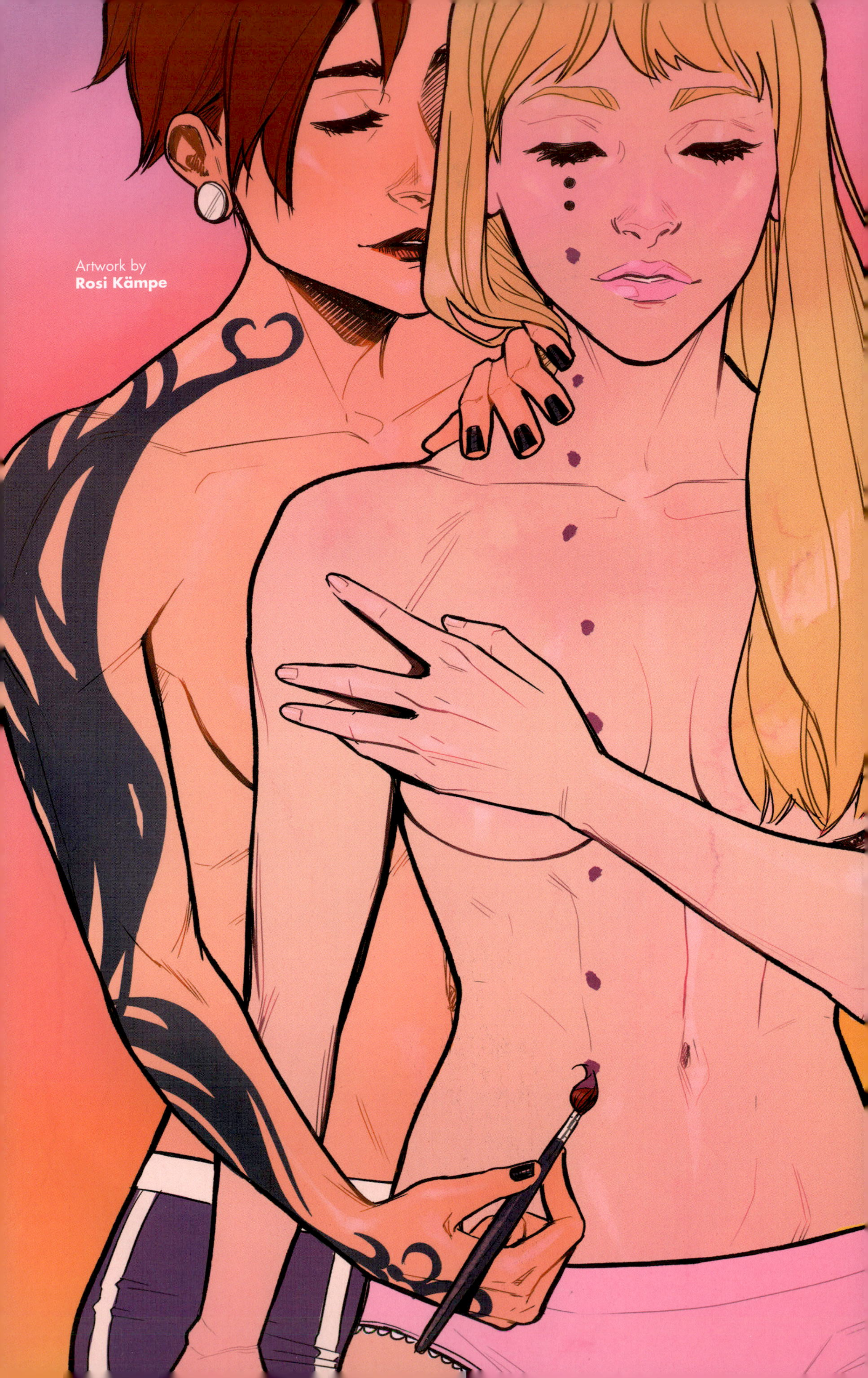

Artwork by
Rosi Kämpe

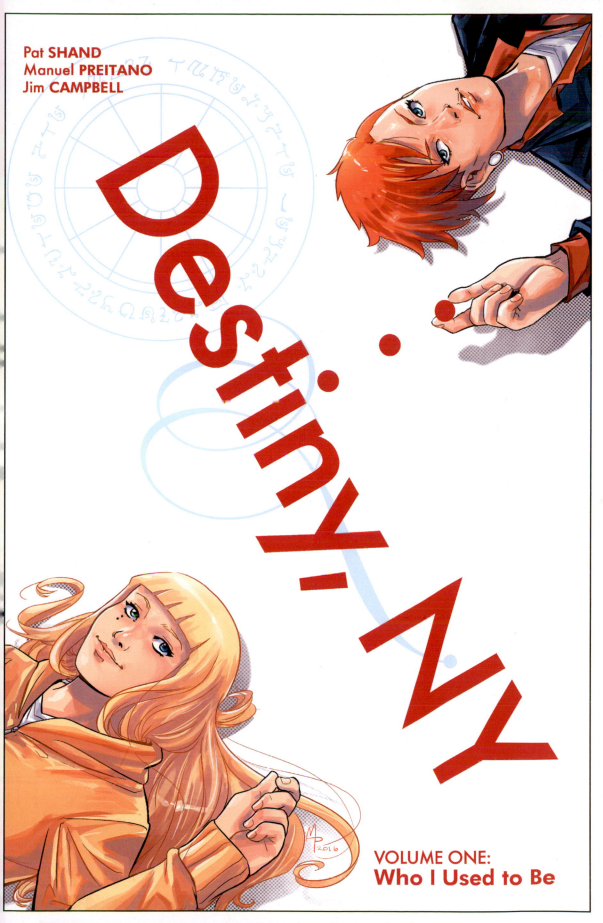

Pat SHAND
Manuel PREITANO
Jim CAMPBELL

Destiny, NY

VOLUME ONE:
Who I Used to Be

Original *Destiny, NY* Volume 1 cover by **Manuel Preitano**

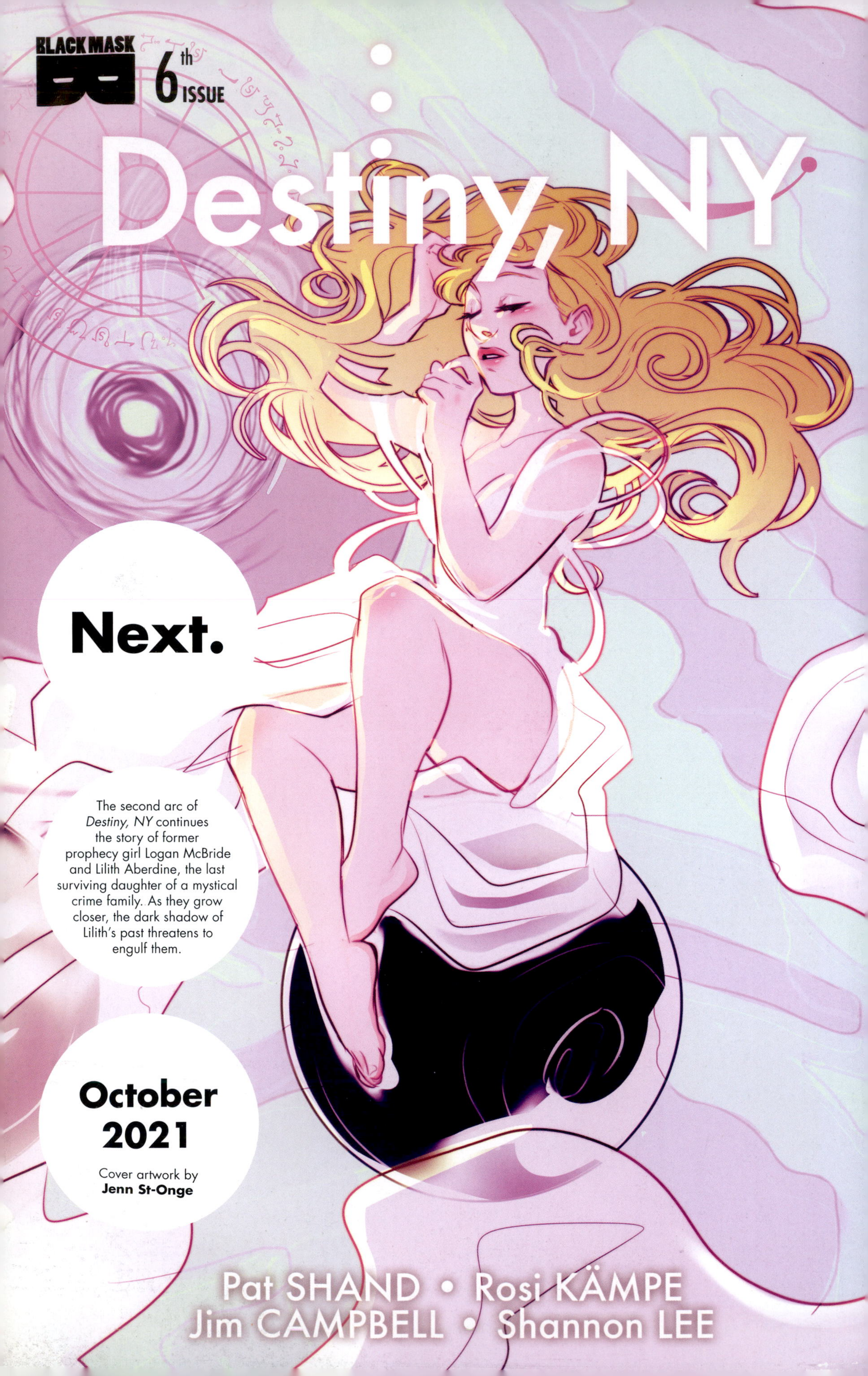
BLACK MASK
6th ISSUE
Destiny, NY
Next.
The second arc of *Destiny, NY* continues the story of former prophecy girl Logan McBride and Lilith Aberdine, the last surviving daughter of a mystical crime family. As they grow closer, the dark shadow of Lilith's past threatens to engulf them.
October 2021
Cover artwork by **Jenn St-Onge**
Pat SHAND • Rosi KÄMPE
Jim CAMPBELL • Shannon LEE